Two Thousand Minnows

Acknowledgments

When writing a love story about a family and all their ticks, it's only fitting to start my dedication to my mother, Ardell, who shared all of her gifts and talents with me. Thankfully, she gave me everything she had and more. For without her, there is no me.

And to my father, Bill, who sadly broke my heart in half when he passed away in 2005. Although he could never bring himself to read *Two Thousand Minnows*, he was my biggest fan—proudly handing the book out to strangers (literally, waitresses), bragging, saying, "This is my daughter," as he handed them the book. He told me laughingly, "If they ask if I read it, I just tell them, 'Hell, I don't need to read it, I lived it.'"

My final indulgence ends with a big hug and huge shout-out to all my brothers and sisters, Shelly, Mark, Beau, and Melinda. Thanks for all the love.

Two Thousand Minnows

1

"Hey Sandra, wanna go fishing?"

Dad is standing by the crooked screen door watching the dark sky threaten to rain. He looks like a bored little boy who wants to go out and play. I do too. I am seven and a half and tall for my age. I don't know how to fish. I saw Dad get mad and throw his pole in a creek once. But that was a long time ago when we used to live in Phoenix, Arizona. Things were different then; a little louder and a little more rocky. But we're here now, in the mountains of West Virginia. No one knows us, and no one cares. It's slower around here and a lot more quiet. So quiet that my head doesn't know what to do with itself. Back in Arizona I knew what to do, how to act, and what to look out for. But here it's different. Dad says we're starting over. I've never started over before. It's sort of like being lost. I look around all the time, trying to find something familiar. So far I don't recognize a thing.

This cabin is my new home and it's not big and it's not roomy. It sits across from the river and says *Go ahead and play*. Even the ratty furniture invites me to jump on it. The brown couch with soggy cushions has been jumped on at least five hundred times, I can tell. The walls have been painted so much they don't even know what color they are. And the green chair now rocks so far back that the wall has to stop it from throwing me to the floor. The tired old woodstove stands alone in the living room. I still have no idea how it works. The house is cold—not chilly—and the light has trouble shining in, because of all the trees I guess. The carpet is wiry and bald in some places. It feels like lots of boots tromp tromped across it. To the right of the living room is a small dreary kitchen. The cabinets hang loose and the floor has scars all over it, probably those boots from long ago. They say it was a hunting and fishing cabin. I guess cabins aren't like houses. They don't have to be pretty, and they get worn out.

The back door opens wide to three crooked cement steps, and a thin dirt path cuts through the grass that's in its way and circles all the way around to the side of the house. The backyard is not a backyard at all, it's a mountain. This mountain has vultures, big black ones, with dead wrinkled red skin for heads. I stay out of the backyard when they land. The other day, I saw one as tall as Mark. He's my little brother. He's okay, but he's still kind of small, and I have to be careful with him. He's five, shy and quiet. He mostly stays out of Dad's way because Dad yells at him more. Shelly's my little sister, she's six, and I don't have to be as careful with her. She's always scared, she's prissy and she acts like a girl. Not me, I hate wearing dresses. I'm what they call a tomboy. All that means is I'm tough, I never say *No, I'll get too dirty*, and I always want to climb.

Off the kitchen in the back, through a faded green curtain, is a large closet made into a bedroom, with a set of bunk beds and a twin. This is ours and the twin is mine. Off the other side of the living room is Mom and Dad's room. The bathroom sits in a tiny hallway, and that's it.

"Are you coming?" Dad is halfway out the door. I run to my closet bedroom and grab my dirty blue tennis shoes.

Mom stands behind Dad and nags, "Bill, you be careful out there. You don't know anything about this river." Mom used to sing for nightclubs, but now all she gets to do is hum once in a while. She's decided to give it another try with Dad and not sing anymore. I bet it's because of the baby. They split up back in Phoenix. Mom just got tired of it; all the fighting and stuff. She's not happy yet, but we've only been here a little while. She probably misses all her friends.

"What in the hell are you talking about? I practically grew up on this river." Dad scratches his head. "As a matter of fact, I lived here every summer till I was about sixteen. Dorothy and George brought us here right after school was out." I see his face settle back into his thoughts, and I don't want to know what they are.

"All right Dad, let's go." I pound out of the screen door across the dew wet grass, dropping one of my tennis shoes as I go. The hill slopes down hard and fast to the road and I have to watch it. My feet can easily get away from me. If I lose my balance and go too fast, I might end up in the road when one of those mean coal mining trucks flies by. They sound like they're in pain as they bounce hard down the road. Some of the coal flip-flops off the back, glad to be free. The trucks go about a hundred miles an hour and they don't watch for kids. Heck, they'd squash me like a caterpillar. I've seen them do it. I don't know why those dumb old caterpillars even try to cross the road. They should just be happy where they are.

I wait and watch. The road's clear, no trucks. Dad forgot his jacket; he turns and runs back to the house. I can't wait, I can't, I love that river. My feet scurry across the damp road; I can smell the wet tar. The air smells too...damp, like rain. Then, as if stepping onto a cloud, the sand covers my feet and the road is gone. I manage not to step on sticks, walnuts, or rocks as I dig each toe in deeper than the other. Now Dad's right behind me. He unchains the upside-down boat from the tree, and with a heave we flip it over. He drags the boat down the bank and into the river. The river slaps the boat on the side and then nudges it hello.

"Go ahead, get in. Make sure you stay in the middle and go all the way to the back."

I trip over the pole, lose my balance, and fall into the wooden seat. Dad rolls his eyes but doesn't say a word. He shoves the boat, avoiding the cold water. The boat rocks hard, then swishes and rolls as we settle down.

The clouds drip a drop or two of rain. I say nothing. Maybe he won't feel it. He rows us out into the middle, and suddenly I'm lost in this still place called Fort Springs. Back on the bank the trees sway just a little, and the clouds reflect in the stillness of the river. The birds seem to be hiding from the rain that is coming.

Dad dips his pole with a single wiggling worm into the water. I lean over and dangle my hand along the sleepy current, wishing I could go swimming, but that's over. Fall is here, so I'll have to wait until next summer. Dad reels up the drowned worm and cusses at him for not doing his job. He toys with a bobber and lets the dead worm go back to work tricking the fish. The raindrops fall one at a time hitting us on the forehead. I ignore them and so does Dad. "Ya know," Dad says as he closes his tackle box, "the best time to fish is during the rain." I'm convinced. After all, the fish are already wet; why would they care if it rains?

We sit there and sit there. Time floats by, along with the twigs, leaves, and river gunk. Dad leans behind his wooden bench and pulls out his BB gun. I don't like that thing. He points at the defenseless tree and snaps the trigger. He misses. He pulls again and a BB flies. "See that? Bet ya I can hit it." I look into the bank at whatever "that" is, and he fires. "Got it." The beer can bounces. He shoots at everything not alive and kills it. I watch and cheer him on. "Wanna try?" Dad holds the gun my way. I shake my head no. His pole lays limp over the side of the boat; it's done fishing. The rain comes and splashes inside the bottom of the boat. Dad aims at a leaf in the water and shoots. He shoots again. The leaf finally drowns. Nothing around us moves. Then up pops a fish alongside us. Dead. Dad looks at me and I stare into the bulging eyes of the fish. He's been hit. The fish must have got it when Dad shot the leaf. Dad slaps his knee, "I'll be damned." He fires again and again. Two, now three more fish pop up like Cheerios floating in milk. "Sandra, who said you had to fish with a pole?" Dad rows to his catch and nets them into the boat. "I told you the best time to fish is when it rains. Nobody's out and you can shoot all the damn fish you want." I laugh and laugh. I can't believe how many fish must have been swimming around under us the whole time, and then bang! Dad shoots them. My hair is wet and Dad is drenched by the time we get back to shore. He puts the fish on a stringer and pretends this is his catch for the day.

As we walk up to the house, old Mr. Grimes can't believe his eyes. "Son, you catch all those?" Mr. Grimes gimps off his porch and heads our way. He's been here all his life. He tells me that every time I see him.

Dad smiles back. "Sure did." He holds out his victims. "Want'em?"

"Why sure if you're not eatin' em'."

Dad hands them over, stringer and all. He pats me on the back as we walk away. "I hate cleaning fish."

"But Dad," I giggle, "shouldn't you tell him to watch out for the BBs? What's going to happen when he bites in and breaks his tooth?"

Later that week, Friday night, I finish dinner and help Mom clean up the kitchen. It's a quiet night. Dad is out, maybe at work. Mom isn't herself; she isn't funny or kind. No jokes tonight. I keep to myself. I can't figure out why it's so weird. The air has that thick electric feeling in it, a bad night feeling.

"Mom do you want to color?"

"No, I'm tired, why don't you color with Mark…?"

The night is moving slowly and I pray it's my imagination. I stay alert and cautious. I don't want to ask where's Dad. If I do, she might say "I don't know" with *that* voice. The cold and dead sound that says nothing. Her voice is the key and I'm afraid of it. She stares away as she speaks. It's better to stay in the dark and act surprised later. Time to go to bed, and that means stay awake and wait.

Shelly and Mark fall fast and hard to sleep—they know deep down inside, but they can use sleep as a way out. I can't, it's my job to help. God is trying to talk to me but I won't listen. Dad promised out loud that he wouldn't drink anymore. I am going to believe him, I have to. God is the problem; He keeps making it hard. God is still trying to warn me; I hear him but I won't answer. If I answer it will be true, and if I answer I'll be scared out of my mind. He'll make it happen for sure if I answer. "Shut Up! It is not going to happen."

The car pulls up and I feel Mom shrivel up inside when the car door slams. She stays in her room. The electricity is here. It is buzzing, humming, and now the door opens. No time to feel. I check out of my body and get into position. Ready…hold on. I have to pay close attention because my timing is crucial, and it can save my mom's life. I turn to Shelly and Mark all the way awake, propped up tight on their beds, and snap, "Shut up! I told you, if you guys scream it'll make it worse." They don't know how Mom feels when they scream. I do. It makes it hard for her to defend herself.

I listen. He is calling her names, asking questions that he doesn't want answers to. "*Please mom, don't say anything*!" I send her thought messages. I know better than to come out of my room. He'll start throwing things when he sees me.

I leave my bedroom, but my body stays in bed with Shelly and Mark. I help her think. I slow him down. What kind of hitting is it? With his hand or his fist? I listen, trying to slow him down with my thoughts. If it's his fist we need the police. I forget about the neighbors who always called the police; we have no neighbors now. What am I going to do? I have to get her out of the house. I move like a snake into the kitchen. He can't see me. I open the door to the outside. I know she won't have time to turn the handle. She sees me. She knows what to do next, get out of the house! Dad is dragging her out of the bedroom by the hair. She needs to stand up. She's screaming. I hate it when she screams. Now Mark and Shelly are screaming. I can't stop it, they are not supposed to scream. She's running for the door. I look at Shelly and Mark, but they don't move. Dad lunges and grabs for her. Mom makes it out!

I block the door with my back up against it; he is pressing against my body. I will kill him. He will sleep tonight and I will kill him, no question. He smells like the stuff, and he is green just like the devil. I hate this man. Why is he doing this? His eyes meet mine and I stare into his soul. I am more powerful than him. Watch. "Dad, it's okay, Mom's gone, let her go."

He melts like green slime under a rock. "Sandra," he stumbles onto my shoulder. "I am so sorry. I love you kids so much. Your Mother is a whore and she makes me mad, but I love you."

I watch him from my bed with Shelly and Mark crying on my lap. They know the game and they know their cue. Together we plead, "We love you Daddy, it's okay." He continues crying, begging and explaining himself. This is my cue. "Dad, don't worry, it's okay, tomorrow it will be better, we know, we forgive you."

"Forgive me! You little pieces of shit. Your Mother is a cheating, lying whore I'm alone here. You're all against me!"

Now Shelly steps in. "I know Daddy, I know. We will do better, I promise. We love you." She talks really fast, and soon we are all scrunched up repeating our love over and over again. I am out of the room looking for Mom, but I can't look too hard or he'll know. If he feels or sees my fear he'll win. I have to get him out of our room and into his bed. I never had to do this much work before; usually the police come and the baby-sitter helps. I must stay strong. Mom is going to die out there. There are no police, baby-sitters, or neighbors.

Good, he's back to hating himself and wanting us to forgive him. I won't talk this time, we'll all just listen. Mark is sucking his fingers—he has no tears—and Shelly is babbling to herself and listening to him. I am watching. When will he stop crying and just go to bed? I have to get outside and find Mom. It's snowing, and she has no coat or shoes.

He's done, he's gone, he's told us to go to sleep. This is not a good time to disobey. I hear him lock the doors. I get up and unlock the kitchen door, it's close to my bed—not too risky. The front door could have been deadly. Shelly and Mark are asleep. I told them I would go find her. I open my window and call to her. It is black, no streetlights, no moon, no point. I will wait one hour, and then I'll go find her. If she's hurt she won't be able to hear me. I am looking for her out of my body. My head is popped out of the open window, and I notice the tears are warm on my cold face. I want my mom now. There she is creeping toward me. I say nothing. I have to get her inside. I hold her hands and help pull her through the window. She's cold like an ice tray, and I wonder if she could die. I don't know a lot about cold. She kisses me on the cheek and crawls deep into my covers. I rub her body starting with her arms until each part is warm. I listen for her breathing. I do not sleep. I look around the room at Shelly and Mark across from me, they are so small. I see Mom with her beautiful skin and her black hair. I decide I am okay with them around me, and I would rather die myself than see them hurt. I love them very, very much.

2

We've been here over four weeks. The house has settled down and so have we. The hot water works almost all the time. The river is moving slower and they say it will be an early winter. Winters in Phoenix, where I was born, meant nothing but put on your sandals and grab a sweater in case it rained. Dad has been telling Shelly and me about how much fun it'll be riding the bus to school. I used to ride my bike.

The first day of school is here; it's six a.m. and time to get ready. The bus will pick us up at seven in front of the house. How does the bus know where we live? Shelly and I stumble out of bed with knots in our hair and squinty eyes. Mom gets up in about the same shape and starts a little fire; it goes out twice before she cusses loud enough, then it starts. It only warms us up if we're standing next to it. She gets our clothes out and hangs them on a kitchen chair close to the stove so they'll be warm when we get dressed. She makes it a game and we laugh at each other. Mom knows as much about the cold as I do. I thought all you had to do was turn on a heater. Shelly is quiet while Mom rips out her tangles. She's nervous. I rip out my own tangles and all three of us wonder about the big day ahead. Mom starts breakfast and packs us a lunch at the same time. She leans on the rusty sink. I notice that she is getting more tired as the days go on.

I have Shelly with me as we wait at the edge of our front yard. It's too cold to wait outside anymore. I don't know what to do. Do I have to be out here, or will the bus honk if it doesn't see me? I better just wait. Mom watches us from the living room window. I see it! I see the yellow blur way down there. It's coming. What do I do? Do I wave, or what? It's the first time we've ridden a bus.

The first day of school is terrifying. It's the first time we've transferred schools, and we don't even know any of the teachers. Mom can't go with us. She doesn't have a car. So I have to do this one by myself. I don't even know if she knows exactly where we're going. Normally Shelly's the one who's scared all the time, but today we are both frightened and nervous. The bus door opens with a loud sigh, and the brakes blow out hot air while the bus impatiently waits for us to get on. I hold Shelly's hand, and she squeezes mine back as we step onto the bus. Mom had given us a long hug and stern orders. "Sit together Sandra. Don't leave Shelly alone, and walk her to her class first. Remember to meet in front of the school and don't get on the bus without her. I love you. Watch out for your sister."

As if I would let anything happen to Shelly. She has been my little sister forever. I know how to take care of her and I know more about her than anybody. Shelly's stomach hurts all the time. She's afraid of Dad and she doesn't like to talk very much. I will take care of her, I always do.

We enter the bus, me first and Shelly behind me. I have to make sure it's safe. My body feels like it's going to be sick; but I'm the only one who knows that. Everyone gets quiet and stares. They are all so much bigger and older than us. A very tall boy scoots over. "Here ya go." I am horrified. I can't sit next to him! I have to sit with Shelly, but there's nowhere for us to sit together. I sit down next to the boy and put Shelly across the aisle next to me. We look straight ahead with our hands folded in our laps.

"Hey, where ya'll from?"

The whole bus listens for my answer because they know that we're not from around here.

"Arizona." I say without looking.

"Whatch' all's names?"

"Sandra, and she's Shelly." I wish he'd shut up but I'd better be polite. "What's yours?"

"I'm Bob, but everyone calls me Bobby."

Shelly stays folded tightly in her seat.

"Ya know ya talk funny but yur real purty. If anyone bothers you, you just tell me and I'll take care of them, ya hear me?"

I think he wants to be my boyfriend. He's a nice boy, about eleven with thick, short, blond hair and big brown eyes. He smiles the whole ride. Everyone knows him. I think he's popular. And we're the pretty new girls who talk funny.

Shelly trusts no one and I don't blame her. The bus bounces back and forth up the hill to the front doors of the school. There's at least twenty more buses all lined up in the parking lot. The kids are loud by the time the bus stops, and I can barely hear my thoughts. I don't know what do to first. I take Shelly to class. No one's there but a couple of kids drawing on the chalkboard. She doesn't know where to sit or what to do and she looks at me with cold blue eyes. I don't know what to tell her. I point her to an empty seat close to the door. I feel sorry for her. I know she's embarrassed, just like I will be in a few minutes. I think knowing what she's going to go through is harder than going through it myself.

The school is big, ugly and brick, the closest thing to a prison I have ever seen. It's not a happy place. No running, no laughing, no personalities. "Yes, ma'am" and "No, sir" is all I hear in the halls.

I step into class a little late in my new black and purple velvet dress; it's a little too fancy as I notice the kids sitting down in front of me. My long thick brown hair feels extra heavy and my face starts to get hot as I stand next to the teacher who is introducing me to the class. They all say "Hello" in unison, and I learn how humiliation feels. Along with the hello comes a hubbub from the boys. They think I'm pretty. The girls don't. The teacher puts an end to all that. I take my seat making sure I don't make any eye contact. I sit in the back of class, alone in my own world, ignoring all the strangers, trying to be tough. I'm so worried that Shelly is suffering the same way I am. I can see the teacher's lips move, but I can't hear her words because a falling feeling has taken over my brain. Is Dad home? Are they fighting? If I know they're okay I can calm myself down. I spin around and around in my head finding nothing to hold on to. I think of Shelly, her eyes gray with fear when I left her alone in that classroom—everything is bad and everywhere is dangerous.

"Turn to the next page," a voice whispers. I snap back into reality. Some girl is asking me where I'm from and I tell her Arizona.

She looks at me weird and cocks her head, and with the strangest twang she says, "Is that down there by Florida?"

I am so stunned by her voice I don't even hear her question. "What?" I whisper.

"Yeah, that's down there by Florida," she repeats.

Hasn't she ever looked at a map?

"Attention!" Mrs. Tart stands up from behind her desk. She's dressed for church in a yellow high-collared dress and shiny black high heels. Her long thin hands clap. "If anyone disrupts the class, you'll get a swat with the paddle, I promise you that." My eyes almost fall out. I don't remember teachers hitting. She can't hit me.

God, you promised no more hitting. Is this your way of tricking me again? Every time I make a deal with you, you do the opposite. I've asked a thousand times, and every time I beg for help it happens anyway.

God's trying to hurt me. But I'll show him. I won't talk to him, and if I do I'll ask for the opposite to happen, then it'll be my way. But how do I say the words, *God, please let my dad hit Mom.* I don't want him to hit her. But if God hears me begging he'll do the exact opposite.

I have to quit thinking. It hurts and I can't figure it out. I don't know what to do. Besides, I need to see Shelly. I want to go home *now.*

After watching the long, skinny, black second hand tick a million times, the bell rings and I'm free. I forget my new deal with God and accidentally pray Shelly will be waiting for me outside. Finally I find her at the door. We don't even talk. I find the right bus and we go to our seats. She puts her head on the windowsill. She won't look at me, and I know why. If she does, she'll cry.

3

Winter passed us by all the while Mom's belly is getting bigger and bigger. I wake up early because it's so hot I can't sleep anymore. It's still dark, but I know that morning is just around the corner. I get dressed and then go across the road to the river. This is my first time being alone. I love the river. I could get lost in the current or the trees that sing with the wind. The little creatures who live in the river are my favorites, and I like to watch them swim and shuffle and dart through the water. I decide to catch crawdads, and grab my dented empty bucket. I feel alone and quiet. The morning isn't completely here—no one to consider or watch over or figure out. The water is perfectly still and it's much cooler by the riverbank. I take my time crawdad hunting. I know I'll disturb the beauty when I plunge my bucket into the water, and when I turn the rocks over I'll lose the clearness. I understand beauty and the emptiness of alone is soothing.

I have my favorite yellow sweatshirt on. It's six times too big and soft and everyone hates it and that makes me love it even more. The more they comment, the more I wear it. Mom, Dad, Shelly, and Mark all plot together to destroy it. I protect my sweatshirt with the same passion I protect them.

I'm at the river over an hour, lost in perfect quiet. Finally, I'm bored with the crawdads. Now I dare myself to catch the magic of the minnows. Minnows are impossible; I know that from experience. I crouch down letting them get used to my shadow, and I wait until I have so many in sight—there must be at least two thousand. Then quickly, without breathing, I drop the bucket into crystal water and swish out my trophies. I wait for the water to settle inside the bucket to see my prize. They're all there, inside the bucket, all two thousand minnows. Some people would call it luck, but luck means you don't know what you're doing. I call it magic and magic takes practice. No one in the history of Fort Springs had ever caught minnows. At least not that I know about. It's the perfect morning.

"Sandra Lee Vaughan! What the hell are you doing? Get your ass over here!" Mom never talks to me that way unless she's really pissed. She isn't dressed, she's in her nightgown. Why is she in her nightgown outside and why is she screaming at me? I don't have time to figure it out. I grab my trophy and slosh it as I run to her.

"God damn it, Sandra you scared the shit out of me. Who do you think you are?"

"I just wanted to catch some minnows." I try to show her.

"I don't give a rat's ass if you were trying to catch whales." She huffs and puffs away down the hall and slams the bathroom door.

Mom forgot how to catch minnows ever since we left Phoenix, that's all.

Dad ignores the morning's events. Normally he'd jump in and help Mom make sure I understand just how much trouble I'm in, but I've noticed that Dad's acting different now that we are living in West Virginia. He's funny and he plays with us again, but he's still kind of mean to Mark. Insults are his favorite game. He likes to put us down and then be nice. I watch him carefully. I know I'm his kid, but it's Shelly who makes him proud. If I am not watching him, I'm trying to be his friend. Sometimes it works. I finally figured out why he likes Shelly and Mark better: they look like him, blond and fair skinned. I have dark hair like Mom, which makes me more like her. It's true, I'm older, fatter, and dark haired. I'm doomed. I hope the baby looks just like me.

Mom told us that she has to go to California where her sisters live to have the baby. She doesn't trust the doctors here in West Virginia; and she doesn't like the hospital. It will be safer for the baby if she has it back in California. We listened and agreed with her.

Mom prepares us for when it is time to have the baby. Each day after lunch we took off for our baby walk. All five of us would walk for hours exploring another new path off a road that led to everywhere. We would find ourselves lost in the trees, leaves, and moss. The woods were quiet. We had no one around but us, and it was perfect. We took turns telling the baby what we saw with our eyes. We had games that involved the baby. The funniest part was feeling the kicks. Mark swore that the baby was laughing. I don't know for sure, but I do know that the sound of my voice seemed to make the baby move more. We told it how it felt out in the world, what things smelled like, and what colors we were seeing on our walks.

As we walked barefooted on the tar roads, the tar would heat up in the afternoon sun and we would run to pop the tar bubbles with our big toes. By the end of summer we would have permanent black feet. Our mission was to save the woolly little caterpillars from being smashed by the coal mining trucks. We kept a count of who saved the most each day. I figured that with those walks, we saved a million caterpillars from death. And then those that didn't make it, they were given a proper burial off to the side of the road in the briar bushes.

Once we got home, Mom would start dinner and we would try to scrape off the unforgiving tar. That kept us busy for about an hour. After dinner we played with the baby. Mom just laid there and laughed. We would try to figure out what kind of music the baby liked best, then we would sing a song or tell stories. I felt the baby kick, but mostly I felt it move and flutter around. I would try to see inside my mom's belly. I would lay there, with my head on Mom's belly, while she stroked my hair and I pretended to tickle the baby's hand.

Dad's family is coming to visit for a while this weekend. I love that because no one has to be afraid, and everyone behaves. I can laugh and have fun when my uncles get here. Usually Mom's happy about them coming, but this time she doesn't seem to care. Maybe she's getting more pregnant, her belly is sticking out. Maybe it's the baby, she looks really tired. I'll help her out, I don't mind. I love to cook.

Mom has something on her mind. She's so quiet lately, and it scares me because I can't figure it out. She's sad, tired, mad, and miserable all at the same time. She loves her hair brushed. Today I'll brush it for a whole hour. She's in the bathroom staring again.

"Mom, what's wrong?"

"Nothing honey, I'm fine." She splashes her face.

I don't believe her. I sit on the edge of the tub.

"Want me to brush your hair?"

She looks down with that could-you-leave-me-alone look and answers, "Sure honey, but not now, later."

They're here! They're finally here: Grandma, Uncle John, Uncle Brooks, and Cousin Paul. The car pulls up slowly in the driveway. It feels like I've been sitting outside all day. They're all here to play, laugh, swim, and keep the peace. They don't know about the peace part. We're going to have fun. The car is full of suitcases, shoes, pickled beans, cucumbers, and canned vegetables. They're going to stay a lot of nights. We jump off the porch, we can't help it, we're loud and excited. Grandma hugs each one of us and looks us in the eye. I can feel her heart swell up when she sees us. We're so special to her that even the sight of us gets her a little teary eyed.

John and Brooks have Mark in a headlock, and now he's on Brooks's shoulders, and I see Mark beaming. Shelly is shy, and so Grandma worries about her.

"You know if that child would eat more greens she'd be fine."

Mom grabs three more jars of pickled something from the car and walks Grandma to the house, "You know Dorothy, Shelly's a big girl and I really don't believe in forcing someone to do or eat something they don't like."

Grandma thinks Mom's crazy and eating something green will cure shyness, being too skinny and having freckles. Shelly knows that the next few days are about to gobble her up. She'll have to eat beans and I can't help but laugh. Shelly eating a bean is the most painful, dramatic, and pathetic experience. She looks to Mom for help, but Mom's hands are tied. Dinner with Grandma is funny. We'll all sit around eating fresh broccoli and raw radishes and, of course, "*raw is better*," they say. Shelly will close her throat, clench her teeth, and finally choke and gag.

Grandma trots to the backyard to inspect the weeds that have taken over the garden. She cusses and fools around with a tall plant and digs her fingers into the soil. She's going to plant some new stuff later.

"Rhubarb!" Grandma tugs on a weed like she's just struck gold. "My goodness will you look at this, it must have come back from last year."

I bite my tongue. All I see is a huge ugly-looking, purplish-green celery thing. No kidding, it looks just like weeds do. Horror fills Shelly's mouth, it hangs open wondering do we really have to eat that too.

Dad dismisses the weed. "I'm not gonna eat that."

Shelly, Mark, and I exhale with relief. For a minute there I thought this ugly thick weed was our next meal.

Grandma mutters to herself, "Well, I'm not going to waste this, I'll eat it by myself, damn fools."

By now it's time for lunch and all the guys take turns showing poor Shelly how to eat a bean. "Ummm, look Shelly, they're really good." Brooks turns toward her and shows her how to chew. Brooks is tall, thin, and crazy. He's seventeen or so. He's so nice he'll do anything for you. Everyone is *darlin'* and no one is a stranger. He's more cautious than John but dares life just the same.

Shelly sits there with the *I don't care, I can't hear you* attitude. Now it's Uncle John's turn, and he talks like a baby, "C'mon Shel, eat a green bean for your old Uncle John." As if she can't understand him. John is taller than Brooks and has thick blond hair. He's always trying to grow a mustache and Dad always tells him, "Boy, all you got there is peach fuzz." John doesn't talk as much as Brooks, but when he does, he's just plain funny. He'll fight anybody and win every time according to him. He's younger than Brooks by a year or two, and he loves being Grandma's baby and Jack's little brother.

Now it's time for Dad to step in, "Shelly Rae just eat the damn things."

With her lip tight she gurgles, "Nope."

It's only a matter of time. Shelly throws up, and the game is over, a game that Shelly wins every time. The losers walk away with their heads down. Don't worry we'll try it again tomorrow without fail.

Grandma shakes her head and mumbles to herself as she clears the dishes, as if somehow she's failed at being a grandma. It's so funny to watch the passion built up around this damn bean. I eat my beans, or should I say I swallow them whole. All I have to do is swallow about six of them and then I'm off the hook. Mark, on the other hand, will eat them for two reasons: one Grandma will kiss and praise him endlessly, and two the men will pat him on the back with a *that-a-boy*. Mark shines, and green beans hang from his mouth.

"Shelly," I say with a frown, "I told you all you have to do is swallow them like a pill. And the green ones, well, just cut them in half so you can get them down."

She looks at me with little tears filling her eyes. "I know Sandra, but I can't."

I'm sick of it; it's as if someone's going to win a big prize if Shelly eats a bean.

Mom grabs the hose by the throat and grumbles in the distance while filling the dog dish with water. "Would you just leave my kids alone for God's sake?" Grandma didn't hear her since she's in the house, but I did.

The next morning I can hear a slight hammering in the distance. Is that Paul at the river and up a tree? I push my bangs back and rub my eyes.

"Mom, can I please go see what Paul's doing across the street?"

She doesn't have time to answer. I am out the door pulling my shirt on as I run across the yard.

Paul hears me panting beneath him and looks down from the tree.

With nails hanging from the side of his mouth and a hammer above his head, he yells down, "I'm building you a swing."

He's really building me a swing, my very own swing. Paul's my cousin; he's about fifteen, full of magic, and he's on my side. Like an older brother. He looks like a monkey up there barefooted holding on to the tree trunk. I watch him. He's halfway up, and has nailed together a few pieces of wood that work as stairs. I want to marry someone like him. He pounds a small slat of wood every foot, and after he pounds another one in the tree, he can climb on that one and reach for the next place. When he's reached the top, he yells down,

"Hey Sandra bring me that rope."

"How?" I whisper to myself. I really want to but I don't know how.

"Just take one end and tie it on your pants and start climbing up here."

He's so smart. I tie the rope end to my belt loop, and start the climb. I feel myself effortlessly go up the tree, and now I see the rope following me. This is amazing. I'll be swinging pretty soon. All we have to do is tie the rope to the giant tree limb. I'm watching myself as the new staircase carries me to the top. I'm a hundred feet in the air and I'm not scared. I keep climbing. The tree stays perfectly still and holds me, it's not going to let me fall. I want to say thank you, but I don't have to. The tree hears my thoughts.

"Keep going Sandra you're almost here." Paul is calm.

"Here you go." I reach out to him.

"Stay there I'll come to you and get the rope."

He's on the last big branch straddling it with his legs. If the branch breaks, which it won't, but if it did, Paul would fall on his butt, straight into the water. I am at the top of the main trunk. He scoots off the overhang and reaches me. He smiles the Paul smile and assures me I did a great thing. He bends his body down and unties the rope from my belt loop without an ounce of fear, then slithers away to tie the knot. My job is done but I am not leaving. I hold on and watch the tying of the knot. He tugs and spits, "If we don't tie a good knot it won't last, and we want this to last forever."

I couldn't agree more. I watch carefully so that one day I can tie one of these important knots. We both come down the tree, me first of course, him teasing me all the way down. We sit down in the sand, our cutoffs full of bark and dust, then look up at the magical swing.

"Paul, do you think the tree hurts with all those nails in it?"

Paul shifts his body, looks up at the trunk, and nods. "Yeah, it probably does, but I did ask the tree first. It said it wouldn't mind." Man, am I glad he asked first. I was worried about that old tree.

By late afternoon Paul's the hero. We're all at the river and the boys compete at who's the best rope diver. They run down the riverbank and jump on the rope, grab the third knot which is the highest, and fly into the river. Somehow they pull themselves up into a ball then let go upside down and dive into the water. I can't do it, Shelly won't, and Mark is too small.

We try another trick, two people at a time. This is great. I team up with Paul, and the hardest part is running at the same speed in order to grab the rope and swing out. His tan body, strong arms, and fast legs threaten my attempt. I hope I can grab the rope before he flies away without me. He grabs the top and I grab the bottom. Our bodies slam together, and before I know it we are out, up, and over the river. "Let go." Paul screams. I don't know where the courage comes from, but I trust him and without a second to question, I let go and fall from the tree. I see the branch above shake me loose, and water splashes a deep crisp hello. Paul waits for me to rise from the water. He shakes the curls loose from his head and blinks the water off his eyelashes. I smile so hard I feel my cheeks lift. Paul races me back to the shore; he slows up, I might win. Then for no reason, he grabs my ankles, pulls on them hard, and back under the water I go. My hair is everywhere. I reach for a quick breath and close my eyes and from the bank, John and Brooks cannonball me. I give up immediately. They'll drown me if I don't, and I still can't touch the bottom. After they all dunk me, throw me, and finally leave me alone, I start swimming back to shore. Paul's cutoffs are floating in front of me, John is on Brooks's shoulders getting ready to jump, and me, I float back to shore slowly, barely moving my arms, and fiilled with pride, joy, and love. I did it, I'm not chicken.

"It's time for lunch," Grandma hollers from the house. We eat outside, soaking wet and dripping. There's not enough room in the house—some of us eat on a big white picnic table in the backyard. The backyard is really a garden that Grandma tends. After lunch she teaches me how to plant, what to plant, and why it is so important to water and get rid of those damn weeds. Her hands are soft on top and scratched on the bottom.

Mom stands up and excuses herself. "I'll get the dishes you stay out here with the girls." Mom is not a country girl, she's a city girl trapped in the mountains with a bunch of hillbillies, and she could care less about tomatoes, worms, when to plant, or when to pick. Mom likes swimming pools, new carpet, sunglasses, and tanning.

"Sandra, get me my bucket and some paper bags. It's time to pick some of those tomatoes and the green beans."

I never have figured out how she knows, but she knows when to pick like the second hand knows time on a watch. "Now listen, you pick the tomatoes I tell you to, and put them in this paper sack." Grandma bends over, her butt high in the air and her hands searching the dirt for weeds. "And Shelly Rae, you can start picking them beans over there." She points without looking.

I guess she figures that if Shelly picks em' she just might make friends and eat em'.

After we finish the hard part, we sit down in the hot sun, drink ice tea with sugar, and shuck the beans. Mom doesn't mind shucking the beans. I snap off the ends with my nubby fingernails and slowly pull down the string.

"Now the way I see it, you and Jack can stay as long as you need." Grandma scoops the good beans off the table into the paper sack.

Mom chokes as if all her air had been cut off. "Oh now Dorothy this is just temporary," she sips hard on the iced tea. "I really appreciate it, but I don't think I can live here in the mountains."

"Well that's all fine and good..." Grandma leaves it alone.

"Dorothy I love it here, don't get me wrong, I'm just not used to it."

Grandma knows that, she's just snooping around. She's the one who's comfortable out here sweating, shooing flies, and shucking. Mom's okay with it, but it's not her thing. Grandma likes women's work. Mom has always taught me that there is *no such thing as women's work*. Grandma shows me different every chance she gets.

The night is finally here. The night chirpers are singing extra loud; they call them locusts, but I've never seen them.

Dad yells out, "Snipes! It's time to snipe hunt." He turns to his brothers, "John do you think we should take the kids?"

John with a serious look says, "Well Jack," his thumb rubbing his bottom lip, "I just don't know. It's not a thing for kids. We were much older before we got to go snipe hunting. What if one of them damn things gets loose?"

Dad thinks about it, "Sandra do you want to go?"

Oh my God, do I? I can barely get the answer out of my mouth.

"Okay, but you kids stay right behind us, you understand me?"

We nod yes with our mouths hanging open.

"Okay here's how we do it. I'll hold the bag—Shelly go get four paper bags, not the big ones the little ones, those sneaky bastards will escape out of the big bags."

She runs into the house. I listen carefully with all my might. Mark is ready.

"John, you take Sandra. I'll take Mark, and Brooks you take Shelly. Paul will be lookout, he'll scare those little bastards to us. Shelly!" he yells into the house, "bring a flashlight."

The hunt begins. My knees are nervous, so I stay close to Uncle John. Paul's gone into the dark somewhere, I sure hope he'll be okay. We head out toward the woods because snipes live in cold dark places somewhere in the woods; step-by-step we look. Brooks starts calling out to the snipes. Paul is nowhere. It's dark and the only thing I can see is the movement of the ground when the light hits it.

Uncle John is telling me not to worry, he wants me to help. He says it would be better if I hold the bag, but I don't want to hold the bag.

"Here hold it, I've got to watch out for the rest of them." He puts the bag in my sweating hand.

Dad wants Shelly to hold the bag, but she won't. He gives her the flashlight, and she tiptoes behind him. "Shel, no matter what happens, you keep the light straight ahead." We keep walking, calling, and watching for the snipes; we have been warned.

Brooks creeps behind me, and John whispers, "If you see one, put the bag down and watch out for your fingers, they can take one off." Mark looks down at his fingers.

"What do they look like?" I wonder out loud.

Brooks looks at us with Mark on his shoulders now. "No one really knows. See they've never been caught before."

I am going to be the first one to catch a snipe! This is no longer a game, it is a challenge. I'm determined, I want to be the first. Now the questions are swirling through my head. How do we catch one? How big are they? Do they really bite? I want all the answers, I need to know. Dad is crouched down. Shelly is holding onto his neck and he is telling us to stop! I don't breathe, I stop.

We hear a rustle in the woods, it has to be Paul. Paul is scaring the wormy things toward us. I'm afraid with excitement and it feels better than a roller coaster. Shelly wants to go home, and her feet start heading that way. Mark's laughing so he won't cry. "Be quiet," I have to tell him. Then Paul starts screaming. One of them bit him!

"They're coming, they're coming, get ready." John squats.

I don't know what to do, they never got around to telling us that part. I wait, the sweat beads on my forehead. The grass is tall and briars surround us. Dad's got one! Shelly is running around and Brooks is helping him hold the bag with a vicious animal ripping and tearing, trying to get out.

I pray that it won't escape. I am very aware of my feet dancing around the twigs that feel like snipes. There's snipes everywhere, but it's dark and I can't get a good look at one. Hell, I don't want a good look at one. Chaos and confusion rustle in the bushes, everyone is everywhere. Meanwhile, Paul is crawling out of the bushes, bent over and holding his hand. He's been bitten. I knew it. I see a little blood. We have to get home. Dad has lost the varmint. He's out of breath and beat.

Brooks holds Mark and admits his defeat, "I had him Jack, I had him, what happened? Did you drop the son of a bitch?"

"No, this one was big and mean. I couldn't hold him, he fought his way out. He's somewhere around here."

Paul jumps out of the way pushing Shelly, "There it is," John shouts from behind. "Run!"

No one is left, I am ahead of everyone, knowing that that thing is on my heels. "Mom, Mom," I holler deep and loud, "Help…"

We all make it to the porch, our hearts racing. We beat Dad and the guys back to the house. We're in shock. Mom is trying to listen to us flapping away.

Dad and the gang are at the side of house; they're on the ground roaring, laughing! "Did you see Shelly's eyes when Paul said 'they're coming'?" Dad rolls over holding his side.

"I thought Sandra was going to kill that paper bag." Brooks is cracking up so hard he hits John in the leg.

John ignores the punch. "I swear to God, those snipes couldn't have caught Sandra, she looked like her ass was on fire."

We've been had.

Dad shoves me in the arm. "We got you."

"No you didn't," I stutter, "I knew you were kidding." I try to defend us but they got us good. They lied, cheated, and bullied us. I had no idea that snipes were a fake. I really thought we were snipe hunters. As the laughing and joking continues, I start to get mad. Enough is enough, they got me. If I was from around here, I doubt they would have got that far. I would have figured it out. How was I supposed to know they don't have snipes here, heck they have everything else. Buzzards, bears, snakes, moles—besides it wasn't funny anymore. I was really scared there for a minute. I'll never admit it, but I was.

We all sit on the porch making each other laugh as the night passes. Everyone has their own version of the story, and I make them laugh so hard they beg me to quit. The chirpers quiet down. The night air smells sweet. This is a good night. I don't want this one to end.

4

The next morning, Grandma has to go. She kisses us good-bye, but she leaves the "boys" behind. I realize that they are here to take care of us when Mom has to go. Now it's for real, it was time, she's leaving in a few days and it hurts to know she is leaving.

"Mom, how long will you be gone?" I watch her scramble the eggs.

She whips the bowl hard. "I don't know, it depends on the baby." She looks away.

Paul and I are up early and leave for the river. He wants to be an artist. He's got long hair that drives everyone crazy. His whole head is curls—thick, long, dark, and brown. We walk and talk. He makes a lot of sense to me, and he wants to talk to me. I can tell he cares about what I think. Once in a while I try to sneak a touch of his hair, no one in my family has curly hair. He talks to me about himself and I understand most of it. But mostly I listen. We can make each other laugh.

This day we take off in the rowboat. He unties it, I get in, and he shoves us off. He usually rows from the center and I balance myself in front. Laughing is mostly what we do. The middle of the river is my favorite place, and the current gurgles beneath the boat. The fish jump every few minutes and the sun shines on my shoulders. Paul drifts back and forth into his thoughts as he paddles from one side to the next.

"Hey San, I want to tell you something very important. Do me a favor and never forget it."

I can see that this is serious. I agree, after all Paul is my friend and if he says it's important, then it is.

"Never believe what you read, never believe what you hear, and only believe half of what you see."

I'm immediately confused. "Say that again."

He does.

"But how can I do that? I have to read in school and I have to listen to my mom and dad, and my eyes are my eyes."

He looks at me and holds onto my warm shoulders. "It will make sense to you later, I promise. Don't try to figure it out now, but you will when it's time."

I repeat it out loud for him a dozen times, and after each reciting, I still don't get it. It feels big. But I promise him that I will never forget.

That night I think of Paul's important words, and I remember a terrible fight in Phoenix, with the police and everything. My babysitter Thelma said, "When two people really love each other, they fight." She was holding us so tight that we could barely breathe; she was so scared that her voice was shaking. I *had* asked her why Dad was hitting Mom. She said it again, "When people love each other like your Mommy and Daddy, they fight. But that doesn't mean they don't love each other." I didn't expect her to lie to me. The worst part was I knew better, and that was the first lie I ever heard. I guess Thelma didn't know better.

That was the closest thing in my life I could relate to Paul's instruction. It felt good that I had something to understand about his puzzling quote. He'd told me not to try to figure it out, but that was impossible.

Two days have passed and it's time for Mom to go and have the baby. Of course I'm worried about her and when she'll come home. Dad's taking her to the city and he'll be back. In the meantime Uncle John, Uncle Brooks, and Paul will stay with us. I feel okay with that, but I can see it isn't okay with Dad. He sternly threatens them with their lives if anything happens to us. "Don't you guys screw around, those are my kids."

Uncle John gives Mom a big hug and wishes her well. Mom's eyes start to water—she trusts my uncles more than Dad. She whispers her worry to me as she holds onto my neck, "Sandra your father won't hurt you kids, you know that, right? I'll be home as soon as I can, and I need you to please watch out for your sister and brother." She leaves me standing there with nowhere to go, the lump in my throat hurting. I can't cry, she needs me to be strong. God, I wish I could cry. Mom dashes off quickly to say her good-byes to Mark; he's hysterical inside, his face says so. He knows that his only friend is about to leave him. She grabs his face and kisses his cheek. Shelly breaks up as soon as Mark does. Mom rubs her hand down Shelly's back, her voice cracks just a little. "Shelly, you help your sister with Mark and stay with him." Mom's in the car looking straight ahead, her glasses cover her red nose and swollen eyes. Dad throws the last bag in the car and we can't pretend any longer. She has three broken hearts waving softly when they leave the driveway.

Shelly finally answers Mom back, to herself, "I will Mom, I won't let him be scared." She knew Mark like I knew her, inside and out. Is Mom really going to leave us?

I feel so sorry for Mark, I can see him hurt inside so bad. His body's small and his tears are big, and of course he's always burdened with being a big boy. He isn't a big boy today. Shelly holds him with her stiff arm around his neck. It looks like a headlock, but it's her way of using him for support as she stands there scared.

Shelly is a shy little girl who doesn't like strangers, none of them, even the ones that are family. She likes me and Mark. The boys are trying to cheer us up and offer us fun things to do or fun foods to eat. Nothing sounds fun. We all walk into the house and sit on the couch, Mom's couch. "I guess this is what it's like when a Mommy has a baby," I answer Shelly's question about why Mom has to leave. "I can't remember what happened when you and Mark were born, my memory doesn't remember." I sit there smelling Mom on the couch. We all sit there not crying. All three of us hurt at once.

It takes forever for night to come. The boys make hot dogs and hamburgers. We even get to sit outside to eat dinner. We sit out there afterward, barefooted, popping off the weed tops between our toes, listening to the chirpers and smelling the river. The boys play cards and pretend to care about who's winning or losing. It doesn't really matter.

Days come and go. If the phone rings it's like a thunder storm. I run to hear who it is, and each time it isn't her. Why won't she call us? Is having a baby that hard? I guess it is. The phone becomes the enemy. No one talks about Mom. The house feels empty, and like a tin can being kicked down the street, the emptiness echoes. She's so far away I can't find her. I know one thing, she's not looking for us either. Maybe she likes the baby more and forgot about us. I don't like to think that, but maybe it's true. I won't tell anyone that I think that.

Dad came back two nights later. I thought maybe, somehow, Mom would change her mind and not go to California. He walked in. We all held our breath hoping she was behind him.

Dad said in a stern voice, "Your Mother will be fine."

John and Brooks made a joke and tried to shift things away from his entrance. It didn't work.

A whole week passes and the boys take the Greyhound bus home. I'm sad to see them leave, but things aren't that much fun right now. Tonight I'll cook dinner; SpaghettiOs , and hamburgers. My hamburgers don't turn out like Mom's; her hands make them quickly and round, I struggle with round. I have to put the hamburger down and mash it into shape and then I get a knife to make it round. It's like Play-Doh, but for real. No one says anything at night. We eat and clean up. I do the kitchen by myself, it's better if I'm busy. After dinner I throw the scraps out for the dogs, and then I'll get their dog food ready. I hate dog food, the can is so hard to open. But as I look into their eyes, waiting for me to get the stupid can open, I remember when Big Foot and Little Foot were born.

Sugar Foot was pregnant, and it took forever for her to have her litter. I watched and waited every day, but nothing. We had made her a special bed in the living room close to the woodstove. She stayed there, not with Mom and Dad like normal. I got up one morning, and stopped by her bed on the way to the bathroom, to say good morning. I reached down to pet her, and holy moly there they were, shiny and so tiny, two puppies, a black one and a fuzzy brown one. They were only the size of a candy bar. I ran so fast to Mom, I woke her up before the bedroom door was open. "Mom, Sugar had her babies. Come on." I pulled on her hand hard, dragging her to the living room. Mom and Dad stood over Sugar Foot. Dad reached for Sugar and Mom reached for the twins.

"How you doing girl?" Dad patted his Sugar Foot.

"Oh my God, they're so tiny, is that all of them?" Mom gently put the babies back.

Little Foot was half the size of Big Foot and looked just like her mom, black and short-haired. Big Foot was brown and fuzzy. Not only did he have lots of fur, but he also must have eaten all Little's food when they were inside Sugar. Naming them was easy, heck they practically came out with name tags on.

"That's all Mom, there's only two. Can we keep them?" I squeeze her hand extra hard. Mom made the decision right then and there.

"Sure, why not, we can't split them up."

It was the happiest day of my life.

5

I didn't sleep well last night. I tossed and turned all night, I think it was the bad dreams. I miss Mom so bad. I'm glad that morning is finally here. I drag myself up and look down at my nightgown, darn it I must have spilled grape Kool-Aid on it last night. Shelly and Mark are already up fighting in the bathroom over toothpaste. I make myself some toast and sit at the table stabbing at the hard butter. Why does Dad always put the butter in the fridge? Mom doesn't. I hear a car, it's probably Dad back from work. I sit at the table kicking my legs and scratching off the burnt parts of my toast. Uncle John says burnt toast is good for you, it'll put hair on your chest. I don't want hair on my chest. Grandma walks in the doorway. My face lights up like sunshine. "I didn't know you were coming today."

Shelly and Mark run out like the wind is blowing them toward her. "Grandma! Grandma!" they hug her like Mom.

"Sandra, you help your brother and sister get some things, we're going to Grandma's for a little while."

That's good, now I can rest. She'll take care of us. She's taking us to her house for awhile, just until Mom gets back. But inside I know Mom's not coming back. It has been too long and she never called. I remember Phoenix, and the way it was, how happy she was, laughing all the time, being silly with her friends. I heard her as we were leaving

Phoenix with her friends all around, telling them how she hated saying good-bye. She didn't want to go, I could tell. She's probably too afraid to come back.

Grandma packs us up and carts us away. I still don't understand what's going on. Dad didn't tell us this part and neither did Mom. At this point I don't care, I don't want to be here without Mom. It's too hard. Grandma is doing Grandma stuff, talking a lot and asking stupid questions that she already knows the answers to. She has Mark up front with her and is loving him every mile we drive.

Dad just sat on the couch as we left. He said it would be a few days.

What is a few days? I feel so confused. I get to Grandma's and put my stuff in the room that Shelly and I share. Mark gets to sleep with Grandma. I wish I could, but I'm too big. It is time to go to bed, she makes us go to bed early, and thank God, because I am so tired. It feels good to sleep with Shelly; we used to sleep together in Phoenix, in our bed.

The next morning Grandma wakes us up, she's nervous.

"Girls, Girls, get up it's almost eleven o'clock. Are you okay? I've never seen you kids sleep so much. Mark and I have already had our breakfast and picked some tomatoes." Shelly is panicked that she's missed breakfast. If she has, then that means it's time for lunch and that is when Grandma really pushes her to eat those beans. Breakfast is safe. But in this situation I will have to stick up for her. I won't come to her rescue too soon, but I'll help her toward the end of each meal. We're safe—she's going to let us have breakfast late.

"I slept like I rock," I tell Grandma. Something about her house always makes me sleep. I love it here. All I have to do is answer questions and she does the rest.

Three days later the call came, we're going home. I don't know what they talked about, but I do know that Mom is home. *I want to jump out of my skin.* I can't believe it, she really came back. Grandma tries to slow us down. I shove everything into the suitcase and claim we are packed. Shelly and I are in the car waiting. Mark comes out with Grandma. I can't wait to get home.

I think Grandma is driving too slow. We are over the mountains, and that means we only have one hour to go.

This is the happiest day of my life, I keep thinking to myself. Mark has a grin and Grandma talks him out of his blanky for a while.

Shelly seems quiet, I don't know why. Actually I don't care. I get to see Mom and the baby. The baby, the baby is going to be there, I almost forgot. Is it a boy or a girl? I hope it's a girl.

Grandma pulls up in front of our house. We break the rules about the car being stopped and shut off before you can get out. We're out and running to Mom on the porch. I see her standing there arms folded and her face like stone. We grab her by a leg or hip and we hug her tight. We're so happy. "Where's the baby? Where's the baby?" we scream.

She pushes us away and looks down at us, very serious, almost scary. "He died about two hours after he was born." She turns away to face the door.

We search for what to do next, cry or question or wonder about this horrible thing. And then she just says, "And I don't ever want to talk about it again, do you understand me?" Her stern voice crashes through the screen door. She walks into the house and we hear loud sobs from her room.

We stay outside. I'm alone. I know there are people there but I can't see them. I have been lifted from my body and I am gone. I don't know where I am. I can't see anyone, not Shelly, not Mark, not Grandma; no one is with me.

When I come back, I'm at the river, alone, by the big tree. The swing drifts back and forth caressing my thoughts. I'm crying hard inside, but nothing's coming out and I feel emptiness. I keep seeing Mom on the porch with no baby in her arms and her big, loud, and horrible words: *There is no baby, there is no baby.*

I scream out, *He didn't die, that's why you went away. He was too strong to die; the baby couldn't have died. We took good care of him.*

Then I see Paul, he is floating around my head saying, *Sandra never believe anything you hear and only half of what you see.* Shut up, shut up,

I beg. At that moment, I hit the ground. I know something, something that I was not supposed to know. I can't believe Mom. How can I not? I lower my head and stare at the ground. I lift my head slowly, things look hazy, and I'm looking at myself, another Me—an eight-year-old girl with my favorite faded yellow sweatshirt and a happy face. I have split in two. She looks at me, I have to do something. I can't live with this. My mom is hurting and I am dead. I put the girl away, I will never play with her again, she was nothing but a stupid little girl. I had to put her away. No one is ever going to find her. I tell her to get into the tree and never come out. The tree will be safe and warm, and when the time is right, I will come back for her one day. But for now, she's too little for this stuff, she's going to be hurt. I won't let them hurt her anymore, it's not her fault. She doesn't want to go into the tree, but I beg her to get in. This is the end of her. I'm not going to play anymore. I'm going to fight. The hole in the tree is just big enough for her, I know that, because I used to play in the hole myself. She gets in, she turns, and she looks back at me, her eyes so sad I look away. And there she stays. I sit beneath the tree with my fist digging into the dirt while the earth rumbles below me. I can't change my mind. The ground is hard, it tries to trick me, *let her out*, it shakes. I sit still shivering, my eyes moving fast as my heart stops searching for the truth.

I'll be the one who lives with the lie, and she, in the tree, can live in the truth, and the baby can live with her. I have no choice. As much as I tried, I can't hate her; I love her and I want her to stay safe and happy. I walk away with my head down and my heart clumped in my hand, dripping blood through my knuckles caked with dirt.

I am back at the house, but the house is still and Mom has that "voice." You know the voice. It's away from you and freezing and doesn't have life to it. I find that with this voice it's best to stay away. I have questions, lots of questions, but I know better than to ask her anything.

Eventually, four weeks later, I forget all of my questions. I have shoved them away like a bully who I hate. Mom's sick and we know it.

Shelly and Mark are on their best behavior. It is not that we think *we're* in trouble, but more of a sense that we are *all* in trouble. I wonder how long it will take for Mom to be better.

This is more than a cold. She is weak, ugly, and her eyes are always ready to cry. I watch her face, I watch it carefully. Her chin has that "I am going to cry at any minute if you look at me" look. It's as if the nicer you are to Mom, the more you make her sad. Shelly and Mark play outside mostly. I, however, am a bitch who has just had pups. I don't play. I just watch out for *my* pups. I have instincts that tell me to stay away but not too far. It's almost time for school to start and I can't ask Mom about it; it would be one more thing that will make her cry. It's been over a month and we've all learned to shut up and shut off. If we need anything, we take care of it. If we have questions, we keep them to ourselves. It is a house of robots.

Mom doesn't talk anymore, and we, well, we just keep waiting for her to come back. Dad is there with us but not often. I barely see him, and he, too, tries to be nice to Mom and has learned to shut up. I was right, there is not going to be any more fun. The days are long and dread has new meaning in my life.

Dad is taking all of us to Aunt Alice's house. Maybe this will make Mom feel better. Heck, I don't know anything right now. I help Mark and Shelly pack their clothes; it seems like we're packing a lot lately.

6

We're now on a bus without Dad, heading for California. Mom won't explain things like she used to, she just says, "We are going to California," and that's it.

We do it, we just get on a bus hand in hand with Mom. The bus ride that will take many days has just begun. It's a long ride and Mom never talks to us other than, "Do you have to go to the bathroom," or "Are you hungry?" I'm scared inside because I know that this is bad, and she's not telling us what's happening. All I can do is sit there and be good. Good is not breathing. I can't ask any questions, and I can't make a fuss. I have to pretend I'm okay. I sit with Shelly, and Mark sits with Mom. I want to sit with Mom. Shelly wants to sit with Mom.

The bus ride to California takes more than a month, but according to Mom, it's only four days, and Aunt Revell picks us up in downtown Sacramento right on time. She has a big blue van that holds a lot of people.

It's nice having a whole seat to myself. Aunt Revell is a very happy person who means well. She has a half smile and a half pity look on her face. "You must be exhausted, are you okay?" She directs the question to all of us, but mostly to Mom. She keeps the happy face on for us, and the concerned look is for Mom. "Ardell, what's wrong, are you sick?" she asks.

"I'll be fine, I'm just a little tired," is Mom's worn response.

Surely Aunt Revell knows what is wrong, after all Mom was just here having the baby. Nothing really make sense, and I'm scared again.

We enter the lovely, well-organized home, and all six of her kids are there to greet us, the cousins from West Virginia. I can practically hear Aunt Revell briefing the kids before our arrival. Be nice and don't ask too many questions, they'll be tired and nervous. Just act normal.

Some of them want to play, while the older ones ignore us. It's very loud here and I don't like it loud; loud makes me scared. I don't know these people. I can tell that Aunt Revell has fallen in love with us. She looks so deeply into me that it's a little uncomfortable. I think she can read minds.

"Time for dinner. Now don't be shy, just help yourself and eat." The gang takes their familiar places, shoving and cutting in line. There is a buffet of choices: spaghetti, corn bread, and salad. The corn bread seems to be the favorite. Aunt Revell notices that we are not going to push our way in the line, and we are not comfortable making our own plates in a stranger's home. She immediately handles the situation.

"Move over Steve and let Sandra sit on the counter. Julie, why don't you take Shelly in the family room and get her a plate? Mark you little sweetheart, come with me and we'll sit with your Mom at the table." Aunt Revell takes his hand and reassures him, "Do you like spaghetti?"

Mark nods yes.

I sit with these very large people called cousins and I twitch and fidget; I feel self-conscious. I really am hungry and my stomach growls, which makes things even worse. No one laughs, but I know they want to laugh at me. Someone is asking a nice question. I answer and eat at the same time, "Yeah it was fun on the bus." But the question I have is, *Why are we here?* And my only concern is, *How long are we staying*? The corn bread is good, I mean *really* good. Now I know why everyone fights to get to the corn bread. This feels funny, I want to go home. If I ask Mom, she'll cry or yell. I guess I'll just wait.

It's time for bed and I really don't want to stay the night here. There are too many people, people I don't know, and I feel that I am in the way. I pray with all my heart that I can sleep with Shelly. *Please don't make me sleep with one of these cousins, or worse, alone,* I silently repeat to myself. Once again Aunt Revell senses our moods and comes to the rescue. "Okay, Sandra and Shelly will sleep in Julie's bed, and Julie you can sleep on the couch. Ardell, you and Mark can sleep in Jeff's room, and Jeff you can sleep on the other couch." She perfectly resolves the problems. Julie and Jeff look as if they just got some candy, for them sleeping on the couch is a treat.

Aunt Revell tucks us in and says a loving good night. I am softly crying to myself, and as Aunt Revell leaves the room, she notices that I'm sad. "Sandra, what's the matter sweetheart?" She waits for an answer.

Shelly tells her, "She wants her shoes."

Aunt Revell is confused. "Why, sure honey, here you go, they're right here." She picks up the black patent leather buckle shoes.

"Mom just bought her those shoes and she wants to sleep with them," Shelly explains while I sniff away my tears. I carefully and purposefully tuck my shoes under the covers with me. I'm exhausted and I want my mom, but words alone can't explain my sadness.

The next morning we watch while the cousins get ready for school. This is an amazing sight. In a house built for five, there are six kids plus three more, all needing things. Breakfast is all over the place, clothes are yanked from the dryer, some people iron and some people don't. The ones who don't iron brush the wrinkles off with one hand and eat toast with the other.

Some walk and some get picked up for school. I don't understand how it all happens in such a short time. Shelly and I stay out of the way of the tidal wave. When I finally get to the bathroom, it's as if a bomb went off: toothpaste everywhere, piles of underwear, towels hanging, and the toilet seat is up.

Aunt Revell and Mom are secretly working things out; they've been working on it for days. This is when they go into the other room and ask us to play outside. I wish Mom would talk to me. She is still very sick, I think she's sad but they keep calling it sick. I'm not sure what the difference is anymore. At least she's talking to Aunt Revell. Aunt

Revell is a really nice person, and I can tell she feels sorry for us, the more she does the scareder I get. Mom's not going to die is she?

Mom has announced that we are going to Aunt Carole's tomorrow for dinner. She wants us to get to know the other cousins—three more names to remember: Darla, Ross, and Jason, the baby.

Aunt Revell drives us to Aunt Carole's promptly at six to arrive at six thirty-five. We enter, we give pretend smiles, but we're ready to size up the situation. Everyone has a job to do to get ready for dinner. The organization is remarkable, especially compared to Aunt Revell's. Dinner comes and goes with a blink of an eye and now the kids get to do the dishes. All adults leave the mess behind. By now Aunt Carole is having a secret conversation with Mom. I am starting to get very nervous about these secrets. Mom always said she hated secrets. But now I doubt her words. This is not like Mom. She won't talk to us, heck she won't even look me in the eye.

Darla washes, Ross rinses, and Shelly and I dry—the worst part of dishes. Darla is making us do the drying, but worse, she wants us to put away the dishes. We don't know where they go. After the dishes we have been instructed to watch TV, quietly. I am just sure I do not like these people in the slightest. I watch TV with the kids not because I want to, but because I have to. I really want to know what Mom is talking about, I can tell it's serious. I pretend I have to go to the bathroom and I try listening at the wall in the dining room. I can't hear a thing. I have to find out what's going on. What is Mom doing? She's hiding things from me, that's what she's doing. I decide to try it again, but this time I'll take a glass in the bathroom with me. I grab a plastic tumbler next to me and go back to the bathroom, I am being watched but I don't care. The glass doesn't work like it did on TV, but I probably need a real glass. The night continues to grow and so does my curiosity. But the lid is tight on this secret.

Mom finally comes to our rescue, "Come on kids, it's late and we need to get back." I can't jump up fast enough.

The next morning at Aunt Revell's all the cousins begin the early morning race to get ready for school. Mom is nervous and jumpy.

After some of the kids leave for school and Aunt Revell departs with her share of kids, Mom has to speak with us. Everything is so serious lately, Mom doesn't speak *with* us, she talks *to* us.

"Hey guys, come here."

This is not a good way to start a talk; I know this because of the tone.

"Listen to me carefully," she says, "and remember it will only be for a while. I don't feel very well and we need to get you back in school. Grandma doesn't like kids that much and she can't take all of us." My heart quit beating. "I need you and your sister to stay with your aunts. Sandra you'll go to Aunt Carole's, and Shelly you can stay here with Aunt Revell. Mark and I will go up to Grandma Lois's and stay. This will just be for a little while, just until I feel better and can figure out what to do. Please be good girls and don't let me down. Mind your aunts and be big girls. You know I love you…please do this for me…"

I can't believe her. A little while means absolutely nothing, it's like air. "But Mom, when do I get to see you?"

"I'll be back soon," she says in a foreign language, "I'll come and visit you all the time."

The lump gets bigger and takes over my whole throat. I don't know if I can ask the next question.

"When can I see Shelly? Will I get to sleep over with her?"

"I'm sure you can." She looks away, she doesn't know. Her stab at the truth is vague, distant, and far from the Mom I used to know.

I have never had to say good-bye to Shelly and Mark before. Mom and Aunt Revell drive me away without Shelly. I sit in the car showing Mom what a good girl I am, but inside I want to fight somebody. Mark sits in the back with me, and I can't look at him. I'm so mad inside. I know she's sick, but why is she hurting me? I can take care of Shelly and Mark; why didn't she think of that? Or why doesn't she let us go to Grandma Lois's with her? We've been very good, on the bus, staying at Aunt Revell's, and we haven't asked for anything, not even a question. I don't understand this; why didn't she talk to me first? This is not my mom.

In my mind, I slip away, back to Phoenix, as I contemplate who my mom is, and then further away from this stranger calling herself Mom. I remember the good times when the Easter bunny used to bring us colorful baskets filled with treats. I'd open my eyes in the morning and somehow he would sneak in and right there next to us on the nightstand was the basket. We ran, tripped, and fell into Mom's lap. "Look Mom. Look!"

"Oh my God, he came again." She would sift through the basket and steal a piece of candy from all of us. "Hey, Mark you get out of there," She would tickle Mark's neck as he started eating M&Ms for breakfast.

Shelly and I knew better; you have to eat breakfast first.

I remember, "Eye Winker Tom Tinker, and tickle, tickle, tickle," that was Mom's favorite. Or the butterfly kisses she gave just before she left for work to go do her show. Mom was a star, she twinkled when she was up there on stage. She always stood in front of the other singers and dancers. I was a star too back then; just having her for a Mom meant I was special. At night she came home with a little sweat hanging onto the ends of the danglies from her hair that was falling down and she'd peak in the bedroom and think I was asleep, I wasn't. She used to drive with one hand, sing to the radio, and wink at me. She never had time for bad moods, being sick, or frowns. She was sassy, cute, pretty, and smart. Everyone came to Mom for answers. Her friends would come over on the weekends, sip cold Cokes in the backyard, and kick their feet in the pool while we swam around their feet and pretended we were sharks.

"Sit up straight," she would remind Shelly and I at the dinner table.

"I want to be a dancer." Shelly would say with a mouthful of mashed potatoes.

"Sweetheart, you can be anything you want."

I challenge, "Yeah but what about an astronaut?" I smack my food.

Mom shoots a look and my mouth stops smacking, "By the time you guys grow up, even girls can be astronauts, firemen, and truck drivers." My eyes got wide as she talked about a world that wasn't true.

"You guys can be anything you want when you grow up, anything. Don't ever let anyone tell you no. If you want it bad enough, you can have it. Just believe in yourself because I will always believe in you." She stroked the back of our long hair and then stabbed her T-bone.

Mark wasn't listening. He couldn't; the dog was begging for food down below. I would hear her say it over and over again for the rest of my life.

The drive drags on and on. Mark wants to play. I don't play, all I can think about is Shelly. How is she? Is she feeling as sick as me right now? She can't be left alone with those people. Who's going to take care of her? She's too shy and too little to stand up for herself. They better let me see her, or I will run away and find her. I pay close attention so I can find my way back to her.

When we get to Aunt Carole's, I don't know how I'm supposed to hold up. The gathering of aunt, uncle, and cousins is perfect and polite; they are overly nice as I stand there being welcomed into their home. Now it's my turn to act like this is okay, as if it's perfectly natural to not sleep with my family or be with Shelly for breakfast in the mornings. I hate this whole situation, I hate Mom.

It will be easier and better if I'm mad rather than sad, because this kind of sad is bigger than an ocean full of tears. Besides, this is not just a bad dream, it is war. God is not my friend. I'm alone, alone with these new people who pity me while they pretend they want me to live with them. I'm not fooled. I yell at myself, *I am staying here for awhile, that's all.* I must stay safe in my head otherwise I might crack and go flying to my mom and beg her not to leave me. *I won't listen to these people. I won't like it here. I won't like them.*

I can't look at Mom, because if I do my throat will clog up, my ears will hurt, and I will feel the tears fill up my eyes. She better not look at me. She better just leave me alone. After all, I'm the one who has to deal with this mess. I want Dad. That's not entirely true, but he wouldn't like it if he knew I was here. I know it's not right to hate, but I do. No one knows I do, but I do. I can't stay here. My body can, but I can't. I don't have to stay, Mom can't make me. I leave my body and no one even knows I'm gone. I watch her from a distance. Is Mom going to forget about me?

"Sandra, do you have everything?"

I don't look back, my body tightens at the sound of her soft voice. "Sandra…"

I continue to walk forcefully to the odd front door. I hear her stupid question and I want to scream back, *No, Mom, I don't have my sister and brother.* There's no need for Mom and me to say good-bye, I can't.

As I enter the home I re-enter my body. I must face the truth, the new rules, and the new family. Maybe I can do their dishes forever. My body says, *Don't look at me.* My heart says, *I hurt so bad I want to be alone and die.* Aunt Carole says, "Darla why don't you show Sandra to your room where she'll be staying?"

Darla obeys and announces, "Here it is and you can have that side of the bed, but don't touch my stuff." I have to share a bed with a stranger. My knees buckle but I politely agree.

Darla is tough, one of the toughest girls I have ever met. She doesn't feel like a cousin, certainly not the ones I knew back in West Virginia. She smiles but she's thinking something entirely different. At first I have to see if she has a knife behind her back. She's had about as much time to adjust to the new living arrangement as I have. She has one thing on her side: dominance. I have none. I'm her new chore girl. But I don't care. This is a big fat joke and I hate everyone; that is *my* little secret. If I stay far enough away from this horrible new life, then I simply won't feel it. I can fly away at anytime.

Days pass like old tar bubbles growing on the side of the road, and Darla is showing me the ropes. Along with those ropes is a small detail that seemed to slip through the cracks: these strangers are Jehovah's Witnesses. Mom has lost her mind. Does she know what she's done to me? Does she care?

Not only can I not see Shelly and Mark, but now I have no more birthdays or Christmases. I can't even talk about my birthday or

Christmas. Around here it is a bad thing, and those who do celebrate are wrong.

"Okay," I agree with my words, but inside my head I go to Grandma and she says I don't have to believe these people. I don't go to Mom like I used to. I can't find anybody but Grandma. Grandma is always there to talk to me and help me. She knows how scared I am and how much I miss Mom, Shelly, Mark, and Dad. I quit wondering when somebody will ask me how I feel or if I need anything? I just can't wait for night. Night is my time when I leave my body and find Grandma. Sometimes I feel her waiting for me in her big, green La-Z-Boy chair, sneaking a cigarette until I get there, then she puts it out quickly as if I didn't see it. She has a blanket waiting for me, and there I am all crawled up on her lap. She never says too much, she just holds me until morning.

Morning…morning! Oh my God Darla has wet the bed. Mark doesn't even wet the bed. I never met a bed wetter before. I heard of them, but I never knew one, especially one this big. I hit the floor as I get tangled in the damp sheets. I can't get up quick enough, I can't get to the shower quick enough. I want to run for my life, but I stop in my tracks.

"Don't tell, please don't tell. I am sorry, I'm sorry."

This is the first time I have ever heard *please* or *sorry* from Darla and especially in the same breath. Darla is running around the room white as a ghost. This is some type of mad ritual she conducts. The Wicked Witch of the West is melting before my eyes. I feel sorry for her, but at the same time I'm grossed out. I sleep with a bed wetter. Another one of those little details that just seemed to slip by.

Meanwhile, she has some kind of race with time. She wants to hide the evidence and take care of it herself. She knows exactly what to do next, thank God, because I certainly can't help. I watch this tornado blow through the room and destroy the night's accident in less than three minutes. "Sandra, promise you won't tell anyone, please. It's not my fault. Aunt Revell used to wet the bed too when she was little."

Her words are like candy to a baby, they fall upon my ear like magic. Dominance just took its first turn my way, and I am holding onto this one. It's survival. "Don't worry, I won't tell." It will be my pleasure to hold on to her little secret.

Darla leaves the scene of the accident and heads for the shower. Aunt Carole says nothing as she casually walks in our room and grabs the accident. She must be psychic.

They want me to start school in a few days. I remember last year and how tough it was. I was a wounded solider who wanted to get out of battle. Besides, this is Darla's school, and I can tell she doesn't want me to hang around her friends.

We will dance the dance and pretend it's fine around Aunt Carole. Later, Darla threatens me like she always does. We walk to school together as far as Aunt Carole can see, but at the first corner it all changes. I walk through those gates alone. I think it gives Darla pleasure seeing me so nervous. I never ask for her help, but, then again, I never thought I would have to. She doesn't like me. She doesn't tell me that, but then she never acts the way she really feels. Darla always keeps me in the dark. She likes to see me trip. But then I have her little secret tucked up under my sleeve.

7

I have to go to the Jehovah's Witness meetings too. Another little detail that slipped through the crack. It's Sunday morning and time to get ready for the meeting.

"Aunt Carole, do I have to? I'm not a Jehovah's Witness," I continue to pray, "and I don't know what they are."

"Sandra I think it would be best if you came along. You can just sit there and listen, you don't have do anything."

"Can't I just stay here? I promise I won't touch anything."

Just then Uncle Mal comes into the house wiping the grease off his hands with a filthy black rag. "What are you doing? You don't need to drag Sandra off to that meeting. Hell, she can stay here with me. The poor girl isn't going to convert." Uncle Mal loves cussing on Sundays just to make Aunt Carole's eyebrows stand up on edge.

I can see Darla peering at me with one eye. That's all I need, her pissed off because I get to stay home with her daddy. Uncle Mal wins and the rest of them waddle down the street behind the mother duck. As for me, I am a dead duck. Darla will probably kill me in my sleep tonight.

Time passes like it always does...slowly. Sometimes it feels like I am watching a tree grow. Aunt Carole is still the sergeant around the barracks. She secretly likes me and we both know it. I am not sure how I feel about the strange household with these strange people I call family. They are nowhere near the family I have in West Virginia. I was special in West Virginia, and I had no doubt about who loved me and who I loved. My uncles are dear to me and I to them. This is a new place and I don't fit in. I miss Grandma.

I find that the less I talk the better it is. I have many questions, but answers are hard to come by and not common around this house. Kids are not as special here in California. We are *managed.* "I managed to get the kids to bed," or "I managed to fix dinner and get their showers over."

Darla is starting to call me her best friend. I don't like that word, it makes me very uncomfortable. It sounds as if the other people in my life don't matter, but I keep my mouth shut. If I am Darla's best friend, so be it. It's a lot better than being her enemy. Darla is the toughest girl in the neighborhood. She has an edge to her and a way of keeping me in line. I am her toy, her friend, and her enemy. Days with Darla are never predictable. One day she's boy crazy the next day she's not. She wants a boyfriend so bad, but she always pretends she doesn't. It is plain crazy. In the presence of adults she always says the right thing, but in the real world between us, she says the truth. She's two-faced and I've seen them both.

I like her, but if I cross the line, the same line that is invisible and in constant motion, she'll hit me, or tell on me. Or kill me.

I can't go to Aunt Carole. Either she's too busy or Darla is watching my every move. I am stuck in the middle here with my true feelings. And I really don't have it in me to tattle; I wish I could. I try to deny it, but I hate it here. God told me it's wrong to hate, but I can't help it, I still hate everything.

Three months have come and gone and another Sunday shows up. They're back from church and the rest of the day is spent playing Jehovah's Witness games. I don't know what is worse, the chores or the games. This is Aunt Carole's last attempt to win the day. We sit cross-legged in the living room by the picture window. Ross has the same look on his face as I do; what a big waste of time. Ross is lean, polite, and awkward in his tall growing body. He's handsome. He looks like himself, not like the others; he's fair with straight blond hair. Mom and Aunt Revell love Ross. He's special to them all, including Aunt Carole. It's probably because he's the first one born, and they all had a little something to do with him growing up.

I make the best of it while we pick a card and answer questions about who did this and who said that, but all of us drool as the other kids ride by outside on their bikes. We must play for at least one hour, or until Uncle Mal saves us. The board game continues as we take turns answering the questions. Once you answer correctly, you move your man. I stay in one place and lose willingly. I will not be brain-washed into a religious experience, and that's what this is all about. Besides, Mom said I don't have to be anything if I don't want to, not a Witness, not a Mormon, not even a Baptist, whatever that is.

"Last year for my birthday," I brag, "I got my favorite doll and a new coat." Darla tries to ignore me but her interest is piqued. "And," I scoot up, "on my birthday I pick out any kind of cake I want."

Finally Darla retaliates, "It's wrong to celebrate your birthday. You're not supposed to. You're supposed to celebrate Jehovah everyday, but not for yourself."

I think about it for a moment. "You mean to tell me that I don't matter to God because I don't think like you? That's stupid!"

"Yeah, well you live here now and Mom will make you. And who knows when your Mom is coming back for you." Darla sits back on her hands after that slap.

She's right, I don't have any idea when Mom is coming back, and I better shut up or else.

I am not going to make it much longer. There are punishments for everything around here, not being a Jehovah Witness, not getting the dishes clean, and of course, punishments for speaking your mind. There is even punishment for asking too many questions. Uncle Mal was in the Air Force. *Force* is the word around here.

I have been here for months. I am starting to forget about my other life. When is Mom coming back? Doesn't she realize how hard it is for me to stay here? How long is she going to leave me and Shelly here with people who speak differently? And they lied. I haven't seen Shelly once yet. No one around here will tell me the truth.

"Please, Mom, come back, I've had enough, my head really hurts and I'm scared I'll never see you again. Please…I miss you and Shelly and Mark. Get better soon, please, Mom." As I end my personal prayer to whoever will listen, my heart pounds with the sadness I have held in all this time. I'm pretending I'm okay, but most of the time I'm not.

Aunt Carole reminds me I have to write my mother. I don't know how to write my mom, I've never had to do that. Once I wrote my Grandma, but that's it. *Dear Mom, How are you? I am fine…* I scream at the blank paper before me while I hold the pencil that is too big for my fingers. *Dear Mom I am fine, thank you so much for leaving me here. I really like not being with Shelly and Mark and boy it's fun around here. Tell Mark I miss him and…*

Aunt Carole looks over her shoulder and sympathizes with me. She can feel me struggle. I write little words that have no meaning, and address them to the place I've never seen. I can't wait to think of two more sentences so it will look like a letter.

Ross runs in for a drink of juice, the sweat rolling from his sideburns. He's been playing tag football in the front yard. "Mom, when can Sandra come out?"

"In just a few minutes, she's almost done."

Mal stands in the hall and shouts, "Ross, I thought I told you not to run in and out of the house."

"Yes, sir, I won't do it again."

Aunt Carole stays out of it but her ears perk up. Mal, a short, dark, and average man, is yelling at Ross, a tall, blond, and above-average-looking guy. Mal is hard on him, and according to Mal, he's going to "straighten him out." I feel sorry for Ross; he tries so hard, but it doesn't matter. Mal can't seem to like him the way he loves the other kids. Mal is always mad at Ross because he's not his real kid. Aunt Carole had him when she was unmarried and very young. Her mother wanted her to give him up for adoption, but Aunt Carole refused. Mal calls him his son out loud, but that's not true. Even if I were blind, I could see that for sure. The truth is getting slippery the more I grow up. Even I can't tell the difference sometimes. I remember Mom always saying to tell the truth, but now I have trouble telling what's true. I pretend I don't see it, I just jump in, and I ask a stupid question or make a silly joke. I stay in the dark most of the time, and once in a while I pop out long enough to smooth things over around here.

Finally, Aunt Carole has approved my trite letter and the stamp has been licked. I can go play now. I run out and grab the ball from Ross and play a game of catch with him. One by one the other kids have shown up in the front yard. I hear from the distance, "Hey Sandra you look like a potbelly stove." The others laugh and I don't.

I remember when I was in West Virginia and those kids at school used to tease the black girl in my class for being black. It just isn't funny to laugh at someone. I felt sorry for her and I used to run to her rescue, but no one is running to my rescue. I hold my head high as I run into the house shouting back to them all, "Sticks and stones may break my bones, but words will never hurt me." I am reminded by the cross-eyed look from Aunt Carole to "slow down..."

I find peace in the backyard, alone, where the sheds and big trees hide me. The grass is thick and thicker in patches along the sidewalk. It's cooler back here. I love the shed; that's where I can be alone. Sometimes I hear Darla calling for me, but I stay hidden behind the shaky wooden doors. I know there's spiders in here, but I don't answer. And eventually she gives up. Later on when things settle down and my head quiets I find a way out of the backyard through the fence and into a vacant field and no one knows where I came from. I just act like I was down the street.

Today it feels good to be alone with myself. I wonder about my family so much that it hurts my heart: Uncle John who always had something nice and funny to say; Uncle Brooks who cared so much; Grandma who had a pink rainbow of love that rolled off her shoulders;

Paul full of wisdom and magic. My poor old Aunt Mozell who was so mean for so long, I think she forgot how to smile, but there was no doubt she loved me. Not like Aunt Carole who's not really mean, she just acts like she is. But that could just be the fact that I am one more kid in her house. It is worth it, just to sit here in the grass behind the shed and remember the laughs.

"Saaandra," I hear from the distance. I snap back, "I'm in the backyard," and I run to her leaving my thoughts behind. The other rule is to never, I mean never yell "What" from a distance. If Aunt Carole calls, you'd better run to attention, soldier.

"Hey there," she wipes her hands down her sides, "your mother will be here in a couple of days."

My eyes get so happy that it's contagious and her eyes get happy too. I say nothing, but my heart is melting. I have some questions but not right now. I just want to be happy for a few more minutes. A couple is two days, and a day is twenty-four hours, plus twenty-four, which equals forty-eight hours. I simply can't wait, nothing is going to bother me. Darla will try to blow my happiness away, but there is not a chance in hell, I mean in heck. The kids are still teasing me, but I don't listen to them. I get to see Mom. I'll do anything. That includes dishes by myself, folding clothes, and cleaning up Darla's room.

8

Mom pulls up with Shelly and Mark in the car. She looks better and she's just the way I remember her. She's so pretty. I hug her around the waist. She smells the same, I love that smell. I don't want to let go, but I have to, big girls don't hold on to moms forever. Oh, how nice it would be if they could. Shelly stands next to Mom, she is quiet, so quiet that I'm worried about her. I wonder if her little home away from home is as quaint as mine. She'll tell me all about it later when we're alone.

What's weird is Mark, he looks so different. He's not smiling and where's his blanky? "Mark where's your blanky?"

He mumbles his answer back. "Grandma won't let me have it anymore."

I try to assure him, "That's okay." Who is this Grandma Lois, telling him he can't have his blanky? I don't like Grandma Lois, she sounds so mean. I'll find him another blanky, but I know it won't be as good.

Mom takes us into the house and she wants to talk to us. My stomach is doing that upside-down thing, and the blood turns cold in my skin as we walk hand in hand to the door. I repeat over and over again to myself, "I will not cry, I will not cry..." All three of us sit on the bed and she bends down on her knees and begins to tell each one of us how much she loves us and why. "Now you guys, you have all been very good and I know things are tough right now, but you must never lie..."

Before she can finish I am in shock. What in the world is she talking about? We've been without her for months, this is the first time we have all been together and she wants to talk about lying. When I finally return from tracing off in my head, I hear something about biting off the eraser of a pencil.

And before my eyes there's Mom hysterical, crying about some dumb pencil. "Your Aunt Carole has told me that last night when you were watching TV, someone bit the eraser off a pencil, and when she asked who did it, no one admitted it." She continues on and on about the seriousness of lying and how could I? She never really said, but I knew it was only a matter of time. "And Darla told your Aunt Carole later that night that it was you who bit the eraser."

I fly off the handle and hit my head on the ceiling. The disbelief oozes out of my body. I want to crawl under the bed. Is Aunt Carole completely heartless? My only day with Mom, and I have to spend it in trouble and looked down on. I'll never talk to her again. And where's my real Mom? This isn't Mom. She'd never react like this over something so stupid as a pencil eraser. Besides, I didn't mean to. I haven't done anything wrong and I have been really good this whole time.

Why is she crying now? This is crazy. I've ruined everything. Poor Shelly and Mark, now they are guilty of my crime too. But Mom is the one who's messed everything up. We're the ones who have to be separated and live with strangers. Strangers who live in lies and can't wait to ruin other people's fun. "Okay Mom I bit the eraser off, I was watching TV and I accidentally broke it off."

"But why did you lie...?"

"I don't know." Now that I think about it, I did. It's the first time I remember ever lying. I never had to before.

Mom lowers her head and continues to sob. At first I feel horrible for disappointing her and dragging Shelly and Mark into this mess.

But as I hug her and apologize, I can feel her body and I know she's still not feeling well. Mom is on the edge, her heart hurts and she misses us. Her tears are about much more than this, exactly what I don't know. The pencil is not the truth behind her tears. Aunt Carole gets to make a new rule, and Darla can gloat all day as she hides behind her innocent goody-two-shoes show. I'll be stuck with a sad Mom, instead of a laughing, telling stories, and playing tickle games Mom, from back when I didn't lie.

Before I know it, Mom is bending down saying her good-byes. "Hey you guys, I don't want you to get your hopes up, but I think we'll be living together soon. Aunt Carole is helping me look for a place."

I believed her this time; she looked me in the eye. I could have jumped to the moon. Is it really over? Have I made it through this nightmare? I don't ask when, I know that time has no meaning. Mom kisses my cheek a long time and slaps me on the butt.

"Sandra, I'll be back. Be a good girl for your Aunt Carole, I can't handle any more bad news. Okay?"

She's gone before I can say, *Yes Mom…I love you.*

9

Mom is really coming back. All the way back, her smile, her laugh and mostly her love. I can't wait to talk to her. I am going to tell her all about living here. But mostly I can't wait to stop living here with all the rules. Mom is a straight shooter, she tells it like it is and she loves to laugh. I'm going to be just like that when I grow up, sassy, smart, and confident. I'm finally going to be living in my own skin again. "Thank you Aunt Carole," I whisper as I swiftly pack my clothes.

The house Aunt Carole found for Mom, to my surprise, is across the street. The words echo in my head. *Across the street.*

"Sandra, is that all your things? Aunt Revell will be here with Shelly in a few minutes." Aunt Carole is fussing around like it's her that gets to move out.

Aunt Revell arrives on time without a minute to spare, and she's got Shelly, Mark, and Mom in the van. Mom looks to me and smiles a beautiful smile, she loves me I can tell. Shelly and Mark jump out and run to me, even they love me today. As Mom gets out to say hello to Aunt Carole, she says a strange good-bye to Aunt Revell. I hear her say, "Yes she had dark hair, she looked like Sandra."

The words slide down my back like ice melting on a hot day. What did Mom just say, *she*? I must have heard it wrong. Why is she talking about the baby? She never says a word about the baby. She had dark hair like mine? I wonder what she was like?

For the next three days we set up house with anything loaned or free. Everyone helps, including Darla. I think she's happier now that I'm sort of gone. We'll always be friends, but I'll never trust her completely. That's my rule. I like my Aunt Carole and my cousins from over here. I can leave and go home. I don't have to learn any more rules.

In this neighborhood our house is considered haunted. I quickly put an end to that silly rumor. The house isn't so bad—it's rickety, it needs paint, but it has character and a crazy floor plan. It sits high on a tall porch, the windows are old, and the bedrooms never really end, they just seem to slip into the next room. It has a great service porch that makes sneaking around easy for me. Part of me is a little embarrassed about living in this tired little house, but then who cares, I get to sleep with Mom and wake up without dreading the day.

"Sandra you better get your ass up—we have lots to do today."

I laugh to myself; even hearing her yell sounds good.

"Mark put down the damn dogs and take them outside." Mark drops Big on his head.

"Shelly you too, get up and get dressed."

I roll my eyes and get out of bed, thinking yeah sure that'll take Shelly an hour right there. I hear Mom scoot the kitchen chairs up to the table.

Shelly is much more relaxed and she is funny again, telling stories of her experience with the Bratty Bunch. She tells us endless stories of how the older boys beat up the little ones; Jeff and Julie are human punching bags. The noise was the hardest thing to get used to, and she never slept. She was mostly scared of the oldest boys.

I have a few stories of my own, but they aren't as funny. Mark is still a little different. He's a lot quieter. I think he's still scared that we won't be together, and he doesn't like talking about Grandma Lois. I don't know what's the matter with him for sure, but I know this, it's not a good time to tease him. I'll leave him alone, but I keep my eye on his mood. I think he'll be okay.

Everything is almost back in its place. We don't talk about West Virginia, I think we're too afraid. I know I am. I figure the less we talk or think about it, the less chance God is going to make the bad stuff happen. But mostly, I just want to stay as far away from Him as I can, maybe He forgot about me.

After a few weeks, I love it here. I can feel the magic in this house, which feels like an old man with laughing eyes who is watching out for us. He is a safe old house. I can almost hear him giggling with us at night as we sit there being silly. Sometimes I can hear the house talk to me, quick warnings, a nod of approval, or maybe just a happy sigh. Being in this house is like having a grandfather who protects us. No one seems to know the secret but me. I wonder what it would be like if Dad was here too. I wish he was here kind of, I miss him. I hear Mom shutting up my thoughts with her, "And people in hell want ice water."

As summer continues, we play in the sprinklers every day. Ricky next door has a crush on Shelly, and I have a crush on Tommy down the street. I talk Shelly into being Ricky's girlfriend. I always talk Shelly into one thing or another. If Shelly had it her way, all she'd ever do is say Nope. She's a sissy. Actually, we call her Penelope Pitstop, named after the cartoon. Penelope is a girlie girl who runs on her tippy toes and she always wins at the end. When Shelly runs in a game of Tag or Red Rover, Red Rover, her legs kick high and her heels practically hit her in the butt. Shelly's always getting hurt. I think she's faking. But one thing she doesn't fake is how smart she is, and if I forget, there is always the memory of Dad telling me so. I can hear him yelling at Mark, "Why can't you read like your sister?" Mark is "Mark the Fart," and me, well, I am still the "Potbelly."

On a good day we all get to walk six miles to the pool at the park and swim by ourselves. Today happens to be one of those very special days. On this kind of day we'll do anything Mom asks without a wrinkled nose or eyeball rolling. Mom asks me to do the dishes. "Sure Mom, my pleasure... Can I put those groceries away for you?" She sees through the act, but she also takes advantage of the fleeting moment.

"All right you guys, watch out for your brother and someone stay in the shallow end with him. Here Sandra, here's $1.25. Each one of you can get a soda and a candy."

"Thanks." I look over at Shelly who wishes she got to hold the money. "Put it in your pocket." Mom stuffs the money in my hand.

"Mark, where's your towel?" He grabs it off the floor.

Mom makes us take care of ourselves and come home on time, actually she's adamant about it. She puts her foot down when it comes to that.

We walk the long walk. I think it's over five miles. The time goes fast as we walk, not run, around the pool, swimming and diving in the cool water. Four o'clock, time to go. If we're late this will be the end of our escape. We exit the pool and say our good-byes quickly and hop home. We have to hop: one, because the ground is so hot, and two, because we'll be grounded if we're late. Thank goodness our bare feet have toughened up so we can take the gravel shortcut. When we reach home, I pray I don't see Mom on the porch biting her lip. She's not, we must be on time. Mark starts complaining and dragging his body as if he's being tortured. His dramatic exaggeration is a sure way to make Mom laugh.

"Dibs on the shower!" I scream first as we hit the front porch. I drop my wet things on the steps outside and head straight for the shower; there is nothing better than a cool shower to get the chlorine off my body and my hair. I hate the stringy feeling my hair has after the pool. The only thing that could top off the shower is BBQ hamburgers. I grab a towel and run to my bedroom. I dig in my drawers and find just the right underwear. My hair smells fresh, and I put on a loose tank-top and baggy shorts. I hear Shelly from the bathroom, "Mom, where's my clothes?" I laugh to myself—I know that trick—ask Mom where they are, and maybe she'll go get your clothes for you.

"In your drawer where you left them..." Mom yells back.

I sit on the porch and my feet feel the cooling cement. I wiggle my toes as I tug and pull at the knots in my hair. I can feel the drops of water fall onto my shirt. The comb has to have big teeth, or forget it, I'd be here all night. The sun is lowering and the shadows of the trees are just about on my lap. I'm worn out from all the swimming, and Mom is going to treat us with BBQ hamburgers.

Our towels lay there next to me, drying, but they won't dry until tomorrow when the sun is hotter. In the distance I see a man walking. The sun is behind his head, but he is heading up the drive. I have to squint. I look harder, it looks like my dad. No way, this can't be. I scramble to my feet. It is! It's Dad! He's coming up the driveway. I panic, stand up, and kick open the front door with my foot. "Mom…Mom, Dad's here…Get out the back door!"

"It's okay," she says, "I'll be fine." Mom barely raises an eyebrow, but her mouth drops her smile. The water at the kitchen sink moans as she turns it off.

Shelly and Mark trip over each other to get dressed. Mom goes to the bathroom. I run outside to greet the stranger and welcome him here. His shirt is open and he is sweating.

He smiles at me like he just got back from the store, "Hey San. Got a drink of water?"

I melt, I can't help it, I love him so much, it's true, I did miss him. I just don't want any more fighting.

"How did you get here?" I ask.

"Walked."

I can't help but laugh.

"Where's your mother?"

"She's inside."

He climbs the last step and gives me a hug. "How are you, sweetie?"

While I stand there being hugged I am not sure how I am, nobody has asked that in awhile. I wait a second then hug him back. He stands there as if he just got home from work. By now Mark has peeked his head out of the door, his eyes as big as flying saucers. I hold back my tears, practically choking. Shelly sees Mark's chin start to quiver, and her eyes start to tear. Then a couple of my tears fall onto my cheek. How can it be? How can Dad just be here without us knowing he was coming? I don't care, I'm happy to see him.

Mom, however, shows no sign of life. Her body tightens as she forces her face to say Hi. She stays in the doorway of the kitchen with her hand holding up the doorjamb.

Dad stays still in the middle of the living room. "I like the place."

She keeps her distance and squints her eye, "Yeah we're just waiting for the new furniture to delivered."

"Well, I hope they get here soon." Dad cracks back.

Mom's body relaxes a bit and her hand lowers, I don't know what she is thinking. Her body is not a welcome sign, but her face lightens up just a little.

Dad makes a move toward Mom. "I really missed you and the kids."

She looks like she's going to run. "Well here we are."

He looks like he's trying to catch a nervous cat. Mom waits, she stays in the doorway. Dad says nothing and gives her a hug.

Suddenly I remember the baby not coming home and Mom's face. The memory of how we got here invades, the bus, saying good-bye to Aunt Alice, and Grandma. How much has changed and how much time has passed. The room starts to tilt and I can't get back. I can see the words falling out of Mom's and Dad's mouths but I can't hear them.

I snap back and hear Dad. "Now have you guys been good for your Mother?"

No one answers the question; we all know it's not a real question.

He's acting like everything is fine, we're all acting like it's fine, so it *must* be fine. Dad tells us stories and keeps us laughing for hours. We eat the hamburgers and Mom stays mostly in the kitchen breathing out loud.

We tell Dad all about our school, teachers, friends, and cousins. We catch up by flipping tales back and forth. Mom won't be a part of this exchange, and I really wish she could. I can hear her in the kitchen wrestling with pots and pans, she's so noisy.

Nothing is said between them, and nothing is said about the past. And with that, we begin another new life, again. It's our second time around without him, and with him—this starting over is getting to be normal.

Mom works at night and Dad looks for work during the day. Everyone is on their best behavior. Mom and Dad are starting to be friends again. I hope it works out. I have noticed that they're beginning to laugh a little. This is great because you can't laugh unless you're happy. We have rather quiet nights around the house while Mom is at work.

Tonight he tells us he's going to cook us our favorite—fish sticks and canned corn. He's very excited about this perfectly prepared meal. "Stay out of the kitchen," he reminds us.

I look at Shelly, she looks back at me, we have no idea what is going on with Dad. He's never been quite this nice about dinner. The fishstick dinner is the only meal we all agree on. Shelly runs our lives with her *I don't like it*, or her constant, *Nope*. I remember when she discovered that she didn't like watermelon. *That's not normal, no human can possibly hate watermelon.* My conclusion was that she was making it up. She's picky about everything from socks to dessert. If Shelly hates it, we don't get it. We sit there watching her face for a verdict. Once she even had the nerve to decide that she hated pizza. I had had it. I was fed up with not being fed my favorite foods. *Shelly you will like pizza.* After our little talk that day, she changed her mind. Shelly likes pizza now. As far as beans, I couldn't argue, I let her have that one.

"Hey, you guys, dinner is ready."

Mark and I are extra hungry and bump into each other as we race for the table. Dad has already set the table, this isn't like him. I sit down in my seat and notice something fishy is in the air. Dad joins us at the table with his hairy chest and freckled arms. He waits for us to eat first; this, too, is strange behavior. I reach across the table and dish up my plate. Mark struggles with the corn and it falls off the big spoon onto his plate, some of it hitting the table. Without thinking we all stab our forks into the fishsticks and smash them apart.

I can't believe it. Shelly gags. I sit there with my mouth open and my nose wrinkled. I investigate further with my fork. The fish sticks aren't the normal ones, these have the heads still attached with the cooked eyeballs. Sure enough, he's played one of his jokes. Only he could find something this disgusting. Where did he find these?

Dad sits there laughing and pounding the table. Tears run down his face as he watches us squirm. "Go ahead and eat them, they're perfectly fine."

Now I want to laugh too. Is he completely crazy? There's no way we'll eat them. He's still laughing and teasing us. "Just cut off the heads and feed them to the dogs, the rest is fine." He shows us how it's done. Mark is getting scared, and Shelly's head is turned away from the table. He's got to be kidding, but now he's really mad. I wish he wouldn't do this. Now this is going to turn bad, really bad. Dad turns sharply and continues to explain why we must eat this mess on our plates. The mood has shifted just as I expected. I try to bring the fork to my mouth and eat a tiny part, but they're not even cooked all the way. There is juice running out of them and my stomach is turning. I wish Mom was here, she'd stop this nonsense.

Dad starts out kidding, but then it always turns serious. Finally, Mark is breathing hard while Dad is trying to regain control at the table.

"Mark, get your ass to bed if you're going to act like a baby."

Now this is Dad.

"Get your ass in bed!"

Mark jumps from his seat and takes his hurt feelings out of the room. I watch and try to eat the corn. I think we can stop it if I eat. It doesn't work. I feverishly shove cold corn in my mouth as I wait for the fish sticks to jump off my plate. Shelly is so mad her face is red. Now I'm really scared. When Shelly gets mad she's liable to say anything. I put one more spoonful of corn down the hatch and pray she'll behave. Nope. Shelly gets up and throws her fork on the ground. I gulp and reach for some milk. She stands up and leaves the table.

"Where in the hell do you think you're going? Get your ass back here!"

She exits without a twitch and his warning is left there on the floor with her fork. I slowly wipe the milk mustache off my face and wait for him to go after her. He just sits there beaten at his little game.

The house stays pretty calm until Mom gets home that night. Something's gone terribly wrong. It's only a matter of time; ticktock go the beer bottles. We've been waiting and wondering when the "Big One" was coming. It's here.

The air is clammy, and the sweat drips as the wave slowly builds up. Where do I position myself? I memorize all the doors for escape. Shelly and Mark stay in the back bedroom. I press my ear against the door and listen. Mom doesn't have a chance to put her purse down.

"Ardell, I am sick and tired of this shit! You and the kids don't care about me!"

It's time. I slip on my armor.

"Bill, just knock it off. What are you talking about? I hear her open the fridge and pop open a soda. She has no idea how mad he is.

"I am sick of living here with your sisiters coming over and telling you you're something special. Well you're not Goddamn it!"

"You're going to scare the kids. Why don't you lower your voice."

What? She's not supposed to mention us; she knows better than to bring up the kids. That will only make it worse. Shelly and Mark hear his voice and know that this is their cue to hide. There is silence, horrible silence. Mom has shut up, but it's too late. The bomb's gone off.

"You're nothing but a fucking whore and you'll always be a whore!" He yells at the top of his lungs. Mom stands there defenseless. He sees me watching him from behind the crack of the door and screams, "Get out of here!"

I slam the door. Shelly finds a new strength; she must have reached deep inside herself as she opens the door and throws a coat hanger at him. I can't stand the screaming. Mark is flipping out, he doesn't know what to do, he can barely breathe.

"Mark calm down," I tell him, "you're going to have an asthma attack.

Shelly continues pacing holding her head. "Dad stop it, stop it."

I take my stand behind the bedroom door and plead. I wait for the next sound, him hitting her. Dad hits her, I hear her wince in pain and get up.

Then the unexpected happens—Mom starts yelling back, in a loud growl.

"I hate you, I really fucking hate you! Why did you come back anyway? Just so you could push me around...Does that make you feel like a big man? Leave you fucking coward! I don't need you. You stupid son of a bitch all you do is feel sorry for yourself!"

I can't help myself, this is too much. I open the door. Shelly snaps, something inside her decides to fight with me this time. She starts screaming louder than both of them. By now Dad is hitting Mom and throwing her around the living room. Mom scrambles to her feet and makes it to the porch. Shelly is hitting Dad, and I have to get some help. How? I can't be in two places at once. The neighbors hear and see the violence, and now Uncle Mal and Ross are at the door. Mom is a mess, and Dad has stopped hitting her. He never hits her in front of others.

"Come on, Bill. Let's go outside and cool off. You don't need to hit her anymore." Ross is blocking the front door as a reminder that Dad is not going back inside.

Mom is crying. She pulls it together enough to check on us. "Are you guys all right?"

Shelly and I nod our heads.

"Where's your brother?" Mark is still in the bedroom. She dashes across the broken furniture and the smashed knickknacks. "Mark, come here, I'm okay, don't worry sweetheart." They both sit on the bed hugging each other. "I'm sorry I scared you."

I can still hear Dad on the front lawn. "Fuck her, I don't need her."

"Sandra, pack you and your sister some clothes, we're not staying here." Mom gently picks Mark up and holds him to her face. "Honey, we're going to sleep at your Aunt Revell's. Go get your clothes on, I'll be right here." We leave through the back door and walk in the pitch dark to Aunt Carole's house. She is waiting for us.

"Take us over to Revell's." Mom reaches for Mark's hand.

"She already knows you're coming. Sandra, why don't you stay here with me tonight there's not enough room?"

I really don't want to, but now is not the time to argue.

"All right, but can I ride over with you and Mom?"

"Sure."

We load into the car, Dad finally sees us leaving and starts screaming again. Mom is so mad she would kill him this time if she had the muscle. We pull into Aunt Revell's driveway and wake the sleeping house. Everyone is nervous and scared of what Dad might do.

"Ardell, do you think he'll follow you here?" Aunt Revell twitches.

Mom is trying to be strong, "I really doubt it. He'll probably just go to sleep." The phone rings and Mom jumps. "Hello? Oh sure. Here Carole, it's Mal."

Aunt Carole talks into the phone, "What's going on? Oh, he is? Well that's good. Okay, I'll be home in a few minutes. Yes, I'll have Sandra with me."

In the meantime Uncle Doug has woken up the bigger boys, Steve and Alan. They have to watch out for my dad. This is all so humiliating. I really don't want to drag all my sleeping cousins in on this. Julie slowly wobbles out of her bed to see what's going on.

"Honey, you go back to bed, everything is fine. Your dad is a little upset tonight." I hold my thought tight. That's a lie. He's not upset, he's the devil.

Aunt Revell continues unfolding the hide-a-bed for Mom, Shelly, and Mark to sleep on.

"Sandra, you go home with Aunt Carole. I'll see you in the morning." Mom says with a brush to my hair.

Aunt Carole tries to make me laugh. Doesn't she know you cannot laugh for awhile after Dad does that?

10

Everyone still sleeps except for Aunt Carole and me. We sit together not talking. We know that soon it will be time for the Dad Show. This is a very touchy time. This is when we walk through the graveyard and wait for the corpse to pop out and get us. Sometimes it does and sometimes it doesn't. I can hear Aunt Revell pull up with Mom. Aunt Carole runs outside giving advice to Mom. I watch Mom listening and defending him at the same time. Aunt Revell has to go, she waves a sorry sweet good-bye to Shelly and Mark. She can't see me on the porch.

We begin the walk home down the long driveway. It's like it's Dad against us. And Mom's dreams versus Dad's anger. The gravel beneath my feet is extra loud this morning. Here we are, Mom holding Mark's hand and Shelly and me right behind them, a family holding on for dear life. No one talks as we walk this road. We have walked it before, and the rule is no talking. Shelly and Mark look like they just woke up, and their hair has that funny puff to it. Mark shuffles with Mom as we get close to the door. I wish we could hide for good this time.

Mom opens the door; Dad pretends to be asleep on the couch. This is good. We all have a chance to act like nothing happened. It gives us all time to get to our rooms and be safe. Mom gets in the shower, and I play lookout for her. Of course I know nothing will happen in the light of day, but I still play a little game of what-if. What if he does try to hurt her? Then I'll jump on him and beat him. I will be stronger than him and I will win. In this game he is not drunk, he is weak and I can beat him

"Time to eat," I hear from the kitchen. All I really want to do is to lay here and listen to my music. I pull my body up from the bed and drag myself to the door. Now I open the door and decide what face to put on for him. *Please, please let him stay on the couch and eat over there.* My heart stops as I wait to see what's going to happen— will he come over to the table or will we be spared? *Good, he is going to stay over there.*

Shelly and Mark sit with me at the table, Mom is in the kitchen, and nobody wants to be here. I know why it's hard for Mom to look at us, because when she does, it hurts. And when we look at each other, it hurts too. I don't look at Dad because I'm afraid he'll read my mind and know how much I hate him. Dad gets up and walks to the table to get his food. I suck my whole body in, begging that he won't talk to me. He always talks to me first, it's his way of communicating to the rest of them.

"Sandra, wanna give me the ketchup?" Aren't cha gonna put ketchup on those eggs?"

"Yeah, Dad," I reply politely. I want to scream, *I hate ketchup on my eggs! Don't you know that by now?*

Secretly the entire house exhales at the same time. We have now been released from doom and the day will go on. What a beautiful day it is. Mom will go to the bathroom and finally fall apart.

Later on she forgets her fear, the terror that filled her last night and sings, "Okay you guys, it's time for bed. Brush your teeth and I'll be there in a minute,"

Mark wanders off to his room and Shelly and I jump into our beds. Mom comes in, happy to see us.

"Sandra, it's going to be fine, don't worry," she whispers in my ear.

Baffled, I look into her eyes. I think it's nice of her to say that, but it's not true. I want to believe her, but she's not looking me in the eye.

After a "Big One" it takes a long time for things to get back to normal around the house, everything's still a little shaky. One night after dinner he says he is going to take Shelly and Mark out for ice cream. I don't go. I don't know why I don't go, but I don't. They're gone an awfully long time. And Mom is already mad at him. She starts biting her bottom lip and pacing around a little bit. I can't help but catch on to her nervousness, it fills the house. We walk over to Aunt Carole's and sit with them while we wait. Mom and Aunt Carole sit in the kitchen talking. We haven't been there but a minute when there's a strange loud knocking, sort of a banging, at the door. Darla goes to get it and starts screaming. I never saw a house move so fast in my life. Aunt Carole must have jumped over the kitchen table through the wall. She is the first one to the door. When I finally make my way to the disturbance, there is my dad laying in the front yard holding his arm, blood spurting out of it like a hose turned on full blast. I stand on the porch watching him roll around on the ground delirious, trying to talk. Some stranger is there interpreting.

Mom is on the ground with him screaming in his face, "Where are Mark and Shelly!" I'm so scared. Were Shelly and Mark just as badly hurt? Were they already at the hospital? The man has the answers but no one is paying attention to him. Mom is out of her mind, screaming for her babies. I'm crying for my dad whose arm is spilt open from the shoulder to below the elbow. His shirt is torn and his sleeve is gone. Uncle Mal is trying to help Dad and I leave my body and begin searching for Shelly and Mark. I hear from across the yard, "Your children are fine. They're at my house with my wife, waiting for you."

Mom stops and looks at the man. "Take me to my kids, now." She jumps into the car and leaves with the man.

Dad is still in the yard bleeding. I can't help him. He lays there screaming in pain and blood, but he's so hurt I'm afraid of him. All I can do is watch Uncle Mal load him into the car, while Aunt Carole brings out towels for the blood. "Dad I love you, you're going to be okay."

"I love you too," he whispers. He reaches his good arm to me, "I'm sorry about this." And they drive off.

Mom is gone and so is Dad. I stand in the yard looking at all the blood on the grass, not sure what just happened. Mom returns and runs into the house, "Carole will take me to the hospital. Shelly's cut her chin and I think Mark is pretty bruised."

"Are they okay, Mom?" I want an answer now.

She doesn't answer me. I run out to the stranger's car and see Shelly and Mark just sitting there. Shelly has a cloth on her mouth and Mark is shaking. "Dad hit a telephone pole and we wrecked the car."

"Are you hurt?" I lean in closer through the car window.

"No, not really." Shelly takes the washcloth off her bleeding chin.

"How's Dad, is he okay?" Shelly is shaking and stuttering.

"No his arm is all messed up." I talk slow so I don't scare them anymore, "Didn't you see him?"

"No, when we hit the pole," Shelly starts crying, "the car spun into a neighbor's fence and we landed out in the road. Dad was asleep and we couldn't wake him. So, I got Mark and we ran to a house for help."

Mom is back, she's ready to go. The man helps move Shelly and Mark out of his car to Aunt Carole's. Shelly finishes the story.

"I guess when Dad woke up he got a ride to get Mom, but we never saw him. The man must have told him where we were. Sandra, it happened so fast. One minute we were eating an ice cream and the next Dad yells for us to get down. That's how I hit my chin. Mark was in the back on the floor behind Dad."

I never saw Shelly be so brave. She sat there with a bloody rag on her face telling me the story. She got out of the car, got herself and Mark across the busy intersection safely, and ran and found help for Dad. Alone with Mark she waited for Mom and never cried. She was really brave. And Dad, poor Dad, they never did figure out how he got such a wound. They say it was on impact and that his arm took all of it, that's why it wasn't a cut. It was as if the arm blew open. It took one hundred and seventy stitches to close him up. The next day he started crying when he saw Shelly. He put his good arm around her and said, "Thank you honey." He nudged Mark, joking, and said, "Bet you next time you'll think twice about an ice cream." He smiled as Mark's eyes watered up. Mark didn't like to see Dad hurt.

11

Everyone is sitting in the living room waiting for me. Mom is rubbing her fingers back and forth and Shelly staring out of the window watching a bird. Mark is chewing a gigantic piece of gum with purple all over his lips and face. And in the middle is Dad clipping his toenails. I drop my books on the TV. "What?"

"We're having a family discussion, sit down."

I sit next to Shelly on the chair arm.

"Kids your mother and I have decided—we're going back to West Virginia. Were going to take the money from the accident and go back there to open a hot dog stand in downtown Charleston. Your mother hates working nights, and I hate working at Weinstocks. It's just not enough money."

This is not a real discussion because I don't get to say anything. But my stomach never lies, and I know we're in big trouble. This will change everything. Mom sits there in her body, but she too has left the room. I see that stare, that horrible scary stare. I don't want to go. My head starts screaming—there'll be no neighbors. Who'll help us? No one knows us, I can't go back, he will kill us. Back to West Virginia, I can't believe it.

The weeks have passed beyond my control. We are preparing to leave for West Virginia. *Why*? They can open a hot-dog stand here.

Besides we are rich. Dad got three thousand dollars for his arm when that guy hit them. I'm so scared. Doesn't anyone see that Dad got here and nothing changed? It's still not safe. Why are we leaving? Can't anyone see what a giant mistake this will be? I want to talk to somebody. I want an answer. I don't want to go.

I keep waiting for one of the adults around here to question this stupid move. They are not questioning anything, they just keep smiling the pretend smile. Aunt Carole won't even look me in the eyes. Shelly and Mark think it's going to be fun driving across the country. I guess they forgot the Greyhound bus. I didn't.

They want to leave soon so they can get us into school. That's a big fat joke, those schools are too hard. I wish somebody would ask me what I want. I'd tell 'em. I would say, *I want to stay here in California. I don't want to be alone in the mountains*. No one's going to ask. Mom has painted an old travel trailer and put her sense of humor into it. I must admit it looks great. I love the little turtle she painted on the back and the bright purple isn't half bad either. I know we're going to look stupid going down the road, but it doesn't matter. It's not like we'll see any of those people again.

It's been close to two years since we came to California, and today we leave. I'm not excited, but everyone else seems to be. I look at them all running around smiling and laughing at the big adventure we're going on.

In my head I'm screaming—*Does anyone know how far West Virginia is from here? What is this dance that these people are doing? Are they crazy?* Three weeks ago Mal almost kicked Dad's ass, and now he's saying good-bye like they're brothers or something. My cousins are just stupid, they have no idea what's going on, they're just here to say good-bye. Aunt Revell is sad, but more like a sad movie. The truth is in Aunt Carole and she tries to hide it. I can see it spilling out of her eyes, she knows, and so do I that we are about to go nowhere. I see her hug Mom and whisper something to her, probably a warning. Aunt Carole pats and hugs each one of us—I think she held me a little longer. But she had to let go, I think she's going to cry.

"All right you guys, we better leave," Dad announces and off we go. Why, I don't know.

It will take exactly three days and four nights to get back to the mountains. Not only is that a fact, but it's a goal. We must stay on time. Where is the clock that determines our arrival?

"Where are we going?" Shelly blurts out. Thank God, someone is going to ask. West Virginia is a big place.

"Honey, we're going to Grandma's first then we'll see from there."

I do like it at Grandma's, but it's kinda weird for Mom. I think she feels uncomfortable staying at Grandma's.

Day one of the trip and the backseat is getting crowded. The dogs, Sugar, Big, and Little, don't make it any roomier. Mark is with Dad, driving the pickup truck with a camper thing on the back. Dad made it and it looks like it. Mom painted it purple for the laugh of it, and I can see a lot of people laughing as we go by. Thank God I'm in the van behind the turtle Mom painted. It's not bad driving with Mom and Shelly, I like it. "Front seat, front seat, I called it," Shelly screams as she runs down the driveway. I lost and nothing makes me madder than losing. I hate losing. I can't believe that I didn't remember to call the front seat. Shelly sits in the front seat. As I sit in the backseat I notice a lot of things about my mom: her dark, thick hair, her round pretty face, her little hands and her smile. I study each line and curve.

"Mom, do you think I'll look like you when I grow up?" I ask.

"Yes, I think so, but you won't look exactly like me, you have a little of your Aunt Revell in you."

"Shelly looks more like Dad, huh?" I point out.

I love the fact that I look the most like Mom. Shelly is by far more beautiful than me, everyone knows that. But at least I look like Mom. Shelly knows she's more beautiful than me and smarter than Mark. This is the way it is for her. She's liked by everyone, treated special, and school comes very easy for her. Mark and I struggle with sounding out words like C-A-T, and yet Shelly just seems to know them. I don't ever hear her sounding out her letters. We never talk about this strange occurrence between ourselves, but we all know our place. I think Shelly is a little uncomfortable with the extra attention she gets, but don't think for a moment she can't use it against us. Especially if it has to do with her getting her way. I'm leaning forward trying to hear Mom's story.

"Sandra scoot back, you're pullin my hair," Shelly screeches. If she screeches loud enough Mom will get mad and make me scoot back.

"Just move your hair so I can hear," I demand. I lean back just enough so my arms don't rest on the seat.

"Stop it," she yells again.

"What in the hell are you two doing?" Mom yells.

"Sandra won't scoot back and she's pullin my hair."

"Sandra just scoot back," Mom says with "fed up" in her voice.

I scoot back in a huff wishing I could yank her hair right now.

Dad is pulling over, it must be time to pee or change passengers. I hate that part, I like staying with Mom, but I bet it'll be me who has to move.

Now I'll miss all the laughs with Mom. "Sure Dad, I'll ride with you." I cover up and keep the peace. I'm the only one who actually thinks about his feelings. Everyone else just gets to be scared or intimidated. I, on the other hand, care about not hurting his feelings. They never say thanks.

My hands grasp the large pickup truck door handle; it takes two thumbs to get the door open. I put one thumb on top of the other and push with all my strength. The seat is scorching; it has that plastic material that gets really hot. I test it with my hands before I jump in. The smell of old and new cigarettes is blowing my way. The ashtray is always full. "Dad can we dump this?" I plead. He reaches down and fights with the hooky thing that holds in the ashtray. Finally he unleashes it and bends out of the truck ready to dump it on the ground. "No," I yell, "you can't litter." I reach over the seat to him, grab that nasty thing, and try not to breathe through my nose while I run it over to the garbage can. Mom and Shelly and Mark look to see what's going on. I hide what I'm doing just to make them wonder a little. The truck is full of junk. Positioning myself in the torn seat, I clear a path for my feet and my butt. The eight track is all ready to blare Blood Sweat and Tears. How weird that Dad has this tape, I wonder where he got it. I sit up and pull my shirt down in the back so the sun-beaten seat will quit burning me.

"Want to listen to that tape?" Dad pops it in, "Sandra, this is my favorite song." I watch him with a smile on his face and rhythm in his fingers. I sit back checking the temperature of the seat and listen carefully. I love music. I continue to listen, my mouth drops and suddenly I see a deeper side of Dad. The song rocks and rolls in the cab.

I'm not scared of dying, I don't really care,
if its peace you find in dying and dying time is near,
just bundle up my coffin cause it's cold way down there.
Troubles are many, they're as deep as a well,
I can swear there ain't no heaven, but I pray there ain't no hell.
But I'll never know by living, only my dying will tell.
And when I die and when I'm dead, dead and gone,
there'll be one child born in this world to carry on, to carry on.

The words echo in my heart. Am I the child born to carry on? Is Dad ready to die? Or maybe he knows how mean he is and hates it too. I look deep into my dad and can't help but love his crazy sense of humor, his toughness, and his hairy, freckley, happy belly. The man can't scare me as much as I love him. *He is my dad and I wonder if it's all his fault.*

The ride is long and tiring. I almost feel safe enough to sleep for a while. What am I thinking? Am I crazy? I know better than to let my guard down. I must be tired. I refocus my eyes and try to stop them from crossing. I wish I had something to drink or that we could stop and get out for a minute. The conversation between us has died down. As I look out the window I feel the hot wind brush against my face. I search the desert and its flat empty space, which has no end. How did this part of the world get so flat? Ahead in the distance where everything is sort of bluish, I see some mountains. "Hey Dad, what mountains are those?"

He answers quickly, "Those are the beginning of the Rockies. We'll be heading through those tomorrow."

Mom hates the mountains. I hope he's still in a good mood tomorrow when we drive through them. I hope he doesn't try to scare us. My mind replays the scary drives in West Virginia. I'm seeing the fear tighten in Mom's face as Dad laughs his way down the mountain, getting close to the edge with no guardrails. Mark is on Mom's lap sucking his fingers, and he is terrified—the whole car is terrified. Shelly screams at Dad with begging in her voice, "Please stop it." I pray my twisted prayer and know that this will be over soon, and that there is nothing we can do as long as everyone is freaking out. Best to leave the fear alone and pretend it's okay. There is a game you have to play with Dad, and I am the only one who plays it. No one knows that I'm the one who stops Dad from being so mean with my magic.

"Dad, I'm getting hungry. Can we stop and get a hamburger?" My mouth waters at the thought of ketchup and pickles.

"Yeah, we'll stop at the next town, it's about fifty miles."

I ask how long that is and Dad tells me how to calculate mph. I give him the answer, about an hour. "You got it," he agrees. Thank god because if I was wrong it could have been a verbal beating. I can hear him telling me how stupid I am. I hate it when he has to teach me something.

We stop for lunch and we still have a lot of driving before we can stop for a motel. I decide to stay with Dad and not complicate things. Mark is sleepy and Shelly still has the front seat. I want to talk to Mom, but she just gives me the be-a-good-girl look. I finish lunch quickly so I can go play with the dogs for awhile. I like taking them for a walk in between stops. I walk around the gravel yard next to the truck stop and wish I was a truck driver. "I'm going to be the first girl truck driver. I bet you I can do it." I turn around with my new discovery and trip over the cement parking curb. I catch my balance with the other foot as it slams the ground. I turn back to see what tripped me and there before me is a ten-dollar bill just staring at me. I cock my head, close one eye, and look around to see if anyone is watching. I grab that dirty ten-dollar bill and throw it in my pocket and run back to Mom. "Mom, look what I just found."

"Let me see. You found that?"

"Yeah, right out there on the ground by the parking thing." Shelly and Mark can't believe it, and Dad wants it. But it's mine, all mine. I can't help but notice Dad's head is turned toward the ground where I found the ten-dollar bill. "So you say you found it over there, huh?"

That night we find a cheap motel to sleep.

"Yeah, the motel has a pool, and we get to swim tonight." I dance around the backseat. All of us are happy, but I'm the one who says it out loud. I've been swimming since I was two years old. Dad always says I was the easiest to teach to swim, I practically swam before I walked. I get so proud of myself when he says that.

Dad pulls up to the office and we get in our positions; everyone has to hide. As soon as we turn into the parking lot we put the dogs down on the floor. We go down on the floor with them. I curl up on my side and Shelly does the same. It smells like old tennis shoes and mildew. The stains and crumbs keep our mind occupied while Dad goes into the office. It takes forever. We can't wait for the car to start moving toward the room. Dad always asks for something in the back. I never quite understand why we have to hide, maybe it's cheaper if they think it's only Mom and Dad. And whatever we do, we mustn't let them see the dogs. I feel sorry for the dogs, they never get to go out and play. Mom, Dad, and I each take a dog into the room underneath our coats. I feel a little scared I might drop the dog or the dog might bark and then what? I get scared I'll screw up and we'll get caught and kicked out, or that Dad will slap me for screwing up. Or worse, what if we don't get a pool? So far we've never been caught. It's such a relief to get into the room with all the dogs. It feels like the make-believe game where I have only so much time to run and hide from the car lights. The blood pumps extra fast through my body when I play that game, just the same as hiding the dogs at the hotel. It's over, we made it, no one knows, and now we can go swimming.

At dinnertime we all walk to a Big Red's Steak House. This is weird; we never eat at a sit-down place. It's nice to eat something different; I've had hamburgers for so many days I lost count. I love looking at the big menu. It's so big that Shelly and I share holding it, we have to so it fits on top of the table. I notice that something is odd about Dad and he has a smirky look on his face.

"You guys order anything you like, tonight it's on me," he laughs. I can't believe what I just heard. Am I in heaven? Normally we can't order the things on the first page, and we have to try to order from the children's menu. But always, always, nothing over $4.00.

"Okay Dad," we all nod. I know something is about to happen, my stomach is telling me so. We all order and Mom helps Mark, who has a hard time talking out loud to the waitress. I love it myself. "I'll have a steak with French fries and no soup," I communicate with confidence. The waitress is so nice and pretty. I can see her loving the fact that she is talking to us. I make eye contact and thank her.

The food is great, I feel full, I can still fit in one more French fry, with ketchup of course. We eat a fat happy meal and the end is near, time to go. Then Dad waves the waitress over. What's he going to do? I feel the redness starting to cover my face. She comes to the table promptly. Here it comes. He asks for the manager, I can't believe it. "Sir, is this your restaurant," Dad asks sarcastically. I panic. I knew it, I knew it…

"I am the manager, sir," he explains.

"Well, then, why in the hell when I ask for well-done steaks for my family do I get rare?" Dad attacks, catching the poor man totally off guard. I can already see that Dad has won, it's only a matter of time. Mom rolls her eyes and buries her shame. I am aghast at the whole scene he's making, a rude, nasty embarrassing scene. The manager tries to question—why did the whole family eat their meals if they were not satisfied in the first place?

"Are you calling me a liar?" Dad raises his voice. Intimidation is the next punch, and all that's left of this poor man is to the count of ten. Dad has won again. I feel so sorry for the manager and that nice waitress. They did nothing to deserve this, and she was so sweet and thoughtful, asking us what we needed all the time. I want to get out of here right now. The whole restaurant turns their heads and whispers as we leave. And just for an encore Dad bellows, "This place is a disgrace, can't even make a simple steak. Come on, let's get out of here."

Mom follows, caught between a hard place and Dad. She waits until the glass doors shut behind her.

"Oh that's great. You are one hell of an ass."

Dad laughs and keeps walking and chewing his toothpick.

"I mean it, that's not funny." She wraps her sweater tighter around her body. "Next time you want to pull a stunt like that, let me know first."

Dad laughs a little more and chuckles, "Hey, it was free wasn't it?"

She stomps out Dad's fire. "That's bullshit."

We say nothing as we get ready for bed. No one is safe from the wrath of Dad, not even strangers who bring us a nice meal. I shake my head. Shelly crawls in bed with me. The dogs curl up at the foot of our bed. Mom and Dad share with Mark. Mom whispers, "Sleep tight, don't let the bedbugs bite..." Just one big, happy family going to sleep.

The next morning it's up and at 'em, time to go and beat the traffic.

What traffic? I think to myself, for God's sake we are in the middle of a damn desert, on our way to the Rocky Mountains. I'm losing my patience with this whole trip.

12

The days weave in and out as we near the Ohio border. Shelly is in charge of the peanut butter and jelly-stained map that guides us through the boredom. She pulls gently, trying not to tear the sticky part of the map folded together. It gives her something to do rather than talk. She opens it all the way and finds where we are, this takes about a half an hour.

"Shelly, give it to me, I'll find it," I say.

"Nope, I'll find it".

"Come on, I'll give it right back."

"No."

"Mom, make Shelly share the map."

Shelly continues to struggle and fight with the damn map. Not only do we have the map to kill time, but we have the dogs to torment, fighting for space, the annoying games of copy cat, and of course, the radio. Mark's favorite time killer is blowing on the window and scribbling a happy face. I love pretending we are racing across America with all the other cars and we are ahead. Shelly talks and talks and talks. She can actually talk to herself if no one is listening. If you don't listen she doesn't care, she still has a good time.

We get to Chicago, time to straighten up and be good. Maybe six hours or so, and there we'll be, at Grandma Dorothy's house. It's been forever since we left West Virginia. Mom sits up and breathes out, her bottom lip sucks in and her mouth says stuff without talking. She looks pissed but she's not, it's a sort of confused, irritated look. No one is in trouble, exactly, but you could get backhanded if your timing is off. Poor timing is dangerous. For instance, if I call Mark a baby, because he is, this could go unnoticed. But, if my timing is off, I could actually get backhanded across the mouth in a split second. At any other time this name-calling is no big deal. Another example is teasing. Don't tease Mom during this time; normally you can tease her and she'll tease you back, but not now. Time to straighten up and "be good" translates as, talk low, no fighting, and watch out for the backhand. The concept of being good is not just mere words, it is now an action.

The last five hours are going to be quiet while everyone goes into their heads. Daydreaming is what most people call it, I call it preparing. No one talks, we just think about whatever comes to mind. I think that the last time I saw Grandma she was holding back the tears as we left. She was being strong, but I know she was breaking inside. I wonder if she ever thought she'd see us again. I personally can't wait to see her and those loving eyes. I hope she makes chicken and dumplings. She always does for special occasions; this is one of those special occasions I am sure. I can see her in the kitchen fussing around and yelling at Duke to mow the yard. Duke always has to mow the yard when we come over.

Mom is still chewing her bottom lip. We must heed the warning while Mom is lost in her own thoughts. I keep my eyes on the road noticing the trees and their beautiful colors starting to shine. The season is changing and so is our life, and who knows what's going to happen this time? For that fact, who knows where we are going to live? I don't think Mom knows either. That's probably why she's so quiet. Or maybe it's the baby. That's not very good to think about, so I'll forget that.

I think I'm starting to recognize the highway a little bit. Dad is still up ahead leading the way to Grandma's house. Mark is in the front seat asleep, he looks so cute sleeping—his little fingers. Mom reaches over and covers his legs. Shelly is kicking her feet back and forth, she is nervous, probably anticipating those damn beans that await her. I know that Grandma would not make her eat beans on her first day back. I can tell that Grandma loves us so much that all she wants for us is to be happy. It would break her heart if she knew the truth about us. I mean all the bad stuff that has happened. I have a feeling that maybe if we all live closer to Grandma it won't happen anymore. Dad is never mean or drunk around Grandma. CHILLICOTHE SIXTEEN MILES, we'll be there in about a half an hour.

The daydreams start to vanish and reality wakes each one of us with a pat on the head. Everyone in the whole car is stretching, yawning, and itching to get there. Shelly has to pee, but we won't stop this close to Grandma's. I want some dumplings. Mark is thirsty after his nap.

There she is on the porch as if she could sense us coming down the street. *How does she do that?* I wonder to myself. I have my hand on the door handle, I'll get to her first.

"Grandma, Grandma!" I scream as I run to her arms. She holds me as she searches out the rest of her little angels.

"Where's that Mark?" she spouts as she walks toward the car. "There you are." She reaches for his tired body that grew so big while we were gone. She doesn't even ask for some sugar, she simply steals a kiss from Mark. I can see Mark with that adorable smile covered up with embarrassment. He looks at her out of the corner of his eye.

"Come on, y'all, get your clothes and those dogs, I got some supper ready," she orders with love in her heart. Her babies are back and ain't nobody or nothing gonna take them away. She cocks her head in a teasing way, as she goes to the kitchen. I am her little eater and my mouth waters waiting for the special announcement. If I would have asked Grandma what's for supper, well now that would be rude, and with Dad so close I don't dare start off rude. Instead I'll follow her. "Grandma, can I help you?" I ask with a motive.

"Why sure, you can set the table. You remember where everything is, don't ya?" she smiles.

I reach up over the counter for the plates as I smell it, yes, I bet you it is chicken and dumplings. Grandma lifts the lid off the big old pot and as I lower myself down from the counter in perfect timing, there it is, a big pot of steaming, thick, rich, delicious dumplings. I put the plates on the table and wait for Shelly to get out of the bathroom. "Shelly open up," I whisper.

"Just a minute I'm going to the bathroom." The door opens. "Grandma fixed the dumplings." Relief takes over Shelly's body. We head down the hall to the kitchen. Duke sits in the recliner smiling and asking stupid Grandpa questions. Grandma remarried when George died, and the way I hear it, it was a good thing that George died. I don't know for sure if he should have died, but Duke is much nicer than George from what they say. George was Brooks's and John's real dad, but he was my dad's stepfather. He is not my grandfather according to Dad. Dad never says too much about George, as a matter of fact no one does. Aunt Mozell hates George. Aunt Mozell doesn't hide her feelings, it's best not to mention George around her or Dad. Mom tells us stories about the horrible way George treated my dad. And even though I didn't know him, I get mad hearing about him hurting my dad when he was a little boy.

"All right you all, wash your hands, supper is ready,"

"Me and Shelly already did," I say as we scoot up to the table. Mom is in the background correcting me, "Don't you mean Shelly and I already have?"

I acknowledge my poor English. After all, I know what she's trying to do, she's trying to establish that we're not going to use the word *ain't*. Mom hates the word *ain't*. The hillbilly vocabulary is just a word away. It's hopeless, but she'll give it a shot for a while and then she'll give up. I can't wait for my accent to come back. It's so fun to pick up new words like *dinner* for *lunch*, and *you all*, and *ain't*. *You all come on and let's git us some dinner, and I ain't gonna be late.*

"Ardell, why don't you let me git them dishes and you take a shower? I'll put the kids to bed." Grandma can sense Mom's exhaustion.

Tomorrow the whole family will come over and welcome us back. Dad's outside with Duke catching up. After the dishes are done, Shelly and I go outside to sit on the porch and watch night fall and the lightning bugs slowly struggle to light. Mom has taken Mark to bed with her and Dad will join them soon. It's quiet on the porch and the only sound is the squeak of the back door opening as Grandma comes out to have a sit. Duke knows it's his cue to leave us alone. He exits, without a word, to his chair and TV. Grandma squishes in the middle of Shelly and me.

"Girls, I've missed you something terrible. Grandma worries something awful about you so far away in California." She spits with contempt, pulls out her secret Salem cigarettes, qualifies how bad smoking is, and lights up with relief. "Girls you don't need to say nothing to your Uncle Brooks about me smoking." We know that.

The next morning we wake to Aunt Mozell in the kitchen clanking around loud enough to wake the neighbors, as Grandma puts it.

There is nothing worse than waking up to Aunt Mozell first thing in the morning. As a matter of that fact, there is nothing like Aunt Mozell. She's an antique, a legend, and she speaks her mind. As Aunt Mozell demands her hugs from us, Mark puts it best: terror written all over his face, he runs to Mom.

Shelly and I don't have that luxury, and must politely give away our hugs. Smothered in the overlapping folds of her arms, I can't help thinking to myself how wonderful she smells. How can such an ugly woman smell so good? I give her an extra hug just so I can smell her scent. What is it? She smells sweet, loving, pure like honey. That's it, she smells like honey before it's put into a jar. I see Dad turn into a little boy right before my eyes as he sees his Aunt Mozell. Something inside him melts as she returns the look.

"Jack, you come over here and sit next to your Aunt Mozell," she orders with pure old-fashioned love and a frown. Dad has the same look on his face as he walks over to his aunt, the same sheepish, shy, coy look Mark has when Grandma teases him with her love. Jack is the nickname Aunt Mozell gave to Dad when his love for Cracker Jacks outdid him. The name Jack stuck and everyone in his family calls Dad Jack, except for Mom who calls him Bill. But only Aunt Mozell can say Jack with true conviction. I think Dad loves Aunt Mozell more than his own mom. I don't know for sure, but something else sings between them that isn't there for him and Grandma. Aunt Mozell asks all the important questions with a certain abruptness.

"So now that you and the family are back home, what are ya going to do next?"

Dad fidgets a bit and in the background Grandma defends.

"Now Mozell don't start with all those darn questions."

"We're all family here, no need to hide from it. All I want to know is what is Jack going to do next? Where is he going to live? Can't stay here forever."

The room is at attention as the truth floats through the air. I sit in the chair wanting desperately to go to the bathroom and brush my teeth during this adult conversation. Plus, I really don't want to know the plan; I want to pretend we're staying at Grandma's for a while. I am stuck in the chair, however, sitting straight across from Aunt Mozell who has the floor at this time. I can't escape, it would be way too bold to interrupt and cross in front of this touchy topic.

Mom butts in, "You know Mozell, Bill and I were thinking about opening a used furniture store, maybe antiques or something."

There she sits questioning, with her drooping left eye, crooked smile, and wiry hair sticking straight up, disapproving. Dad has turned into a small boy waiting for a lecture.

He sits up and says, "You have no idea how much of that kind of stuff is up there, we're going to make a fortune."

Eventually we go back to the mountains, same area but a different town. They say it will be different. I can't help but get scared as we drive off to those mountains. But here we go. Dad pulls up to a large, white, dreary, cold house. It has been rented; I think Grandma rented it for us. In less than four hours the house is unpacked, and here we sit in a still house full of empty dreams. Dad is on some tirade about opening a business and getting rich. I don't know what it means to be rich, but I do know that we have no money and asking for anything is out of the question.

Dad looks for furniture and Mom finishes unpacking the measly boxes no one wants to touch. It takes but a day to put all that small stuff away. "Don't unpack your toys, just leave them in the box and use it as a toy box," Mom explains.

I start exploring my new neighborhood. There's a nice boy who lives down the street. I think he's a rich kid. I'm not sure, but he has a mini bike, a big house, a horse, and nice clothes. Dad says he's going to buy me a mini bike one day.

I develop a curiosity, maybe even a fascination, with these incredible bones I keep finding on the property. I take over the shed and it's now my laboratory. Everyone needs to stay out of my lab. I make this quite clear to Shelly and Mark with a quick threat, "Don't even think about coming in here, it's mine." They don't challenge my authority. I have no idea that later that afternoon I would find my biggest treasure.

I have moved to new territory. I'm getting tired of these little bones. Now I'm an archaeologist and I'm looking for dinosaur bones. I have over fifty bones and eventually I will put them all together. As I sit on my knees digging and digging, I hit a hard pack of dirt. I take my finger and clear a path. I can't believe it, this feels like a skull.

I dig with purpose, I am finding a skull. I can see the headlines now LITTLE GIRL FINDS MILLION-YEAR-OLD DINOSAUR BONE THAT STUMPS THE COMMUNITY. I am lost in fame and fortune as I carefully unbury my dinosaur bone. Finally, it's uncovered. I must be at least ten feet into the earth. "Mom, Mom." I scream, running to the house with my find. She meets me at the porch, Shelly and Mark close by. "Look what I found." I hold up my dirty two-foot find. Her face scrunches, she is dumbfounded by the skull. "I think it's a dinosaur," I pronounce.

"Well, I don't know what it is, but it is big, and it is a skull."

Mark's eyes are lit up. I can see he's happy for me.

"I like your bone, can I help dig?" he asks softly.

I think about it, "Yeah, but you have to be careful."

Shelly is less interested than Mom. Mark and I go out to the back and I continue the dig. I tell him all about how I found it and what might still be down there. I dig forever, but I can't find any more and it's getting time for dinner. I walk carefully to my lab and put my find next to the others on the workbench in the shed.

"What's this one?" Mark reaches up onto the table.

"Hey, don't touch." I screech, "This is important stuff." His hand slowly lets go and falls back down to his side.

Dad gets home and we eat dinner. I can hardly wait to show him my find. "After dinner" he says.

"Come on Dad," as I reach for his hand, "let's go." He and Mark follow me out to the shed. I struggle to reach the string that turns on the light, and as I spin around to see Dad's face, he gives a condescending snicker.

"What?" I stamp my foot.

"Well Sandra, that's a nice horse head you got there." He can barely hold back the laughter. Now he's crouched over laughing, and embarrassing me with each roar. I think to myself he doesn't know what he's talking about.

"I hate to tell you this sweetheart, but next door used to be a veterinary clinic. What you have is nothing but a bunch of old dead farm animals." He leaves with a pat on my shoulder and heads to the house to tell Mom what a fool I am.

I wonder if I can sleep out here? I know the whole family is laughing at me. Mark stands next to me and looks up, he knows I'm humiliated. He tells me with his eyes that he's not going to laugh at me.

I decide quickly that I'm now studying to be a vet, not an archaeologist, and that this horse head is a good sign. I stay outside and work on cleaning up my find. Mom hollers for Mark to come take a bath, and I stay focused on painting my treasure. Mom hollers for me next. "Just a minute, I'll be right there," I holler back. I am finished. I load up the skull and walk in with it tucked under my coat. I head straight for my room where I proudly present my new piece. I am ready to defend my find, one large, very shiny, freshly varnished horse skull. Mom enters my bedroom and sees the skull on display like a treasure from the sea. She complements my hard work, says "good night," and shakes her head. She thinks I've completely lost my mind.

Weeks have passed. It's okay around here. I run downstairs, "Can we go look for bottles now?"

"Yes but you have to take your brother; I've got to go with your father," Mom bargains.

Now *this* is what I live for, bottle hunting. The two-lane highway is full of them. We pack a small lunch and begin the journey. Exploring is my game. I love to make believe and get rich at the same time. We walk up the road, heading somewhere past town, chatting back and forth, deciding who's the boss and who will lead. Without saying it, I am the boss, and I will lead. Being the oldest has its advantages and its responsibilities. For instance, if a car goes crazy on the old country road while we're walking, I am the one who will save us. I keep a watchful eye out for us and our safety. That's why I have to lead and be the boss. The first mile or so is dead, there are no bottles. We all know that, because we were just here a day ago. So the chitchat continues and we keep half an eye on the ditch. We walk at a faster pace through this stretch of road. We take turns pulling the metal fold-up cart—empty is one thing, but full of bottles is a chore. We get past the dead territory and begin entering fresh road. A serious tempo takes over and searching becomes the theme. We all know that the more bottles, the more money, and the more candy or toys we'll get.

"Mark the fart," Shelly and I start teasing.

"Shelly MO-belly," he laughs back at her. We all think of what we're going to call me, but "Sandra" doesn't really rhyme. Laughing is all we can do. The freedom of walking the two-lane, windy, damp country road is exhilarating. Shelly starts with "A hundred bottles of beer on the road…" and soon we all sing it with heart to the end. Mark dashes off into the ditch. He sees something, the first bottle of the day. Up until the first bottle is actually captured, we are not real sure what kind of day it will be. He pops up with a Coke bottle that has been buried for years. I don't know how he saw it. He carefully reaches over the cart and drops in the first five cents. We then follow our mission, money motivating our every step. "I am going across the street," Shelly yells. I feel a whisper of fear, I really don't want her on that side of the road. It's more dangerous if she's on that side; the cars might not see her, and if she's over there, how can I protect her? What if she gets hit by a car or one of those trucks? Now my slight fear has turned to terror, I'm out of control. I know she doesn't have to mind me, only Mark has to mind me. What am I going to do? "Hey Shel, I really need you over here on this side so we don't miss any bottles."

She argues back, "But I can find some here too."

"I know, but we'll come back on that side and we can all look over there at one time." My logic gets through to her. I hear her, "Okay," and I breathe a sigh of relief as I watch for the enemy while she crosses back to my side.

I see that we've passed the old farmhouse with the barn that leans to one side. I love that old barn, it has so many stories and looks so tired, yet it still stands. I measure our distance by that old house, and we are far from home. By this time the bottles are practically jumping into our cart. I'm trying to count, but it's too high for me to count, so Mom might have to help us when we get home. I don't know my times tables very well. Shelly does, but she doesn't want to count right now. I look back as Mark squeals, he's got another one. He runs to catch up. He shows me the prize, but this one is tricky. "I don't think so Mark, this is a beer bottle, only the ones with longer necks get money." His face is embarrassed. "Here, I'll show you the difference." I reach in. "This big one is worth ten cents, and pop bottles are worth a nickel. But this one is nothing." He barely gets it, and neither do I. But I do know the rules as they apply to bottles, I am an expert hunter.

In the middle of a field I see an oak tree that looks like a great place to stop and eat our peanut butter and jelly sandwiches. We all squeeze between the fence post. As we kick our way through the high, soft grassy pasture toward the grandfather-like tree, Shelly starts singing, "Lions and tigers and bears, oh my." We start skipping to the words and pretending we're in the *Wizard of Oz*. I plop onto the ground and lay back, enjoying the wispy clouds above and the smells of fall. The tree looks brilliant from down here. Shelly gets the lunch out of the dingy, wrinkled paper bag. All I can think about is, I hope Mom put enough jelly on them, for some reason she's stingy with the jelly part. Which means it doesn't go down very well, and we are left thirsty on the rest of our hunt. First bite tells the story. We will be thirsty.

I notice that my legs are getting a little tired. As I notice, Shelly says it. It's odd but I know we can read each other's minds, especially when we have to. "We should keep going you guys." I stand up. "Let's go to the second curve up ahead, and then we'll head back on the other side." They don't want to, they want to go home now, but my bossy position, not to mention my greed, gets me my way.

The cart is almost full, and we still have the other side to venture. This is a good day's hunt, almost too good. The cart weighs a hundred pounds already. The second curve granted us another four bottles. I'll be the one who picks when and where we'll cross the road. I have to be careful because it's not safe to cross the road on a curve.

We all make it across the street, and now it's time to search out the bottles. The way back is always a little different. Mainly because we're getting tired, and the cart is no longer an option for Mark to pull, it's up to Shelly and me. Fighting starts over how far the next person will pull it.

All the while, finding more and more bottles, the dreaded walk back becomes the thread that binds us. While the bottles continue to call to us, Shelly pulls her last pull.

"Help, I can't do it!"

"Come on, I did, it's your turn," I beg. But no amount of strong-arming or fighting is going to get her to pull her turn.

The cart is winning. Finally it is time to take serious measures. Shelly and I must pull together. And we have to quit finding bottles.

I take the last seven bottles and stack them between Mark's arms and balance each one for the long walk home. Shelly and I work together and pull the beast down the road that seems to stretch against us as we tug home. "Yes, I see the bottle, but where are we going to put it?" I snap at Shelly sarcastically. "Okay, let's take a break. Mark put your bottles down." Smash—they hit the ground. We're too exhausted to care that Mark just broke thirty-five cents.

"Here's what we'll do. We mark where we are and quit looking for the damn bottles. We'll come back and get the rest later." It's a great idea and we all know it. Shelly finds a paper cup and we proudly poke it on the fence. Our territory has been marked and saved for another day. All we have to do is get this load back to the house and cash in our reward.

Mom is in the road watching for her children to return. I hope we aren't late, I never thought about time. Shelly is cheating, she's not pulling very hard anymore, I can feel the difference. She denies the accusation as we huff and puff our way home. We get in the yard where Mom waits to greet us. Or kill us, we aren't sure. I see in her eyes we're late, but not in trouble. She's astonished at our treasure. We all sit down and sort the nickel bottles from the dime ones. Mom helps us count. "$5.25, my god you kids did great. I don't even have that much money." She laughs with a frown.

All of us say at once, "Here, Mom, you can have them."

"No I'm just kidding…" She plays.

"It's okay Mom, you can pay us back."

Dad still doesn't have any antique furniture, although he looks all the time, and without the furniture we can't open a store. Mom says he's "crazier than hell." He's getting grouchy and the house is getting quieter and quieter. Uncle Brooks shows up for a visit from the Navy. He looks so goofy with short hair and the Navy uniform. But it's the same old Brooks, laughing, joking, and playing around with Mark.

Dad tells Brooks all about his *new* idea. "It's an abandoned old mansion from the Civil War that sits in the middle of town. I want to turn it into a hotel and restaurant. I met this guy who owns it, and he'll give free rent until we get it up and running. It's perfect."

Mom listens with one ear, she's heard about it all week.

"We're going to be rich, man. I mean it, it's perfect for us. And it's exactly what this town needs. I've been talking to this guy, Mr. Stowe, he's the owner or something like that, and he'll let us rent for practically nothing. Then all we got to do is watch the money roll in. I figure it'll take a couple of months to get things rolling, but hell, I got time."

"Jack, it sounds great. Wish I could stick around and help out, but I only have one week's leave. Then I'm out to sea."

Within a day or two it's time to pack up. Moving is just something to do, it's no big deal. And thank god we didn't unpack our toys because now all we have to do is load up and we are out of here.

It's a cold, crisp New Year's eve day when we move into the mansion—and it *is* a mansion. Dad showed us the place last week from the road, but it was too far away to really see it or believe it. In our tiny caravan of truck, camper, and van, we creep up the long curvy driveway big enough for one car, through the giant trees that block the sky, and up to the traditional white-with-black trim mansion. The wraparound porch alone is bigger than the old house. Heck it's bigger than Grandma's house. Big Foot jumps off Mom's lap as soon as she opens the van. Sugar Foot won't get out. I don't blame her. This is too big, it's way too big for us.

"I don't know what he's thinking. I'm not going to live here." Shelly leans against the van and nods her head. Her eyes alone can't see the whole thing. She tilts her head upward and says nothing. She's stunned. I think Mark wants to run. I will not go in this place alone, not without the lights on first, people close by, and the dogs. Everyone moves slowly and cautiously. We have to, the house, I mean mansion, will swallow us whole. I've never seen such a big place, and I never thought I'd live in a place that has its own name. This is Oak Terrace.

Dad fumbles with a black skeleton key that looks like it's straight out of a horror movie. I can't believe this key works. The word *skeleton* can't be good. I watch with intrigue—will this key actually open the door? The side door we enter is to the left of the porch. The porch has two massive entry doors, but for now we'll just use the smaller door. It's open! Dad is first, of course, and Mom's next, so if someone is going to die, it'll be one of them. Shelly, Mark, and I huddle, but once we're in, we loosen up. We enter a kitchen, the first of two big kitchens. The stove over in the corner looks like a car and the sinks are the size of bathtubs. I shake my head at the thought of how many dirty dishes the sinks can hold. No one leaves the group. We move together, figuring out where we are. I feel like we're breaking into someone else's place, and we might get caught. The first kitchen has five separate doors. Dad picks the swinging door straight ahead. It leads to two formal dinning rooms and a foyer. The ceilings are grand, they have pictures on them. Mom said something about murals. I say, how the heck did they paint upside down?

"My god, look at this." Mom moves gingerly to the parlor, or lobby, that sits in the center of all four entry doors, two to the right and two straight ahead. She points at the spiral staircase just like the one in *Gone with the Wind*. My eyes follow each beautiful stair, up and up to the chandelier that reaches to the stars. I must see the upstairs. I hear Dad down below.

"And look, it already has a front desk for checking in guests. Solid oak. Ardell, can you believe this place?"

"I know, it's beautiful, but can we pull this off?"

I can count the bedrooms, all sixteen of them. But I can't count all the bathrooms because I get lost from one bedroom to the next and forget my count. Each bedroom has its own decor. Nothing is the same, each closet door, which I will not open right now, is carved with a particular detail, and every bed is different. I investigate further, door after door, so many doors, that eventually I end up where I started. "Dad, can I have this room?" I yell down. At this point I realize everyone's left me. The creepy crawly's race through my skin. I run down the stairs, skipping every other one, past the murals and back to the kitchens where I hear voices. I pound through the swinging door, and nobody's there. I stop and listen. I can hear them but I can't see them. "Hey, where are you guys?"

Shelly pops her head out of a smaller brown door through the back part of the kitchen. It looks like a closet. I step over the doorjamb. Mom and Dad are staring, just standing there staring at the billions and billions of dead black and yellow bumblebees the size of golf balls. Each step I take sounds like Cracker Jacks under my feet. The bees are everywhere. They must have all decided this would be the place to die, year after year after year. I knew the skeleton key was a bad sign. Dad starts laughing, "Well, Mark, I know what you'll be doing for the next few days."

Mark checks to see if all billion bees are dead or if they're pretending.

About that time Brooks walks in, he has no trouble finding us. "Hey ya all." He lifts his feet. "What in the hell...?"

Dad turns around, "Yeah, must have been some party, huh? Mark's going to clean this up, and this will be our living room. Up those stairs are the kids' rooms."

Shelly looks to Mom and I look up to God. Mark just keeps looking for the one bee that might not be dead.

"Jack, what's the rest of the place like?"

"Not too bad. Just needs a little elbow grease, that's all."

Mom returns to the kitchen where the bees aren't. She rolls her eyes at the amount of elbow grease she needs. Dad takes Brooks on the tour of the nice part of the mansion. We stay back and digest the servants' quarters, our living room, the dead bees, the wooden staircase that leads up to the three tiny bedrooms, and the filthy kitchens filled with cobwebs. "Mom let's go see our bedrooms."

Mom leads us up the wooden staircase, single file. I hold my breath and don't touch anything as we climb to reality. The creaking of the stairs is ignored because of the smashing of dead bees under our feet. My eyes do not deceive me. This is not like what I saw sixteen rooms ago.

Dad says we'll live in the back here, the servants' quarters is what they call it. It's like a secret hiding place for the blacks who worked here a long time ago. You go through the second kitchen, through a small door that looks like a pantry and opens to a small living room. Then there is a narrow staircase on the other end of this room that leads straight up to the three bedrooms. Once you get up there, it's mine and Shelly's room first, then a hall with a banister to Mark's room. Then back into the hall to Mom and Dad's room where there is another staircase that takes you down to a service porch, which goes outside. I don't know how they built this place, and I cannot for the life of me figure out how I end up outside when I come through the kitchens. But this is where we and the dogs live. Of course, we don't show this part of the house to anyone.

13

I clean the yards and rake leaves all day long. Mark and Mom work on bees. If you get too tired of one chore, there's another one to follow. I pop my head into one of the massive kitchens to see if the coast is clear. I'm hungry and I want some Cheetos, but I don't want to have to help in the kitchen. Good, no one is here, all I want is the Cheetos and a drink of water. I tiptoe through the kitchen to the stove, the bag of Cheetos is laying right there. The stove wants me to clean it, and the Cheetos want me to eat them. I grab a handful and run. If Mom is in there cleaning the stove or something, she might see me and ask me to help. Besides, it's a holy terror in there, freezing cold, grease, and hard work. I am just fine raking leaves.

I love making huge piles of leaves and swinging from the hanging branches into the soft crackling cold leaves below. I was trying to teach Shelly, but she's so scared she probably won't let go in time and she'll land on her butt. I look around at the grounds; I must have filled twenty bags of leaves so far. Dad is going to pay me a nickel a bag. I rake harder, seeing the nickels piling up.

"Hey, what are you doing?" Shelly runs down the hill to me.

"I'm raking, what does it look like? What are you doing, nothing like always?"

"I was helping Mom and Mark with the bees."

"Dad's going to pay me a nickel a bag."

Shelly's eyes get big and she grabs a rake laying on the ground. "I'm going to help."

"No you're not, this is my job." Next thing I know Shelly's running up to the house screaming, "Dad, Sandra won't let me help."

Dad stands tall on the porch with Ajax all over him. "Let your sister help and quit fighting, or I'll come over there and put my foot up both your asses."

Shelly rakes slowly and steals all my hard work. I care, but it's still better than cleaning those old black iron stoves.

Later that night we eat hot dogs with Tater Tots and ketchup, and everyone is exhausted. We work from the time we get up until dinner. Dad has decided to open up the restaurant first, then we'll open up the hotel part later. I have a sick feeling about this. I hope we can pull it off.

"Ardell, I think a buffet will be our best bet," he says. Mom agrees. They both decide that in the worst case we can support a buffet. Dad said I could waitress if I want. I don't want to. I hate serving and being nice to people for no reason. I can't do it.

Mom and Dad continue to work hard on a menu and ideas; they interview cooks and help. I lay in bed with a weird feeling in my stomach listening to them figure things out. I know if this doesn't work we're in big trouble. And I also know we don't have much money left, regardless of how it looks to other people. We're renting this place, and not for much, is all that I've heard. But it's an exciting time, having all this great energy and positive thoughts running wild. We all get to throw in our two cents. And if you have a good idea, it's worth a listen. I'm really looking forward to the new life. Just like they said, "Happy New Year."

We get ready for bed, Mom lets the dogs out, and we brush our teeth. Dad watches TV while the bedtime buzz flutters around him. We come back downstairs to watch TV for the last half hour, before Mom puts her foot down and marches us up to bed. She opens the door and claps for the dogs. She claps three times and in bounces Big.

Sugar is outside by the driveway, it's dark, she won't come. Mom claps and demands, "Get in here." Nothing. Sugar won't come. Now I'm up, I'm curious, Mom goes outside barefooted. I watch her from the door, she walks over to Sugar, Sugar is alone. She starts yelling and clapping for Little, she's worried all of a sudden. Next, we're all outside yelling, clapping, and whistling for Little. Sugar doesn't look good. Mom searches frantically. Sugar must have told her something is wrong. We look under the car, in the bushes, and around the back. Little is all black and so is the night, no moon.

"Oh shit!" We all hear from the parking lot. We run to Mom's voice.

She bends softly and slowly down to the ground. She picks up Little, all two pounds, and rubs her with her hand. I see her from the side, I can't be sure, but I think she's sick.

"Bill, get over here, something is wrong with Little."

Dad shoots over to her and nods, "You better get her to a vet now." Mom leaves, no shoes, no purse, and her baggy T-shirt with Little wrapped tight to her chest. Dad stands with us while she speeds down the driveway and turns left toward town. My thoughts are with them, the fear that Little is sick starts to scare me. What if something happens to her? No, that's crazy, she probably just got sick and the vet will fix her.

An hour goes by. We wait for Little and Mom to return. Sugar is a wreck; she paces, pants, and sits by the door waiting for her daughter to get home. Big sleeps, he sleeps hard, he never sleeps this early. I hear the car door slam, Mom's home. The kitchen door opens, and she should have walked in the living room by now. She doesn't. Dad gets up and meets her in the kitchen. "Wait here," he says. We don't, we follow him. Mom leans over the table and weeps, she doesn't want us to see her. Dad stays back, he waits a minute and then asks, "Is Little . . . ?"

"No, she died in my arms before I got there. She just closed her eyes, there was nothing I could do." Mom sobbed and we listened. The tears filled the kitchen and no one moved. Little was alive not two hours ago, playing. I can't believe that in a blink of an eye she's dead. She'll never sit on my lap, be my baby when I play house, or look up with her black eyes and say she loves me.

The next day, we hear that three boys had been arrested for poisoning six dogs last night. They went up and tricked all the neighborhood dogs with a treat that they had poisoned. All the dogs that ate the hamburger laced with poison died. The vet said Little never had a chance, she was too small and too weak to fight it. Nothing ever hurt that bad, and nothing makes sense about the night that three boys decided that killing Little Foot would be fun.

We're going to open for business soon, and the place is really starting to shape up. I think the yard looks great. We've made friends just like I thought. Kids are slowly popping over for a visit or a sled ride. I'm popular again and I like it. Shelly and I just sit bundled up on the porch, waiting for the brave souls to introduce themselves. We laugh at the nervous boys who struggle to find an excuse good enough to say hi. Mom said she'll make hot chocolate for them when they come over. Dad wants to charge them a dime, of course. The sledding here is remarkable. Normally, when I've sledded before it was fun but not like this. This hill takes your breath away every time. Shelly will not go down on the sled, she just doesn't like going that fast. I love standing at the top deciding which dangerous path I will take and which way to go down, either on my butt or on my stomach. The stomach seems to be a little more comfortable, and I can roll off before I hit the bottom.

Today two boys come by, I think it's odd, they just walk up and plop their sleds down without even saying hi. They jump on their sleds and away they go to the bottom in a flash as they fly across the street below with sparks flying from the runners. Once they're on the other side of the road, they use the wooden fence to stop them. Each sled bounces hard off the fence, throwing the boys into the air. I think they're dead. But they simply get up, knock the snow off their pants, and go home. These guys are tough.

I am so tired, I must've walked up that hill a hundred times today. I can feel the sweat under my hair as I pull off my hat. Shelly and I have decided that the ride is not long enough to warrant such a painful hump back up with the heavy old sled. Shelly rides the plastic saucer, one because it doesn't go as fast, and two it's not as hard to get it back to the top. I'm noticing that my feet are getting numb. Mom says it's time to come in if our feet get numb. That's easy, I just won't tell her.

Dad casually walks up the front porch steps after sweeping. He says, "Sandra I'll be back. Watch your brother."

I am just twenty feet or so away from the top of the hill, the takeoff, pulling the good sled behind me. Shelly stands above me at the top.

"Get ready here I come."

"Go ahead, I'll move, take the slow path," I yell up to her. I make sure I move all the way over and dig my foot into the snow with my heel, this will hold me on the slope. I look up and see her smile as the pink saucer bounces off the edge. She'd better balance or she's going to fall off. Oh, but that's Shelly, she always falls off early. She rolls into the snow and wipes the cold sprinkles off her face. "I'll wait for you here," I say with relief, just the excuse I needed to rest some more before I tackle the last of the unforgiving hill.

The last twenty feet are the hardest, it's when the slope turns into a steep slant and the icy part won't let you walk. I look away from Shelly who's halfway up to me, and turn to the top.

Oh my God! Mark is standing there with a sled that's as big as he is. My heart stops. "Mark, don't! Wait for me, that sled is broke!" I'm begging, but he won't listen. He's got a crooked little smile and the sled in position. "Mark, *no*!" I drop my sled and run with all my strength. I can feel my legs are heavy but I keep running as fast as I can. But Mark thinks it's funny.

"Bet ya can't catch me," he yells down while sitting on top of the sled as if it were his magic carpet ride, and then he pushes himself off the mountain. I stand there next to the path and try to catch him or grab him and pull him off as he goes by. I miss, he's going faster than I can reach. He looks at me with excitement and a giant smile as he slides by. I don't want to scare him, but the steering bar doesn't work on that one. "Mark roll off, get off!" I'm screaming. He's heading for a tree. He freezes when he realizes he can't steer away from the tree. I freeze too. All I can do is watch. Mark is in slow motion as he hits the tree with the sled. The crash throws him into the tree head first.

I must have been already running. I hear Shelly moaning at the sight, but she is too far away to get to him. I don't remember running. I hear Mark screaming, "I can't see, I can't see help me." Blood is everywhere.

"Mark it's okay." I lift the bloody hat from his head. My God, I wish it was me. "You're not blind, you're not blind." I reach down and pick him up.

Shelly is screaming for Mom. I hear nothing but Mark's pain. His arm is broke and his face is a mess. I'm afraid he might die. The crack in his head won't quit bleeding. I have no idea how I will get him up the hill. The hill at this point has a mind of its own, it won't let you walk up it. Instead, you must bend forward and crawl. The hill never lets you forget you just made it to the top. I manage to carry him from the tree, up the hill, and to the porch without breathing. I think Shelly's pushing me from behind, but I can't be sure. I just keep telling him, "You're okay, Mark you're okay." I don't believe it…but it has to be true. Dad storms out of the front door, and flies off the porch with Mom in his back pocket. He sweeps Mark from my arms and into the car. Shelly and I are left there crying. I'm in such shock that once he is out of my arms, I feel the blood drain from my knees. I can't tell if I'm scared or sick.

Shelly is consoling me, " It wasn't your fault, I saw the whole thing. You tried to stop him." I can't stop crying, which makes Shelly cry too.

They finally return with my broken little brother in Mom's arms. He is one big bandage. His arm is broken for real and he has stitches. Dried blood everywhere reminds me this is not a bad dream. Dad lightly lowers his baby onto the couch. Dad is the most frightened I've ever seen him. He doesn't even get mad at me. But if he does, Shelly will stick up for me. I think everybody blames themselves: Dad for leaving him out there, me for not getting to him in time, and Shelly for going down the hill before I got all the way up there. Mark is hurt and we all hurt with him. Dad makes a bad joke here and there trying to ease Mark's pain, but the painkillers are what put Mark to sleep. I go over to him and ask if I can see his head. He shows me the stitches and tells me with a look that he's very sorry. I am so relieved he's home. I don't ever want this to happen again. Of course, Mom is done biting her lip, and she just wants to baby Mark and make it all better.

While Mark heals, planning and fussing continues on the home front. We have decided that Louise will be the cook. She has been here all week preparing delicious dishes. She must weigh three hundred pounds and is a homemaker. She grew up here in West Virginia, and her cooking is good, old home style, which is exactly what Dad wanted. However, we get the final say as to what will be served. I'll tell you right now, stuffed cabbage is not going to make it, nobody in our family likes cabbage anything. If Shelly and I had it our way, it would be hamburgers, meatloaf, and spaghetti. Dad pulls up with a carload of boxes. He has bought dishes, utensils, and linens from some restaurant supplier. The dishes are used, it's all used. I don't really like the black-and-white pattern on the dishes. I don't know, it's just too plain.

Dad signals with one finger, get out here and help. He's outside by the side door that leads straight into the first kitchen. "Yeah, I'll help." I drop the broom and go running. Unfortunately for the next five hours I'll wash, rinse, and put away all those new/used dishes. I still can't believe this whole business thing is really going to happen.

It's the grand opening and the lights are on for business. A few curious people show up and then a few more. I'm surprised and embarrassed at the same time. We stay in the kitchen, laughing and giggling at this unbelievable sight. People actually coming to our house to pay for a meal we helped cook. Mark goes to the couch, he's tired and ready for bed. I'll go upstairs with him in a minute. He doesn't like sleeping alone back there, heck, I don't either. When I peek around the corner, I see Mom and Dad and they look happy.

"I want to see." Shelly pushes me. She laughs at all the people in the dining rooms eating. Louise is frying more chicken and stirring the gravy as Dad comes in to refill the buffet trays. He is as happy as a pig in shit, he says. As he whizzes through, he mumbles something about raising chickens to cut the cost. I'm so happy for him.

"Maybe this is going to work after all." I shake my head, wondering.

Weeks have passed and now we are open six days a week for business. I can't wait for the first hotel guest. Everyday at three in the afternoon Louise shows up for work and we start heating the buffet trays. Shelly and Peggy, the waitress, prefill water glasses, and I help knead the biscuit dough. Dad has decided that Louise is eating too much. Mom thinks he's crazy.

I have been invited to stay with Louise and her family for the weekend. I'm thrilled to leave by myself for a whole weekend. I go with her and meet her daughter Sam. She's my age and has three horses. She looks like she has three horses. Her hair is long and stringy, her freckles are from the sun, and she wears cowboy boots. She's been riding horses since she could talk. She has a heavy accent and skinny legs, and she assumes that I am a country girl like her. I shouldn't have told her I knew how to ride. We start out for just a little walk toward the barn. Then I open my big mouth, "Yeah I been riding since I was six." The only part I don't tell Sam is that it was a pony around in a circle.

"Come on, we'll throw on a couple of bridles and head up the pasture." She slaps me on the back.

I can't tell if anyone is watching this horrible rider being beaten by this horse as I slap up and down hard on his back. After a half an hour or so the horse's sweat and my bruises aren't mixing very well; horseback riding is not fun. Trying not to hurt him I carefully pull the ropes to the right, and head back. Sugar no sooner feels the tug to the right than he completes his turn back to the house and begins to gallop. The gallop turns into a full-blown run, and this horse is not going to stop for the fence or the barn door. I close my eyes and let go. From where I land, on my ass, I look up at Sugar; he is above me, stomping his foot.

What now, is he going to trample me, too? I scramble up to my feet and notice my own foot—it's jammed under the rusty old barn door and the cut is deep. I don't bother to complain because I really don't know what just happened. Sam rides up laughing on her mean horse, as I stand there with the nice horse.

"I forgot to tell you, Sugar has barn fever."

"What the heck is barn fever?" I sit down and listen, while I examine my half-amputated middle toe.

"Awe, that's just when you turn a horse back, they go a little nuts gittin' back to the barn, cause they know they's goin to git some grain." Sam certainly does seem to know a lot about horses.

"Time for dinner," I hear from the house.

"Wash up and sit down," Louise can't help fussing in the kitchen. She could care less about the excitement that nearly cost me my life. I can hardly wait to eat lunch.

And what does Louise fix? Cabbage. I hate that stuff. I think she did it on purpose. I hold my spoon with a limp hand as I force myself to ask, "What is in this?"

"Heck girl, ain't you never had stuffed cabbage? Well, it's got hamburger and tomatoes..."

Sam hasn't missed a bite. And that night, wouldn't you know it, Louise baked the leftover lunch and called it dinner. This time it's baked stuffed cabbage. The only difference is the pan she cooked it in. I want to go home now, I'll never spend the weekend here again, I can't be friends with anyone who loves cabbage, rides bareback, and spits like her brothers.

14

Friday morning and I am going to ride my bike around the neighborhood with Shelly and Mark. We have so many friends, but no one really stands out. We have a lot more fun by ourselves. People here don't really have a good sense of humor. The kids are a lot like their parents. All they talk about are the bad things like no money, or things like, *My older brother got a job at the mill.* Who cares? It's time to play, and play is what I want to do. These kids really don't know how to play or make believe very well. I spend hours looking for baby animals that have lost their parents or rabbits who hide in the briar bushes. I teach Shelly and Mark to risk their lives riding downhill fast, or climbing trees with old dead branches that may not hold us. I listen to Shelly and Mark all day as we walk around exploring old homes that are haunted.

Today Shelly rides Mark on her bike; she has a banana seat. We've heard stories in the neighborhood about a strange little girl. On the corner of Price Street, down the hill, we see a little girl about Shelly's age in her front yard. We ride up and skid to a stop. "Hi, what's your name?" I ask politely. We had seen her before, but she's never outside in her front yard.

"My name is Polly." She looks away.

"Wanna go for a ride with us?"

"I can't, my mom won't let me."

"Well go ask her," Shelly says.

"Ma ain't home. Besides I gotta take care of my sister. She's sick."

"What's the matter with her?"

"She ain't right."

I'm hearing something she's not saying, so my curiosity is full blown.

"She will die if she gits a cold."

Now I'm intrigued. Here is a little girl who has a sick sister and who never gets to leave the yard, and if her sister catches a cold, she'll die.

"Want to see her?" Polly offers.

All I can think is, what a weird thing to say, *Want to see her?* It sounds like she's some kind of animal. Then it dawns on me, this must be the strange little girl we've been hearing about. "Yeah." We put our bikes down and walk a slow walk to the back of the house. I'm acting like this is no big deal, but inside I'm nervous. I don't think Shelly and Mark are hearing Polly's words the way I am. I turn around to see where Mark is, and there he is, tight behind me. I think he might be sensing what I'm sensing. This is not normal. I feel like we should be getting our tickets to enter the freak show. Polly opens a door off the back of the house that leads straight into a little girl's room. There she is, smaller than Mark, about the size of a three-year-old and all curled up in her bed. She has a big head, a really big head. I can't see her face. I must have stared for ten minutes. Her arms are thin and her legs are folded together. Her skin is exactly like a newborn baby's, with that purplish color to it. She is in a pink baby doll nightie and she is asleep.

I get a little closer and move around to the other side where her face is laying. Mark follows me. I peek around the covers—her face is that of an older woman. I am afraid. This is too horrible for me. Mark wants a closer look and Shelly wants to get out of the room now. Mark is in shock, I think he's scared stiff. I have to tug on his sleeve to get his attention. I'm stunned at what I'm seeing. I whisper to Polly, "How old is she?"

Polly blurts out at the top of her lungs, "She's twenty-five and she don't ever wake up but to eat, she just sleeps. She don't even know me."

I now want out of here fast. I don't understand it, and I am afraid this is not something her mom would appreciate if she comes home. I'm praying I don't have a cold. This half-girl-half-lady lays in bed and never wakes up, but if she catches a cold she'll die.

As I ride away from this scary sight, I can hear Mark and Shelly asking all sorts of questions, but I'm lost in my own thoughts. Maybe that's what would have happened if our baby hadn't died. Maybe that's why the baby did die. I've always heard about birth defects, but I had never seen any. I guess being born normal is a hard thing after all.

I haven't thought about the baby in quite a long time, but I can't help thinking about it now. I mustn't start or else I'll get that sad feeling in my body. Once in awhile I do let myself think about the baby; I pretend I can hold it. But then it ends with a clank as I remember Mom's words, *The baby died and I don't ever want to talk about it.* I know it's wrong, but I do miss the baby. Will I miss the baby forever, or one day will I just forget about the whole thing? Like when I was born, I can't remember that. I wish I could have held it just once, then I bet I'd forget the baby. I think our baby would have been about as big as Polly's sister. I don't understand why it died. It felt so healthy when Mom left. I have to stop this right now. The more I try the harder it is as my mind continues to wonder about life and death. It feels like I should cry but I can't, I don't have any tears. What does that mean? I don't understand, I mean, I don't understand what happened at all. What did God do, give us a baby and then change his mind? I'm getting sick to my stomach. Does God really sit up there and decide who lives and who dies? Or who lives with a birth defect? What if Shelly or Mark were like that? I certainly wouldn't show them off to strangers like Polly did. I'm not comfortable with this day at all. I wish I'd never seen that little girl.

Mark is moved and so am I. We must find out what happened to that little girl. We ask every single person that crosses our path until we get the whole story. Some people say that it was because the parents were too old to have kids. Others say it is a rare sickness that allows only the brain to age while the rest of the body stays as a baby. The mom must really love her baby a lot. The baby wasn't supposed to live past a week or two. But the real weird thing is that the mother of the sick girl is the grandmother of Polly, the little girl we met. Polly and the sick girl are not sisters, that's her aunt who lies in that bed. When Polly was a baby, her real mom left her with the crazy grandma, who is dedicated to keep her twenty-five-year-baby alive. No one really knows if Polly knows that her mother is not her mother, but rather her grandmother. But everyone we talk to that day, from young to old, they all agree it's the freakiest thing they ever saw. Mark is really bothered, it really scared him.

Tonight I just want to be left alone, I get upstairs and fall away to sleep. Sleep is what I need when I start to feel this way.

The next day Mom feels my forehead and notices I don't look that good. "I just feel tired," I answer Mom's question. The truth is I still have a stomach ache. I hate being sick, and worse, I hate admitting it. If I do, then I have to stay in all day.

The day is beautiful and I won't let being a little tired stop me from enjoying the day. Besides, I need to get out of bed, I can hear the birds calling me.

I eat a little breakfast and race upstairs to get dressed. Everything is fine, but I still feel a little out of sorts. The sight of that little girl won't leave me alone, it's like a nightmare in the day. I try to make myself quit thinking about it. Now it starts up again, the same feeling I had last night is in my body. I have questions and I want answers. I can't help it; this sick girl has got me thinking about the baby and I can't quit it. "Where exactly in heaven is the baby?" I want to know. "God, can you hear me? I want you to bring back my baby." I can't believe I said that.

I'm mad now and I don't want to play with Shelly and Mark. I'm irritated, and I want to be alone. "Get out of here!" Shelly and Mark look at each other with hurt feelings and think I'm crazy. "I'll hit you if you don't get out of here, I don't care if I get in trouble." Now they know this is one of my more serious moods and they better get away from me. I take off down my secret path out the back porch, where all the poison ivy is. I talk to myself and pick a fight with the weeds. I'm in a terrible mood and I really don't care. It's been a long time since all that happened and I promised myself I wouldn't think about the baby or feel this way. It's not okay to remember or relive that day. But for some reason the thoughts just keep popping into my head. The more I think about it, the madder I get, none of my favorite things are fun. I usually talk to the wise old tree and count all the branches; I swing from the low ones and fly through the air. I find leaves with pretty designs and bury the rotten nuts that hope they can be a big tree one day

But not this day, this day is mine to think what I want. As a matter of fact, I think I'll get some poison ivy. I grab the vicious plant and smooch it all over my arms. See if I care, I hope I get poison ivy all over my body and have to go the hospital. I don't care.

I realize what I'm doing is wrong, but I keep screaming and fighting with the weeds. "Weeds are dumb, so are flies, locusts, and poison ivy. Besides, why did you make all this ugly stuff anyway, God? I thought you were good. I find all the ugly stuff and throw it and stomp on it. I stomp the ground, I even stomp on the flowers, I stomp on it all. I wrestle through the woods, rip the bark off the trees, peeling their skin back, hoping that the sun will make them rot. I hit the young leaves and make them fall.

After a while I'm tired. I am half sorry and half not. I know I'd get in trouble if anyone saw me acting this way, but the only one who is watching is God, and I don't care. I sit down and pick up a small twig and make circles in the dirt. Life is all around me, it's loud, and the questions won't shut up. I make the circles deeper and deeper. I finally notice the tree with the bald spot and the pain it must be feeling. As I wake up to the destruction I have caused in the woods I love, it feels like a bad dream. I am ashamed and exhausted.

I climb to my feet and try to tell the woods how sorry I am as I try to fix the broken flowers and patch the tree bark. I have to go now, I can't bear to see what terrible things I have done. As I escape out of the woods, I apologize to each thing I've hurt and brush it with my fingers. I hurt inside too. Suddenly, I remember what else I have done to myself. I must get this poison ivy off me. I need some cold water and soap. I have to get these clothes off. Nothing scares me more than getting poison ivy. I run with frightened tears. This is a part of me that no one needs to know about, I tell myself as I run scared. I shouldn't think about the baby, it's not good to think about the baby. My head swirls with pain and sadness, I must forget about this. Shut Up!!! I have a headache, I have to undo my thoughts, I feel like my mind is in knots.

Just as I get to the back porch, I hear a chirping, a constant chirping from the ground by the old briar bushes. I must investigate.

Oh gosh, there's a baby bird with no feathers and no mother. I search the sky and trees above for her, but there is no mother bird. I have to save this bird. Maybe God will forgive me if I can save it. That baby bird will make a delicious cat meal. I rush into the house and upstairs without a word to anyone, heck Mark and Shelly are still scared of me. I rip my clothes off and find a pair of cutoffs. I find a washcloth in the dirty clothes and wash my arms quickly and carefully. I go to the closet and find a shoe box—I save shoe boxes just for emergencies like this. I run to the bushes and there he is, with his big yellow mouth and gray pink skin. He fits in my hand, my hands are still wet, water dripping between my fingers. The baby is quiet. I put him down next to the tree and hide behind a small bush. I give the mother bird one last chance to claim her baby. I carefully roll the baby in my hand and warm him. All baby birds are boys because they're so ugly. And all baby rabbits are girls because they're pretty. I go back to the woods and find the perfect bedding for my new baby and create his home. All the while he is in my hand breathing up and down. I complete his shoe box with just the right amount of grass, twigs, and flowers—you have to put a few flowers in because that will make him heal quicker. Then I announce the new addition to the family, and no one argues or raises a brow. This is common. I love finding animals or birds; they all know that any animal I find I will heal, and let go.

It's too soon to tell but I think this is one of those colorful nice birds. I forgot the name but it's not a sparrow or a blue jay, I don't like blue jays. They never say thank you and they're always grouchy. Weeks have passed and this little guy is going to be fine. They usually die right away if they're not going to make it. But this one is worthy of a name. He's a happy bird and very colorful. He loves worms and bread. I think I'll call him Tweedy. Shelly will not help with baby bird until he has feathers. Mark always wants to hold the tweezers and feed him. I keep him upstairs where all of our bedrooms are, that way I can hear him call for food. He knows me, and although it may not have anything to do with me, I call it love.

He's outgrown his shoe box and he's now hopping around anywhere he pleases. His home is primarily the upstairs hallway. That's where the meat slicer is. Don't ask me why it's upstairs instead of the kitchen, but I've heard Dad say something about the health inspectors. It's kind of weird to think of the meat being sliced upstairs where we live. Mom is no housekeeper either, she likes the house clean, but she hates doing it. Dad stands with no shirt, sweating, his red hair flicking back and forth, slicing meat in the hall. The same hall we keep the dirty laundry in. A lot of dirty laundry. Dad stands on top of the laundry while he whistles the same tune over and over. Tweedy stands on top of the slicer looking out the window. I don't eat the roast beef. People have no idea that my bird, and the laundry, all share something in common with their roast beef dinners.

"Dad don't," I order him, as he taunts my bird with fat from the roast. Dad ignores me. "Dad don't, he can't digest that fat, all he can eat is worms and bread." I leave to go get a fresh supply of worms. Tweedy eats about ten worms a day, and I'm running out of places to dig them up. I leave for about half an hour and return to feed him. I climb the stairs with the old butter container full of worms. I walk over to his box—he is not there. I look around the hall, on all his favorite perches, and nothing, no bird. Then I turn around to the meat slicer; there he is laying on the counter next to it. He is dead. I look at him and try to make this not be so. But he is dead, there's nothing I can do. I fill up with rage and hate so fast I can't even stop to think. Before I know it, I'm in the kitchen, it's three o'clock and everyone is busy. Louise, the cook, notices me first, and the look I give her is deadly. I storm across the kitchen to Dad. "Are you happy you killed him?" I scream at Dad. "I told you not to feed him the fat!"

Dad looks at me with a blank stare and a grin beneath his face, but no one sees his grin but me, and I know it's there. He pretends to be innocent. Mom rushes in to control her daughter.

"Now honey…sometimes these things just happen…"

I shut her out of my mind. She's not going to treat this like one of those things, one of those things we just let be and never talk about. Damn these people. I snap my arm back from Mom, "You killed my bird." I stare him down. I see that he has no regret in his eyes, he's playing some kind of game. I won't let him hurt me, if this is his game, I will win. That's what he wants, he wants me to cry and carry on. I turn around and despise them both. Mom, for not being able to see what this has done to me, and him for still being the hateful bastard I know he is.

I go to my bird and tell him how sorry I am for leaving him alone with my dad. It was my fault, I should have known better. I will never trust Dad again, no matter what he does. I know Mom wants to come talk to me, but I send her the message, *Leave me alone. You're not my friend.*

I need to bury my bird. I don't want Mark to see Tweedy dead. I try not to cry as I take him and put him in his little home, which is now a coffin, and go into the woods. But I finally give in to the tears as I approach the old damaged tree. The lump in my throat hurts, it's so big. God knows what just happened and I don't have to talk to him either. I'm alone, burying my healthy, dead baby bird. Is this how Mom felt? No she wasn't mad at death like me, she was more of a shell left over after being cracked wide open. That was all Mom was, an empty shell, after the baby died. Dad well, now that I think about it, he never cared one way or the other.

I go to bed early. I will not eat with them and I don't understand why things can't be the way they used to be. I slip under my covers farther and back into my past. I remember when I was little and Dad used to play with me and make me laugh. Mom used to roll up my sleeves and roll down my socks before I went outside, her hands were so soft and then the little pat on the butt when she was finished. I could jump on her lap and she would rescue me from the monster or love me to death. I remember swimming with Shelly. I remember holding Mark on my lap as he wobbled back and forth. Mom would buy us donuts on Saturday morning to eat with our cartoons, and sometimes she'd lay on the floor with us just to sneak a kiss. Dad would look at me with wonderment and praise he loved me everyday back then. I have to go to sleep now...

15

The business is not doing so well, we're having trouble paying all the bills. I hear Dad raise his voice while Mom lowers hers. They are going to have to let go of the waitress. Peggy is sweet but mousy, we call her the "four-eyed doorstop." All she does is stand there, propped up against the dining room doors, waiting for a customer. Her shyness doesn't add to her character, in fact it makes it easier to joke about her. Martha keeps to herself as she observes the tension. Her eyes are black with wisdom, and she has skin to match. I try to time it just right so I can sit with her for a while.

"Martha, do you want all the big pots?" I eagerly wait for her answer.

"No child, just two, and I could use those wooden spoons while you's there."

I trip over my shoelace as I fetch her the tools. She cooks and prepares food without a blink, it's like breathing for her. She cuts, pours, and stirs while she tells me a story. She is the first black person that has been my friend. I am often hypnotized by her large hands and her big heart. I can see her smile from across the kitchen as she orders me around. She doesn't say so, but I know she's teaching me to cook. I grab the pans from the top shelf and stand at the stove stirring the steaming pots.

She tells me her favorite foods are collards, black-eyed peas, and grits. I lose interest as she describes the delicious delicacies. "Then if you add some bacon or ham hock wit' dem peas, it salts 'em up real good."

I am so glad that this is not a part of our menu choice. Martha has a bunch of kids and lives out on a farm somewhere. She likes my family and knows it's just a matter of time before this job ends. But she's positive and kind, and says the Lord will take care of us. The Lord practically sits in the kitchen while she peels potatoes. Her love for the Lord is as real as a sunset and just as powerful. Her full bosoms and round face are a testimony in itself. I pay attention when she talks, her voice doesn't allow anything but the truth.

"Child, you mustn't be afraid of getting your hands dirty, that be with cookin' or just plain hard work." We continue to sit at the table while the white biscuit dough dries on her black hands. I realize we're different: she is wise and I'm young.

She looks into my eyes. "When I was a young girl, and you know how long ago that gotta be, I watch my mama make biscuits just like this."

The dough dances around the floured bowl as if she was asking it to move. Her fingers are covered with the soft white clouds as her hands play quietly inside the bowl. Each wrinkle, of each finger, says hard work. But as I watch the dough turn hard in the crevice of her knuckles, all I can think is, I want to be like her when I grow up. She is happy, and loving, and true. I never have to guess with Martha, either she tells me the truth or she's quiet. I think Dad knows of her power too, he's never disrespectful or rude. He says yes ma'am or no ma'am. She has many more stories, but she won't tell. I wish she would tell me who she is and where she came from, but that won't happen. I accept it, but I'll always wonder. I can tell her feet hurt all the time, but she doesn't complain. I see the pain in her eyes but her smile hides it. I love this woman. She reminds me of thunder clouds, dark, powerful, and beautiful. She tells me less with words than she does with her eyes. I want to touch her, maybe rub her tired feet, but I can't. I know what she needs, and I rush to the cupboard. "Is this what you need?" I reach for the baking soda.

"My child, you must be readin' my mind." I clear away her last mess as she begins the next. It's like a ballet, and I'm her feet. We pretend I'm just learning to cook, but her wink tells me thank you.

Every night her husband picks her up from work, he won't come in, he just sits in the car. I never heard his name or met him, he's just Martha's Husband. I ran out once to say hi, but he doesn't say hi back. He's a small man with two wrinkles down from his eyes. He's dirty from sweat, his shirt says so. He isn't mean, he's uncomfortable or shy. Seeing him hurts my heart. I don't even ask him his name, maybe he doesn't have one, maybe he's been a husband, a daddy, and a miner so long he forgot his name.

It's Wednesday night, about 5:30 p.m., and I leave with Martha. She has to go get her kids, or at least some of them. Martha says I can go to church with her tonight, a revival she calls it, if it's all right with Mom and Dad.

This night is muggy and unforgiving. It's at least as hot as it was all day. I sit with my hands folded together as we leave the long driveway. I know I'm going to a world I've never been to before. The car ride and the church alone are enough to scare me. Mom says we're not religious, and God doesn't really come from church. Church is what people want, but God is everywhere. I look back at the mansion called Oak Terrace, my home, my secret home as we drive to the farm. Martha hums and her husband pretends not to listen. I sit with my mouth closed and my eyes open. I feel safe, but I also feel uncomfortable, just like her husband. I don't think he likes it very much, having this white girl in his car driving through town. Martha just hums and says nothing. The drive takes forever, but finally we get to the old farmhouse. It's nice and organized. The wood pile is close to the front door, and chickens run free. A couple of her sons are on the porch, and her daughter runs out with a toddler. Every single one of her children has her smile. They already knew the white girl from town was going to church with them.

I'm honored to be a part of this family for the night. However, my butt is sticking to the seat and my back is sweating. I can't get out of the car, I have to wait while Martha gets the last of her kids ready. The father exits the car with no good-bye, but that doesn't bother me. I sit there with my hands still folded. I notice the blood to my hands has been cut off, I let go of my grip and shake them back to life. None of the kids come to say hi, but I catch them sneaking peeks at me. I wonder if this is a good thing after all.

"Boy, you put down that dirty old knife, we's goin' to church." I hear Martha, but I don't see her. I won't let my nervousness be noticed. I sit there trying to be comfortable, hoping I can stay next to the window. Finally, Martha comes out, she's got on a pretty hat and has a happy baby girl in her arms. She walks with a hobble that reminds me her feet hurt.

"Kids, this is Sandra, she's goin' to church with us."

"Hi Sandra," they all sing.

Everyone is so dressed up, I look terrible. I feel stupid, I didn't know I was supposed to dress up, I wish she would have told me. Her oldest daughter Mary asks me what grade I'm in. I answer. The ice-cold tension is broken for a moment. The baby girl gets passed around like a hat and everyone has a giggle. I sit next to the baby while Natalie holds her. I try to say hi, but the baby doesn't want anything to do with the stranger. After a while, the drive becomes a laugh. I'm being questioned and throwing the answers right back. "Mrs. Marter is my math teacher too and she is mean."

"You got any brothers or sisters?" I hear from the front seat. I am taken back by this question. I think about it long and hard—this is the first time I've had to answer this question, since the baby died. "I have a brother and a sister." My answer feels like I'm lying, or at least not telling the truth.

"You da' oldest, ain't you?"

I find the answer in my head, "Yeah." I like Martha's kids, and I feel fine now that we're not strangers. I think they like me too. I'm starting to relax a little bit.

Here we are, the church stands tall. I feel butterflies in my stomach. The kids can't wait to get out and run with their friends.

The car stops in a parking spot along the dirt road, and everyone bolts. They forget I'm there as they greet the congregation. I open the car door and peel my legs from the torn seat. I now must admit to myself that this was a horrible mistake. I'm embarrassed and alone with a hundred strangers. Martha notices me, at the same time Mary remembers, I am back here. She grabs a friend's hand and they return for me.

"This is Sandra. My mama works for her mom and dad at the old Oak Terrace."

"Oh yeah, I heard someone was trying to reopen that old place. Is it haunted?"

I try not to choke, but I'm focusing on the girls. "Not really."

The gathering is amazing, a spectacle, a sight. Hats, gloves, and smiles, that's all that stands out. It is still hotter than hell, I mean heck. Groups of six or more turn their heads as I walk up with Martha. Martha is welcomed, and widely respected. People want to talk about me, but they don't dare. Acceptance is the only way to describe this meeting. They accept the heat, each other, and me. My head is a little dizzy with all the laughter and gossip. I stay close behind Martha, while Mary and I follow her into the church. I feel bad for Mary, I know she's being polite by staying with me. I can feel her eyes wandering around the crowd, looking for her friends, and the boy she has a crush on. I'm a third wheel.

"Honey, you sit here with me." Martha squeezes my tense shoulder to her hip. I feel like the ugly duckling, and she has tucked me safe into her feathers. It's time to sit down, no one says anything, it just happens. The group disappears and the laughter dies down. I want to sit down and melt away. I'm trying not to fidget with my insecurity.

The word, *gospel* rings out and is pronounced with heart. The preacher enters from the front of the church wearing a very nice robe and collar, I know he's got to be sweating. The hankies and homemade fans start to make their way out of pockets and pocketbooks.

I wish I had one of those fans. "Praise the lord," he continues, and from then on it's no longer a church meeting, it's a miracle. I don't know what he's saying but it is the truth. The truth has no regard for doubt, and truth is a source of power—it's some kind of key that will set you free. He's the preacher and this is preaching. Everyone becomes one, as we all go into a trance. I am scared of this, but at the same time I am a part of it. The intent is to bring God and Jesus into the room, doubt must leave, and only those who believe are welcomed.

I believe.

Sisters and brothers dab the sweat and fan themselves as the truth becomes alive. All I can think about are lies, my lies, the lies I have seen, and lies I haven't heard. Then, without warning, a song is born, and the choir is standing and swaying back and forth. This is something else. I haven't heard music like this since my mom used to sing at the club. I am stunned, my heart is touched, and the words, *gospel, truth, and believe,* have whole new meanings. Tears fill my eyes. I feel light and mighty, I feel the power. Maybe it's the power in the room, maybe it's God, or perhaps it is Jesus. But there's something in the room. I bet it is the truth. The words to the songs pour out of people's mouths, as rhythm breathes through their bodies. I'm not a stranger any longer. I am touched, my eyes are filled with tears. I want the tears to stop, but the music is controlling my heart. The preacher is sweating and the roof is vibrating. A woman steps into the aisle and shakes with the power of the Lord. The Lord is in her soul, and she yells the truth, then falls back into her seat exhausted.

I am now praying not to be touched by the Lord in this way. It would be so embarrassing. Others are falling over, crying and having visions. I am blessed, but not like that. I hear music, but no instruments, just music.

There is no way to tell when one song starts and another one ends. I pretend I know the words. As I clap to my own rhythm, once in a while I have to stop and start over. I'm touched but not like they are. Grandparents and babies alike are touched with this fever. I don't say anything, I'm just moving with the music.

I'm not sure when the sermon ended, but it did, and the next thing I know, we're in the car riding high with the Lord. I can't wait to get home and tell Mom what I saw. Martha drops me off with a wink and off she goes with her family and the Lord.

Mom waits in the kitchen for me and my story. I tell her about the Lord, the people, and the singing. She listens, almost with a puzzled look. "That's nice honey, I'm glad you had a good time."

She doesn't care too much about the Lord or worship, it makes her a little nervous. I keep the story short and quick. Besides, it's not like I was saved. And she wouldn't have it anyway; being saved by the Lord is for people who need it, not us.

16

Dad is not himself and Mom is biting her lip a lot more these days. She's worried that if we do fill up with guests, how will we accommodate the bedding? We don't have enough sheets for all the rooms. This is a pickle or a jam, one of the two. We all take responsibility for making this business work. Mom is going to let me greet the guests. I hope we have some. The phone isn't ringing.

We no longer can afford to pay Phil the waiter either.

"Here you go." Dad reaches out with his last check. We all stand there not wanting to let go of Phil and his nice polite personality.

Shelly gives him a hug as she says good-bye. "Don't worry, Phil, I'll watch out for the frog bubbles myself."

Martha doesn't cook as much; Mom is taking that over too. Dad still pushes forward *knowing* that things will pick up.

Grandma is coming for a visit, it's been quite a while since we last saw her. Now that's someone who believes in the Lord, not like Martha but close. I sit patiently in the largest front yard between the two long driveways singing, "West Virginia, Mountain Mama, take me home, take me home." I know every single word, and I sing this over and over. I lay down on my belly and daydream of Grandma pulling in the drive at anytime. I run my hands through the long, thick clover patch and inspect each leaf as I search for the four-leaf clover. I already know my wish. I'll wish for lots of business to keep us going. But I keep picking the ones that trick me. As I separate the top clovers from the bottom, I pray I find just one. There has to be one among all these clovers. I know it exists, and if anyone needs to find one, it's me. I smell the thick air with its moist, fresh-cut grass scent—I love the smell of fresh-cut grass. I hear a bird singing his song, along with a couple of squirrels that bravely squeal back and forth, pretending I really don't scare them. This is a beautiful morning in the clover patch. I envision cars pulling in anytime, asking for rooms, and a meal. My thoughts of business keep my fingers moving carefully through the clovers. Finally, I have to sit up, all the clovers are starting to look alike. I must refocus.

I think out loud, "There is a four-leaf clover in this patch, and when I find it I will get my wish and luck is sure to save us." Just as I finish my sentence, a voice comes to me, "A clover can't save you." I shake my head and listen again.

Silence is all I can hear. "What?" I ask the voice.

"You will be saved, but by the Lord, not by a clover. I made the clover you search for."

I'm in a clover patch talking to the Lord! Now this is a little strange. I don't believe it. I feel it's true because of the truth and its power. It seems to have a voice, maybe the truth can talk. It's the same power I felt in church the other night. I know I'm crazy to think that I am talking to God, but he started it.

The "Voice" is deep and certain, it drowns out all other sounds and it begins again. "You are saved."

I heard it again, it's so loud and crisp. Doubt does not exist in this voice, like the doubt that had to leave church the other night, just like the preacher said. I believe that God has spoken, and I listen some more.

The "Voice" from outside my head speaks again but this time it scares me, "You can't hide from the truth and you will know it." Wow, this is crazy, God sees me and just starts talking to me. Why is he talking to me? I shake my head in disbelief, I'm too afraid to move and then I notice the clovers. Maybe the clovers aren't magic after all,

I never realized that before. The "Voice" leaves me without a doubt, I listen some more, but I know it's gone. I can feel it.

I scramble to my feet the same time I see the large, white car round the street below, and I wait to see if it will go straight or turn; it's coming to the drive. Grandma is finally here! I run up the yard to meet her at the top of the drive. She parks as I grab for the car door handle. I like being the first person she sees. "Grandma—"

She cuts me off, "Lordy, lordy Sandra, is it hot!

She better not be saying Lordy around here.

She fans herself, "Would you help me with my bags?" She knows I will, but she still asks.

I pant like a puppy, "Yes."

Dad has stepped out onto the porch. "Hey there Dorothy." He waves as he comes to greet her. I see her wince a little bit. He doesn't call her Mom. I think he is still mad at her for not treating him very good when he was a boy. The way I heard it, Grandma had him when she was sixteen, and back then grandmas couldn't have a child without being married. So they hid her away until she had him, and then she left him with her parents, my great-grandma and great-grandpa. I never got to meet them, but they were the nicest people in the world according to Dad. They say that Grandma fell in love with a high school football player and accidentally got pregnant. She was in love and thought he would marry her, but he didn't. He and his family moved away that same summer.

Aunt Mozell said that his family didn't think Grandma was educated enough for them, and they wanted better for their son. Aunt Mozell also said, *To hell with them, their loss*. After years of living with his grandparents who raised him as their own child, Grandma showed up one morning when he was ten, and said, "I am not your sister, I am your mother, and we are going to live with George." It was that simple and that was that. George was mean and a drinker. My dad loved his grandpa, and to this day he still hates the man called George. So I think he is still mad at Grandma for doing that. I can't be mad at Grandma, she is the best grandma in the whole world.

"Ardell, the place looks great. I can't believe all the work you all have done."

Mom is thankful someone can tell the difference from when we first got the place. It's been less than a year, and we really did do a lot of work. "Are you hungry?"

"No dear I stopped on the way, but I could use a drink of water."

"I'll get it." Shelly runs.

"Let's go sit a spell." I gradually lead them to the porch, my favorite place to sit.

Grandma tells us of the family, one by one. She loves to report and compare notes. Shelly runs back with cold water spilling over the sides of the glass. We all sit there listening to the conversation back and forth between Mom, Dad, and Grandma. This is adult conversation and all we do is listen.

Mark interrupts, "Grandma I have a scar." He pushes his hair back with both hands.

"Oh honey, in another year we won't even see that nasty thing. Now come here and let Grandma kiss it."

Mark likes showing off his battle scar. It's practically the first thing he does when someone new shows up. We sit there listening to the weather forecast by Grandma and all about the crazy family members.

Grandma reaches in her pocketbook and digs for her wrinkled hanky. "Jack, I heard from Marty, she's going to have another baby, she's crazy, having so many babies with that fat, lazy husband of hers."

Dad just nods and looks over to Mom for help. He stands up and leans on the railing. "But Dorothy, he only has one more year until he has his master's in psychology."

"Well, that's just fine, but it don't put food on the table."

Grandma doesn't like college or understand it. Only a few people in our family went to college and she wasn't one of them.

The day continues and I can't wait to get Grandma alone to myself. Martha shows up for work. I wave to her and run to see if she needs any help. I really worry about her feet.

Mom introduces Grandma to Martha. Grandma stands there with disapproving eyes as this black woman comes into our kitchen. I notice Grandma's polite tone, but she is thinking something else. "Nice to meet you and what do you do?" The condescending remark hits Martha right between the eyes.

"I am the cook." Martha stands up with confidence and respect. I can't believe Grandma asked that; she knows who Martha is. Mom and Martha go about their business, prepping and cleaning around the kitchen. Grandma wants to help, but this is not a family dinner, this is a business. She doesn't understand the difference. She searches for an apron, "Is this all right to use?" The apron is Martha's.

I rush over to the drawer by the sink, "Here Grandma, here's one." I notice Martha is getting the stepladder. That's my job.

"Ardell, these dirty dishes are getting hard, I'll just soak them, it'll just take me a second." Grandma rolls up her sleeves. Martha catches the remark and moves out of the way. I always wash Martha's dishes when she's done with the biscuits. This is a mess; Grandma is not helping. She's hurting Martha's feelings and taking up too much room. "Martha, is this the pot?" I ask from behind the pantry door.

"It's fine, I'll use the one over here for the dumplings."

"Dumplings," Grandma whirls around as if that's her cue. "I'll do the dumplings."

"That's all right, Mrs. Vaughan, it's fine. All I got left to do is the biscuits, the rest is already cookin'."

Grandma watches Martha's hands reach in to knead the dough.

"You're not going to eat those dumplings tonight," she whispers. "I'll make you kids something else." She pats me on the back.

I am sure Martha hears her, but you'd never know it, Martha would never let me know. She keeps her distance from me, and Grandma. I'm confused by this part of Grandma. Mom leaves the kitchen to go find Dad.

All three of us are alone in the kitchen. I feel so bad with this part of Grandma, I can't believe she doesn't like Martha. Martha is my friend. Grandma tightens up inside and closes off any signs of kindness. I am watching Martha, who ignores the hateful looks and goes about her business. But Martha doesn't really ignore it, she just pretends it's okay. I hear my Grandma's thoughts. She is uncomfortable and scared of this black woman, and keeps calling her a Negro. I want her to stop it and be nice. The more she thinks, the colder it gets between them. I try to show Grandma not to be afraid. Martha shoots me a look, *It's okay Sandra, don't you worry about me.* This hurts even more. I'm standing between my Grandma who is the nicest person in the world, and Martha who is my friend, who teaches me stuff all the time. I can't stop this, I'm stuck in the middle and I can't choose.

"Sandra, help me dry these dishes while I straighten up this dirty kitchen." Grandma hands me a dish towel.

I turn to my friend who is standing alone at the stove. I am supposed to stand up for her, her feet will start hurting, I am her feet.

I hear Dad call for Grandma. I think Mom is making him get his mother out of the kitchen. Grandma looks behind to see if I'm coming. I don't want to leave and have Martha think *I* think like my Grandma, but at the same time, I can't hurt Grandma's feelings by staying with the *Negro.*

Mom tells Martha she's sorry without words, and I look back to Mom for help, as Grandma swings us both out the door.

It's going to be a long weekend trying to think, like Grandma, that we are living happily ever after in this mansion. The mansion we can't afford to live in, the cook we can barely pay, and the restaurant that doesn't serve. Grandma skirts around our part of the house and pretends we live in the good part. She practically closes her eyes to the truth, when she goes to the back, the servant's quarters, where we live. She stays in the parlor and makes believe that this is where her grandchildren live.

"Mark, you come over here and sit next to Grandma."

He hesitates while Dad's voice inside his head reminds him not to sit on the good furniture.

Not only can't we sit on the good furniture, but the carpet is an issue too. If we go into the parlor or entry hall, we'll get it dirty, and we don't have a vacuum to clean it. Grandma sits there in heaven, tapping her dirty shoes on the carpet, "Shelly, are you ready for school to start?"

"Nope!" School in West Virginia is not a great topic for any of us, but especially Shelly.

"Now you're going to have a wonderful time in school, aren't you?"

"I guess so," she lies. It's normal that Grandma makes Shelly say yes, when Shelly means no.

I try one more time to defend Martha in Grandma's court of law. "Grandma, Martha showed me how to make biscuits rise by adding a little less flour. She taught me to make gravy from scratch. And, did you know that if you add sugar instead of flour to the pan when you're baking a cake, it won't stick, and it'll taste better."

"That's nice Sandra, but I don't use sugar, I use flour around the cake pan." She shoots me the Look that cannot be denied. Martha's hands are black and that means she's dirty. Martha cannot be my friend, she is black and that is all Grandma can see. Martha could have saved my life and it wouldn't be good enough for Grandma. I decide I better not tell her about the Gospel night, the clovers, or the Lord.

I can especially see it in Mom's face as she races through the parlor and up the stairs to make up the guest beds.

As we sit there tonight, each one of us does our best not to spill on the tablecloth, or the carpet. She wants us to eat in the dining room like a real family. We have to break our own rules in order to make Grandma comfortable. We normally eat in *our* living room in the back on the scratched-up coffee table. We don't ever just go into the kitchen and eat out of the refrigerator—that is the restaurant food. It was a long meal in the fancy dining room.

Grandma leaves early Sunday morning, she's going back to Ohio to work on Monday.

"Bye Grandma, I love you."

She waves and blows kisses all the way down the drive. I watch her leave, as I exhale all the pretending out of my body.

"San, let's go for a bike ride," Shelly and Mark yell from the porch.

Dad steps in, "Not right now, you guys. Your mother and I need help around here."

I knew that was coming. We're down to one week before the state fair and we need to clean the yards, dust the banister, and sweep off the carpet that Grandma got dirty. I'll be glad when the fair is over.

The mood around the house is empty, we are all tired of doing this alone. The fair will be over this weekend, and until then we are slaves to the house, the buffet, and the hotel rooms. It's so hot and muggy that no one moves real fast.

Mom says I can go ride my bike for an hour. I don't let the words hit the ground before I am gone.

I leave down the steep driveway and feel the speed as the pedals go faster than my feet can keep up. I untangle my hair with one hand and steer with the other. I let go and ride with no hands, coasting for a while. Usually, I go to the right and see a friend or two, but today I just want to ride. I go to the left at the bottom, into a new area, this is a lot more wooded. The houses are farther apart and no one is out in their yard. The farther I go, the less homes there are and the darker it is.

The trees are thicker and sun is in patches on the ground. I race to each sun patch, and ride proudly through it. I ride from one to another, quickly and slowly, playing endlessly with the blacktop. Every once in a while I notice how far I have gone and what time I think it is. Suddenly, I see a black snake coiled on the side of the road. I avoid hitting it with my front tire but happen to wake it. It must have felt me go by. The snake becomes alive with anger, it slithers next to me as I ride. I do a double take to see whether this is my imagination or whether this snake is actually chasing me. He *is* chasing me. I grip the rubber on the handlebars and pedal as fast as I can, knowing that he can't catch me on my bike. I look once more to confirm my cleverness, but oh shit, he is right behind me. My heart is pumping as fast as I am, and my hands are sweating. I try to think of what to do, I can't pedal any faster. I try. I try to lift my body and pedal with all my weight. It doesn't matter, he is still two feet behind me. Is this a dream or am I really going to die? I see a house up ahead, maybe I can get some help. I start screaming for help. The snake is up on its tail going fifty miles per hour and barely behind me. I'm so scared, I put my feet up as I go down hill, surely I'll lose him now. No. He's still there. I time my feet perfectly, as I regain my pedaling. I can feel him biting my heels at any minute. I scream, pedal, and pray. Up ahead I see a strange little wiry man, standing in his yard burning leaves. All my blood is racing through my body, which is trying desperately to get away from the black snake. I can't go this fast much longer; I can feel my legs starting to give out. I have to make it to the house. I pump, push, and pray I make it. If I turn back to see the snake, the snake might get me. I have to make my decision; keep going straight or turn.

I turn, almost lose it, the handlebars shake wildly as I zoom past the man. I turn sharply around the man and skid into his driveway. I pump the pedals and slide the bike. Magically I fly off it and land hard into the porch steps.

I scramble to my feet and want to plow through his screen door. Huffing and puffing, I see that the snake has vanished. I made it.

I feel sick in my knees, a weakness takes over my whole body as I pick up my bike and walk toward the man.

"Ya know, those darn things can catch a fox. It is the fastest snake in these parts. They call it a black racer snake, and its poison is deadly. I knew whatcha was hollering about." He bends over and shovels some dirt onto the smoldering leaves. "Didn't anyone tell you about these snakes?"

I catch my breath, and listen to him. I notice that my knee is bleeding, and I'm far from home, where I'm not supposed to be.

He continues, "The best thing to do is go crooked and turn around. The snake can't turn around quite as fast, and it'll give you time to get away. The more you try to outrun it the more it wants to catch you."

I want to pass out, but I can't, I have to get home. The tears well up in my eyes, the crotchety old man has made his point.

"Come on girl, let's get you home. I'll throw that old bike of yours in the pickup and give you a ride home."

As I jump into the truck, I know I shouldn't because Mom is going to kill me for going this far into the woods. But if I don't, I'll have one pissed off snake waiting for me. My side hurts, I have to take a ride. I say nothing more as the truck clunks and chugs me home. Ignoring my wounds, it's the shaking I am concerned about.

"Here ya go, now you be careful, young lady."

Mom steps out onto the porch ready to kill me for being late, when she notices my face and the stranger lifting my bike out of the back. "Thank you," I say to the nice little man.

"What is going on?" Mom looks to him for the answer.

"Your girl ran into a little trouble. I am sure she'll tell you all about it."

Mom puts her arm around me, and we walk into the house. I lift my shirt to see the gigantic, throbbing bruise on my side. "Oh my God, what happened?" I look down and see that the bruise covers my ribs and part of my chest.

"Mom, you know the black racer snakes that people say can outrun a fox? Well, it chased me forever, and that man helped after I crashed my bike into his porch. I couldn't get away. It chased me as fast as my bike could go and it never slowed down. I flew off my bike and landed on my side when I hit his porch steps."

Mom is more concerned with my bruise than she is with the story. "Now honey, think about it, a snake chasing you, don't you think it could have been your imagination?" She continues to dab at me.

I suck in some air and want to blow "No," back in her face. "Mom I'm not making it up, I swear."

"Okay honey if you say so."

I get so mad inside, she never believes me, like when I told her about the Lord talking to me the other day, she just nodded her head and blinked her eyes real slow. If she had it her way, she'd tell me the baby was my imagination too, the endless ride to California, and the fighting, when she lies in the snow with a bloody lip. Yeah it's all my imagination. When you're a kid, they always call truth your imagination.

That afternoon, Martha comes by with her husband to pick up her check. Dad goes out to the car and all I can see is his head low and shaking her hand like he's apologizing. I knew that things were tight and that Martha might have to go, but I had no idea it would be this soon. I run out for my good-bye, but her husband's dark stare prevents my tears from falling. Martha gives me her hand and I squeeze it with all that I have. It's the second time I ever got to touch her. She smiles into my eyes, I don't want her to drive off. Love bumps me out of the way and the car pushes by me and she's gone.

17

Days pass and the fair has opened. The traffic is jammed through town, and Dad cusses out every single person as they pass us by. Shelly and I sit on the porch sweating and flicking bugs off us. *Please God let someone come to Oak Terrace, please...* Nothing is said between us, but we know we're in trouble if we don't get some business soon.

All we can do is duck and hide from Dad and Mom.

"Goddamn it, could somebody around here shut the fucking door."

Dad said *fucking*. Shelly and I look at each other with wide eyes, this is serious. Our whole existence is based on cars. Cars mean business, and so does Dad. Every wall that we cleaned, each meal that we cooked, and every time we raked the yards boils down to this fair. The fair is going to promote us and save our ass. We need the business like a dog needs a bone. I wish so hard that sometimes I forget to breathe.

Shelly and I escape the frustration inside the house and go out to the porch. I undo the tangled rubber band from my hair. It only makes the knots in my hair worse. "Want to kill some spiders?"

"Nope." Shelly scoots around to the other side of the porch where the shade is.

"I'm thirsty, go get us some water," I tell Shelly.

"Nope."

I'd rather sit here thirsty, pulling at the knots, than venture into the hell.

"Get some from the hose," Shelly points out with her skinny finger and wrinkled nose.

She's right. I hop off the porch and reach for the hot hose. I decide to let the water run down my legs until it cools.

"Don't let Dad see you wasting the water."

She's right again. I quickly gulp the warm water that tastes like hose, and shut it off. I kick some leaves on top of the evidence and go back to my perch.

"Here comes a car," Shelly squeals.

I hold my breath, "Please let this be a customer." I can feel the whole house peeking through the curtains, praying to itself. The car is slowly pulling up the drive. This is not a good sign—when a car goes that slow, it means one of two things, either they're lost or looking for directions. At this point we have two kinds of customers—U-turns and directions. Only when the car gets to the parking lot can we tell for sure if they're customers. The car continues through the parking lot and down the other drive.

"Goddamn it! It's another one of those U-turn people," I hear from inside, right on cue. "That's it Ardell! If one more person pulls a U-turn…"

"Sure and if you do, then what? We'll have no advertising at all, at least maybe they'll remember we're here."

"I didn't bust my ass so they can do U-turns and get through town quicker."

Mom lets him ramble. Dad has forbidden us to give out directions to anyone.

"Goddamn it, get your asses off the porch. "

Finally! A customer has pulled in and is walking up the front to the porch door. Just like they're supposed to. Shelly and I watch from the side. It's about four p.m., and a whole family unloads out of their new car. The mother and father are average looking but one of the two boys is cute, really cute. Blond hair and tall. He's around my age. I duck behind Shelly, I think he saw me.

"They have money." Shelly can tell the difference.

I stay close to the corner of the porch. "I wonder how many rooms they'll take, I bet ya three."

"Let's go see, we'll pretend we're coming in for a drink." We sneak around to the side of the dinning room doors, off the porch, and listen. "Hi there, can I help you?" Dad reaches in his pocket and rattles his change.

"Yes, how much are your rooms for the night?" The man eases his way to the desk.

Shelly and I look at each other, we forgot about the cost, we listen carefully.

"That's eighteen dollars for a single and twenty for a double."

The man knows Dad is ripping him off. We stay back and cheer Dad on.

"That'll be fine. My wife wants to stay here and get to know the locals of this town."

I think to myself, *Then you really are at the wrong place.*

"We'll need three rooms."

"I told you so, I knew they'd stay." I bump Shelly in the arm.

"Sure." Dad reaches for the calculator underneath the cash register that doesn't work. The nice rich family stomp up the staircase and their footsteps echo in the lobby. They think we're some kind of poor oakies and the wife is going to save us. All that's going to happen for sure is, she'll be glad she lives in the city.

"This feels dumb." Shelly laughs.

I agree while we run up to Dad. He smiles and brags.

"And that's how it's done."

Soon a few more stragglers show up for rooms. They are burnt by the sun, and tired of the dust at the fairgrounds. Dad sticks to his guns with his outrageous room rates. Mom is in the back planning how she'll clean the sheets tomorrow morning. Mom a maid? I can feel her hating the thought of cleaning already. She doesn't clean for us, let alone strangers. Not to mention, she's already in the kitchen doing all the cooking by herself—the buffet opens in an hour.

Mom and Dad still think I'll be the waitress tonight, even though I said no when she dressed me up earlier and did my hair. There's not a chance in hell I'll go ask that family with the cute boy, *Can I get you anything else*? They must be crazy if they think I can possibly handle that kind of humiliation. I don't dare say anything now, but I will when the time comes.

Oh my gosh, I can't believe my eyes as I look at all the people, each guest, including the cute boy, has joined us for dinner. Even some of the local oakies are here tonight. Mom is sweating bullets as she sees all the people. Only God knows if we have enough food. That does it for me—I will not wait on people and run out of food all in the same night.

"Sandra, take this out for me."

I grab the steaming tray of gray stuff and carefully load it into the rack on the large buffet table. I notice that all the buffet dishes look the same, brown and gray. I can't stand looking at this food. Dad is throwing another basket of rolls on the table to make it look fuller. We are down to pork chops, liver and onions, potatoes, all kind of potatoes, and frozen vegetables. Desserts and biscuits went when Martha did. This poor excuse for a buffet is all we have left, and Dad pretends it's just fine. Both Shelly and I have to do the refilling. Shelly refills the water, she's had a lot more training with water glasses than I did. I get to refill the liver and onions or pork chops.

I tiptoe into the buffet room when I think no one is looking. Small beads of sweat drop to the floor with each step I take. The chance of meeting a customer face-to-face is more than I can bear. When I grow up, I will never be a waitress. The buffet is open for three hours. It's the longest three hours of my life. Shelly stands there with a half full pitcher waiting to fill a glass or two. Mark sits at the small kitchen table watching us run around like fools. Mom stays in the kitchen digging deeper and deeper into the refrigerator for more gray and brown stuff.

Dad silently prays the customers will pay and leave soon. Mom hands me another tray of gook and brushes my fancy hair out of my eyes. We are all sweating by now.

Twenty-five or thirty customers and only the four of us to create, serve, and refill. Each time I enter the buffet room I can't help but notice the mounds of dirty dishes, the stained tablecloths, and all the dirt on the floor. And of course, poor Shelly still standing there clutching the water pitcher with both hands. I accept my humiliation, and remind myself I'll never see these people again. I'm starting to think like Dad.

That night, all the kids sit on the front porch. It's so hot that no one can sleep. Oak Terrace does not have air-conditioning. Mom usually sprinkles us with cold water from the ironing bottle when we go to bed, but she can't do that for the customers. Shelly and I join the guests on the porch to chat after we have helped clean up the buffet and turned the tablecloths over for one more night's dining. We pretend that we don't know what they're talking about when they mention how hot it is upstairs. The guests smoke their cigarettes and brush the hair from their eyes as the large night bugs whip by.

"Hey, what's that?" Todd the cute boy points over my head.

"Oh that! You mean that right there?" I can't believe he's talking to me. "Those are bats, they live in the chimney." As soon as I say it, I feel stupid. The crowd begins to get nervous; I, the dumb country girl, act like they're my pets. I try to take it back. "I'm just kidding, they're chimney birds."

The concern on everyone's face disappears. The adults decide to retire for the night. "Now Todd, don't you and your brother stay out here too late, we need to get back to the city early."

The bird bats are still circling above the light, grabbing every night bug they bump into. Shelly and I know better than to sit right here. I casually twist and roll my long hair down into my shirt. Shelly mimics me. We have heard of bats attacking and getting tangled in long hair, Dad told us that.

Todd rolls his gum back and forth in his fingers and says, "My dad is a doctor. He works at the hospital in Charleston, and Mom stays home and works on the city council."

My mouth is dry as I think what we do for a living. I try to imagine Dad as a doctor.

"Yeah well, we're from California."

"California! Why did you come here?" Todd puts his gum back into his mouth.

I pretend I don't see that. "Cause Dad likes it here better." I feel like bragging a bit, but the words have nowhere to go.

"Your Dad likes running a hotel?"

"Oh yeah, he used to run a big fancy high-rise in Phoenix, Arizona." The part I forgot to mention is that he was a newspaper deliveryman and a doorman.

"How come you left California?"

"Shelly, get us some water."

She turns sharply, ready to spit out nope. I try desperately to change the subject.

She looks at me with hate and grits her teeth, "Okay, does anybody else want some?"

"Yeah, I would."

"Me too."

"Sure, if you don't mind."

She walks into the kitchen, beaten by my manipulation. I caught her off guard. Now I think to myself, I hope she doesn't make too much noise, or Mom will make us come in.

"Saaandra," I hear from the kitchen. Darn it, I knew it, it's the evil call that means it's late and you have to come in.

"Is that your Mom?" Todd asks.

"Yeah, I'll be right back," I hop up, grab my hair out of my shirt, and run barefooted through the lobby. I don't have to watch out for my dirty feet, they'll never know it was me. "Yeah Mom?"

"Honey, I think it's time to come in."

"Mom, please, we're just talking on the porch."

"I know honey, but others might be trying to sleep."

"We'll be quiet, *I promise*."

She gives in, and Shelly overhears my good work. Shelly counts one more time to see if she has all the waters.

"Here, give me some, I'll help."

The night is starting to quiet down and the bugs are all gone. Only a distant chirp can be heard here and there. No one wants to say good night, but all of us are tired.

"Well, I think it would be great to live here in the mountains." Todd spits out his nasty gum. Shelly watches the gum land on the stairs.

I want to agree, but he doesn't know all of it. "Yeah, it's so much better than California." The truth is we are poor and I am doing my best to deceive them and myself. Dad is not a doctor, Mom is not a volunteer anywhere, and this could be our last month at Oak Terrace. The restaurant barely serves, and the hotel sleeps only these few customers. I'm saved from the truth by the final call from our parents.

The morning wakes me, and I wake Shelly. All I can think about is whether the customers are still here. I don't want to say good-bye. I run to the window that looks down on the parking lot to see what cars are here. Dad's down below, with no shirt on and no socks, dumping the garbage. The rich family's car is gone and so is the panic. I can relax a little bit now that I don't have to pretend Oak Terrace is doing well. Mark is already downstairs eating his cereal and milk. I go to the refrigerator. Empty, the entire refrigerator is empty. How are we going to pull this off another night? I wonder as I pour the last two bowls of Cheerios. We all sit there quietly, waking up to another morning in the large kitchen at the small table. I'm tired of working, but playing is not an option until the fair is over—the same fair that we haven't gone to. We get to go next year, when we have some money.

Mom comes in with her arms loaded. "Hey you guys, you finally woke up." She smiles, "I'm going to need some help this morning." No one is surprised. That's all we do right now is work.

Cooking, cleaning, dusting, sweeping, and helping. I hear Dad upstairs slicing the last of the roast Mom cooked this morning. "Oh shit." Dad screams. We drop our spoons and run upstairs, it sounds like he got hurt. Maybe he sliced his finger. As we round the top of the stairs, we see him staring at the floor. "What is it?" We gather closer for a better look, and there they are, a dozen or so baby rats. They lay there, squirming around, looking for their mom.

"Go get a shovel."

Mark looks at Dad like he's lost his mind.

"Dad, don't kill them." I stand in front of Mark.

"What the hell do you want me to do, let them grow up so I can kill them later?"

"Can't you just let them go outside?" I plead.

"Sandra, they'll make it back into the house. Besides, if there's this many in plain sight, there're probably hundreds already here."

The thought of hundreds of rats, not mice, but rats, running through our bedrooms is making me sick. I look to the meat slicer that we hide in the hall from the health inspector, and the baby rats on the floor next to our dirty laundry that we can't wash—I realize we are closer than ever to being finished.

"Never mind, I'll shoot them with the BB gun." He gathers up the potentially threatening creatures and proceeds downstairs to execute them out by the briar bushes.

Dad knows that if the health inspector ever got a peek at the rest of this old mansion, the violations alone would close this place down. As I listen to him shooting the rats, I remember the day old Mr. Stout caught Dad off guard and almost came into our living quarters. It wasn't Mark's fault, but he was the one who opened the kitchen door. No one ever enters the house off the back porch or the kitchen. That's off limits to friends, deliveries, and especially Mr. Stout. But that day there was an error in our plan and we almost got caught. Mr. Stout came up the driveway opposite how you're supposed to come up to the house. Dad was in the back burning some leaves and only Mark was inside.

Mr. Stout purposely came to the wrong door, he came to the kitchen. I saw the whole thing. I dropped my rake and ran like the wind to warn Dad. Out of breath, I yelled, "Dad, get to the house, it's the health inspector." He took the warning like a baton and ran faster than me up the hill and to the back porch. He managed to get in through the back porch door and stop the health inspector just as he was entering our secret living room from the kitchen, which could have led him upstairs to a mess.

"Hello Mr. Stout, can I help you?" Dad blocked the door. Behind him was our living room with both the dogs and the endless dirt and Mark wanting to suck his fingers because he was scared. He knew he might get a whippin' for this. "No sir, just thought I'd get your signature. Well, let's go into the kitchen." Dad tightly closed the door behind himself and led Mr. Stout to the table. Nothing more was said, and a beaten Mr. Stout left Oak Terrace through the correct door. Dad forcefully reminded us, "You guys will get us shut down if he ever gets back here. It's illegal to live here with the dogs in this mess so close to the food area. We have to act like this is closed off and it has nothing to do with the business. Do you understand?"

I catch my breath—reality hits me when the last BB is fired. I try not to think about the baby rats dying. Mark and I look for more babies that might have been born in our growing laundry pile. I pray to God this is my imagination.

18

School will start soon and Oak Terrace will end, there is no way to keep this alive. We can't serve a handful of people this winter and pay the bills. Dad said it's the people around here who won't support us. According to Dad, the town is too scared of change and too dumb to know a good thing. Dad is defeated and Mom is relieved. The problem is where will we go next? This is the first time we have ever packed without knowing where we are going. Dad says we are not taking all the restaurant stuff with us, only some. I don't know what that means.

The house is just like it was when we moved in, cold and lonely. I feel sort of sad as we gather up our belongings, I think the house is going to miss us. Our last days are painful. We know that even if the whole town comes over for the buffet, we still won't have enough money for next week. I want someone to shoot the buffet and put it out of its misery.

"All right, you guys, I found a house out in the country, and we are going to run the snack bar in the bowling alley."

Mom has heard this before and wants more details.

"Look, Ardell, I ran into a guy I know, and he needs help with the bowling alley. It's perfect. We'll keep all of the profits, and this place already has business. We don't have to beg for customers, we can make a killing. This is exactly what we need." Dad continues chattering for hours about the new business as we pack up only what we need.

"Sandra, we'll pay you for working after school and weekends. Shelly, you can pour the sodas, and Mark, you can help your mother with the hamburgers." He laughs and wishes all our problems away. "And, guess what—you guys can ride the school bus from the new house."

"Keep packing," is all Mom can say. We are about to throw in the Oak Terrace towel and begin a new life in a bowling alley. Dad drives us away, with hopes and dreams fueling the car, the car that barely goes thirty miles per hour. We are down to just a few loads, and this time it's our turn to go see the new house. I sit there with the two dogs, Big and Sugar, on my lap, poking their heads out the window. I think the dogs are worried we might go for another one of those long rides. I laugh to myself as I think of the dogs who put up with so much. The car goes slowly down the driveway and so do our plans for a rich life at Oak Terrace. We failed. But to Dad, they failed *us*, and we'll get them back. We'll show them…

We take a right off the highway at the Organ Cave sign. This takes us onto a country road that winds in and out of the farms and cattle ranches. At a beaten-up old barn we turn left onto a one-lane dirt road. After about three miles of dust and potholes we pull into the driveway of the brown farmhouse.

"Dad, is this it?"

"Yeah. And the bus will pick you guys up right in front."

As we all ease out of the car, the dogs run to each tree and check out their new territory. New territory is nothing new to us. The house sits firm and stout, with an unfriendly feel to it. I notice that the front porch is moldy and dark, not the warm sunny porch we had at Oak Terrace.

"Sandra, come here." I run to Shelly's voice, which is around the other side of the house. "Look, our very own pond."

I look at the pasture with cows, horses, and a green pond. I immediately recognize this is a watering hole for the animals, not a pond.

"Oh yeah, that's great." I whirl around and stomp off.

Meanwhile, Mom is in the house fussing and spitting cuss words about how much work we have to do. I go to the house from the back door and enter the kitchen. The rust spots on the floor where appliances were tell me that we are the first to be here in a long time. I can't believe how cold it is. I can see in the living room there is another one of those potbellied woodstoves like we had at the river. I shudder at the thought of trying to warm this house. Dad walks in and buttons up his coat.

"Dad, where is the kitchen stove?"

"We'll have to get one later." He walks to the living room and squeezes Mom's shoulder as she opens the droopy curtains. "Let's go see the rest of the house."

Dad leads the way through the living room to the hall and up the staircase. We walk slowly up the wooden brown stairs; they whirl up to three bedrooms and a bathroom. The house gives no signs of welcome. I can't help but feel unwanted as I try to make friends with this old, cold place. Dad opens the bathroom door, it's olive green. He then inspects each one of the bedrooms, and lets us pick our own. Shelly and I share, Mark gets his own, and Mom and Dad take the biggest one.

"Sure glad we got you guys those sleeping bags for Christmas last year."

He is joking, but no one can laugh. We will be sleeping on the floor and a cold one at that. I look out the window of our bedroom and notice all the dead flies. I see the icky green pond and the ivy that strangles the front porch. This is not a nice house.

"Let's go and get the rest of the stuff out of the truck." Dad ignores the cold draft and the yellowing paint. Mark is stuck at his doorway staring at his room. He's not excited about sleeping alone, I can tell. Shelly and I leave footprints on the dusty old floor. The cracked wooden floor frowns at us as we leave. We march behind Dad and hold onto the handrail going down. The rail wiggles and warns us not to hold on to it for help.

"What's that?" Mark points to the giant cellar door with the chains and dead bolts. I can barely look at this door, and Shelly keeps on walking past it. It sits alone in the middle of the downstairs hall. The door is dark, almost black, it is thick and heavy. The sliding dead bolt means business; it would take both hands and all Dad's strength to open it.

"I don't know, but listen," Dad warns. Shelly stops in her tracks and turns around. "The owners told me we could have this place, but we must never open that door. I am telling you guys, don't play around here, just leave it alone. The guy was serious."

Oh great. Now we get to live with some kind of children-eating monster. *Don't go down the cellar.* This is right out of a horror movie. The warning is not a threat, like there might be a secret treasure, but more like *it's for your own good.* We all look to Mom for relief, but she has no sign of kidding about her.

I knew it, I knew when I walked in that there was something strange about this house. I go out the front door onto the moldy cement porch to get the stuff out of the truck. As soon as I get off the porch, I have a sense within me that is much different. When I was in the house I felt a heaviness, but outside I feel lighter, like I can breathe better. I shake off the heaviness and reach for a box of toys in the truck. I feel someone looking at me and turn around quickly. I see a movement upstairs, a curtain moving slightly. I tell myself it is Dad.

"Sandra, I'll get that, your mother needs help in the kitchen."

It wasn't Dad up there. I'll ignore it this time, but I am going to have to watch my back. No one else seems to feel the eerie presence.

Shelly is quiet and Mark sticks close to Mom. I feel nervous, I can't venture up those stairs alone. As far as the cellar door, well, if we go around through the living room, we're safe.

"Mom, come here." We hear Mark in the hall and both of us run to him. "Look, I can see my breath." And sure enough, the sun has set, the cold from outside is in the house, and I can see my breath too.

Mom doesn't think this is funny, winter isn't even here yet, this is still fall. Dad already started a fire over an hour ago. This is another not so good sign. I ignore that too.

Monday morning and the bus will pick us up at 6:30 a.m. I didn't even know what 6:30 a.m. meant. But now I do. It means we get up in the dark, jump into cold clothes, and run downstairs to try to keep warm by the stove. We take turns peering out the window looking for the bus; we have to take turns because of the cold. Mom lets us eat our cereal in the living room where it is warm. I think that's where Mom sleeps at night.

The bus pulls up by the mailbox, and the dogs run outside with us. We're the first ones to get picked up. I don't understand why we can't be last, after all, we'll go right by the house again. "Hey, Miss Bus Driver—" her name is Dottie, but she likes being called Bus Driver—"how come you don't pick us up on the way back?" As soon as I saw her turn around, I knew this was not a good question.

"Because I am the bus driver and that is the way I do it. Do you want me to forget to pick you up? I can do that, you know."

I melt in my seat.

"It was just a question…I don't know why she has to be so mean." Shelly nods as she takes my side.

Every morning thereafter I stand my ground waiting outside so Bus Driver won't forget us.

"Sandra, get in here, you can see the bus from the window."

"That's okay Mom, I'm not cold."

I stand there with my coat buttoned up to my neck and my books inside my coat keeping them warm. I stand there by the mailbox demanding that the bus stop. I pat myself on the back each time it does.

The bus door squeaks open and I help Mark up the big first step. As we take our seats in the middle of the bus, Shelly and I sit on our warmed books to keep the cold plastic seats from freezing our butts.

We can't wear pants to school, we have to wear dresses; ladies wear dresses and boys wear pants. I hate that rule too. Mom got us some tights, but it only helps a little when your legs are freezing.

Dad has started training at night with the owner of the bowling alley. In a couple of weeks, we'll take over running the snack bar. Mom lays on the couch mostly, she is tired. Tonight we are having Spaghetti and grilled cheese sandwiches. Dad managed to get us a kitchen stove, but only the top part works, the oven doesn't. Before that we had bologna sandwiches and Fritos for dinner. Mom cooks our meal while we huddle next to the woodstove.

It was easy to set up the living room; all the furniture we have goes next to the woodstove.

It is getting colder, and Halloween is just around the corner. I don't really like the idea of being in this house at Halloween. Mom and Dad are both working at the Lewisburg Bowl. Mom goes to get Shelly and Mark from school so they don't have to ride the bus home, but I do, because I'm helping after school with the Halloween party. The days are much shorter, so when I do get home, it's close to dark. It's been about a week now since I started to go home alone, and so far it's okay. I stay in the kitchen where it's safe and do my homework while I wait for Mom.

This particular day is a Friday, and Fridays are the most fun. I laugh with a couple of friends while we put the final touches on the signs and banners. I can't wait to tell Mom I have a boyfriend named Kyle. The bus ride home is slow like always, and the whole time all I can think about is the big party at school next week. And, of course, Kyle. He is the cutest boy in school. Today at lunch Patricia gave me a note from Kyle. "Do you like me, I like you, circle yes or no." I circled yes so fast I ripped through the paper. The bus finally pulls to a hard stop at the mailbox, and I say good-bye to everyone, even Mrs. Bus Driver. I don't have to, but today I am extra happy and carefree. Kyle likes me.

I cross the front yard and pretend I am not going to look at the upstairs window, but I do. The dogs greet me and the window is clear.

No ghost. I laugh to myself. I come in the front door, which I hate, but I don't have a key to the back door. I stand on the hardened cracked front porch trying to fumble my key into the door and not scare myself with the "gonna get you" game. As I enter, I drop my books and papers at the bottom of the stairs. There is no way I'll go up there alone, that is my rule. I politely route myself through the living room so I don't have to go past the chained up, dead-bolted cellar door. As I get through the living room and am just about to enter the kitchen, I see the ghost.

Not just any ghost, but *the* ghost, the ghost I have been ignoring all this time. He is a tall man with a chain around his wrist like he broke free and his clothes are torn. He just stands there in the hall as if it is his prison. I am so stunned that to run is impossible. I can't even scream. I think for a minute that I have talked myself into this sighting, but he won't go away. I stand there frozen as long as he does. I stare at this soft, cloud-like image of a man with a sullen look on his face. It looks like he wants to say something.

I think I must be crazy for not being more scared, but his face doesn't look like your typical monster on TV. It is more an old and tired face.

At that minute the dogs start scratching at the door. I jump so fast that I think I bump my head on the ceiling. The man has disappeared. I am free to scream and run. I run to the road without my coat and pray my mom will be driving home now. The longer I wait, the more frightened I get. I tap my foot endlessly avoiding any sounds of him inside the house. He can't talk but he can make sounds.

A car passes me and slows. "Hey there, you're gonna freeze out here. What ya waiting for?"

"I am waiting for my mom to come home." The truth is I would have gone home with this nice farmer lady if she'd asked. I try to keep her there with my questions, "Where do you live? Oh yeah, I see that house on the school bus." I ask so many questions that the poor woman finally has to be rude.

"Well now, you get in the house and wait for your Mama." She drives away.

It's getting later and later, and I don't know where Mom is. Maybe she had to work late. I turn my head to the window to see if he's still watching me. He is not. It's dark and I still don't have my coat. I have the dogs close to me and on my lap warming me as I sit on the mean porch. I sit there safe and terrified, wondering who he is and why he isn't in heaven. That ghost must be why they chained the cellar door, but don't they know, ghosts can go anywhere they want? Never mind, I'll just sit out here all night if I have to. I hear the phone ring—it's probably Mom. She'll worry if I don't answer, but if I answer I'll have to go inside. I will not go in, I'll just wait here with the dogs. I sit there with my legs folded tight, as the wind blows and the house creaks. "Oh thank God, there she is. I know it's her because the car only goes twenty miles per hour, all the other cars fly by.

"Sandra Lee, where in the hell have you been." Mom starts talking before the car door is open.

"I've been right here."

Mom snatches her purse and tonight's hamburgers.

"I have been calling you to tell you I was going to be late."

The cold makes it tough to stand up. "I didn't hear the phone. I was on the porch."

"Honey, what's the matter with you?" Mom rubs my arms. "You're freezing, where's your coat?"

"It's in the house."

Mom turns the cold, rusted doorknob. "Why aren't you doing your homework?"

"Mom, I saw a ghost."

"Oh Sandra, that's just your father filling your head with nonsense."

"Mom, I promise, I saw him. I'm never going to come home alone, ever."

"Okay, you don't have to, I'll pick you up after school."

Mom doesn't want to believe me, but she doesn't argue either. I made my stand. And so did the ghost.

Mom passes out the hamburgers while we gather in the living room where she starts a fire that won't heat the rest of the house. Going to the bathroom is a chore. Dad says at least it's not an outhouse. But this is the closest thing to an outhouse. It's so cold in the bathroom, and it sits next to the cellar door. So if you go to the bathroom, not only do you freeze to death, you're scared to death. When you do get out of the bathroom with your life, you automatically get to be closest to the woodstove. It's an unwritten law in this house. You take somebody with you when you go to the bathroom. We never know where we'll find Mark in the morning, but it won't be alone in his bed. I like it when he stumbles in with me; he's warm and I feel safe from my bad dreams.

The dreams are usually the same, a cave I can't get out of, a raging river dragging me, I can't swim hard enough, or just falling fast, knowing the ground is next.

Mom lies on the couch and we listen to the TV tally the deaths in Vietnam. Every day they count how many soldiers are dead and how many are missing. The rabbit ears fall off the TV, and somebody has to hold them in place while the picture decides if it will return. Mom exhales a sad breath as the reporter stands in the war zone explaining the attack.

"This is bullshit," she says. "No son of mine will ever go fight a war." Mark looks up. "I think President Nixon should get his ass over there and fight," Mom throws the blanket over her legs and feet, "then we'll see how long he can drag this damn thing out."

This reminds me of the time when I was little and she and I sat there watching TV together when Mr. Kennedy died. Mom ran over and picked me up and took me away from the TV. She held me so tight she scared me. That was a scary time, and everyone in the house was sad. I was sad too, but mostly because the world was sad. I didn't know what dead was, but I knew it wasn't good. I think I was about three. And everything changed the day I saw that man get shot. I only saw it once but I do remember the funeral and the sadness came right through the TV. People were scared and talking about it all the time. I knew the name *Kennedy* like I knew the word *toy*.

That night I go to bed thinking of poor Mr. Kennedy and all those 64,000 poor soldiers whose moms are crying right now. I think war is the dumbest thing God ever invented. I don't understand how one man can kill another, I really don't understand this at all. Mom just gets upset if I ask about the war. And Dad, well, I don't know if he knows there is one. Right now he is trying to figure out how to broast chicken without burning himself.

Mom doesn't have to work this chilly winter Saturday morning and we all get to stay home while Dad works with the new guy, Tim.

Dad said he is not real smart, but he isn't afraid of cooking the chicken either. Dad came home the other night and could barely get his story out as he sat at the table laughing.

"So, I'm pouring sodas in the front, and Tim is working in the back with the fryer. He's taking orders from the window and we're busier than hell. The bowling leagues are switching over. All of a sudden, I hear Tim holler from the back, 'Oh no, lordy help me.' Now here's a guy who can barely say two words, a shy son of a bitch, hollering. I go back to help him. I think that damn fryer got him, and there he is, bent over the sink poking at the drain hole. 'Tim,' I say, 'What the hell are you doing?' He turns around, and I swear to God, he has dropped his glass eye down the sink drain. The man is squinting at me with one eye and the other is filled with tears. 'Oh Bill,' he says, 'you got to help me, my ma paid four thousand dollars for my eye and she'd kill me if I's lost it.'

"What am I supposed to do? I can't laugh. I ask him, 'What the hell were you doing with your eye?' He says, 'I took it out to clean it and I dropped it.' At that point Dad is laughing so hard he's got tears in his own eyes, and he can barely finish the story. "Then I had to call a plumber to come fish the guy's eye out of the drain pipe. Do you have any idea how many calls it took to get someone to come out and get Tim's eye? Meanwhile, the poor son of a bitch couldn't wait on customers with only one eye. By the time the plumber got there, I was running the back and the front, trying to hide Tim from anyone seeing him."

By this time, all of us are on the floor laughing, seeing Dad with the one-eyed cook trying to explain to the plumber, "You've got to come quick, my employee lost his eye down the drain."

The morning continues as Mom announces that Brooks will be back from the Navy soon, and he'll be helping out with the bowling alley. Mom cooks breakfast, which is a little unusual. We go play for the day. It's really our first day of exploring since we moved here. All the other times we are waiting for Mom, running from ghosts, or at school. We climb over the rancher's fence that seems to be ours. The back of the house leads straight up a hill where the cattle graze. They say that Indians used to live there. I believe them.

On this particular morning we enter the feeding area and skip through the high grass and mud puddles left behind from the cows. We throw rocks as far as we can into the pond and fling dirt clods at each other.

We leave the barn behind as we open the gate and mosey up the hill where we see some of the cows. They turn their heads and decide we are not food. They ignore us and we ignore them.

"What's that?"

"I don't know, it looks like a black cow laying down." We strain our eyes trying to see the foreign object up the hill. We pull each other up the hill closer and closer to the mystery. I find arrowheads and put them in my pocket.

"I got one too," Mark yells from behind. I don't even bother to look, I know he does not, I am the only one who finds arrowheads.

The sun is up for sure, and Shelly takes off her sweater and wraps it around her waist. I pull off my sweatshirt with one hand and hold down my T-shirt with another. We are free. It feels so good to be alone again, wandering around, exploring. Mark and I try to push each other into dry cow pies. They won't hurt us, but the thought is thrill enough.

Wet cow pies are off-limits.

Finally, we have reached the black unidentified object—it's an old tractor tire. Disappointing, now all we have to do is go back down the hill. Then I get a flash from heaven. "Shelly, help me lift the tire."

"Nope."

"Come on, darn it, I need some help. If we lift it up on its side, we can let it go down the hill." The idea sparks something inside all of us. Shelly and I get on our knees to unbury the old rotten tire, it's been there forever. Mark joins us with a handful here and a handful there as he scoops away the dirt. I handle the weeds that have grown around the tire and make it impossible to lift. Shelly and I stand on the tire with both feet and bend to the other side, holding our butts out as anchors. "One, two, three." With the help of a tree branch and plenty of digging it's out! Shelly and I fall on our asses with the sunken treasure. I stand up and brush off. "Now, let's put Mark inside and roll him down."

Shelly cocks her head to one side and declares, "I don't think that'll work. You better try it without him first."

I hate to admit it, but she's right again. I don't know what'll happen. All three of us stand there with the tractor tire bigger than us and a hill that goes on beyond forever to the fence where the gate is open. Now it's time to test our rocket ship and let it fly.

Shelly is on one side and I'm on the other. We push with all our might and let the blackness roll. It rolls and wobbles a bit at first but then after the first ten feet when the incline begins, this tire is an energy machine. I hold my breath and grab Shelly's arm as, down below, the blackness picks up more and more speed. By now I don't know if what I'm seeing is true—are those cows entering the gate we forgot to close? Oh God, please let this be my imagination. Mark starts laughing.

I want to cry—the monster bounces into the sky after it hits the small boulders buried underground. The tractor tire hits the ground with such force that it shoots into the sky and lands below with more speed. The tire has a mind of its own. No one or nothing will stop it, not even the poor cow who doesn't know what's about to hit him. Bouncing, pounding, and burning down the hill, this tire has been freed, and it wants to go forever. I turn my head as I know this locomotive is only seconds away from hitting the cow or the fence. Either way, there is going to be hell to pay.

Just as the tire makes its last attempt to get away, it slams into the side of an innocent victim. The cow yells out as the air is knocked completely out of her. I don't think this is funny—I think we'd better run. Just as our feet get fired up to take the hill ourselves, we have more than fear to motivate us. Mr. Farley, the farmer, is crowning the top of the hill on his tractor. Only God knows if he saw what just happened to his poor cow.

We don't give it a second thought, as down the dusty tire trail we bolt. I know he saw, I know he did. That's why he is chasing us. Behind me is a lunatic on a red tractor pounding after us. "You little brats, that's it, I'm going to kill you..." And in front of me is a mad cow, who's catching her breath. And of course, the dead tire, guilty of committing such a violent act. I pray Mark can keep up, but if he don't, it ain't my problem. Right now I have to get through the gate and across the fence. Shelly is in my back pocket, running for her life. The old man yells cuss words and threats as I pass by the aching cow at the gate. All I need now is for the cow to charge me. I grab the top rail and sling myself over. "Mom, Mom help..."

"What in the hell...?" She sees the tractor coming full speed toward the house with Mark in front of it, crying. Mom grabs for Mark. The man and his tractor will not be stopped.

He pulls up to the fence, "Ma'am, I have had it with your children. This is not a playground. They are not allowed on my property."

"I understand," Mom is firm and her feet are planted, she's not moving, "but this is not all your property, the way I was told. You are allowed to use the upper pasture for grazing, but my children can play there, too."

"Oh, does that mean they can harm my cattle?"

"Mom, it was an accident, we didn't mean to..."

"Of course not, but you are not allowed to harm my kids either."

"Well, if I see those kids hanging around my cattle, I will not be responsible for what happens next."

However, it isn't our fault that all of his cows get loose the next day, and run all over the neighbors' lawns and the ditches. Mean old Mr. Farley goes by us on his horse—we're in the front yard playing with the dogs—and he gives us the same look that the Wicked Witch of the West gave to Dorothy when she tried to take the ruby slippers. He wishes us dead, and we laugh as the cows stand around in people's yards eating grass and stopping the traffic. It takes all of one day to round up his forty head and lead them back to the upper pasture.

"You kids better keep that gate shut." He slaps it closed with one hand, and with the other he tugs his cows on a rope. He pounds his boots into the ground, jump-starts his tractor, and off he rides away sneering. Mom pops out of the house, "You guys leave that poor man alone. You hear me?"

19

On the weekends around here at the bowling alley, I run the soda machine and am known for my cherry Cokes. The high school gang hangs out at the bowling alley, and my popularity soars. The jukebox plays "A Horse with No Name." I know the words forward and backward, but I have no idea what they mean. "A horse with no name," why don't they just give it a name? And then there is Cher's song, "Cherokee Nation." And "Squeeze Box." What's a squeeze box? I just sing along, pouring cherry sodas, pretending I'm in with the teenagers. The secret to my cherry Coke is simple—I add twice the syrup, one squirt in the bottom of the cup, then I put in the ice, and then I add syrup again on top of the ice. But no one knows how I do it.

Shelly has taken to the broaster. I get a little nervous that the thing might explode and burn her, but she seems to have everything under control. Mark is Mom's little helper, he is the pickle man. For every two pickles that go on a hamburger, he sneaks one in his mouth. No one seems to mind as they watch him add the final touch. Mom has to wrap it though. No one except her or Dad seems to get the art of wrapping a hamburger or hot dog. I tried, but mine looked like a mess with the orange paper hanging off one side. I don't care. I like the soda machine, it's closer to the counter.

Dad has started to take his bowling very seriously. He even comes in early before we open, just to work on his arm. "Ardell, I need to get a bowling ball. Chet knows a guy who will custom make a ball for me. I think it's around eighty dollars." He waits for her response.

"Are you crazy? We don't have eighty dollars. If you didn't notice, we're broke, and things are a little slow around here." She pops off and out of his sight.

I wipe down the tables and think about how much eighty dollars is. That's two new bikes, or maybe a minibike. That reminds me, Dad said he was going to buy me one for my birthday. My birthday has passed.

Dad says no more and lets Mom cool off a bit. But this is not the end of this little talk, I can feel that in my bones. Around three o'clock to my surprise, Kyle arrives and he's alone. I drop my cleaning rag and act like I don't see him.

"Sandra, I thought you might want to bowl a game." His jeans have holes in the knees, that's cool, and his T-shirt hangs loose around his neck. He's cocky and confident, like this is natural—just go to the bowling alley and talk to your girlfriend.

"Uhhh...sure, let me ask Mom." My stomach is up in my throat. I run to the back where Mom is trying to broast chicken. She hates that damn machine. It looks like a robot with steam. It has a mind of its own. When the pressure is at full maximum, the red light goes on, and danger becomes real. I stand back, I don't trust that thing. Dad and Shelly act like they're best friends with it. I won't even introduce myself. Mom puts on the gloves that practically cover her body and begins to gently release the valve. No talking is permitted during this procedure. I stand there waiting. Will she make it out alive? is what I'm thinking. Broasted chicken is what we are famous for, and we have to cook it just right.

"Mom," I ask when she's safely got the chicken out of the contraption, "can I bowl a game with Kyle?"

"Who's Kyle?"

I look away and hope she'll remember that this is my boyfriend.

"Ohhhh, you mean Kyle from school, the boy you like."

"Yeah, he's here and he wants me to bowl a game."

"Sure honey, ask Chet if it's all right. Tell him I said it was okay."

I want to brush my hair, but I can't around the food. Chet is doing his daily crossword puzzle, his glasses barely hanging onto his nose. I stand at his counter trying not to interrupt his concentration, and wonder about his nose hairs. When he glances up, I ask, "Chet, is it all right if I bowl one game with my friend?"

He slowly looks over his paper and across me to Kyle. "I know that boy, what's he want bowling with you?"

"I don't know." What does he want me to say, Kyle likes me? I can hardly believe it myself.

"All right then, Kyle, I know your daddy." He grabs my favorite shoes from under the counter. I have my own shoes that nobody wears but me.

Chet sharply asks Kyle, "What size?"

He answers with the same confidence and cocky tongue that he came in with, "Size ten sir, thank you." Kyle reaches for his dollar.

"That's okay," Chet turns over the newspaper, "this is Sandra's game."

"Wow, you get to bowl for free." He touches my hand accidentally.

"Not all the time, but most of the time." I stumble over my words as I analyze his touch—was it on purpose?

"You're so lucky."

I say nothing and try not to laugh at his interpretation of lucky and then look for the alley with the most privacy and walk toward lane number ten. Chet watches me like a hawk, and then, with a disapproving eye, he turns on the lane. He knows what I'm doing.

"Thank you, Chet." Kyle is in awe of my power.

With a snap of my fingers, the lane is ours. I put my shoes on, praying I didn't wear socks with holes in them. I didn't. But he did. Doesn't matter though, Kyle is the cutest, strongest, and most misbehaving boy in school. I can't believe that I'm actually bowling with my boyfriend. But boyfriend or not, I am not going to let him win just because I'm a girl. I stand there matching the little diamonds to exactly where I want the ball to hit. I become one with the pins, and I count off my steps and release. The ball rolls and hits my target, but it's off slightly to one side, probably a half inch. I get eight out of ten. Kyle looks concerned—he knows this isn't a game he'll win easily. When it comes to competition, I have no mercy.

I take my next turn, and miss. It's okay I tell myself, I'm just warming up. He says nothing as he takes his place on deck. I notice right away that he didn't write down my score. As he returns from the deck, I mark his. After the third frame he asks what his score is. He didn't want to keep score, I guess. "You have fifty-six and I have forty-nine," I tell him. "I'll keep score." After frame five I start to get thirsty. The pressure of being alone with my boyfriend is much worse than the game itself. I want some space, I feel nervous and anxious.

"Hey Kyle, want a cherry Coke?"

"Sure." He returns to his chair where I just happen to be standing. He did it again; he touched my hand. This time I'm sure of it.

"I'll be back in a minute." I want to stay but I need to go. I can still feel where his hand touched mine. I think he was going to hold hands with me. "Mom?" I can't find her—she must still be in the back tackling the floured chicken parts— she says a prayer before scalding the little guys. "Can we have a Coke?"

"Yeah but only a medium."

I carefully create the cherry Coke of a lifetime and return to my man. I feel so weird. I have goose bumps for no reason. Kyle takes his special drink and sucks away. When I sit down next to him, I think how lucky I am to be his girlfriend and hope he tries to hold my hand again. My eyes are locked on him. He must have noticed because next thing I know he reaches over and kisses me on the mouth. I have never been kissed by a boy, not even on the cheek, let alone on the mouth. I hope no one saw, but he doesn't care, he just sits closer and grabs my hand and pulls me next to him. I look behind me to make sure Chet isn't cleaning up an alley or something. I know I'll get in trouble. Then it happens. Kyle puts his arm around my neck and kisses me again with his tongue. It feels like twenty or thirty minutes, he just keeps kissing and kissing me. I'm not sure if I like it. I want to pull away but something says stay. I'm so curious. He stops, and I sit there with my mouth half open, my eyes telling him I had no idea what that was.

"That's a French kiss."

His hand is holding mine; I can feel his pulse in his wrist. I don't say anything, I just sit, looking at him with my mouth still open. Kyle stares back at me with a question in his eyes. I think he thinks we're going to sit here and make out. I'll get killed if my dad walks in and sees me kissing him. I have to bowl. I bowl my turn and do lousy, but who's bowling? I'm back on the bench remembering the best kiss in the world. It's the last frame and soon he'll have to leave—I want this game to last forever. Heck, I want his kiss to last forever. As I return to score, he stands up and we meet in the middle, he kisses me again quick as lightning. I am starting to get bugged, I don't like all this kissing whenever he feels like it. He's not even looking before he kisses me.

"Sandra." He moves away a little bit. "I have to tell you something, I came here today for a reason." He moves back a little farther. "I came here to see if I like you or Marcy better." Kyle takes both my hands. "I like Marcy." He drops my hands, they land in my lap.

I have no words for what I feel. I'm not mad, I'm not sad, I'm not anything, I'm blank. I look at him and how cute he is. I feel a tug at my heart. I wish it was me that he liked, but what do I do? What do I say? I don't even know what I just did.

"Marcy says she'll go back with me, but I had to come here and see who I liked better." He reaches for his coat and sips one more drink off his cherry Coke. "You're really nice, but I have to break up with you."

My eyes blink twice. "Okay," I tell him. I prepare to bowl my last frame. I have to strike to beat him. But he's getting ready to go. I look up to see if this is a bad dream. I reach for my ball, I hit a grease spot and it slips from my hand and smashes down on my middle finger.

All twelve pounds land smack on my finger and I think I broke it. The pain is immediate, the nail is throbbing.

"Are you okay?" Kyle reaches for my hand. "Here, let me see…Oh, wow, you better go show your mom."

The tears and the pain are beyond my control. I don't want to cry in front of him. He picks up his blue sweatshirt and goes to the counter for his shoes. I am sitting on the bench crying to myself, the same bench we were just kissing on. And now I realize that most of my tears are for him, not my stupid finger. I finally go to Mom for comfort.

"What happened, honey?"

"I dropped the ball and smashed my finger." The tears start up again.

"Come here, we'd better get some ice on it." She fusses and carefully wraps it with a cold cloth, in the same special way she wraps a hamburger. "Now you just sit here, and we'll see if the swelling goes down."

Chet walks over and checks on my finger. "That's a bad one. Maybe next time you'll pick a better ball." He squeezes my shoulder—he is not talking about bowling. Chet knows my heart's broken, and it helps that he knows the truth.

20

Dad builds his game and his confidence each day. He runs up to Mom like a little boy showing off his grades; hoping that she'll reward him with a brand new, custom-made ball. Of course it will improve his game. Dad bowls with passion and determination. He will be the next year's Honky Tonk winner of the Tri-State Tournament. It's a cash pot worth up to a hundred thousand dollars. He and Chet plan for the big day way in the future. Dad's got what it takes; he has found his calling. The scorecards pile up as if they'll be worth money one day. Dad talks endlessly about his new average and what that means. "Sandra, when I win the championship, the first thing we're gonna do is buy you that minibike. Cash."

Two days later Brooks is calling. He's at the bus station waiting for someone to pick him up. Dad throws down his towel. "Ardell, I'll be right back. I'm going to go get Brooks. That next batch of chicken will be ready in three and a half minutes."

"Bill, you get your ass in here and get the chicken first. Brooks can wait a minute."

She's right, and Dad resumes chicken duty. I run over to where Shelly is doing her homework. It's about six o'clock and we rarely go home without Mom or Dad. During one or the other's shift break we'll finally go home, usually it's when Mom's shift ends around seven o'clock. "Shelly, guess what? Brooks is back. Dad's going to go pick him up."

"Can we go?" Shelly yells into the back, "Dad, can we go with you?"

"Yeah." He pops out with his paper hat on. "Get your coats."

Shelly and I try to sneak out without Mark.

"Hey, let your brother go too, what's the matter with you girls?"

Mom hands him his coat from behind the counter, and the three of us pile into the backseat and wait for Dad.

He pulls out onto the snowy road, and we hear the crunch of fresh snow smash underneath the tires. I love that sound. Dad tests the slick road with a tap on the brakes and sure enough we slide a little to the left. He always does this. He pretends it's a safety requirement, but really he just likes to spark up the ride a bit.

We reach the bus station and there's Uncle Brooks, a smile from ear to frozen ear. He's in his Navy blues and a black sailor coat. "Hi, y'all." He climbs in the front seat and throws his bag onto Mark's lap. "Here you go, boy. See if you can hold that for your old Uncle Brooks." He's twenty-six, so I guess he's right, he is old. Boy, Mom and Dad must be really old; I think they're about thirty or more. "How ya doin, old boy?" He grabs a cigarette from the cluttered dash. "Jack, I could hardy stand it. I thought I'd 'bout go crazy stuck on that damn boat. Canned this and canned that, I haven't had a vegetable in over a year. Ma would keel over if she knew what I ate. And guess what Shel? I had plenty of beans. I even brought some home for ya."

We all laugh.

"I'm going to have Grandma make us a big old pot next time she comes for a visit. And if you're really good, I'll let you pick what kind." Poor Shelly doesn't know if he's kidding or serious, she stays out of this bean tease.

When we get back to the bowling alley, Brooks asks Dad what the hell he's doing. Dad grins. "I told you I had my own business."

"I'll be damned." Brooks grabs Mark and his bag from the backseat, and we head straight for the door, the cold cuts right through us. Brooks follows Dad to where Mom is ringing up a customer.

"Ardell, don't you look beautiful? I missed you all." Brooks reaches over the counter and kisses her on the cheek. All three of us fight for the stool next to Brooks.

"Tell us a story about being on the ship."

"Oh, you guys, I got to rest up a bit. I'll tell you a wild one tomorrow." He takes off his coat. "You like that coat, Sandra?"

"Yeah, but it doesn't look very warm."

"Oh honey, this is one hundred percent wool. This coat will keep a polecat warm in Alaska. Go ahead and try it on."

I reach for the coat and wrap it around my shoulders and punch my arms through. It fits down to my knees, and it's just as warm as he said. The smell of his cologne and the warmth of his body heat is still in it. Uncle Brooks is the nicest uncle in the world, that is, except for Uncle John. I sometimes try to figure out who is the nicest, but it's impossible to choose.

Shelly wants to wear Brooks's coat, but no way, he gave it to me. I dance around teasing her about how special I am. The coat is mine, it's all mine, and so is Uncle Brooks. He spins around on his stool and gives me my own special smile. The smile that means I'm his favorite, I know I'm his favorite. Besides, I was the firstborn. I return his smile with all my heart; I love being in his big old coat. He and Dad continue chatting. I hear Dad dogging the Navy, the same Navy he's never been in.

Dad enters from the back with a plate of chicken. "Brooks, what are you going to do now that your ass is free?"

Brooks swallows hard, "Well, I was thinking about checking it out around here for awhile. Jack, I learned electronics in the Navy, and I have a couple of bucks in my pocket."

Mom steps in and reroutes the conversation so Dad will get off Brooks's ass and let him breathe a little. Mom knows exactly how and when to get the victim out of Dad's web. Besides, Brooks is my hero. I'm glad he'll be staying, my buddy is home safe.

I wish all this adult stuff would end so we can get onto the important stuff—like stories. I can't wait to hear stories and play with Brooks.

"Sandra, get your things. It's time to go."

I pack up my school books and grab my coat. I whirl back around as I realize that I still have Brooks's coat on.

"Oh Sandra, go ahead, I'll get it from you later." He squeezes my shoulder and kicks me in the butt.

Mom interrupts with logic, "You'll freeze without it, Brooks. She has a coat."

Brooks looks past Mom and straight into my eyes, "No, I insist. Sandra, you wear it home for me. I'll be there later with your Dad." He finishes with a sly wink. The coat wraps around me twice and the arms hang to my knees. It's my coat. At least for tonight.

For awhile, Brooks looks for work and helps around the snack bar. He feels the same way I do about the chicken broaster, but he's a man and he'll do it anyway. I can see him in there alone nervously double-checking everything on the machine. I sit with Chet watching him beat today's crossword puzzle. Dad walks in from the cold with a deposit bag from the bank. Brooks turns on the monster and walks to the front; he has to talk to Dad.

"Jack, I got an interview later on today. Ever heard of a guy named Moss?"

Chet overhears like always. His ears perk up to listen, so do mine. "Yeah, I know the asshole." Dad half ignores Brooks's good news.

"Well, he's got a couple of warehouses, and they need a dock loader. I think it pays pretty good."

"Do what you want, but remember, the guy is an asshole. He's got more money than God, and he thinks he is."

Brooks leaves right after the lunch rush. I help restock and clean up. Shelly and Mark bowl a little. The bowling alley is empty and even more empty when Brooks is gone. No one talks very much. I can see the pressure cooking in Mom's eyes—we can't afford to pay Brooks. She knows it and so does Dad.

I ask Mom for a quarter to play the jukebox, but my timing is off. She snaps back, "No, we don't have any money." She isn't really talking to me, she is talking to herself. I back away and pretend I never asked.

About then, Uncle Brooks bounces in and plops on a stool at the counter. Mom's at the counter, shoving the last of the napkins into the silver holder. I stop reading all the songs I won't be playing. Brooks has good news. "I got the job."

Mom breathes a sigh of relief; she sounds like the broaster when it's done. "When do you start?"

"I have to get some paperwork filled out and then wait for the drug testing results."

"I told you, the guy's an asshole," Dad hollers from down on the lanes.

After we eat dinner at the snack bar, we sit waiting for Dad to take us home. Mom needs to work the late shift so she can do the bills. I've noticed a few things: we don't use the sesame seed buns anymore, we ran out of small paper cups, and it doesn't look like we are getting any more, and the chicken comes in a different bag. Things are getting tighter. However, Dad did get his custom-made ball, it's green. Green is his favorite color. It's best if we leave Mom alone when she works on the bills. Yesterday, I also noticed that the meat delivery guy took Dad outside. I don't know what they said, but it wasn't good. And Mr. Dawson wasn't as friendly to me. Usually, he cracks a smile and gives me a wink. Not yesterday.

"Come on, guys." Dad throws away the newspaper and grabs the keys. "Let's go, your Mother isn't in a good mood." We follow him out the door and I turn back to tell Mom good-bye. We drive home in Brooks's new car at thirty slow miles per hour. The house is its normal, unfriendly, cold self. The cellar door spits its warning, the ghost stays out of sight, but I can still hear him.

Dad turns on the TV and we go upstairs in a pack to get ready for bed. Dad said we can watch an hour of TV, and then we have to go to bed. I put on my nightgown, run down the stairs, and plop on the couch with Shelly and Mark.

"Jack...?" Brooks's hand offers Dad a beer.

What's he doing? We don't drink beer around here, he's going to cause trouble.

"Nothing like a cold one on a cold night." Brooks snaps the pull ring back.

My throat lands in my stomach. I can't believe what I'm seeing. Doesn't Brooks know how Dad gets when he drinks beer?

Dad looks at us because we are staring at him, waiting to see what he's going to do. I know what I'm going to do—I'm going to go call Mom. And right then with a smack, my bedroom door upstairs slams shut. Everyone jumps and looks at each other, I sit back down and listen carefully to the upstairs. Brooks stands there with the cold one still in his hand and looking upstairs.

Dad shakes his head, "Nah, that's okay, you go ahead."

Brooks sits down, "Must've been the wind," and drinks Dad's beer first.

All of us breathe out at the same time. I thank God under my breath. I watch Brooks drinking beer, waiting for Dad to change his mind. What if he does when we go to bed? I don't know what to do. He has a whole six-pack, and I know one thing for sure, people don't drink one beer like you do when you drink a Coke. "Dad, can I call Mom?"

"If you want to, go ahead. Ask her when she'll be home." He continues to flick the TV back and forth.

I go to the kitchen and dial hard with my finger. "Hi, Mom."

"What are you doing?" Mom sounds surprised.

"Nothing."

"Is everything okay?" Her voice drops a bit.

"Yeah, when are you coming home?"

"I'll leave here at ten."

"Okay, I'll see you later." I want to tell her something, but I don't know what. Maybe I scared myself.

"Honey, you guys go to bed soon, you have school tomorrow."

I hang up and think how much I love her. I can't wait for her to get home. I really don't like being without her for very long. I watch the clock more than I watch TV.

Dad is bored with *All in the Family* and claps his hands. "That's it, you all need to go to bed. Your mother will kill me if she sees you kids awake."

We slowly drag our feet and think of fifteen things we have to do before we go to bed. Mark doesn't wait till later, he immediately comes in our room to sleep. I try, but the thought of Mom not being home keeps me awake.

I tell myself that I'm just scaring myself for no reason, but the reason won't go away. I listen carefully for our car. I know the sound. I wait and listen. The listening starts to drive me crazy. I decide I have to see what time it is. I challenge the stairs alone and tip toe down. "Dad, can I get a drink?" I know he'll say yes, but I ask anyway. Anything to pass the time and get me out of my head.

"Sandra, why didn't you get one from the bathroom?" Dad is tired and not in the mood for a lot of chitchat.

"I forgot."

"Go ahead, but then get your ass in bed."

I go into the kitchen and look at the clock. It's eleven o'clock. She's late. If she left at ten, then she should be home at ten thirty at the latest. Where is she? Does Dad know she's late?

"Dad," I say to him, "tell Mom to come give me a kiss good night when she gets home." I am scared, really scared. I can't stop it.

"Okay honey, good night." He doesn't get the hint.

I walk upstairs and feel an eerie sense; I turn around to see who's there, no one. Of course not and none of the windows are open either, it's winter for God's sake. I know it was him who slammed the door shut. I may not be able to see him right now, but he's here, watching. He's not going to hurt me, he's just here. I think he's on my side, I can feel it.

I lay in bed for what feels like hours, and now I know Mom's in trouble. I can't help myself, I dash downstairs. The living room is dark, the TV is off, and Brooks is asleep on the couch. Dad's pacing, looking out the window and has the Worried Look on his face. He sees me at the hallway door where I stand like a soldier, frozen, waiting for my orders. He wants to say *Go to bed honey*. But then a car pulls up, it's not the right sound and *slam* goes a car door. Dad is already at the kitchen door to meet her.

She is cold, wet, pissed, and scared.

"Ardell, what in the hell?" Dad acts a little mad, unlike a few minutes ago.

"I'll tell you what in the hell, I ran off the road in this Goddamn storm. That car is a piece of shit. I hit an ice patch and spun out twice before I hit the ditch. Didn't you even wonder where the hell I've been?"

I'm behind Dad, listening and worrying. I want to hug her, but now is not the time. She hasn't even noticed me yet. Now her eagle eyes have landed on the empty beer cans and a silence takes over— it's so loud no one can speak.

Brooks stumbles into the kitchen in his boxers, scratching his head, "Ardell, are you okay?"

"Hell no, I'm not okay. I've been standing in the cold after I crawled out of the car window, stuck in the ditch, you asshole." She gives Dad and Brooks a dirty look. "Thank God for this farmer who saw me freezing my ass off." Mom kicks off her wet shoes, and they land by the oven. She sees me now and tries to calm down. It doesn't work.

Dad keeps a safe distance, "Honey, I'm so glad you're not hurt." He lowers his head, he knows he waited too long. "I would've come looking for you."

"Yeah, right." Mom shoves her way past the two idiots and bends down with her hands on my shoulders. My knees are wobbling and they feel like water. "Come on, Sandra." She's not going to talk anymore, she's too mad.

21

Weeks have passed and the only good thing happening around here is that Mom isn't mad at Dad. Business is slow or, as they would say, it's dead. I don't like that word. The money is tight, real tight, and I can hear Dad wishing again. He wishes all the time lately.

"Ardell, I think I can do it." Dad throws down his pencil.

"What in hell are you thinking?" Mom is waiting as she dries her hands over and over again. "You're really going to enter the Honky Tonk?"

"If I can get my average to two hundred and thirty I can qualify. Right now I'm around two hundred and ten."

"Well, it would sure be nice if you won the $100,000, but we don't have the money to get you there."

Dad picks up his scratch paper and shows her his figures. "I can do this. I'll take sandwiches and sleep in the car. The way I figure it, all I need is a hundred dollars. Ardell, we have no choice; this place is going to take us down with it."

Mom is reluctant and desperate at the same time. "All right fine, but remember that this is your idea, not mine." Mom wants a signed confession in blood. She shoves the paper back across the counter to him.

Dad bowls day and night getting in shape for the tournament. Chet coaches and encourages with a strong belief that Dad will win the pot of gold at the end of the rainbow. The fever is so high that even I believe that he'll win. It is only a matter of time. I'm in my head spending the money and living in a nice house with a good car and lots of fresh food. I practice being snotty to my friends. I'll show Elizabeth who's got money; I can't wait to show off and have more friends than her. Dad's wishing about winning is starting to feel like reality.

"Dad, you want me to bowl with you?"

"Not now honey," he throws his hand towel my way, "I have to concentrate."

"Okay." I understand and walk back to my seat at the counter. Mom works the counter and the chicken window while Dad is hard at work bowling for our lives. His crackers and Coke sit next to him while he throws another strike. "Goddamn, I'm good." He snaps his fingers against his thigh. "Hell, I'm ready now."

I watch with big eyes and bigger hopes. Every strike means I'm that much closer to being a snob. Dad wipes the sweat from his left hand and talks to his ball as he sizes up the next strike. I don't look this time, I listen, I know the sound of a strike like Mom knows the words to her songs. The sound has perfect rhythm to it. Each pin hits the next with a tap that echoes, the ball hits a certain place in the back board, and the pins follow its lead. Dad is the conductor of the lanes, and the ball is the conductor of each pin, and they have to fall. This is more than a game—it is a chance to prove who we are.

"Bill, your elbow is curving to the outside, and your release is off to the right." Chet observes cautiously.

"Oh shit, Chet," Dad throws away the advice, "I'm consistent and my average is up to two hundred and thirty in less than a month. I think my arm is just fine."

Chet addresses him with a fatherly voice and stern eyes. "Bill, you better remember one thing. Bowling here is one thing, but you're going to be bowling with a hundred and fifty of the best bowlers in the Tri States. You're going to have to get used to competition."

"Hell, Chet, I'm not afraid to compete. I'll join the league this week and we'll see."

Dad does just that—the Monday night advanced men's league. It's about ten minutes to seven and he's down in the pit meeting his team. I've never seen him on a team before.

I ask Mom if I can go watch, and she nods her head. I drop my duties behind the counter. Mark and Shelly join me after they realize it's boring over there at the counter.

The air is thick with competition. Chet was right, it is a lot different. The team crowds around each other shaking hands and smiling about nothing. I watch the Olympics of Fairly West Virginia about to begin. Dad is nervous I can tell, he has a funny look on his face. Shelly and Mark eat like we are watching TV. They don't know that Dad has to prove himself tonight.

The first bowler is up; he's on the other team. He lines up his release and slowly walks off his steps. I want him to miss, or at least get a split. He bowls and gets an eight, this is an easy pickup. Dad looks straight ahead and focuses on only the pins that he'll be hitting next. The guy is tall and lanky, probably goes to church twice a week and has two kids. He is nice and not committed to the game like some of the others. There are five on each team, and half of them are out for blood.

I heard Mom say once that the men around here know their balls better than their wives at home. I am stunned at how much emotion is in the air. I bet I could capture it in my cup. Bowler number one finishes his turn and picks up his spare. It's going to be a tough game. Now it's Dad's turn. The expectation is high, not only from himself, but from the other bowlers—they know he's going to the Honky Tonks. And it's not just two teams playing against each other, but all of them against Dad. Each of them wants to show him he's not good enough. This must be some sort of man thing. It looks like they're there to encourage him, but not really—they're fake smiles, with little knives behind their backs. I can see it, I hope Dad can. He stands with his back turned to the crowd and his face toward the pins that hold his fate. The pressure is about to burst inside me. I want this to be over. He stands there a little longer than normal. I close my eyes and listen.

Shelly eats her last bite while teasing Mark.

Mark socks her in the arm, "Quit kicking me under the table, I know it's you."

"You're nothin' but a big baby." She hits back.

I say nothing as the ball is about to be released into the air. I hear it hit the lane and the furious ball rolls. It takes what seems like forever to reach the target. And finally with a roar, the sound of perfection is not my imagination. I open my eyes and each pin is dead. Laying there helpless and waiting for the stretcher to pick them up.

"Nice one Bill."

"Yeah, those pins didn't have a chance." Dad gloats with a hint of bashfulness. He is so relieved to open with a strike.

As he returns to his seat, he throws a quick smile our way. Meantime, the men put down their knives and pick up their balls. It's war and Dad has thrown down a strike. The game continues, and it takes a long time before it's Dad's turn again.

"I got to go to the bathroom," Shelly says. We get up and go together. We walk with a wiggle in our butts to show off. Chet can't help but snicker. Mom is still slapping hamburgers away at the grill. Tonight's a busy night, and whenever it's league night, both of them have to work. I open the bright orange bathroom door and take a giant step in. Shelly follows.

As we come out and start our silly wiggle walk, the front door opens and in comes Mr. Moss. He's extra tall tonight, and he has on his black, long wool coat—he's the only one in town who has this kind of a coat. I can't help staring, and his eyes meet mine and then skim over me to Shelly. He winces—it's the girl who took the crown away from his niece. The whole bowling alley feels him before they see him—every single person looks like they got caught with their hand in the cookie jar. This man has power and control. I wonder if it's his money or if he really has a special power? I know he owns everything and threatens everyone, but is that enough to rule the town, like people say?

He walks over to Chet and says a few uncomfortable words and moves through the bowling alley like a snake. Shelly and I stand where we are and watch him. He hovers over the crowd and checks on all his people. He shoots a look of contempt toward Dad, but Dad loves it. He's the only one who likes challenging him, from a distance of course. The balls move slower down the lanes, and the conversations die down to a murmur. It looks like he's looking for someone.

"He's probably getting ready to evict someone," I whisper to Shelly. Mr. Moss walks back through the lobby area and right over to the snack bar. Mom's back is turned and she jumps at his presence. I can't hear them but I can see her shaking her head no. She has on that very polite, "you're-an-asshole" smile. She returns to the chicken broasting area. I hope it's not us he's looking for. He exits the building like a king, while a handful of peasants beg for his friendship. It makes me sick. Shelly and I run to the counter, practically falling over the stools as we wait for Mom to return. It doesn't look good for business if we go behind the counter too much; when it's slow it doesn't matter. But you never know when the health inspector is coming by for a checkup. He and Mr. Moss could be brothers.

"Mom, what did he want?"

"Oh, aren't you the nosy twins. He's looking for Brooks."

"Umm, I wonder what he did."

"Now who said anything about doing something," Mom lifts her eyes and shrugs her shoulders, "he probably wants to talk about work."

We all know better than that. Brooks has been hanging around Mr. Moss's only son, Peter, for the past few months. I bet you that's what it is. Peter Moss is nothing like his father, he is nice.

Mark is falling asleep at the table where we left him. "Go sit with your brother, you guys," Mom plays down the event, "and as soon as your Dad is finished we'll go."

We obey and quickly butt out. I don't know the score, but Dad looks pretty good. He's not too cocky, but he is definitely a lot more relaxed.

Mr. Shift, the gas station guy, is bowling his last frame. With dirt under his fingers, and the crack of his butt showing, he's begging the bowling gods for his next strike. He's found his religion and the pins are his gospels. He takes his stand and barely lines up his release. His count off is four but he lets go at three, this ball is a wild one. I don't even have to watch, seven pins down, but it's a split and there's no way he'll pick it up. Dad says that if you get a split, it's your own fault, you didn't release with the proper attitude. I don't know about that, I see a lot of people with great attitudes that still get a split. The next two bowlers are great, they strike and that's that.

I take a deep breath, it's the tenth frame, the last chance to do anything. Dad rubs his arm. I hope his scar isn't bothering him—I can tell that the nasty scar is bothering him. His back is to us and the familiar ritual is about to commence. He steps off his mark, and I count off his steps for him. He releases the ball with no hesitation, the ball rolls fast. I don't even have time to close my eyes. *Smaaack.* The ball smacks the pins to the right a little bit, and sure enough, it's a split on the last frame. That's worse than a gutter ball.

All he can do is pick it up. He waits on the deck for his ball to return and doesn't think twice about nodding to the others how bad this is. He goes to his mark, and in a split second he smashes that ball down the alley. He hits the two pins and shoots one of them over to the last pin, which falls down without hesitation. But this is still not enough to win. His team has won, but he hasn't. Two of the other guys beat his score by at least twenty points. As they say their good-byes and congratulations, I hear from the crowd, "Oh yeah, he's a big man, he'll win the Honky Tonks." Another man grins, "Hell, my grandmother could bowl better than him." And then a grabby old man in his nineties pops off, "You got to be above average, way above average. Hell they're going to clean his clock up there in Dayton."

Mom wipes the sweat from her forehead, and the damp loose hair curls extra tight around her face. It looks pretty, but she doesn't. She's tired. It's a whole different kind of sweat that dangles, not like

Phoenix after a show. She's throwing hamburgers instead of kisses to the audience.

Dad is the last man out. He takes off his bowling shoes and wonders what happened as he walks up to the counter. Chet acts busy putting away the night receipts, saying nothing to Dad when he passes him.

Dad takes the grill scrubber from Mom. "Ardell, why don't you take the kids home, it's getting late."

The pots and pans are stacked in the back, while Mom scrubs hard on the grill with steel wool. They must get it clean for tomorrow. It's the first thing the health inspector looks for, and it's not out of the question for him to be here in the morning waiting for his chance to shut us down. He loves his job and he hates Dad. "All right then," Mom says, "I'll see you in a bit."

Mom is quiet but cracks a joke here and there along the drive. It looks like she's thinking *what if?* What if we land in a ditch?

We run in the back door—no one uses the front door. If we go in the front door, we pass by the chains hanging loosely from the cellar door.

"Look Mom, I can blow fog from my mouth." Mark blows air out of his mouth and shows her how cold it is in the house. I walk outside and blow. I can see my breath just as good as I can in the house.

"I know honey, it's cold." Mom goes to the wood box and tries to find wood or coal, but we all know we're out. She tips the box upside down, and I hear just a few pieces of ash and dirt fall into the stove. She strikes a match and we have heat for a few minutes. We all gather around for those few minutes. It's another sign we're poor. Mom looks sad and frustrated.

"That's okay, I'm not cold," I say.

"Me neither." Shelly moves away from the cold stove. We try to make her feel better. She really gets sad when we notice things like no food, no heat, and no clothes. I can practically see her heart tear in two. Mark opens the refrigerator, "Mom, I'm hungry."

"Didn't you eat dinner?" Mom struggles. She knows there's nothing she can do.

"No, I fell asleep." There is nothing in the refrigerator at all. It's pointless to open it.

"Honey, I'm sorry but there isn't anything to eat."

Shelly grabs an old paper bag from underneath the kitchen table. "Mom, here's some candy bars Dad brought home. I don't know if they're any good. He said he got them for free. The vending machine guy was gonna throw them away."

Mom looks inside and opens one. The chocolate is kind of white but most of it looks good. She gets a knife and cuts off the bad parts, and Mark happily eats the candy bar. Shelly and I follow his example, "Mom they really don't taste too bad, honest." But truthfully they are a little dry. Mostly I'm shocked to learn that candy bars rot. Mom looks more depressed than ever as she watches us eat those candy bars. She's always fair with us; she has us pick straws in real tight spots or she monitors taking turns with us. She never ever wants to be unfair, but tonight she has to. And I think that's what hurts the most. Eating candy bars for dinner was not her idea of fair.

Days turn into weeks, and weeks turn into early spring and business remains the same. We are broke, and yet somehow it's working out. The snow is melting and the Honky Tonks are only a few short weeks away. When things break around the snack bar, they stay broke. The soda machine is fine.

Saturday morning we go to the bowling alley early. I barely remember the drive it's so early, but leagues start at nine o'clock. It's not our favorite thing to do on a Saturday morning, but we have no choice. Dad turns on the fryer and slowly but surely the grease starts to melt. Mom pulls out the patties and hot dogs that she thinks we'll need for today from the freezer. I chop up the lettuce and Shelly vacuums around the tables and chairs. Mark is not able to reach anything, so he hangs around Chet while he, too, gets ready for business.

The Saturday bowlers arrive on time, filing in with balls and shoes in hand, ready to prove themselves. It's funny to watch. Some teams are here to bowl, but others, especially the ladies' team from the Baptist church, are here for one reason—to catch flying gossip. The teams come from all three counties, it's a social bazaar more than anything else. Everyone acts like they haven't seen each other in years, smiling and patting each other on the back. Saturday leagues are mixed. The teams vary from all women to all men and then both. Everyone is older. Once in awhile there will be a homely younger person. I think the older ones are trying to fix the homely ones up. One thing is for certain, you *must* marry here in West Virginia. It's one of the *most* important things you do around here. I already know I'm not going to marry until I'm at least twenty-five or maybe twenty-six. I just don't want to.

Mom always tells Shelly and me, "Live with a man before you marry him, things change." If she said it once, she said it a hundred times. If she said that out loud around here, she'd probably get tarred and feathered.

The weird thing is, no one looks real happy. When I get married, I won't have that look on my face, the look that says bored or miserable. It's not for me. Mom says they're all backward around here and haven't they ever heard of women's rights. The women are brought up to marry and care for the children, and shut up that's it. She constantly reminds us of who we are and who we aren't. *No girl of mine is going to need a man to take care of her, I'll make damn sure of that.*

It's lunchtime and it's really busy around here. Mom and Dad spit orders at each other. The food orders pile up, hanging in front of Dad at the grill. I like watching the cash register open and close. I hope we made some money today, but every time I think we have, they say "not much." I quit asking. Shelly and I play Old Maid and pass the time. It's still too cold to go outside.

Some of the teenagers are here playing the jukebox and sucking on pop. They all know us, and sometimes I get to listen in on their conversations. I know each one of their names. I practice remembering them just in case they might talk to me. By now, more of the cool ones enter and join the crowd. I decide quickly, it's time to put away the

Old Maid. They might think I'm a kid. Shelly lost so she has to clean up. I sit at the table wondering when I will be a teenager. The front doors open and in walks Regina, her hair damp and curly, her nose red, and her body wrapped up tight in Uncle Brooks's coat. "Shelly, look there's Regina, I think she's wearing Brooks's coat." The closer she gets the closer the truth is: she's is wearing my Uncle Brooks's coat. How dare her; who does she think she is?

"Hey, ya all." Her smile is as friendly as each one of her curls. She is short and happy, and has the curliest auburn hair hanging down to her waist. She's about sixteen and I think she's the prettiest girl in town. I've never seen her without a smile. She's a lot different than the other girls that hang out here. She wants to go to college and move out of these mountains.

But what does that matter? She has my coat on. I sit with Shelly at our table tapping my foot, waiting and wondering with jealousy why she is wearing Uncle Brooks's coat. That's his special Navy coat. Regina walks over and asks, "Hey, ya' all seen Brooks?"

I shake my head. I can't even look at her.

"Maybe he's at work." Shelly offers some kind of an answer.

"Well, that's fine, I'll just wait for him here. What y'all playing?"

"Old Maid, wanna play?"

I kick Shelly's foot under the table.

"No thanks, I'm gonna sit with my friends a spell."

Of course she doesn't want to play Old Maid, how stupid. "Shelly, that was a stupid question."

Shelly has no idea what my problem is. "What?"

"Never mind."

Regina simply sashays off. I watch my coat leave. She won't even take it off. She laughs, chats, and sips a Coke, all the while wrapped in my uncle's arms. The coat fits her just about as good as it does me, in fact, it fits me better. I chew my lip and cuss under my breath. I thought I was special—no one wears his coat but me. And now, Regina. "I'm going to make a cherry Coke." I huff off to the counter where I pray she'll give me back the coat. I stand at the soda fountain hoping that someone will notice me. She's surrounded by six of her friends and one really cute guy, but I know he's too old. Regina turns and feels me staring at her. I'm not, I'm staring at my coat. Maybe Brooks doesn't even know she has it and that's why she's waiting for him. I bet that's it. He took her to the movies and she accidentally stole it. He didn't give it to her.

The cute one, Bobby, speaks to me. "Hey Sandra, make me one of your cherry Cokes."

I make no eye contact and talk down to the sink. "Sure."

Mom slaps me on the butt and smiles.

As I carefully and precisely create the drink, I think to myself, "This is for Bobby, the cute one. I wonder if he wants me to bring it to him?" I will, and then maybe I can sit in.

Just as the last of the bubbles slows down, he gets up. "How much?"

Mom steps in. "Seventy-five cents."

He hands me a dollar and says, "Keep the change." Darn it, he thinks I am a kid who plays Old Maid. I kick my foot on the box of napkins below. I hate being a kid.

Shelly walks up to the counter. "Can I have one?"

"Yes," I give her a dirty look. "But don't ever ask me to play Old Maid again." She looks at me as if I'm crazy—we both know I was the one who asked her to play.

Brooks saunters in and right past me. "Hey Brooks, where ya' been?" I try again, "Hey Brooks." No use, he's on his way to Regina. Maybe he wants his coat back.

"Hey darlin'," he says to her, "sorry I'm late, I had some things to take care of.

Darlin'. He called her *darlin'*. That's *my* name. I look to Shelly to see if what I think I heard was correct. Shelly's eyes are big and she's about to laugh. I don't believe it—Regina is Brooks's girlfriend!

I have to talk to Mom. I jump off the crate and down to the floor and run to the back. I slow down just a little so I don't slip on chicken fat. "Mom," I catch my breath, "I think Regina and Brooks are boyfriend and girlfriend."

"Oh now aren't you Miss Nosy Nelly."

"She's got his coat on and everything."

"You're probably right." Mom squeezes the burger, grease spatters all over. "I know he's been dating her for a couple of weeks."

"Do you think he likes her?" My hands land firmly on my hips.

"Well now, what do you think?" Mom waits a half a second and answers. "Of course he does. Now just mind your business and leave him alone."

I turn and walk back to the front. I have more to say, but she doesn't.

"Hey Brooks," I stand right in front of him.

"Hey there, San, whatcha doing?" He puts his hand on my shoulder and squeezes a little.

I stare at him. He sits there with his arm around his little filly. "Not much, just sittin' around." We haven't seen him in a while. He doesn't sleep over at our house at night as much as he used to. I miss him and so does Shelly and Mark. Our pal is missing and a new thing called a girlfriend has taken over. There's no room for her. I wish he knew that.

The following Wednesday night Dad and Shelly bowl in the father-daughter tournament. They bowl for the trophy; it's about two feet tall, and the winners will get their names engraved. If they win, this will be the second time Shelly's name and picture will be in the newspaper. I have another fit of jealousy as Dad and Shelly throw a few practice balls before the game. I tried to be Dad's partner, but it wasn't my grade, it was hers. She has all the luck. Although, she's nervous as heck, and I don't blame her. She'd better not screw up. But if she does, Dad won't hit her, he'll hit me and Mark. If it was me, I'd bowl so good. I'd probably beat Dad cause I'd be scared of losing, and also cause I'd want to show him how good I am.

Each father and daughter plays against everyone else. It's not a league, it's each two-man team for themselves. All ten lanes quickly fill as it gets closer to seven o'clock. I bite my lip, and when I realize what I am doing, I stop and chew on my hair instead. The fathers are all serious bowlers and the daughters aren't. Dad has a good chance to win since Shelly can bowl. Shelly is still really nervous. We both know this could be either really good or really bad. It depends on Dad. If he takes it too seriously, he might start getting mad at Shelly. Or he could be a good sport and just have fun.

The bowling begins, and I can feel Shelly's heart pound down on the lanes. They have to bowl three games and the team with the highest score wins. There are no second chances. Dad wins tonight's tournament or forfeits his gifts as a bowler. I can't watch right now, Mom needs help in the kitchen. The chicken window is backed up and there must be four hundred little kids here tonight.

"Goddamn it," Mom throws her towel in the sink, "this is the last time I'll do this. How in the hell am I supposed to run both areas?"

I listen and pour drinks, my job is to do all the little stuff and make change. I really want to see the game.

Mom whirls by me on her way to the back. "Here, take this scratch pad and add up the order and then ring in the total. Be sure to count the money back into their hand. Okay?" She runs for the buzzer as another batch of dead chickens calls out. I am scared of counting money, I'm not sure if I'm ready for this.

"How much is the chili dog and fries?" I hear the question but I'm not sure who asked it.

I lean over the counter and there is a boy with a wad of dollar bills. Good, it's only a kid, I can add it up. As I add seventy-five cents and eighty-five cents, I hear cheering from the pits. I can't see what just happened, but I have to start over. "It's one dollar and sixty cents."

"Can I have a small Coke?"

Why did he have me add it up if he wanted a Coke too? I want this kid out of here. Another customer and four more kids. I'm trying to breathe and not pass out. "Can I help you?" Words echo in my head, I hate waiting on people.

"Yes, we'll have four medium cherry Cokes and five French fries, and I'll have two hot dogs."

"What? I mean could you say that again?" This time I listen real hard and write at the same time. This is not fair, Shelly gets to bowl and I get to sweat. Mom is just as busy, and we both need help. The line of customers gets bigger and sighs of impatience get louder. "Can you believe this? A person could get old waiting." That's it! I can't help myself. "You could always leave," I mumble aloud.

Mom overhears and runs in. Her eyes scare me as she gasps at the wall of people and the poor bleeding scratch pad. I have to count the change back and write the orders and pour the drinks. I take a second out and finally get Mark's attention. "Mark, go tell me how they are doing, ask Chet for me." I continue my job without missing a beat when I hear, "I don't want any catsup on my burger." I stop counting and turn my head to see what kind of person doesn't eat catsup on a hamburger. Mrs. Moss. She's puffing away on a cigarette and her feet are too small for her high heels. She's the only woman I know who wears high heels for no reason. I should have guessed, of course, her little niece would be bowling with her brother. I can't believe I'm going to miss this. I'm running out of cups and pennies.

"Mommmm," I yell, "I need some help."

"Get it yourself." She rubs the back of her arm across her forehead.

I'm not the enemy, they are, each and every one of these hungry little monsters with purple and red stuff all over their faces. I reach for the pennies as Mom rips open another box of medium cups. She drops them all over the floor. "Shitttt!" The parents in line are shocked but not as shocked as me. Who's going to pick up the cups? "Mark, get back here."

He runs up like he's in trouble. He starts spitting out the facts, "Dad and Shelly are winning by…"

"By what?"

"I forgot."

"Never mind. Pick up these cups. Quick, just throw them away." He looks at me like I'm crazy.

"Mark, just do what your sister says." The poor guy just went to get me the score and now he's in trouble. He scrambles on the floor as Mom and I trip over him and accidentally kick him.

"I would like no onions and extra mustard." I don't know how to write that down quickly, and my brain can't remember anymore. The people keep coming. And down in the pits, through the crowd, I see Shelly. She's smiling and Dad is patting her on the back. Lettuce is everywhere and now we're so far behind that it's funny. "Mom, can you tell when one order stops and another one begins? I can't."

"Sandra, just do your best, that's all we can do." The buzzer goes off and the chicken people are driving up. Mom leaves the grill, "Watch those, I'll be right back."

"What, watch them burn?"

"Don't be a smart ass." Mom shakes her head and laughs at us both.

I pop the straws through the last seven sodas sitting on the counter and hand out the whole order. "Here you go," I lean over and read Mom's total, "That will be six dollars and seventy-two cents." They hand me a twenty dollar bill. I gulp. Oh no, I hope I don't screw up. This is a lot of money.

I work at catching up, and the end of the line is near when I notice the police come in. They both stand in the center of the bowling alley looking around. This is normal, they usually come in at least once a night just to say hi. But I notice something different about them, they are looking for someone. They hold their hands higher than normal and their eyes are a little closer together. First, they go to Mrs. Moss who sits alone with her hamburger at her table above the pit. I watch through the crowd. People are in and out of the way. I see her lift her hands and shake her head no. They say something calming and walk her over to a corner area. They talk seriously. She grabs her purse and storms out, her fat little feet hanging over her shoes as she bounces out the door.

"What's going on?" Mom stands at the counter wiping her hands.

"I don't know. They just told Mrs. Moss some bad news though."

"Come on nosy, it's none of our business."

Just then the wheels turn, and the police start heading over our way. The entire bowling alley is watching out of the corner of each eye. I tell myself it's a soda they want, but they are still carrying bad news—it's written all over their faces.

"Mrs. Vaughan, is Brooks Vaughan your brother-in-law?"

Mom doesn't want to hear so she won't answer the question. Her lips are tight across her mouth. "Sandra, go get your father."

"I can't—he's bowling right now." I'm not going anywhere till I hear what they want to say. My hands are squeezing each other.

Mom mutters, "Yes."

Mark is on the floor, still trying to pick up all three hundred dirty, smashed cups.

"Mrs. Vaughan, this is serious," the tall lanky officer continues, "he's been picked up on possession of marijuana charges and illegal intent to sell. The guy we found him with also had loaded weapons." Mom and I watch his mouth continue to move. "You can contact him tomorrow."

"Who was he with?" Mom finds a question and blurts it out. Her face goes from mad to ashamed and back to scared.

"Peter Moss." They both turn around at the same time and leave the bad news hanging in the air like a bomb.

She sucks in the bad air and bites her lip. She turns and goes straight into the chicken room. I stand there with my hands folded tight, and Mark just sits still for a second. I want to tell Dad, but that wouldn't be a good idea right now. I follow Mom into the back. "Mom, what are we going to do?"

"Not a Goddamn thing," she is foaming at the mouth. "He screws up around here, and he's going to get himself out. What the hell is he thinking? Drugs in a small town in West Virginia for God's sake. They'll lock him up and throw away the key." She notices that she has now scared the living shit out of me and Mark. "I'm just mad right now." She tries to soothe us and take back her words. "It'll be fine, we'll get Uncle Brooks out. It's okay Mark." She turns around, and at the same time she tries to turn her story around, but she is so mad she could melt the grease in the fryer.

In the commotion I forgot all about the game. I run up to Shelly and Dad. The look on their face is undeniable—they are kicking butt. It's a sight all right. I ignore Mom as she yells for me to "get back here." She needs help and she is still mad as hell.

I hurry back to Mom. Just then I hear it. Yes, she picks up the spare. Shelly and Dad are jumping for joy. I think to myself, he won't be jumping for long when he hears where his brother is.

Mom and I clean up while Mark eats a hamburger, and this time he doesn't fall asleep. "Mom," I ask cautiously, "I want to see them get the trophy. It's the last frame."

"Go ahead," she allows with a huff.

Mrs. Moss's brother Jerry and his little girl are the last bowlers. Jerry has a terrible drag to his right leg. They say it has something to do with a hunting accident. Somebody shot him when he was out hunting with some friends, no one was at fault, they were just drinking. But they still aren't very good bowlers. Chet is behind the booth getting the trophy. The newspaper man is standing real close to Dad and Shelly. Everyone claps and the camera flashes. Shelly is hungry and tired. Dad is ten feet tall and full of himself.

Chet announces: "Tonight's winner is Mr. Jack Vaughan and his lovely daughter Shelly."

He squeezes Shelly and another picture is flashing. I am so jealous, I'd give anything to be standing next to him.

Mom waits until all the bowlers have said their last good-byes before she tells him about Brooks.

"What do you mean jail?" Dad drops the happy look so fast I can hear it hit the floor. "That asshole, I knew he'd get thrown in the slammer sooner or later. It's probably that girl he's been hanging out with. No, it's probably that Peter Moss. I hope Peter's going to bail his ass out, I certainly don't have the money."

Dad huffs and puffs around while he cleans the grill. "Well, let's just see how good a friend that old Peter really is." Dad spouts and spits and yells at Brooks, who's not there, while he attempts to help Mom.

"And what about the weapons in his trunk? Hell, show me a guy in this town who doesn't have a gun on him or in his car. That's a bunch of bullshit." Dad goes on and on, and back and forth, defending his brother and crucifying him at the same time.

Two days later, Regina comes into the bowling alley. She's not herself. Maybe it's that she misses Brooks, after all he's still in jail. Grandma is on her way. Regina goes up to Mom. "Ardell, have you heard any more from Brooks?" Her happy face isn't happy and her curls aren't as curly, she's so worried. She's more worried than Dad. And Dad is pretty upset.

"No honey," Mom tells her, "haven't you heard from him?"

"No, they say I'm too young to visit. You have to be eighteen." Regina is torn up inside and sad on the outside. "Ardell, I need to talk to you."

"Okay, what is it." Mom stops cutting the lettuce and puts down the knife.

"I know this is not a good time, but you see—" Regina puts her head down and a tear falls.

"Regina, what's wrong? He'll be out soon. I'm sure they'll reduce the charges."

"It's not that."

"Oh my dear God. Tell me it's not what I think it is." Mom is full of fear, her eyes say so. Regina sits down at the table.

"What am I going to do? I haven't told anyone."

Mom is without words, her face is white. "Do you know for sure?"

"Yes, I'm three weeks late and I can tell." Regina has a heart full of fear as she confesses, "Ardell, it was my first time. He said I *couldn't*."

Mom looks like something inside is screaming. She doesn't want to panic Regina. She quietly takes control, "All right honey, let's calm down and we'll figure this out. Does Brooks know yet?"

"He knew I was late before he went to jail, but he doesn't know for sure."

22

Regina has been hanging around the bowling alley a lot more with Mom and Dad the past several months. I don't think she knows what else to do. She told her parents about the baby, and I don't think they're real happy about it. Mom told her that she could come and live with us for awhile until she and Brooks figure things out. I think to myself, *Figure out what?* They're going to get married and have a baby, there's not much else to figure out. But at the same time I can sense that she is now a part of the family, and that the baby is my cousin. Oh, wow I didn't even think about that. It's all so strange; Brooks isn't like a real uncle with kids of his own, he's an uncle who's more like a big brother. Things are going to be different. Brooks will get out of jail in a couple of days. I overheard them all talking yesterday. Brooks has one week to get out of town and the charges will be dropped. It turns out that Mr. Moss is friends with Mr. Mayor, and I guess that's all that he needed to get his son and Brooks out of jail.

Dad enters from the kitchen, his apron tied on backwards. His face is as red as his hair. And he's breathing fire.

"That son of a bitch, who does he think he is? He can't make Brooks leave town."

Mom cools him off with words of wisdom. She reminds him sternly, "I know he's your brother, but face it, if he doesn't leave town, he'll go to prison for Christ's sake. And then there is the small matter of Regina and the baby."

Dad slides right on past the baby and into blame. "I can't believe that bastard and his money can own us like this. What would he do if he didn't have all his money? He'd have to scrape by like the rest of us."

"Oh, that's right," Mom has just about had enough of Dad's tirade, "it's Mr. Moss's fault. Hell, he just bought Brooks out of jail, for Christ's sake."

"Yeah, but if his spoiled little bastard Peter hadn't been such an asshole, none of this would've happened."

I move slowly around the tables pretending I'm wiping up spills and crumbs. Mom's right. Brooks has a lot to do with this, and not to mention he's messed up things around here. For instance, we won't be playing outside with Uncle Brooks anymore. Or, I won't be around him and Regina when the baby comes.

"You are the company you keep." Mom can't bite her tongue any longer, she lets Dad have it. "Let's also keep in mind who was with who that night, and what twenty-six-year old angel just knocked up a sixteen-year-old girl." Mom finishes sharply, and Dad fumbles for justice.

They go on a little further; Dad swearing that Mr. Moss's money had something to do with it, and Mom swearing that Brooks's lack of judgment might have had something to do with it. But the most disturbing point has yet to surface: Grandma. Grandma is going to come up here and knock a few heads around. She won't hit anyone, she'll just remind them how disappointed she is. I'll make sure I'm around for that little reminder. Mom tries real hard to keep on her smiling face so Regina won't worry too much, and Dad just slams things down a little harder. I stay out of the way with one ear turned toward the whispering. Everyone has on their thinking caps. They have less than two days to figure it all out.

Mom and Regina sit at the kitchen table. I brush my teeth and comb my hair before I go downstairs. "Regina, it'll be fine." Mom paces in the kitchen and worries enough for both of them.

Regina apologizes with every breath she takes. "I didn't mean for any of this to happen."

"Oh, I know that." Mom hands down some hard advice. "But you're in it, and now you have to live with it. The only question you need to ask yourself is, are you sure you love Brooks?"

I choke on my cinnamon toast and try not to cough while Regina thinks—I mean, thinks hard. That's one thing Mom can always do, make you think. Especially when you don't want to.

Finally Regina answers, "Yeah, I really do. But it's all happening so fast."

"You don't have to get married right away."

"I know." Regina looks more scared about not being married and pregnant than she does about being pregnant. I would have been more worried about pregnant, Mom would kill me.

A dead silence lingers until Mark comes pounding down the stairs. He wants some cereal. Mom helps him with the milk.

Dad pulls in with Brooks, I see them from the living room window. Brooks looks terrible, his face isn't shaved and his clothes are dirty. His head is low and so is his mood. Brooks usually has a big fat smile, but he's not smiling. Dad is still talking to him as they slow down in the driveway. It looks like a very serious conversation, or rather, a lecture. Brooks is listening. When he finally makes it into the house, Regina is waiting with a smile and hug. He sees her and it looks like his heart lifts as he grabs her and twirls her around in his arms. He barely notices us, "Oh, hey, you all." His smile returns to his face like an ice cream to a cone.

"Uncle Brooks, are you okay?" Mark says with a mouth full of Cheerios.

"Oh now, don't you worry about your old Uncle Brooks, hell, I'm fine. It was all just a little mistake, that's all." He rubs Mark's hair backward. "Now you all, stop your worrying."

I open the kitchen door and they are still sitting around the table talking. Mom raises her head and greets us, "Hey, what are you guys up to?"

"Nothing, we're bored. There's nothing to play."

"Why don't you go be bored outside and find something to do?" Dad means it and out we go. I catch Mom feeling kind of sorry for us. I find this so stupid—if we felt like playing we would be playing. Playing is not something you can control, there is no on or off switch.

Mark yells from the grass to the kitchen, "Brooks, wanna come outside and throw the ball?"

"No darlin', not right now."

I knew he'd say that. I bet Regina would love to come outside and play ball right now. Unfortunately their world just got much bigger and playing ball doesn't fit in.

I walk outside with Shelly and Mark, and we head for the fence. That's the best place to hang around. I climb to the top and wrap my legs under the board below. Shelly stands with her arms hanging on the top and her feet on the bottom board. Mark sits on the third board and rests his chin on the top.

"Sandra, do you think they'll get married?" Shelly asks.

"I think they're getting married today, before Grandma gets here."

"You mean," Shelly thinks about it, "Regina will be Aunt Regina?"

"Yeah, but I'm not going to call her Aunt Regina, heck she's too young." I lift my arms and fall backward, hanging on the fence with my legs. "You know, she's only about five or six years older than me." The blood rushes to my head.

"That's weird." Shelly takes a leaf off the tree. "You think she's in trouble for getting pregnant?"

"No, but I bet her mom and dad are mad."

Mark climbs higher to listen better and blurts out, "How long do you think she'll live here?"

"I don't know, maybe forever." I tease him.

"Nu-uhh." Mark fidgets around on the fence and gets a splinter in his finger. "Brooks has to leave town, Mr. Moss said so."

"Well, all I know is I'm not going to get pregnant when I get older." Shelly sums up the whole ordeal. "I'm going to be a dancer when I grow up."

Mark is tired of struggling with the splinter and wants to go and see Mom about it. I want to be a truck driver, but I won't say that out loud. But in my head I want to do a man's job, maybe even be a fireman.

We lean, fall back, and sit on the fence for awhile until it is okay to go back in the house. I know when it's been enough time for the adults to talk. I still can't believe that Brooks and Regina are now adults; heck, a couple of weeks ago they were drinking my cherry Cokes and holding hands in the bowling alley.

Dad and Mom go to the bowling alley. Mom is going to help him open up, and then she'll be back. As soon as the car is out of the driveway, Brooks and Regina go upstairs to their bedroom, he and Regina wanted to be alone so they could kiss. I watch everything change so quickly; Brooks is not himself and Regina is no longer a high school girl but a mother and my aunt.

The phone rings. I race for the phone and knock Mark into the wall. I put the phone down on the table and call out for Brooks. Usually Grandma talks to me forever, but today all she wanted was Brooks. He knows he is in trouble. Brooks is coming down the stairs; he pulls up his pants and tucks in his shirt as if Grandma could see him.

"Hello. Yes, Mother, I will. I am. We're going tomorrow for the blood test and...I know Mother, but there's nothing I can do about it now. Yes, I'll be home after we're married. Mother, don't worry, she's a great girl. All right, love you too. Bye now, see you soon."

Brooks turned into a father and a husband, right before my eyes, and nothing was going to stop him. Brooks heads straight for the stairs and *slam* goes the bedroom door. I feel the door slam and I'm shut out. Brooks has grown up and I have not.

One week passes, and next thing I know we're standing in the driveway saying good-bye to Brooks and his little bride. Regina gives me a big hug and says "thanks." For what, I'm not quite sure, but I know we'll be friends no matter what happens. They kept it simple and got married by the justice of the peace. They plan to go live with Grandma until Brooks finds a job. I'm sure he will, he has to. Nothing ever came of the charges, and as long as Brooks left town that was enough for Mr. Moss. His son, however, was never seen again. People say he was shipped to college where he can't get into trouble. I bet he'll come back one day and claim his rightful fortune, but not any-time soon.

Mom is sad to see them go, but I feel her heart strings pull for Regina and the voyage she's about to embark on. Dad, however, has bigger fish to fry, he's only a few weeks away from his fortune. His last opportunity to get us out of this bowling alley and back into the mainstream. We are all real tired of being poor and pretending we're not.

I see a big house with a swimming pool and my own room, nice things to wear, and a minibike. No one is more excited about our new life than me. Mom is starting to believe in this fantasy too. She can't help it, there's nothing else to do. Dad works hard on his arm and more on his game. No one is more convinced than he is that he'll win the championship.

Weeks roll by and not too much is said about anything but the Honky Tonks. We live, eat, and breathe bowling.

I say very little. Mostly I sit there and wait for the big day to come and our wishes to come true. We pull together and work as a team getting ready to go on the big trip. I'm not sure what happened to change their minds, but we are *all* going to Cincinnati. Mom systematically adds the bills and finds a penny here and a quarter there to support this adventure.

We don't tell anyone what we are doing. As Dad puts it, "It's none of their damn business what we do. The less they know the better." We are banned from talking to anyone about anything. Even Chet seems to be on the other side, we have to be cautious of everyone. It's almost like we have the secret potion and everyone is our enemy, they might steal it. As far as I can tell, we have nothing, but Dad seems to think we have something. He refers to everyone as "vultures" or "they" with one of his eyes squinted. He reminds me of Dirty Harry. He starts parking the car in weird places. I don't ask why. As a matter of fact, this is not a time for questions, it's all about acting. Acting suspicious and pretending not to like the vultures that circle our heads. I look up, and sure enough, not a bird anywhere, but I'm sure they're there, I just can't see them.

Mom is paranoid as she looks over her shoulder, "Bill, you take the kids home and I'll close up."

"Make sure you close out the drawer and bring it home." Dad orders.

I don't get it. What is going on? All we're doing is going to a bowling tournament. Every day the sun shines a little more and the people are starting to look a little more like vultures. I can see it. I think we're protecting the money that Dad's going to win next week. Once they find out we won, we're going to have to hide for a while. But that's okay, I understand now.

Dad is a smart-ass to most people or plain rude. Dad avoids the delivery guys like the plague. I think we owe them money. I think we owe everybody money. He thinks he has some kind of right— I'm not sure what that is.

Chet says a friendly "Good-bye." Dad says nothing at all. I'm very uncomfortable with the way he's treating people. Actually, I am embarrassed. I haven't seen my friends for weeks. No one talks about the future, past, or present. It's more of a minute-by-minute time period.

When we get home, Dad goes to the couch and takes off his shirt. He's watching TV and thinking at the same time. "Mark, go out to the truck and get me my cigarettes," Dad says.

Mark runs out and fetches his cigarettes. I wait for him at the door and grab the smokes from him.

"Dad, you need to quit smoking."

"Sandra, give me those." He runs over and grabs me. I laugh and hold them away as far as I can. "Give me my cigarettes."

"No…you need to quit."

He tickles me as we wrestle for the cigarettes. I break free and run toward the back. He chases me and grabs me a little too hard. "I said give them to me."

And without a warning or a reason Dad takes his fist and smashes me as hard as he can in the mouth. My hands immediately cover my face so he won't hit me again.

"I was just playing, I was gonna give them back." I look at my hands and there's blood on them. My nose is bleeding.

"You shouldn't of…" He forgets what to say next and turns around and walks away.

I just stand there, not knowing what to do. If I tell Mom, she'll get mad and then they might start fighting. I never understand why he has to hit me, I hate being hit in the face. I go into the bathroom and look at my nose. My nose doesn't hurt as much as my lip and cheek. I wash off the blood and watch it swirl down the sink. I guess it was my fault.

Later that night, Mom comes into the bedroom to say her goodnights. "Sandra, what's the matter, you're so quiet?"

"Nothing, I'm just tired."

"What happened to your cheek?"

Shelly speaks the words quietly, "Dad hit her for hiding his cigarettes."

"I was playing around and he got mad."

Mom sucks in some air and releases it with effort. "All right, I'm sure he didn't mean to." Mom sits back farther on the bed.

Mean to, yes he did, I hold the throbbing truth in my hand. It's funny how there's always an excuse when he hits me.

Mom continues, "Listen you guys, things are tough right now and we have to be careful with what we say and do. Just stay out of the way and be good." She tucks us in and leaves. I kick off the covers that she so tightly tucked around my feet and roll over onto my side.

I can't wait till this stupid Honky Tonks game is over. I hope he loses. No I don't, I take it back. God, I was just kidding, please let him win, please.

In the morning we all sit at the kitchen table. Dad leaves tomorrow and I don't know who's going to run the bowling alley.

Dad eats silently and Mom chews on her bottom lip; "Bill," she says, "maybe me and the kids should stay here."

He thinks for a minute, "No, you should come along, it'll be fun. It won't cost any more. I'll still need a room and I'll still use the gas. Besides we could all use a little fun." He takes a bite, and then his voice softens and his words are precious. "I really could use you guys there, this is not going to be easy, and especially alone."

Mom says nothing more, we're going, I can see it in her eyes. I also see that Dad is starting to get a little nervous. His confidence is not as cocky. I feel sad for his mood. I think the pressure is on. He has to perform. "Hey you guys," Dad calls us to him, "talk to the Man Upstairs and let Him know I really need this one."

"Okay Dad," we all agree.

"If we get this one, it's easy street for the rest of our lives. I only want this for us, so think hard."

We have a job, and our job is to wish with all our might that Dad wins this game. Shelly and Mark mumble and sing all day, "Dad's going to win, Dad's going to win."

I, however, take a deeper approach. "God, please, if you have any heart at all, you'll give this one to him. If you don't, well, I can't think about that. God, I'll never be mean to Shelly or Mark again. I'll try to go to church. I'll get all As." As soon as I said that part about straight As, I realized that might be a stretch. "But anyhow, I'll never kill another bug." The list goes on all day as I try to find another trade for Dad's success. Plus, I know if we have money he'll be in a better mood. But then a dark thought rolls through my head like a thundercloud. What do I mean he'll be in a better mood? We had money in Phoenix and things weren't good. If anything, he might start drinking again when he has money. The thought is so twisted up that I am beyond baffled. He'll start drinking again and beat Mom...No he wouldn't dare, he promised, *no more*. And so far it's been good. However, the cloud grows darker and so does my dilemma. I am trapped in my head. Back and forth: do we get rich or do we stay poor? I just don't know what to do. "God let him win, he has to. You have to let him win." I decide right then and there that I'd better stay out of this or I might jinx it. A jinx is a tricky thing, and you never know when one might appear. Jinxes have minds of their own and, according to Dad, you have to out-trick them. But I'd rather avoid them if possible. I try not to see it. I close my eyes and walk away from its taunting—if I look at it, it might grow. I continue throwing dirt clods at the fence. I wish I never started this wishing thing in the first place, I always mess it up. I can't even wish right, I always think too much.

It's time, early morning, and we have to pack the car and get on the road. "Ardell, put the bags by the door and I'll get them."

"Kids, if you have to go to the bathroom, you better go now. You know your Dad, he won't stop."

"Mom, what about the dogs?"

"Sandra, just give them some extra food and leave them outside. They'll be fine."

"But Mom..."

"Sandra, they'll be fine, don't worry."

Don't worry she says, heck I'm not worried, I'm scared. This is it, showtime. I have a knot in my stomach and a frog in my throat. I really don't want to go. I wish I could stay outside with some extra food too.

"Mark, open the truck." I hear Dad holler. He scurries across the yard. Mark rarely says a lot, but he moves fast when it comes to Dad's voice. The thought of a long drive with Dad makes us all a little anxious. Will it be fun or will it be long? We never know. I just hope for the best and see what will be. Besides I don't really care—I quit ever trying to get him to love me. The more distance between, the better. This time's for sure—I'll just be a good kid and I'll stop caring. It's obvious the man just doesn't like me that much. But if he only knew how much I love him.

I take my seat by the window so I can get away from the family chitchat. I already know I don't want to be here. Dad sits ahead of me driving, and all I have to do is keep my mouth shut and look at the back of his head. We pull safely and slowly out of the driveway. His right hand rests heavily on the blue plastic bottle of Maalox; the cap barely fits with all the white drippings down the side. I say a quick good-bye to Sugar and Big as they watch us leave. I tell them we'll be back. Mostly I tell myself. No one talks while Dad drives us to his destiny.

I watch his every move and study him carefully. I realize as I stare into the back of his head with its bright red hair, I don't even know this man. I think I do, but not really. He is my dad and that is all I know. But it's not like Mom, I know her. She's kind and strong. Her face tells a thousand stories. Her moods vary, but her love for me doesn't. I can rely on her—she never breaks a promise. She tries to listen to me and she always wants to laugh.

Dad, on the other hand, is unpredictable. He's usually mad at somebody or something. He likes to laugh, but it's mostly at somebody. He's not moody, but he's mean. He likes to tease and hurt people's feelings. And he loves to disagree. I don't know if it will ever be the same. I used to love to play with him, but lately I can't. I try, but something inside always stops me.

Now there's nothing to do but drive and drive. Mom begs for a break, and we finally get one after another forty miles. Dad is bowling in his head. He wants to get there in time to practice. A sign reads, CINCINNATI 87 MILES. We're close but we're not there yet.

"We'll get dinner later, after we've checked in." Dad reminds us we will get to eat.

Mark is asleep, and Shelly and I watch the lights flash. If I hold my eyes in a certain way, I can blur them just enough so the lights stream along the highway endlessly. I can only do it for a short time, and after a while my head starts to hurt. Time passes while the miles dwindle. Finally, the city appears out of nowhere. The town is bright and loud.

Dad starts biting his nails, even though he has no nails left to bite. Eventually Shelly starts biting her nails, too. I don't bite my nails, I chew on my hair. The two-lane road has become a sea of traffic. I don't know how he can drive in all this traffic. Mom wishes he wasn't. "Let's swing by the lanes. I just want to get a feel for it."

"Hon," Mom tries to explain, "we really need to feed the kids."

"It's on the way, it'll just take a few minutes," Dad insists.

"All right, but let's hurry. We've been in the car all day."

Dad has no idea where he's going and no one expects him to. He picks an exit and asks. And then he asks again. Finally, the last time he gets it. I want out of the car so bad. "What'd that guy say? Turn right at the second light or after the second light?"

"I think it was at the light."

He turns the car and runs over the curb. Bump goes the rear tire. I look at Shelly and we can't help but laugh. Mark stirs a little. Mom grabs the car door with fear, she overreacts sometimes. Dad whistles his way through the crowded streets.

"I see it."

"Where?"

"Up there, those big blue lights."

"Oh shit. You're right, there it is."

Mark's awake. Dad drives a little faster and Mom holds on a little tighter. There it is, our dreams, our future—the key to our happiness and a higher place in the community. The sign reads, "Cincinnati Heights Bowling, Home of the Honky Tonks." Below that a small quote: "Bowling is more than just a ball."

Dad pulls up slowly and the sidewalk practically cracks a smile. Dad tilts his head and blows the blowing alley a kiss, and then he turns around to the backseat, his arm resting on the top. "All right you guys, this is it. Tomorrow our lives will be new. The first thing we'll do is buy a new car and some steak dinners."

"Okay Dad," Mark agrees and reminds Dad, "but I want a baseball and bat."

"Hell yes, I'll buy you two." Dad is extra loud and Mark smiles a little.

"Okay Bill. That's enough. Let's go." Mom is agitated as she rolls up her window.

Dad rolls down his window and whispers a prayer. "Lord, you got to give this one to me. I know you, you bastard. I don't ask for much, but I'm begging this time."

Next thing I know we're looking for a motel. We don't have to hide the dogs—this time only *us*. As soon as we hit the first speed bump, that's it, down on the floor. Mom goes in and talks to the people, then out she comes with a key. It always feels like we just stole something. Dad checks out the coast—clear. We enter carefully and flop on the beds. Mark won't get a bed tonight, he'll get the floor. Mom goes to the bathroom and Dad pulls out his bowling ball and shoes. He checks out his gear and peeks inside the bag as if there might be something in there he forgot. "Hey Shell, come here. Shelly gets up from the edge of the bed. "Here, hold this." He hands her his ball and puts on his shoes and then slips on his glove. I watch with disbelief.

"There, how do I look? Do I look like a winner?"

"Yeah."

About that time, Mom pops out of the bathroom. "Bill, you're acting crazy, now put the toys away and let's get something to eat."

"Mom, then can we go swimming?"

"Oh honey, I'm sorry but I don't think this place has one."

I didn't even think of the pool possibility, but now I don't have to, it's pointless. Mom snatches her purse, and the hunt begins for the first McDonald's we can find.

Dad needs his sleep and we need to get back and hide. As we start back to the motel, I notice a few raindrops on the window. And then a few more. By the time we get to the motel, it's raining hard. I don't mind the rain, I like the rain. Dad doesn't, Dad only likes nice sunny weather. We cover our heads and try to outrun each other to the door. Mom fumbles with the keys as Dad hides us from the manager. We break through the door laughing and out of breath. Mark and Shelly grab the good spots on the bed. I'm stuck at the foot of the bed with no pillow and four feet in my face. This would never happen at home. "Shelly, scoot over." She scoots one inch just to piss me off. She knows there's nothing I can do with Mom and Dad right there.

"Scoot over some more." I push Mark's foot out of my way; the hole in his sock lets his big toe out. That is the last straw. They both know what they're doing. As Mark continues to wiggle his feet just enough to bother me but not enough for Mom and Dad to see, Shelly inches her way over while I struggle to keep my body and legs on the bed. I have no room whatsoever. I lay there watching TV, but all I can think about is that being back home with the dogs would be a whole lot better than this. I've had it. "Mom, would you tell Mark to get off the bed so I can go to sleep." Sleep is the last thing on my mind, but I have to do something. Mom gets up and takes a blanket and makes him a bed on the floor.

"Mark, come on sweetheart, here you go."

Mark looks at me and I wink with a smile. "Good night Mark." Shelly now scoots all the way over and their little game has ended. Eventually everyone drifts off to sleep; Dad is the last, his snoring confirms it. Mom sleeps too. I roll over and look at her, she's tired, I can tell. She's so pretty when she sleeps.

The next morning we all sleep in, except for Dad, he's out getting coffee. He returns with donuts and a coffee for Mom. I see him at the sink, he is sucking on his Maalox like a baby on its bottle. His face is tight and the white stuff leaves a mustache. Dad always drinks that stuff, he says it's for his ulcer. Sometimes he hurts so bad that even the chalky white stuff won't help. I hope I don't have to drink that when I grow up, I won't. He takes another swig and shakes it off, "Ardell, I'm going to register. I'll be back soon." He gathers himself and off he goes. He looks like he's going to war, and his ball is his machine gun.

I sit Indian style on the bed with the covers on my lap.

"Shhh, don't wake them." I wonder why she always says that. They have to wake up sometime. I nod back to Mom.

Dad returns a couple of hours later.

"Bill, how much was the registration?" Mom continues counting her dollar bills.

"Those bastards wanted fifty bucks."

Mom rolls her eyes around twice. She wants to ask something else, but she hesitates instead.

The sun is peeking through a cloud or two, and it feels like a pretty good day to win the pot. We are stuck in the room. Mom would let us go play, but the motel rules she broke won't let her.

"There's a lot of people there, Ardell, I mean a lot. I waited for a lane nearly two hours, I finally gave up." Dad throws his hands up. I guess he's going to pay the registration later.

"I need to lay down, I'm not feeling well."

Mom stops brushing her teeth and spits, "What, you're sick?"

"No, just tired that's all. I'll be fine."

Dad sleeps. I can't believe he can sleep on such an important day. I know I couldn't sleep. There we sit watching *Tarzan* on TV while Dad sleeps. Hours have passed and it's time, time to get him up and take our ringside seats. Our job is to pray and think positively. We have done our job quite well. I hear thunder banging in the distance. Mom and I look at each other. She doesn't mind the thunder, but Shelly and Mark do. I love it. I love the way it feels. Dad rolls over and opens his eyes. We stand there ready to go. The idea of a brand-new bowling alley to explore is more than we can stand. We've been cooped up in the motel all day. Home for us is a bowling alley, full of noise and the crash of those pesky pins. Dad however, wants to go back to sleep.

"Bill, get up."

Dad has a funny look on his face. He rubs his head and sits up in his underwear. His belly hangs over a little bit and his hair is wild like horses. "Ardell, get my Maalox." He grabs it from her, shakes it well, and pops the top. As he slugs it, I hear him grunt under his breath. "Man, I don't feel good."

Mom pretends she doesn't hear. I heard it, loud and clear. Oh my God, the jinx, it's here, I think to myself. Just then the thunder claps, laughing in a mighty roar. Shelly and Mark are in the background, oblivious to the sounds inside the room. They sing "Dad's gonna win."

Dad stands up and breathes. He reaches for a cigarette and then changes his mind.

Mom loads us and our stuff into the car. "You listen to me, Bill, this is it. You have to bowl, do you hear me?" She marches off into the storm. She's so mad that the raindrops won't even land on her.

She waits in the car. So do we. Dad gathers himself and shaves one more time. He shuts the motel door behind him with his shaving kit and keys in hand. The car door opens, and as it shuts, I can see the jinx all over him. I don't say anything, but it's there. It's right there. We drive in the storm with no words. Our hands are folded on our laps praying to heaven above, but our prayers are blocked by the thick darkness of the clouds. I'm scared.

Dad knows exactly where he's going this time. "Hey, I'm going to pull up to the curb, and you can let me out here. I'll wait for you and the kids inside." As the tires hit the curb, he stops and says in a very soft and sad voice, "You guys, wish me luck." He opens the door and we put down the prayers and start wishing all right.

No more do his feet hit the sidewalk when Dad turns white as a ghost. The sidewalk isn't smiling anymore; the cracks are wide as they swallow him up. He stands there while the rain falls on him and then, without warning, he's on his knees, throwing up. He's sicker than a dog, throwing up in the face of the game. We all get out of the car and start patting him on the back, "Dad, are you okay?"

He yells back, "Why, you bastard, why?" He's crying, we're crying, and Mom wants to cry. He throws up while Mom does the count off, and finally she throws in the towel. We've been rained out. I stand there watching him plead for forgiveness from anyone who will listen. People walk by and shake their heads as this broken sick man lies on the wet sidewalk, all washed up. The lights flash on and off from the sign above. His face reflects the crazy colors and his pain, blue one second and red the next.

Mom finally steps in and stops his suffering, forcing him back into the car. She picks up the pieces with ease and with a simple click of the car door she ends the event. This time he is in the backseat and Mom is driving. She pulls away from our dream and off to hell we go. Dad's familiar last words tear at my heart, "I'm sorry." Shelly and Mark clench their teeth shut so they won't cry. Mom's hands are wrapped tightly at the top of the steering wheel—I know she doesn't know how to get out of this place.

23

Mom exits the highway; after hours of driving the road sign ahead reads FAIRLY 47 miles. I don't know exactly where we're going for sure until the sign appears. Of course I thought we were going home, but for what, is the real question. The ride is long and the pouring rain never stops. Dad lays motionless in the backseat. All I can do is find a comfortable spot in my head and stay out of the cold, dark rainy night. Mom drives and drives, and what was once a celebration turns into a funeral. The dream died in a flash, there were no attempts to save it, it simply died. I try not to be scared, but something in the car that night does not let me escape the fear. No amount of talking to myself can convince me that things are going to be fine. I've heard that so many times already from Mom and Dad.

The terror races through me as I realize there *is* no other plan, and without a plan I'll bet we'll be moving soon. I continue running around in my head as the thoughts pour in. School will soon be here again and that will bring up a fight or two. Mom will fight, she'll want us to go to the same school. And then Dad, forever promising her that this time when we move it will be different. There is no difference, except for each school—now that is very different.

At one school, we'd be smart and the work was easy. And at another school, we'd be dumb and the work was hard. I gave up on friends a long time ago, I know they're only good for a few months anyway. And teachers, they mean nothing to me. They don't know me and I don't know them. It's different and the same every time Dad moves us. Pack, drive, and wait to see the next house and school. Never say good-bye; that's just a formality that we don't have time for. Besides, I'm used to being the new kid with no friends, no history, and no neighbors. When I was little, it used to bother me, all the new faces and all the scowling looks, but now I'm used to it. I can actually use it to my advantage. By being the unknown stranger riding into town, I feel a sense of power. They don't know me but they want to, and I couldn't care less because I know that this will never last.

When we move into a new place everyone stares at us when we roll into town; they give us dirty looks, I can feel it. Sometimes I think they know we are coming. No one in the neighborhood talks to us for a few weeks. Not until they are sure we're not murderers or thieves, and then a fellow here and a fellow there might stop by and ask a few friendly questions. Dad's answers are not what they want to hear. They leave and rarely come back.

And then there's money, it's always a problem. We have none. I don't know exactly what that means, but I do know this: we don't ask for things and I hate Christmas and birthdays. I know we can't afford it, but somehow Mom always manages to get us something, even if it's nothing; that is, nothing we really *want*. We always say thank you and pretend it's perfect; none of us would ever dream about showing our disappointment. That would just hurt Mom's feelings and Dad would probably knock the hell out of me. Besides, there's nothing they can do about it. I know it's wrong to bother Mom and Dad for such stupid things like toys, candy, and dumb stuff, but once in a while I can't help it. It's something I must have been born with. "I want," is usually followed by a sad look on Mom's face, or by Dad sternly reminding me how selfish and ungrateful I am.

The car bounces off an exit—Mom needs a Coke. No one moves or notices we've stopped. I drift back into my thoughts and remember last year's Christmas. We were broke, we had just left Oak Terrace, and things were pretty bad. The whole time I remember telling Shelly and Mark that I didn't think we were going to have Christmas. They both looked at me like I just ate a frog. I felt I had to warn them, but mostly I wanted to make it easier on Mom if my suspicions were correct. I wanted us to have plenty of time practicing not getting anything. It would take a lot of effort not to show our disappointment. We were getting good at accepting the small stuff. And not getting new shoes, nightgowns, clothes, bikes, and surprises, but it would take all we had to hide this one. I walked by his room and noticed him struggling with his paper and pencil. "What do you think you're doing?"

"I'm writing a letter to Santa."

"I told you not to do that." I snatched it. "Here, let me see." His list was normal, barrel of monkeys, Hot Wheels, bike, wagon, and so on.

"Mark, do you remember last year? All we got was a sleeping bag, and it was something we needed. This year might be the same, and if Mom sees this she's going to feel bad. Just don't let her see it."

He put his hand in his pocket. "But this is to Santa..."

"There is no Santa. Santa is Mom and Dad. You know that." I dropped his note back on his bed and left the room.

I notice the last turn is up ahead. I quickly put away my memories, but I'll never forget how much I hate to be hit in the face.

The grumpy house sits there with two happy dogs waiting for us. It's such a relief to see Sugar and Big in the driveway. I love the dogs, they put up with so much. They don't get much food, and they always have to sit outside. And when we go across country in the car, they are stuck on the floor, cramped in the backseat, panting. But they never complain and they always have a smile on their faces. How do they do it? Mom wakes up Mark and Shelly. I pet the dogs while I open the other car door for Dad. "Thanks," he mumbles as he crouches over and holds his stomach. His walk is slow and no one bothers to get their stuff out of the car. Everyone enters the house and heads straight for bed. Mark stops at the bathroom and Shelly stops by the kitchen sink for a drink of water. Mom forgets to give us our good night kiss. Dad makes it to the couch as Mom slams her door shut. I go to the window and count stars; I can only count to about twenty before I get beaten by the number of stars I'll never get to.

The following morning the whole house sleeps in. I can't; I wake up at eight o'clock and tip toe down the stairs. I round the bottom and quickly go through the living room. The last thing in the world I want to do is wake up Dad so I go outside and sit with the dogs. They sit on each side of me and smile. Big wants a whole bunch of petting and Sugar wants nothing. I look across the field and watch the cows with nothing better to do than eat. I think how lucky they are, after all, all they have to do is eat and hang around the fields. But then I remember when winter comes, which it will, they aren't so lucky. They stand in the muddy fields with the wind blowing as they crowd together. It's got to be cold for them. I guess even the cows don't have it that nice after all. Winter will be here soon. I hope we don't have to stay in this house when it hits. The thought of this house, the ghost, and the cellar door are enough to make me shiver in the sun. I don't like it here. Big nudges my arm and begs for attention. I think Big and Sugar know we lost the Honky Tonks.

As I pet Big, I hear the creaking of the screen door.

"Hey, whatcha doing out here?" Dad stands there with his belly popping out of his unbuttoned shirt and his freckles everywhere.

"I don't know. Just thinking."

He carefully hops down the two steps with his crinkled-up toes, barefooted. He stands there with a cup of coffee. "How are the dogs?" Sugar runs to him and winds herself in and out of his legs. Dad reaches down and picks her up.

"They're fine, but I don't know if they liked us being gone."

"No, probably not." He lowers his hand to pet Big. "San, I want you to know we're going to be fine. Me and your mother will figure this out. I'm thinking about Florida. What do think about Florida?"

"I don't know."

"The weather is great down there, I hear it's hot all year long. We need to get out of this damn snow."

I shrug my shoulders. "Okay."

"I haven't told your mother about this yet, so just keep it to yourself for right now."

Something inside me knows he's already made up his mind.

"I think it'll be better for us down there. Our luck has to change by now. I can feel it."

Just then I hear the ghost slam my bedroom door. Dad barely notices and shrugs it off like always. "I'm going to have to find out where that damn draft is coming from."

I sit there with Dad knowing he'll never find it. It seems ever since we got back the nameless ghost slams the door a lot more. I haven't seen him lately, but I can feel him in the way when I'm in the hall.

Dad continues to talk all about the next promise of daisies and dandelions. I knew we'd move. It's like clockwork: after every failure we move and this one is no different. I sit patiently and listen to his description of the dog tracks and gambling, the vast ocean that will be our new front yard, and all the possibilities. It's not like he is talking to me. It's sort of like he's talking to himself and I'm just there.

"John has a buddy down there and I know I can find him. John said that we can stay with this guy. You'll love the ocean."

I've never been to the ocean, or if I have I don't remember it.

He continues on, "Sandra, I think this is it. We'll get out of this back hills bullshit and move to a city again, Fort Myers, Florida. Hell, there's nothing here for us. We're better than this shit." He's now convinced himself and he puts Sugar down on the ground. I sit there with more to think about. He steps off the grass and onto a rock with his bare feet. Polio left his feet tender and deformed; the rock was a reminder that he needs to wear his shoes before he goes outside. "Goddamn it. Shit." He hobbles up the two steps and flings open the screen door. I laugh a little as the screen door slams shut.

What is he thinking? Mom will never go for that. I stop myself from complaining and shake my head. Oh well, I guess it'll be nicer than here. Maybe that's where we'll end up. I hope we find somewhere to live soon, I'm sick of moving all the time. But then again, Florida is by the ocean and it could be fun. I've never been there. I might meet some new friends—and what if Dad finds this buddy of Uncle John's and does get a great job? Then a horrible chill runs through my body. I can't lie to myself, I know it's just a scheme and my body won't let me think good thoughts. The chill gathers strength and runs up and down my spine. This is not a good idea, this is not your new home, and you will not meet new friends.

I stand up and brush off my nightgown as I try to get away from the chill. The chill follows me. I want to sob, but I don't know why. The chill is in my shoulders and I want it to leave me alone. I want to go to Mom and tell her, but I can't. I want her to make it go away. But I can't. I can't be scared, I must stop it.

Then I hear Mom in the kitchen, "What! Are you out of your mind? You'll never find Al. And what if you do? What are you going to say, Hi, here I am with my family, can I come in…?"

"Well, do you have any other suggestions?"

An eerie quiet fills the kitchen. "Yes, why don't we go to my father and ask him for some help? He might know somebody who can get us some jobs or something, for Christ's sake."

"Yeah, so you can go sing in a nightclub somewhere? Hell no…your father is nothing but a child-molesting drunk. He barely has a pot to piss in himself, he's not going to help us."

"That's not fair, you stop it right now."

My eyes fall straight out of my head as I sit there listening to our destiny. A child molester, what's that? I scoot closer to the screen door so I won't miss anything.

"Listen Ardell, I don't like this anymore than you do, but face it, we have to do something. We have about three hundred in silver dollars in the strong box, that's it."

"That's supposed to pay Chet for his truck. Besides, do you really think that'll get us to Florida and back if things don't work out?"

Dad had managed to save money the old-fashioned way, some for them, and some for us. Every silver dollar that came our way was ours and would go immediately into the secret box. The rest of the money that went into the register was for them, "Uncle Sam" as Dad put it. By now, Mom is quiet as Dad thinks of the answer.

"Yes, it'll have to. We'll get there and find Al, he'll help us out. If I can't find him or work in two days, we'll come back."

"Come back where? Here? We can't come back here or your mother's. I can't go back there. She's done enough for us already."

"Ardell, we won't have to, Florida will be great."

"What about the bowling alley?"

"To hell with it. We're finished, you and I both know it. We don't have any money to keep it going even if we wanted to. We'll just get in there and clean out our stuff and we won't say anything to anyone. We have to get out of town, there's not a whole lot of choice here, Ardell. We'll pack the truck and the van and move next week. We'll take what fits and leave the rest behind. I'll write Chet a note when we get there and pay him back. We don't owe Mr. Moss a damn thing; if anything he owes us. And as far as this place goes, the bills will get handled once we get settled. Stop worrying, it'll be fine."

Mom sighs and drops her cup into the sink so loud that two of the cows in the distance raise their heads and look my way.

24

I stay outside as long as I can, but I have to get dressed. The sun has warmed my shoulders and the chill has gone away. I can't sit out here in my nightgown all day. I open the door and tell the dogs to stay.

Mom is at the kitchen table. I can tell she's mad, she's had it, and she hates everything. She looks at me with her sleepy eyes and mad written all over her face pretending that nothing is wrong. She avoids eye contact and shuffles around me. She smiles the warning smile—the one that curls extra tight around the corners as if she wants to scream. It's the same smile that reads, *Get ready honey, we're about to leave with your father and God knows where we're going*. She tries to tell me, "Everything is fine, dear," as she brushes her hand through my snarled hair. But we both know I am too smart for that. Beside it's too late, her smile gave it away. I don't smile back as I run upstairs to get dressed. It will be a day or so before they officially announce the decision and our new destiny. In the meantime, I'll pretend that I don't know what's going on and that everything is fine.

The day continues and no one is the wiser. We rest and hang around the house. Dad is still racking his brain while he watches TV, I can see it. Mom leaves for the store and we beg to go with her.

"All right, but I'm just running in for a couple of things. You guys wait in the car."

Mom passes the bowling alley. "Mom, can we stop and get a soda?"

"No."

We all look at each other. She's never said no quite that quick before and especially if it's free. She drives by and barely turns her head as we poke ours out the window looking at our bowling alley and for our friends. "Mom, why can't we stop for a Coke?" After all, a Coke with ice is Mom's favorite.

"Listen, I said no."

Shelly makes a face behind Mom's back and Mark giggles out loud. Mom ignores us as long as she can. She parks the car and tries not to cry. Her chin quivers and her voice cracks. Mark and Shelly think she's crying over them. Her words are heavy and forced as she tries to talk to us. "We have to move again, you guys. We're going to Florida to start over. There is no more bowling alley."

Mark reaches from the backseat and pats her on the head. "That's okay Mom." His hand smooches down her fluffy black hair.

"Honey, I just want you guys to know that we're back in one of those tough spots." She looks at me. When Mom cries it is the saddest sight we have ever seen, none of us can stand it when Mom cries. Our hearts swell up immediately and all we can do is try to make her stop. "Mom, that's okay, we don't mind."

"I know you don't, but I do. School is going to start in a month or so and I really didn't want to drag you guys around this year."

We say nothing, there's nothing to say; it's better if we just let her settle down. The more she talks the more upset she gets. She sniffs a couple of times and wipes a tear or two.

"Mom, are you okay?"

She nods, "I'll be right back." The van door opens and closes. We watch our mom walk away with her head down. Our eyes follow as we realize she is beaten once again.

Each one of us has our own seat, the van is almost new. We bought it from a used car lot a couple of months ago. The van has a lot more room than the car. Dad bought it for a couple of reasons: one, "because we deserve it," to which Mom disagreed, and two, because he thought he was a sure bet for the Honky Tonks. Of course it's better than the car, and if you don't get the front seat, there's always another good seat to choose from. We each sit there with our legs stretched out, thinking about Mom's hurting heart and all the times she tries to do what's best. But this is a mess and we're going to make it easy on her.

"Do you think we'll live in Florida very long?" Shelly asks.

"I don't know, but let's pretend we like it no matter what. Dad said he has a friend there."

"I don't want to go."

"Mark shut up, do you want to make Mom sad? The ocean is right there and we can swim all year. I think we should try to be good and don't ask for anything. If we do, Mom will get upset and Dad will get mad." They both agree, but this is not the first little talk like this we have had. We all sit and wait. "There's Mom, now be quiet."

Mom gets in the van with the groceries and reaches in the bag she hands each one of us a surprise. She got Mark a Tootsie Pop, me a Tootsie Roll, and Shelly a 3 Musketeers. Our personal favorites, God, she's nice. Our eyes light up as she smiles her beautiful smile. I instantly feel how much I love her. She starts the van. "Aren't you forgetting something?" We all say, "Thank you," at the same time. She loves playing this game.

Mom pulls up as Dad is getting ready to pull out in the truck. Mom rolls down her window. "Where you going?"

"I'm going to go to the bowling alley, I'll be back in a while." Dad is vague and that pisses Mom off.

Mom rolls her eyes and rolls up the window. The rest of the day we putter around the house as Mom listens to the radio. I sing the words to "I'm leaving on a jet plane, don't know when I'll be back again..." I love those words, I don't know why, I just do. Mom starts a little packing, mostly sorting what goes and what doesn't. It's not time for us to pack yet. We usually don't start packing until a day or two before it's time. But when the packing begins, the fun ends for a while. No one is in the mood to play or laugh. The questions and curiosity build. Where will we live? What are the people like? Is school going to be hard? How long will we stay? No one asks, but the questions fly around everyone's head. Dad is gone for hours, I wonder what he's doing. I bet he's embarrassed about losing the Honky Tonks. But if I know Dad, he's probably made up some excuse why he lost, and he'll cut them off at the knees if they ask too many questions. I wonder why we don't just stay here and work at the bowling alley. I guess we can't anymore.

Shelly is upstairs in her socks and shorts trying to fit her father-daughter trophy in a box. "I thought I'd start packing up the stuff I really want," she says.

The sight of packing is horrible. I want her to stop it right now. "Oh well, I hate packing." I ruffle through my stuff. "All I'm going to pack this time is my clothes."

"I hate leaving my stuff behind. This time I'm going to try to fit it all."

I look around the empty room and wonder what stuff she is talking about. Packing is an art, except there aren't any brushes or colors to speak of. It's like finger painting without paint. I especially hate all the decisions. First I must decide what fits and what doesn't, what's ugly and what's not, and then, what I need and what I don't. I don't need my horse skull. I made my point and now I can't stand looking at it. As a matter of fact, I can't stand looking at any of my stuff. All I want is to get there and unpack. It's much easier to unpack than to pack. I sit on the floor watching Shelly shove one thing in and another thing out. She struggles forever with her stuff. Mark and I don't.

I hear Dad pull up in the truck. I rush to the hall window, push the cobwebs out of the way and see the truck is full of boxes. That's it, it is official. "You guys get down here and help me." He stands by the truck waiting for us to unload. The first load is mine. I have nine empty boxes stacked above my head. I balance them carefully to the back door where I can finally drop them.

Mom meets me on the back steps. "Sandra, don't hurt yourself."

"I'm not, I can carry more."

"Honey, you don't have to."

"Here Mom, here's a good kitchen box." She reaches for it and agrees. Mark tries to get in on the action, but he's not very good at understanding the importance of the proper box for the proper use.

"Here, Mom, here's one." She takes another one from him with a huge smile. He keeps handing her boxes until she finally has to tell him that's enough for right now. But his boxes aren't what she needs for the kitchen, I know better than that. Thank goodness we don't have knickknacks anymore, those were the hardest to pack. I'd have to wrap them individually or they might break and they took forever; each one of those little bastards demanded special care and understanding. I like packing big stuff like tables, toasters, chairs, and shoes. Shoes are my favorite, all I have to do is dump them in a box and they're done. The big stuff goes quickly and there's not a lot of fussing involved. Dad has to help me fold the top of the boxes. I keep forgetting which two go down and which one pulls up in order to keep the box closed. We'll have the house packed in less than two days.

Once the packing begins, it goes pretty quickly. And once it's almost done, it's lonely sitting around the empty place. I not only see empty, but I can smell it; it smells like rat poison and mothballs. It's large and musty, and it laughs at us. I ignore the empty echoes of laughter by staying outside. The outside is much nicer to me. We never pack the TV until it's time to pull away, we save that for last. Dad is the mover, he lifts all the heavy stuff. The final days go by fast, and we haven't been by the bowling alley at all. I ask if we can stop by the bowling alley and say good-bye to Chet.

"We'll see."

God, I hope he lets me. I like Chet, he was always so nice to me. Mom yells from the kitchen for Dad to come get these boxes out of here, she's running out of room. The upstairs is done except for the bathroom. Mom will do that last, after our showers tomorrow. There is a buzz in the air as the last few boxes go out to the truck. I trip over the boxes and yell at Mark. The echo in the house reminds me that this is it, and my stomach wants to know, what are we doing? Shelly is in the kitchen trying to get the icky black ink off her dirty hands. But it won't come off, it'll have to wear off in time, just like moving. The effects of moving linger, we must wait until things feel right again.

The sun is setting and all that is left are a couple of broken boxes and a few wads of newspaper here and there on the floor. The dust patches indicate what is missing and how dirty the floor really is. I have three paper cuts and six Band-Aids on. Mom is spilling over with stress and whirling in circles as she determines the clothes and bathroom stuff necessary for traveling. Dad is the master when it comes to fitting two boxes in the space for one. It may take him an hour, but eventually he'll talk the boxes into cooperating.

"You son of a bitch..." Dad pushes on.

At this point in moving we must be careful not to screw up. The tension and resistance fight like dogs and cats. Electricity fills the house to the ceiling, and all that Mom and Dad need is one little spark and they'll blow their stacks. If you accidentally forgot where you left your shoes, better to leave them behind. You must make do. This is critical in maintaining a good mood in the beginning and hopefully making a good move. Not to mention staying alive.

Friday morning and Dad wakes us up on cue. "Get up, you sleepy heads, it's time to hit the road." Oh man, I'd like to hit something right now. I roll over and notice that the sun barely shines in our room. I smell toast.

We have exactly one half hour to take a shower, get dressed, and eat. Mom stands behind us with a suitcase ready to pack up the last of us. "Give me that, you can wear that to sleep in tonight." She shoves our T-shirts into the suitcase. She practically rips the towels off our damp bodies. By the time we get downstairs, there is dry, cold peanut butter toast—we ran out of butter—and a glass of water waiting. My mouth is not watering for this breakfast, but I chew on the toast as does Shelly and Mark, there is no time for complaining. The cowlicks in Mark's hair tell the story best, we are leaving in ten minutes. From the corner of my eye I see Dad unplug the TV set, and we're off. I grab the bag with books, cards, and puzzles. This is the most important of all, and it's my job to make sure it gets on board safely. Without these items, I could go nuts; my sanity lies in *Word Search* and *Mad Magazine*. The half hour is over and not a second to spare. It always feels like if we don't get out in time, the house will blow up or something.

It's still early and now I know there is no chance of me saying good-bye to Chet. Dad tried to trick me into believing that I could say good-bye when we left, but no way, not at this hour. I can see Chet standing in the bowling alley before it opens, with his money bag and crossword puzzle folded neatly. I would run in and give him a great big bear hug and say good-bye. I can practically feel his hand on my head telling me, *Now Sandra, I want you to be good and don't worry so much.* Then I would look up and see his reassuring smile under his mustache and the shape of a tear in his eyelash. He'd probably blink it away and pat my shoulder. I love him. I didn't know it until now, but I can already feel how much I'll miss him.

My fairy tale ends abruptly as Dad grabs Sugar and plops her in the truck. Big wiggles his way to the van. He tries to get in, but he needs help. I lift him in and throw the bag next to the front seat. Mom lifts herself in to the driver's seat. "Everybody in?" The door closes. "You follow me." I see Dad's mouth move. Mom nods her head yes, and we leave. Mark pats down his cowlicks while Shelly and I stare out the window and say our silent good-byes.

I look upstairs to my old bedroom window, I wish I could see that old ghost one more time, but he's not there. I wonder if he went back down to the cellar. The house gets smaller and smaller, and I can't help but notice that as grouchy and unfriendly as the house is, it looks sort of sad that we are leaving. Maybe it didn't mind us after all.

We drive out of the country and through town for the last time. While Shelly and I look around, Mom looks straight ahead as if she's never been here before. I can't believe we're not going to say good-bye to Chet, he was our friend. But that's usually the way it goes. Mom doesn't feel like talking and neither does Shelly. I do. My mind relives all the lies as my heart fills up with sadness, madness, and shame. I hate this, I hate the fact that I can't have any friends and Chet was my friend. He watched out for me, and now I don't get to tell him good-bye. He'll never know I cared about him and that I'm not like my dad—I have a heart. I have such a sad place for him in my heart. I don't even know his address, and if I did, I bet I wouldn't use it. How can they do this? Doesn't it hurt them? Or am I just too melodramatic? That's what Mom calls me all the time. Well I'd rather be that than cold and mean. Chet isn't going to know what happened to me, and he'll miss me, he really likes me, I could tell. I bet he's just sitting there right now wondering what happened to us. Why don't they just cut out my tongue? At least that way I wouldn't be able to speak. They might as well just tie me up and gag me for the rest of my life. Because that's how it feels, the pain of not being able to tell just one person thank you or good-bye. When I grow up I'll talk, and I'll tell people how much I love them, and I'll have fifty million friends, and I'll keep them forever. No one will ever control where I go, what I say, or how I act. I will not live like this. Do you hear me, God? I will *not* live like this, I will not!

The road rolls and rumbles underneath me. The steaming, swirling heat waves up in the distance are inviting. Who are they, those invisible waves that disappear if you get too close? God hears me and tells me, they are my body and soul, they are always there. The anger from within me radiates like the waves of rage before me. I have more heat in me right now than any old stupid heat wave. I open my window all the way, endure the heat on my face, and let it blow back in their faces like a torch to a match. They don't say a word. And I dare them, God, the Lord or whoever, Mom, Dad, and the Voice that never shuts up. Lie after lie, just like the road, it rolls on and on, never ending and never admitting...what? I can't tell the difference anymore.

One whole day passes and nothing has changed, we're traveling south to Florida. The engine of the van sits between Mom and me. The cup holders are stuffed with wrappers and half-full drinks; the melted ice has separated from the soda. This heat from the engine continues to remind me of my discomfort. I lightly rest my leg on the hot engine cover to see how long I can stand it. The burning is faint at first, and then it feels cold just before the pain is real enough to move. I attempt it again and again. I win the game—I can go longer than before. But at some point, I always have to move my leg. I reach down to rub the burn and watch the redness disappear. I feel the sweat from the day all over my body, and my hair is getting greasy. I want out of the van. I want to go swimming in a cool river. There are no rivers on this journey, just swamps and alligators.

This part of the day is almost over, and the dirt drifts on the side of the road never end and they never begin, they just continue to drift. I lay my head between the seat and the door, and the vibration prevents comfort or sleep. My eyes roll shut and pop open with each jerk and bump of the road. I look back at Shelly and Mark. They feel the same way I do, dirty and tired. After so many hours we can't get comfortable anymore and we can't complain. Complaining has absolutely no point.

Shelly looks at me, and she can tell I'm not happy. Mark doesn't know, but he also doesn't want to. Shelly is the one who will always notice my mood first and she'll do anything to get me back to happy. She gets quiet and then pretends everything is fine when I can't any longer; she's my shadow side. Shelly squirms a little with my discomfort.

"Mom, can I find a radio station?"

"Sure."

Shelly whirls back and forth and up and down on the knob. She desperately tries to find a station and hopes it will change my mood. The twirling static changes from high to low while voices growl beneath the crackling. "Could you please hurry up, you're driving me crazy."

Shelly spins the knob harder, but no luck. If she can't catch a station in time, she'll have to turn it off. It'll be at least an hour before she can try again. The sound of static is Mom's least favorite thing, other than her feet being tickled. She hates that too. The sun is starting to go down behind the vista on the right of the van. Dad is ahead driving with one arm hanging out the window. Mark teases Big until the dog finally snaps at him. Mom snaps a little too. "Mark, that is enough!" Mark pets Big with two hands nicely. Dad said that we'll take a break around nine and get a cheap motel. And by tomorrow afternoon we'll be there. The drive continues to bore us out of our minds. I stay in my books and flip the pages slowly; if I read too fast then I'll have nothing left to do but think. I want to avoid that as long as possible.

Mom tells us a story of when she was little and used to live by the ocean in Santa Cruz. She said it was the happiest time of her life. Her foster mother was kind, giving and loving. She'd pack her and her sisters a lunch, and they would explore all day by themselves. She learned to swim in the waves and they loved the beach.

"Mom," I interrupt, "what happened to your dad?"

Her face changes shape instantly. "Honey, I didn't know him. He left when I was about three."

"Where did he go?"

"He had to leave California. He was a very sick man back then." Mom keeps driving, keeping her eyes on the road.

"What was wrong with him?"

"He touched your Aunt Carole, and he had to leave California or go to jail."

"Grandpa was in jail?"

"No, he would have gone to jail if he didn't leave California. He was ordered to stay away from us."

"Oh, sorta like Uncle Brooks."

"Yeah, kind of…" Mom ends the conversation and goes back to the happier time at the beach. We listen as she talks about all the fun she and her sisters had.

I'm intrigued by now, my heart pounds for more. "What happened to your foster mother?"

She sucks in some air and blows it out as the words fall. "I don't know. I never saw her again. My mother showed up one day and said, 'Come on, we're going now. I married a man, his name is Red, and whatever you do, don't call him Dad.' She took us away to live with her and Red."

I thought about what-if and remembered how I felt at Aunt Carole's. "How many times did your mom leave you?"

"She left me in an orphanage once, she left me at my foster mother's once, and she left me with my grandmother a couple of times. I was three when she first left me in an orphanage with my sisters."

Her story ended there, but the thoughts of Lois and Red did not, I knew more. Red was meaner than Tabasco sauce on a snake, and Lois, our grandmother, hated kids, she didn't even like us to call her Grandma. There was no mistaking her dislike of children, puppies, kittens, and ponies. She had three poodles that ate dinner at the table with her. We sat outside with tray tables and paper plates, beating off the flies. Their booze was officially introduced at three o'clock every day. They would be sloppy drunk by six and then attempt to spill a little dinner on the table. Grandma and Red would get a little nicer to us around then. It was only because they were drunk and forgot who we really were. I couldn't stand it when they would be like that. They treated Mark like a little baby and teased him. They would make him grab for things out of reach and Red would always make him cry somehow. *What's a matter you little baby, are you a girl?* Then he'd give him a treat. After that Red would apologize.

One time Red grabbed Shelly as she was walking by the dinner table and was going to put her on his lap. I jumped out of my seat so fast, and I grabbed her arm and pulled her back. The look on her face was enough to melt metal. No one ever touches Shelly. It wasn't normal for Grandma or Red to hug or kiss us. I usually didn't have to worry about Shelly, she'd stay far away from them.

The van is quiet. Even the road settles down as memories float in and out of my head. Shelly lays against the window with her mouth half open. Mark plays a little tickle game with Mom as she reaches back for his knee. I drift again into the thoughts of my distant grandparents.

One time, Grandma taught me how to put my shirt on inside out and I'll never forget the lesson, it was fast and to the point. The green shag carpet was worn from the bedroom to the kitchen. Grandma kept one eye on me to make sure I wasn't touching her stuff. Her cigarettes were lying all over the house, inside and outside the ashtrays. The ashtrays were metal and they used to be pretty. But the ashes had melted them away after time and the silver was gray. Mom said Grandma was beautiful when she was younger; I couldn't see it no matter how hard I looked. The smell of the liquor and Listerine on her breath made it hard to listen to her. Her eyes looked like they were bleeding and the wrinkles went on and on. Her body was thin and her face spotted. This particular day Shelly came out of the bathroom and I went in with a clean shirt in my hands. I left the door open, I didn't see Grandma Lois standing there. I struggled with it as I tried to turn it right side out.

"Here, give me that." She snatched my shirt. All I could think was, How come I'm in trouble for changing my shirt? "I'll show you how to put your shirt on."

I stood there in the bathroom with Grandma and her lit cigarette burning in the worn-out ashtray. The knitted, stuffed yellow poodle sitting on the counter holding the toilet paper was my only friend as she began teaching me something I already knew. "Here, now put this over your head."

"But it's inside out."

"Don't you think I know that, just do what I say."

I put the neck of the shirt over my head backward and pulled it down. It made no sense to me at all. But I wasn't going to say that to her. "And now reach in and put your arms through just like you normally would." I did. I then pulled it down around my waist. "See, you don't have to turn your shirt right side in, you can do it over your head and save time." I stood there with smoke burning my right eye and I looked at myself in the mirror. Before I could thank her or turn around to her, she was gone. It was the most words she had ever spoken to me in my life.

She stepped onto the porch later that day with an empty basket, as she made her way to the clothesline. I could tell she wanted to be invisible. Her head was low as she tried to hide her frail body behind the green laundry basket. Mark overkicked the ball and before Shelly could dive into the path of the moving red threat, the ball rolled toward Grandma's swollen ankles. I watched with one eye closed as the ball slowly landed beneath her. Shelly lay there with two new grass stains on her bare knees. Grandma almost reached down to pick up the ball. Instead, she hesitated and rethought her action and quickly kicked the ball back Mark's way. For a second I thought she was going to play, but she walked sternly to the clothesline and ignored the ball and us.

I can feel the heat rising from the engine on my leg. It reminds me I need to stretch my shoulders and lift my sweaty hair off my neck. The stickiness is all over my body. I shift my clothes and my body weight. The van continues rolling away, down the highway. Time moves unnoticed; I go back to my thoughts.

Red was a big mean man, the meanest man I ever saw. I never saw a man look so much like a man. He had a round face and a red nose and not much hair. If he did smile, it was the loudest smile in the world. He had a big belly that stuck way out, more than Dad's. And his pants buttoned underneath his belly. He worked hard in his life, I could tell by his hands. They were kind of curved inward almost like they were stuck that way. And his back sort of did the same. His scowl made Dad look like a little boy. Dad tried to hold up to this man's meanness, but he couldn't. I could see them sitting there staring at each other, one would tell a bad joke and the other would top it. After that they just sat there making up mean stuff to talk about. Red thought everyone was a Nigger, Wop, Jew bastard, or Nip. He pretty much hated everyone except Grandma and the dogs.

Shelly stirs in the backseat, I look back, she's half asleep and half miserable. The stickiness of the van is all over her. Her hair is wet with sweat; she hates it when her hair gets greasy. She should, it is. Mom is still daydreaming. I wish I knew what she was thinking.

I know the old stories about Red beating and torturing Aunt Carole, Aunt Revell, and Mom. But for me the terror was more about Lois and all the excuses they made up for her not stopping it. I look at each person in my life, even those who aren't here anymore, and I watch with disbelief as the old stories continue to echo. The grandmothers used to be mothers and before that they were daughters, and yet each one of them did the same as the one before them. All I know is that it stops here. No man will ever hit me or my kids, ever! The first time he decides to hit me, I'll knock the shit out of him and leave. Plus I won't get married until I'm older, like about twenty-five or thirty. No man will run my life and make me do things I don't want to. How can people let other people run their lives? I don't understand. If I wasn't a kid, no one would ever tell me what to do. I look into the faces of these women from the past who helped create me and I wonder when did they quit fighting for the truth, and for God's sake why? My great-grandmother was a hero, but she hid from the truth behind her flowered apron. And Grandma Lois still hides from the truth behind a highball and cuss words. And Mom hides from it everyday behind Dad. I can't help but notice something is different about me.

Once, Grandma Lois stood looking at us from the top of her tiny back porch while we played in the backyard, and I accidentally caught her enjoying watching us. I looked at her with all the old stories surrounding her, like cobwebs in an attic. I turned to her with a smile, and she slammed the door shut with a curse. *Goddamn it, don't you kids break anything.* She stomped off in her slippers and went to pour herself another stiff one. I heard the ice clinking hard against the glass. The whiskey settled her nerves. But nothing could explain how she could have given up her kids.

25

Tonight we all sleep with the sound of trucks rolling on and off the highway, the gears changing, the brakes squealing, and the air hissing. Lights are flashing from nearby signs outside our window while the guard dogs keep barking back and forth in the distance. I have one eye closed and one eye open. The pillow I share with Mark is all his, and Dad snores just enough to make sure I don't fall all the way to sleep.

Now the sun is starting to break and the flashing signs are starting to die. The truck noise is silent. We eat while Dad smokes up the tiny room. He has his trusty map and he's checking out our route one more time just to make sure we're still on the right track. Or possibly to see if there is some magic shortcut he's overlooking. "By tonight. I think we'll be there by tonight." He stretches his whole body and agrees with himself. "If we get there by tonight, we can stay at Al's house instead of a hotel. I wish I had this guy's number so I could call him first."

I can't believe this poor guy doesn't even know we're coming to his house.

"We need to start driving if we're going to make it by tonight." At first it was just a possibility, but now I can see that this is a challenge, and Dad wants this one, all six hundred miles of it. Meanwhile, the dogs stay on the floor for the next six hundred miles.

The ride practically drives itself; all we have to do is follow Dad and beg for a bathroom break now and again. Mark and I stay quiet while Shelly entertains us with stories.

"How about that school in Roncevert? They didn't even have doors in the bathrooms. Mom, why didn't they have bathroom doors? All they had was ten toilets on one side and ten on the other. So if you went to the bathroom you had to sit next to someone, and then you had to look across at someone else. I never went to the bathroom. The stupid teacher would walk us all to the bathroom and stand there waiting. I don't feel like chatting while I sit on the toilet. It was the weirdest thing I ever saw, and all these dumb girls acted like it was perfectly fine. Mom, they'd talk to each other and go pee, and the teacher would give me dirty looks when I refused to sit on the pot. The bus ride home was the worst part. That's why I couldn't talk to Sandra, I had to go the bathroom so bad that I had to concentrate with all my heart."

Mom laughs, "Yeah I'd see that bus coming down the road and I'd open the front door for you. The bus barely stopped and you were out before the bus driver could stop."

Shelly relives the nightmare. "I wonder who thought of that. Probably some grouchy teacher who had nothing better to do than take down all the bathroom doors and then, when that wasn't enough, they took the stalls. Thank God for Mr. Wiley. He always gave me a pass while everyone was in class. I think he knew I was going to die."

I sit there laughing at all the bizarre rules that school had, including the naked bathrooms. But now I'm left with thinking about the next school and the new rules.

Florida is not going away. We're getting closer as the van keeps on rolling down the highway. In the back of my mind I keep thinking that this will go away. That somehow we aren't going to get there, and that something will change our course. But the miles keep dwindling and so does my hope. Mom drives and so does Dad. The hours move out of our way. Dad pulls into a Jack in the Box, and the clown waits patiently for us to talk to him. We order for ourselves, we've memorized the whole menu. Mom reaches into the strongbox and grabs a few silver dollars. She exhales each time we need to spend money; the money is getting lower. I wish it wasn't, but it is. The strongbox holds our future and the silver dollars are the truth. We have to eat in the van, and Dad says with any luck we'll be there in about six hours. Dad sucks on his Coke as he smiles and waves for us to follow him back to the highway.

Fort Myers, Florida, finally has its own sign. After we eat, each one of us falls deep into sleep. I try not to, but the sandman is relentless. Mom listens to music and follows the highway. The highways in Florida are wide and clean. There isn't much to see on the sides of the roads. All the buildings are built off the highway. There aren't any old stores or houses. Everything looks new.

By the time I wake up, it's a little after sunset. I can't believe my eyes—I can see water. "Mom, is that the ocean?"

"No," she corrects me, "that's the bay and those are swamps."

"Swamps, you mean like where the alligators live?"

"I guess."

I can't believe the swamps are so close to the highways.

I study the landscape and wonder about this new place. It doesn't look anything like West Virginia or California. I open the window and smell the salt air. My hair blows back as the humidity wets my face. The salt air is thick and the palm trees grow tall. I've seen palm trees on *Gilligan's Island* but never from the car window.

We finally reach Fort Myers. The town is beautiful and everyone seems to know exactly where they are going. Dad pulls over to a Circle K and runs for the first phone booth. He flips the pages searching for this Al, friend of John's. "Ardell, I found him," he shouts. Mom nods her head not really caring. Dad dials the number, we're all listening.

"Hi, is Al there? Hey man I'm John Vaughan's brother, Jack. I just pulled into Fort Myers. Oh, he didn't call you? Well, I'm here with my family, and we're thinking about moving here. John said you might be able put me up and maybe help me find my way around." There's a long pause. Dad is starting to bite his nails. "All right, that would be great. Ardell, get a piece of paper." Mom finds an envelope and I hand her a pencil. Dad writes down the directions. "All right, thanks, we'll see you in half an hour."

Mom isn't pleased with the conversation. "You mean to tell me that this guy didn't even know we were coming? Now we're just going to show up on his door step?"

"He's fine, he said we could come over."

Dad's words have nervous written all over them, and Mom knows it.

Dad feels his way through the evening traffic and misses the streets a few times, but we finally find Al's house. He lives on a quiet street. No one is outside, and the porch lights give the only hint that people are home. Dad pulls up and we're behind him. I don't feel welcome and I'm not even in the house yet. Usually people come out and greet us when we come by, especially after a thousand miles. But the porch light flickers with bugs and no one comes out.

"You guys stay in the car while I go say hi." I couldn't agree more. Here's a perfect stranger and five of us with two dogs standing on his porch. The poor guy doesn't even know how many of us there are. Dad knocks on the door and goes right inside. The man pats Dad on the back. We sit there silently. I want to ask Mom what's going on, but heck, she doesn't know. We sit there for a long time watching the front door stay shut. Then the door opens, and out comes Dad across the lawn to the van. He comes to Mom's window. "We can stay tonight and tomorrow we'll leave."

"Let's just leave now."

"We can't, they're already making up some beds. Their kids are asleep, and we have to be quiet, and…we should leave the dogs in the van tonight."

That's all that I heard clearly, *Leave the dogs in the van*. I want to argue, but the facts have already been established.

"Listen you guys," Dad says, "I want you to go straight to bed once we get settled. Do you understand?"

I can't believe it. After all the driving, we have to go lay down. This is more than unfair. Mom knows by the look on my face that this is not what I want to hear right now.

"Now listen to your father, we don't want to be rude. Just go to bed, and tomorrow we'll go find the beach."

We empty out of the van and I let the dogs out for a minute. Mom gathers half our stuff and Dad carries it in. We follow behind him, wondering how we're going to fall asleep.

The wife, Jean, is bouncing off the walls with tension. Her nightgown tells us she wasn't expecting company tonight. And Al looks like Nixon as he keeps trying to act like everything is perfectly fine. Their little dog is the only one saying how much he doesn't like us; I think he was speaking for them. Jean politely shows us her house and our beds. She turned the family room into two giant beds on the floor. I see the beds and know it's only a matter of brushing our teeth before we'll be in them. I hate those beds. Mom shuffles around the strangers and helps get us ready for bed. She doesn't have to, she wants to. She feels the same way I do about visiting with Jean and Al.

Jean comes by the hall and checks on the family that is about to sleep in her house. "I'm really sorry, but I only have three pillows."

"Oh, that's fine, the kids can share." Oh sure, three kids and one pillow, that will be no problem. Mom tosses it our way and says "sorry" behind Jean's back. I want to be helpful, but it's hard.

Dad and Al sit in the living room with newspapers at their feet. Al lights another cigarette and so does Dad. Dad talks about himself while Al listens. "You know Jack," he finally says, "I'm real sorry, but I have to work tomorrow or I'd be glad to show you around."

"Oh, that's fine. I'll just get a map and feel things out."

I keep listening for the part where Al offers Dad a job. But I must have fallen asleep before that part of the conversation. Mom and Jean sit and pretend to be interested in ongoing bullshit. Jean sits at her kitchen counter wondering how long we plan to stay. "I have to work and get the kids to swimming lessons tomorrow, or I'd show you around."

"That's not necessary," Mom says, "we'll be fine. We really appreciate you letting us stay tonight, but tomorrow Jack has a lot of things to do. We'll get a hotel tomorrow."

Jean doesn't miss a beat, "There's a nice one on the other side of town. It's close to downtown and all the bigger hotels. You did say you were in the hotel business?"

Dad grunts, "Yes."

Mom and Dad join us in the family room later that night. I hear them slip under the covers on the floor next to us. I haven't slept that close to Dad, ever.

The next morning we wake to the sound of hair dryers and the smell of bacon. We all take quick turns in the bathroom. When Shelly comes out she announces, "Mom, I need a shower."

"Shelly, just get dressed. We're leaving right away."

"But Mom…"

I feel the same way. What, no shower?

"Do as your mother says." Mom immediately folds blankets and throws us clean clothes. Dad goes out to break the ice cold air in the kitchen.

"Here, you want some coffee?"

"Sure."

"I can make you some breakfast if you like."

"Oh no, we don't eat breakfast, we'll get something later."

What? We don't eat breakfast?

Mom folds the last blanket and without saying it reminds us to put on our happy faces. I pray they won't hear my stomach growling. We have to go through the kitchen from the family room.

Their two kids, about our age, sit staring at us with a spoon in one hand and milk dripping from their mouths. They are barely awake. No one introduces us, and I can only guess it isn't necessary, we are leaving. Mom says no to the coffee Jean offers and goes outside to load the bags. Dad sits with Al for a few more minutes pretending we know what we're doing. "Yeah, we need to get on the road. I have some things to do this morning."

He does not, and Al politely accepts Dad's pretending.

"If you're going downtown, take the 194 to Dayton and swing around the bay."

Dad nods and agrees with Al as if he knows what he's talking about. Shelly and I keep smiling as I count the remaining bacon strips in the pan.

"Okay, you kids ready?"

We stand up directly and follow Dad's lead. Mom comes back inside and checks the family room.

"Thank you so much. I hope it wasn't too much trouble putting us up. You have a lovely home."

The boy and girl just sit there, not moving. They keep staring. I want to tell them to wipe the milk off their faces.

"Bye now, we'll call once we get settled." Dad spouts like a teapot.

As we walk down the sidewalk along the perfectly manicured lawn with the little black man statue in the front yard, we all notice that this is a really nice neighborhood. Dad's truck sticks out like a sore thumb. Al and Jean stay safely by the front door waving at us. Dad has that look in his eye just before he turns around to say his final good-bye. The same look that means he's been humiliated and there's nothing worse than Dad embarrassed. He'll smile right through it, but then he'll blow.

We have no idea where to go, and we all need a shower. This is not a good time to ask about the beach. Dad grinds his gears as we drive out of the cute neighborhood. We drive into a traffic jam and try to find a coffee shop. Dad heads for the tall buildings and the stop-and-go traffic only adds to his frustration. Today is a good day to be real quiet. After about an hour, Dad takes an exit with a Denny's sign. We pull in and Dad walks up to the van, pissed. "Come on, let's get some breakfast."

Thank God, I'm starting to get dizzy. We sit in a booth for six and open the menus. Dad is pissed, he's humiliated.

"Could you believe that bitch. She couldn't get us out fast enough. And then that son of a bitch Al, 'Oh, I'd love to help you, but I have to work.' He was full of shit. He probably thought we were going to rip off her precious knickknacks. I can't stand people like that. He never even offered us a shower or a cup of coffee. They made it perfectly clear we weren't welcome another night. I don't know how people live like that. How in the hell do you make breakfast for your family and not your guests? I'll see that guy in hell. Go ahead kids, order what you want."

Mom quickly counters that with, "How about some toast and cereal, you guys?" We didn't have to answer, we were going to have toast and cereal. Dad talks about Al and his unmannered wife throughout breakfast.

"Mom, can I have another glass of milk?"

"Here, have mine, I don't want any more."

It isn't the same as my own fresh glass, but it will do.

"Well, I don't need that son of a bitch. I'll get a job today. He can kiss my ass." Dad finishes his juice.

Mom reaches for the butter and offers a suggestion, "I'll take the kids to the beach, and we'll get showers there while you look for a job."

"Yeah, that'll be fine." Dad half listens.

Dad continues driving in the later morning traffic, feeling his way toward the skyline. The white sand beaches follow us practically the whole way. Everyone around us seems to know exactly where they are going. People in cars and people on the streets all have a purpose this morning. They have a fresh cup of coffee and determination in their walk. We have wrinkled clothes and greasy hair. I want to go swimming in that ocean; I can hear it calling my name.

Dad finally pulls off the interstate and turns right on a street called Ocean View. We drive along the water toward what he thinks is a shortcut to the city. The street winds around large homes and once in a while I see a maid getting out of her car going to work. The palm trees sway slightly back and forth. I can smell the money mixed in with the salt air. If I look out my side of the van, I can see the beaches. If I look out Shelly's side, I can see the green lawns that lead up to the white homes. I can't help but note the difference. Homes are large and have families that live in them and dads who go to work. Houses, however, are small and the grass never looks good. We haven't had a home since we left Arizona. I want a home again. Dad drives and drives, and we follow him along the confusing streets. Every time he turns up a street to cut over it's either a dead end or it circles us back to where we started. Mom is getting tired of this game.

"Mom, I have to go to the bathroom." Mark stretches.

"Well, as soon as your father gets his head out of his ass, we can stop." Mom begins her search for a bathroom while she keeps Dad in her sight. Mark tries not to squirm too much, but he can't help it.

I notice that Dad is pulling over up ahead. Lucky for Mark, this is a miracle, Dad never pulls over. Dad pulls into a 76 station on the corner. It's real busy and all the pumps are full of cars. "Mark, go ahead."

"Mom, can I go to?"

"Me too."

"Yes, just hurry up."

Before I can slide the van door all the way open, Dad is at the door. Shelly is still strapping on her sandals. That's why I don't wear sandals, they take too long to put on. Shelly looks up, and Mark sits there waiting as Dad blocks the door. "Ardell, this place is a bunch of horse shit. I'm not going to find any work." Mom is speechless, we're all thrown back by his words.

"Do you mind telling me what in the hell you're talking about?"

"We don't fit in here." Dad waves his arm around. I look around at the surroundings, and all I see is nice cars, nice homes and nice people. "It's nothing but a bunch of rich snobs. No one is going to give me a job. We just need to get out of here."

"All right then, where do you suggest we go?" Mom twists her rings around and around and scowls, waiting for an answer.

"Let's go back to Dorothy's, and I'll get a job in town."

Mom turns her head and rubs her face, she says nothing. I wish I knew what he was talking about, he hasn't even tried getting a job.

And then it dawns on me, he's scared. I want to throw up. We drove all this way for nothing. We are leaving now. Is that what I'm hearing? I can't believe it.

"How much money do we have left?"

"I don't know, you count it." Mom reaches under her seat and passes him the box.

He sits on the edge of the van and counts. "We have just about a hundred and fifty bucks. That's plenty as long as we don't eat in restaurants. We'll get an ice chest and go to the store for food."

Great, bologna sandwiches and grape Shasta soda pops, I can hardly wait.

"Yeah, we'll stay at KOA camps and sleep in the van." Dad continues to ramble on and on about his ideas of how we'll make it back to Grandma's, but Mom and I have both left this conversation back at the ice chest. Dad moves out of the way and Mark makes a run for the bathroom. Shelly and I climb out behind him.

"Sandra, are we going back to Ohio?"

"Yeah, it sure looks like it." I turn back to the van where Dad sits with the map blowing in the wind as he beats the wrinkles out of it.

"Where are we going to stay?"

"Probably at Grandma's like we always do."

"Do you think she'll be happy to see us?" Shelly asks.

"Of course she will, but she won't like it if we stay there too long." I open the bathroom door and we both go in. Shelly and I take advantage of the sink and wash up. "Shelly, help me get my hair wet." I lower my head into the sink, and Shelly wads my long hair up over my head and helps me get it wet. We both try to wring it out. I fling my head up and down and my hair flies in the air and soaks anything in its path, including Shelly. Shelly just laughs. "Shelly, you should do your hair."

"Nope."

"It feels good, and we probably won't get a shower today."

We run back to the van, Mom is giving the dogs a drink of water. "Okay kids, we're not staying in Florida, we're heading back to

Grandma's." Dad is gassing up and eating a Zagnut bar. I hate Zagnuts, they are the worst candy bar ever made. I think the only reason he eats them is because he knows we'll never ask for a bite.

"So listen, this time we're going to have to be real careful with the money." Mom says this as if we weren't careful on the way down here. The hamburgers were a treat, I guess. Shelly is miserable and Mark is lost. I am tired of driving, but all I can do is take a deep breath and pray we get out of here. Dad waves the caravan to depart Fort Myers, Florida, where there is nothing but a bunch of rich assholes who won't give Dad a job. Not to mention rude people who only let you stay one night and who don't offer breakfast and a shower to strangers.

26

Now I'm shit out of luck. I've read every comic book and finished all the word searches. I have nothing to do but stare out the window and wonder when I can shower again? The dogs are in a coma, and I can't even tell them how much longer. Mom pulls her hair back and stays hidden behind her dark sunglasses. Dad smiles a big smile as if this is what he had planned all along; drive to Florida, get gas, and turn around. I shake my head and find the strength not to scream. I hate Florida, I'd never live here. I don't care where we end up as long as I can get out of the van. My legs are so sick of sitting. I bet Shelly wishes now that she would have washed her hair. I feel half good, at least my hair is wet. That's what I can do, I'll comb out the tangles. I comb, Mom drives blindly, and Mark and Shelly play cards. We drive toward Georgia all day. I don't bother mentioning that we never did get to swim in the ocean. I lost the ocean hours ago, now it's just highway and tall green grass. I've never seen so much grass, fields, and fields of grass. The sun has disappeared behind the fluffy white clouds. I wonder how much longer it'll be before we stop; I think Dad plans on driving all night.

We continue driving and stopping every two hundred miles whether we need to or not. It starts to rain and for awhile it's nice, a change, but Mom hates driving in the rain, and she gets nervous.

Soon it starts to pour, and the farther we drive the harder it rains. The rain isn't fun any longer, it's scary. I can't see, the windshield is a blur. The car lights are nothing but streams of light falling down the windshield. Mom wants to stop, but Dad won't. He never even pulls over to check on her. She's cussing the rain and Dad. The thunder is here now and it's only making things worse. I feel Mom's fear all the way to my seat. I'm afraid for us. The few cars that were on the road are starting to pull over.

I wonder why we don't. Mom flips around the radio station to find out what this storm is all about. The newsman says we are experiencing a hurricane out in the ocean. Mom has had enough. I can't feel my legs anymore from braking so much and Mark and Shelly are crying. It's about seven o'clock at night, and Mom veers off the highway into a little old market/gas station. It's closed and no one is around. I guess if Dad keeps going then we'll just meet up with him at Grandma's. Dad pulls in and up to the van. The thunder is so loud that he has to yell his words to Mom.

"It's a pretty bad one, huhhh?"

"No shit…I can't see a thing. We better wait it out."

"Okay." Dad parks his truck and gets out. He runs around to the door. Just as I open the door and he climbs in, a lightning bolt shoots from the sky and explodes. His whole body jumps the rest of the way into the van. I pull on the back of his sopping wet shirt to help him in. The lightning has blown up a transformer on top of a telephone pole. Shelly and Mark scream with terror, and I look to Mom for the answer to this one. Nothing lets up, the thunder pounds outside the van, the rain pelts the roof, and the lightning dances around us. My heart is pounding too—Mom and Dad don't know what to do. Where is it safe? If she drives anywhere the lightning could get us, but if we stay it's only a matter of time. Then sharply another warning, lightning spitting as it hits the ground in the parking lot. All I can think is, *What now God? What have we done now? Why are you so mad?* I listen for the answer, but the thunder and the rain drowns out the Voice. I don't know why God is so mad. I can only guess that he's not happy with us leaving West Virginia the way we did. Mom can't take it, the lightning is too close to her kids. "We have to get out of here."

"Okay, but stay away from the power poles and trees."

Mom slowly puts the van into drive and creeps around the parking lot leaving the truck to sit out the storm. "Shit, I can't see a goddamn thing." I wish she'd quit saying "goddamn."

"Here, let me drive."

"No." I guess if we're going to die in a hurricane, it's gonna be her that does it. She gets to the highway and looks both ways, this is not for a car, but rather a decision. Which way will it be safe? She decides to go the same way the wind blows, north. She drives a cautious fifteen miles per hour. We hold our breath as trees and their limbs fall before us. Not only does the thunder, giant buckets of rain, and lightning try to get us, but now the wind is ripping the trees apart. It is safe to say that there is no safe place. The two-lane highway is dark and deserted. Mom prays for a motel where we can find shelter. I keep asking God to stop this, begging him to make the storm turn away from us. But the lightning lights up the sky and says, "No!"

"We better go back to the parking lot. At least it's an open area."

Dad agrees, but there is no right answer. Mom does a big U-turn and back to the parking lot we swim. The parking lot just sits there not welcoming us at all. We wait and watch for the next hit. Here it comes, the lightning strikes, the thunder laughs, and the rain blows with the wind as another tree limb cracks. The signs swing horizontal, and all we can do is wait our turn. We can't move. Mom tries to listen to the radio, but Dad reminds her to turn off the engine. I don't think he wants to know what's going on. How could we have hit a hurricane and not even known it? I shake the thought and brew up all my strength, *I will not die in this van with my family. Do you hear me? I want this to stop right now.* I go further and further into my head, I lift to the sky and follow the storm, chasing it. *You get out of here, I'm bigger than you.* I cuss and yell at the storm that has got us in its grips. I blow back as I fill my lungs and hold my breath, all the while challenging the storm to just try and touch me. The lightning begins to turn into a twinkle and the wind is stopping. The rain dribbles from the sky as the thunder passes us by.

"Ardell, listen, hear that? I think we're in the eye."

Mom loosens her grip on the dead steering wheel and looks around. Shelly and Mark notice it too. I can't believe it, I'm in shock. The storm has slowed down to a muffle in the distance instead of the mighty roar on top of our heads.

Mark is done being a baby and Shelly looks completely spent. Mom is exhausted. Dad rolls opens the van door, goes outside, and steps in a meager puddle to show who's boss. Mom wants to curl up and die.

"Okay, let's go, we might as well get some driving done." Dad pats Mom on the arm and pops over to his truck. Even the truck whines a little before it will start. Dad drives us into the night. His plan is to get us to a KOA camp in the morning where we can take the day off and swim.

The morning comes and our stomachs growl, a good morning wake-up call. Mom has driven all night—she can't take off her glasses, the new sun will blind her. Dad works a deal with the camp leader and somehow we manage to check in five hours earlier than we're supposed to. Everyone runs to the bathrooms with Mom throwing fresh clothes our way. I didn't care if I had clothes or not, I'd rather be naked than dirty.

"Shelly, pass me the cream rinse."

"I'm not done yet."

"I'll give it right back." We both stand in the half warm and half cold showers on a concrete floor washing our bodies and pretending that this is the best shower we have ever had. The rest of the camp sleeps while we are ending our day.

We meet Dad by the truck, he's untying his knots and laying some of the stuff out to dry. I don't think the TV will make it. "Honey, don't worry it'll be fine, we'll let the stuff dry today."

Mom knows that this is not true and she's going to be stuck with moldy clothes, waterlogged papers, and ruined furniture. She stays as far away from the wilted boxes as possible. Dad ends his attempt to save our wet, soggy stuff and calls the time of death, the TV is gone. He takes his shaving kit and a wad of clothes to the bathroom. Mom needs some sleep right after she makes us some bologna sandwiches for breakfast, which is really our dinner. Dad is back and eats with us as he lays down the law.

"Your mother and I need some sleep. I don't want to hear a word out of you guys. Take the dogs for a walk and go play, but by God you better let your mother sleep." He wipes the mayonnaise off his face and slugs down a grape Shasta. "Don't you guys even think about waking her for anything."

I wonder, *not even if Mark accidentally cuts off his foot? Or if Shelly falls into a rushing river and is drowning?*

He flops in the back seat and Mom curls into the next backseat of the van. They both stretch out and fall asleep. They look like different people, they are so tired.

For the next four hours, we are on our own, the camp is ours. The playground, the nature trail, and the pool. Oh shoot, the pool, no one asked about the pool. Can we or can we not go swimming? Shelly and Mark look to me for the answer. "He didn't say we couldn't, all he said was be quiet."

"But we don't have our bathing suits."

I know Shelly's right and we have to fix that. "All right listen, I'll go find them." I have no idea where Mom packed them, but I will find them. All I have to do is be quiet about it. "Stay here, keep the dogs back, and I'll be right back." Shelly and Mark know the risk I'm about to take. I take my shoes off so there won't be any noise and gingerly walk around the bees toward the van. I make my decision to try the box first. I dig and riffle through everything and, there, I find mine. Next I look hard for Shelly's. I find one and now Mark's. I can't find Mark's bathing suit. I have to try one more time. I tip toe through the grass over to the suitcase. This is far more dangerous, it's right next to the van. I open the locks one at time. Click! God I hope that wasn't too loud. Dad stirs and rolls over to his side. Mom just sleeps. I pull everything out and look over the dirty clothes. I can't find Mark's. I look up and Mark has accidentally let Sugar go, she is running straight for the van, she wants to see Dad. She runs and I scramble to my feet. I have to stop her before she jumps in. All I can see are Dad's bare feet hanging out the side door and Sugar going about fifty miles per hour to see her daddy. I can't call her, and I pray I can stop her. I wait for the right second and I make my one attempt to catch her. I lunge in front of her just as she gets ready to jump and I catch her in midair. She yelps. I hold her tight with my right arm and grab the bathing suits with my left. I start out of the danger zone, when I realize I still don't have anything for Mark. I quietly and quickly turn around and grab the first pair of shorts I see, then I run away as fast as I can. Shelly and Mark greet me like any hero of the day.

"Here, give me mine." I throw Shelly her bathing suit and her face drops with disappointment.

"I don't like that one."

"What?"

"That one doesn't fit right."

"Shelly, for God's sake just wear it, no one's here you know."

"Nope."

"Mark, this is all I could find."

He throws his on the ground. "Those are girl's shorts."

"Mark, they are not."

"Yes they are."

"Are you telling me that we can't go swimming because you guys don't like what I found?"

"You found yours."

"Yeah, because mine was on the top. Shelly, just wear it; if you go over there and wake them we'll all be in trouble."

Shelly pouts and stomps off to change. Mark picks up the cut-offs and examines them for cooties. "Mark, they aren't girl's shorts, I don't know whose they are. Just wear them to swim. No one can tell, I swear."

Mark finally agrees and changes his long pants and puts on his girl's shorts. I tie the dogs to the trees in the shade and off we go cannon-balling into the pool at nine o'clock. The whole pool is ours; most people are eating breakfast, I can smell it. We swim and swim and swim. I stay underwater and feel the perfection of my mermaid body in the water. I stay to myself for awhile, lapping up the water and freedom of swimming. The chlorine burns, but who cares. I kick my feet and feel the power of my legs. Shelly is still tugging at her bathing suit and letting me know how much she hates it. Mark has forgotten about his girl shorts, and the dogs are asleep. I dive in and pull my soaked body out of the pool to do it again. I love breaking the water with a dive from the side of the pool.

"Shelly, I'll race you."

"Okay."

"I want to race too." Mark can't race us, we're a lot faster than him. "Why don't you be the judge?" Shelly and I take our mark while Mark sings, "Get ready, set, GO!" Shelly and I pump and kick as fast as we can; she's a lot faster than last year. I have to beat her. I tuck my head and don't look back. I kick with my legs and breathe once in a while, the race is mine. I gasp for air as I reach for the side of the pool and look up to Mark.

"Shelly won."

"No she didn't."

"Yes, she did."

I know what he's doing, he's decided to be Shelly's friend not mine. They do this all the time. Mark and Shelly gang up against me. "Mark, that's not fair, you know I won."

"Nu-uhh, Shelly did."

I swim away from them both, I hate it when they do that. I can't believe that today is going to be one of those lonely days when they won't be my friends. All because I got the wrong bathing suits. I cry off to the side of the pool and try not to let them see me, but Shelly does.

"What's the matter little baby, mad cause I beat you?"

I say nothing because the answer is I am sad they won't play with me. Nothing hurts me more than when they're not my friends. All the time I spend getting us out of trouble, fighting Dad for them, and then this, Shelly and Mark teasing me. Mark doesn't tease as much as Shelly, he mostly just follows her. She won't let up, she really thinks I'm mad that she beat me unfairly. The truth is I'm too sad to care, but if I did I'd beat her ass. She can't swim faster than me, I know that, but what she can do is take her's and Mark's friendship away from me. She knows that's the only way to hurt me, and she does it on purpose. The part that bugs the most is that I can't tell on her. She doesn't have to play with me if she doesn't want to. Shelly calls the shots, and she always has.

I decide to go sit with the dogs. I cry and cry and wonder if I'll ever stop. Sometimes when you start crying for one reason a whole lot of other ones show up. I look up and there's Shelly and Mark playing in the pool that I just gave them. They don't love me, they never have. I wish I didn't love them. Sometimes I think it would be better if I lived somewhere else, maybe then they might miss me or love me. But I know they don't, and what's worse is they don't care. They don't even know how much I hurt inside. I know everything about them, I know before they do. I could die and nobody would ever miss me. Yeah sure, Mom would cry a little bit, but then she'd forget about me. Dad would just be thankful he had one less mouth to feed. And Shelly, well, she'd probably dance on my grave and sing, "Ding dong the Wicked Witch is dead." Mark would miss me a little bit, but only because I'm the biggest and I can save him before he gets in trouble with Dad. I don't have to worry about Shelly, she never gets in trouble. What really hurts the most is that no one cares who I am. I struggle with my words and I try to let them know, but it's Shelly they want to hear about and see, and it's Mark that Mom loves. I try to shine and let them know what a good person I am and how much I love them. But something always gets in the way, and when I want to tell them how I see things, or I have a question,

I get a lump in my throat and I forget how to talk. Then I just feel big and clumsy, begging for attention. I'll never beg again. It's easier to sit here and remind myself, *I am a good person*, and to think my own thoughts safely in my very own head. I know what I'm trying to say and I know what I feel. Right now Shelly has done it again, hurt my feelings for no reason, stepped on my head with her roller-skates and just kept on going. She doesn't even turn back to see if I'm bleeding.

27

It's almost ten o'clock in the morning and we are exiting the highway. There's Duke's local bar on the corner—it's only a matter of blocks now. Duke is Grandma's new husband. I like him, but I really don't know him that well. He's a quiet man with a smile that cracks out of the corner of his mouth. He mumbles, and when I can't understand him, Grandma interprets. She repeats his words for us as if something is wrong with our hearing. She always gets a little pissed when we say "huh" more than twice. He loves kids and dogs, as long as we don't sit in his recliner. The recliner that used to be Grandma's is his now, but she doesn't seem to mind. I do. Duke grew up with thirteen brothers and sisters on a big dairy farm. His brother and two sisters all live together in the old farmhouse on a thousand acres, with a thousand cows.

Duke works early in the morning; he works the big machines on the interstate snow plowing. Sometimes he has to get up at three o'clock in the morning.

Mom pulls in the driveway, so Dad parks on the street. I look in the picture window and watch the front screen door. I wait for it to swing open and Grandma to come out screaming, "Lordy be, what are you all doing here?" as she kisses us to death. But the screen door doesn't open and she's not coming out. Is she angry? We drag our road-weary bodies from the van. The dogs run to the backyard. It's very confusing, where's Grandma?

As I lift a suitcase out of the truck, I look over my shoulder waiting for her voice. Shelly runs for the bathroom, and Mark is lugging a bag of toys across the lawn.

"Hey what you all doing?" Duke is standing in the carport, he must've come out of the backyard.

"Oh nothing Duke, we just thought we'd stop by for a visit."

"Well Grandma's at work."

"Oh that's right, it's Saturday." I can feel the relief soothe my body.

"Well now, come in and make yourselves at home. She should be back around one o'clock." Duke looks at me and grins, making sure that I understand completely.

"Duke, can I call her at work and tell her we're here?"

"Sure, come with me, I'll have to find that number." I follow him to the kitchen, walking by the green recliner. I remember sitting there on her lap when I was little.

"Here you go, she's at the doctor's office today." Grandma works on Fridays and Saturdays for Dr. Schelinger, he's a foot doctor. I always wonder why she works for a foot doctor and every time she comes home the first thing she does is take off her shoes and rub her aching feet. If he's a foot doctor why doesn't he fix her feet? But that's okay, I'll rub her feet for her when she gets home. I dial the number, "Grandma."

"Sandra is that you?"

"Yes Grandma, we're at your house, we just got here."

"Lordy…I thought you all were in Florida."

"Nope, we went there but Dad didn't like it."

Dad appears out of nowhere. "Give me that." He snatches the phone. "Hey Dorothy, sorry we didn't call first, but things didn't work out. Okay Dorothy, we'll make ourselves at home. Yes I'll make lunch. Bye." Dad hangs up and I didn't even get to say good-bye.

Duke goes back to the backyard. Mom shuffles our stuff to the basement and the spare bedroom. Dad sits on the couch and flicks on the TV. Shelly and I go find Duke. Mark is asking Mom questions about where he gets to sleep. Usually he sleeps with Grandma, Mom and Dad get the extra bed, and Shelly and I get the basement. I hope Mark sleeps on the couch and not with us.

I open the back door to the yard. Everything looks normal—there's a garden in the very back by the clothesline, and the grapes are almost purple. The bird feeder is half full of seed, and is hanging in the tree next to a giant tortoise. I blink my eyes and look again. Yes there *is* a turtle. It's about three feet wide strung up in the tree. Duke is standing there with a bucket of blood and a knife. Shelly can't look, neither can I, but what in the hell is he doing? I know that Duke hunts ducks, squirrels, and fishes, but a giant turtle?

He turns around and smiles, two teeth are missing. "Turtle soup."

Does Grandma know he's got a dead turtle hanging in her tree? My thoughts run wild: How could he have killed this beautiful creature? How horrible it must have been to be swimming along and then some old man comes and catches you and hangs you in a tree and kills you. God I wish he hadn't done that. All in the name of turtle soup. There's going to be enough turtle soup for two hundred. Grandma never said she liked turtle soup. I'll tell you right now, there's no chance in hell anyone will make me eat this turtle, soup or not. I'm ashamed of Duke, and I hope that poor turtle can forgive me for being here.

Dad comes out, I'm sure Shelly went to tell him what's going on. He stands there trying not to be touched by the sight of the peaceful old turtle who was alive not hours ago.

"Yeah I got it this morning." Duke pulls up his pants and fusses with his suspenders. "I had to wait until I got home to kill it. I had to shove the knife…"

I close my ears. The turtle was probably tucked in his shell real tight for protection. The thought of what Duke did to murder this guy is enough to make me sick. I have to talk to Grandma.

I stand there listening to Duke tell Dad about ripping off his shell to cut him up for soup. Dad is polite, but inside he is just as sick as me. I pray for the turtle and close my eyes when the shell is removed.

I can feel the pain of the turtle deep inside my heart, I feel it. Dad sneaks a squeeze on my shoulders, and I think it was for both of us. After all the driving in humidity, humiliation, and hurricanes, I cannot believe that this is my welcome home. I'm depressed. I need to go for a walk.

"Shelly, you guys want to go for a walk?"

"I guess..." Shelly isn't pleased either. We don't ask Mom, she knows I need to get out of here. Mom stays far away from what's going on in the backyard, she won't even let anyone tell her about it, let alone see it. Mark hears that we're going on a walk and bounces out of the bathroom.

"I want to go."

We leave the house and head for the hill behind Grandma's. The walk is cooler in the woods, and the walk to the top is steep. No one is there but us, and the squirrels. I can tell they know what's going on at Grandma's, they are yelling at us. "See, they all know about the turtle and they're mad at us."

"But we didn't do it."

We walk up the mountain, our legs burning, as we try to tell the squirrels we had nothing to do with killing the turtle. But all they can smell is death in their neighborhood. Even the blackbirds are diving at us. The echo of squirrels chattering, birds screaming, the rabbits hiding—Mark can sense the mood of the woods.

"It's not our fault." He yells.

They don't believe us. They want us to leave. I want to stay, but it's hard; the tiny voices get louder. The geese below in the pond won't even take bread crumbs from Mark. They swim to the other side and turn their beaks up. I feel horrible, Shelly and Mark do too. We leave the woods early with our heads down. We have nothing to say but good-bye.

Today is the single worst day of my life; my magic kingdom full of small friends has abandoned me. We have been going to these woods for years and we know everybody here. They may never forgive us, but I'll make it up to them.

We walk around the corner and there's Grandma's car. I don't know whether to be mad or glad to see her. I walk in first with my fists closed and my lips together. Mom doesn't know how serious this backyard bloodbath really is. She doesn't know that all the animals in the woods are sad and terrified.

"Sandra, oh my goodness, give me a hug." Grandma squeezes me and grabs for Shelly. I stand there with my arms down at my sides.

She notices slightly, but she needs to know more. I have to tell her. Grandma opens the refrigerator and talks to herself. "Well let's see, what can we make for lunch?"

I stand in the kitchen ready to fight. "How about peanut butter and turtle?"

Grandma looks at me directly.

"Watch your mouth, do you hear me." Mom flips the back of my head.

I nod my head and go outside. I have to bury the turtle. I can't let Duke throw him in the garbage. He's not garbage.

Grandma comes out and sits with me on the porch. "Sandra what's the matter?"

I can't find the words. My throat closes, and although I have plenty to say, all I can muster is, "Grandma please don't make turtle soup, please."

"All right honey…don't you worry."

Grandma goes out to Duke who's cleaning up the mess. "Duke, you have really upset the children. Sandra wants to bury the turtle."

"Why? It's nothing but a dead old smelly turtle."

"You have to bury it. Now call Sandra and go dig a hole in the back of the garden."

He has a shovel in one hand and a gunny sack of dead turtle in the other. I help move the wheelbarrow and Duke begins digging. He digs a great big hole and I approve it. Duke gets ready to drop the sack into the hole, but he catches my look and decides to lower it gently instead. Duke starts kicking and shoveling the dirt. He stands there for a couple of seconds and stabs the shovel next to the grave and then walks into the house. He never says another word about turtle soup.

The next morning everyone takes advantage of sleeping in. I can hear Grandma stirring around in the kitchen. Her ability to be quiet only works to a certain point, then it's pots and pans clanking in the kitchen sink and the cupboard doors opening with a squeak and closing with a thud. I roll over and throw a pillow over my head, but somehow her footsteps creep through the pillowcase and to my ears. She's fully dressed, I peek as she carts a basket in her arms down the wooden basement stairs past Shelly and me, to the washer that sits in a dark corner of the basement where we sleep. By the time she turns the loud knob around on the washer, it's time to wake up. "Morning Grandma."

Her eyes light up as she turns to me. She's next to the washer with her white shorts and green sleeveless button-down shirt and little tennis shoes with dirt stains from the garden. "Good morning to you sweetheart. Did you sleep good?"

"Yeah."

"That's good."

Shelly rolls over, "Grandma, can we pick tomatoes today?"

"Surely, I was waiting for you two to get up and help Grandma."

"Grandma, can I take a shower?"

"Of course, but take a quick one so we don't run out of hot water."

I jump to my feet and run over to the shower. It's a little one that sits in a corner next to the washer. The shower curtain is tan and it's a little too small; it doesn't quite shut all the way. The water pressure is high and if I'm not careful when I turn on the knobs, the water feels like gravel against my skin.

I shower while Shelly waits. Shelly won't go another step until she gets a shower. "Hurry up, Grandma said."

"I am, I have to rinse my hair. Shelly are there any towels down here?"

"Nope."

"Well, could you please get me one?" She hesitates for a minute, "Shelly, will you?"

"Okay...Grandma, Sandra needs a towel," she yells from the stairs. I can't believe she won't even get me a towel. As I'm washing my feet and waiting for a towel, I hear footsteps down the stairs. I turn off the water and pop my head through the curtain expecting Grandma to be there with a warm smile and a dry towel in her hand. But it's Mom. She hands me the towel and waits for me to dry off. I wrap the towel around my damp body, my hair is soaking wet hanging there off my shoulders. Shelly sits on the bed and I stand in the towel. Mom's lips are tight and her eyes are serious.

"Girls you listen to me." She continues in a soft but stern voice. "This is not fair to your Grandmother. We are here out of the kindness of her heart. I don't want to hear you yelling orders and bugging her for things. You'll eat what she fixes us and ask for nothing. Your Grandmother is not here to serve you. We are guests and I expect you to clean up after yourselves and help her around here. I'm not kidding." Mom ends her early morning lecture, which is not like her at all, she isn't normally grouchy in the mornings.

She steps up three stairs and turns around, "And don't forget to make your beds." Mom wants Grandma to stop helping all the time and she wants us to know it.

What is going on? Shelly turns.

"I don't know." I shake my head as she rolls her eyes and shrugs her shoulders.

Mom is up the stairs and out of sight. "I think Mom's mad."

"But why is she mad at us?"

"She's not mad at us, she's just mad. Mom hates staying here too long, and who knows where we are going or when we can leave. We can't go back to Fairly or Roncevert. We don't have any money and Dad has to find a job."

"Well it's not our fault."

"We better just do what she says and stay out of the way."

"I'm taking a shower." Shelly pops off the bed, and I get dressed for the day and make my bed. I leave Shelly behind and go to the kitchen.

"Dorothy, do you mind if I do some laundry later?" I can see Mom's face cringe as the words leave her mouth. Her pride is the real question here.

Grandma answers kindly, she can tell that Mom is embarrassed. "Oh Ardell, now be sure to help yourself to anything around here." That was Grandma's way of saying don't worry. "Sandra, now, what can I fix you for breakfast?" Normally I would ask, What'cha got? But not with Mom standing right there glaring at me. Grandma would tease me with yucky stuff like eggs, mush, or toast and then I would say, "Waffles." But Mom is watching me like a hawk and we both know what my answer will be.

"Grandma, I'm not very hungry. How about some cereal?"

"Now that's not enough, how about some waffles?"

"No, just cereal."

Grandma mumbles as she gets the Cheerios out of her cupboard. "At least have some toast, girl."

I look to Mom and she approves. "All right Grandma." That was the least Grandma could do, it's her kitchen and I am her granddaughter. She has to make me something.

Mom passes Dad in the hall and says nothing to him as he says a cheery, "Good morning." He kicks the footstool out of the way and plops down in the recliner, the green recliner. "Dorothy, we might need to stay here a little while until I find a job."

"Now Jack, you know that's fine with me. Stay as long as you need."

I sit there eating the dry nasty round things floating in a bowl of milk, pretending I don't understand a word they are saying. As I swallow another spoonful of cereal, I gag under my breath, "I hate milk, I hate Cheerios, I only like Cocoa Puffs and Froot Loops." No one hears me and that's good. Dad would have knocked the shit out of me, but at least I said it.

I hear the shower turn off and I jump to my feet and wash my dishes. Shelly is eating the toast and Mark is gobbling up the Cheerios. Grandma is at the stove making Dad some runny eggs and bacon.

"Sandra now you stop that, I'll get those dishes."

I turn off the water and know that Mom is going to have something to say about that.

"Ardell, what can I get you for breakfast?"

"Nothing right now, maybe I'll have something later."

"Are you sure?"

"Yeah, I don't feel too good."

"Well, you should rest. All that driving probably wore you out."

I turn on *Tarzan* and look over to Mom. Now that she mentions it, she doesn't look too good. Grandma's right, she's probably just tired. Mom sits on the couch with her body, but her thoughts are miles and miles away.

"Mom, want me to brush your hair?"

"Oh god, that would be great." She moves to the floor. I sit on the couch and brush her hair from the top of her head down her back. She likes her hair brushed hard on the top and lightly at the bottom. I hold the brush in my fist and make sure I get every single hair. She melts and her back slightly relaxes. I love her back resting on my knees as she touches my foot. She remembers that she loves me as she pats my leg with her soft hands. I am so glad she's my mom, I can't imagine anyone else as my mom. Her hair is thick like mine and her skin soft. She smells like flowers and her smile is back. I haven't seen her smile in weeks. After a while, my arm is getting tired and I switch hands. I can't brush as good with my left. She scoots up and tries to help me get a better angle to brush. Breakfast is done and Tarzan is fighting with an alligator.

"Sandra, go help your Grandmother." She pats my leg twice.

Grandma washes and I dry, Shelly dumps the garbage, and Mark goes to the shower. Men don't do dishes in Grandma's house. Dad opens the paper and searches for work. Mom falls asleep on the couch.

She quickly catches herself, "My God I am tired. Dorothy. I'm going to lay down for awhile."

"Go right ahead, the kids and I'll be fine."

We spend the afternoon in the garden and going to the grocery store. I must get some better cereal. Grandma stops by her friend's house to show us off. "Now, do you remember Marge?" Of course the answer is no, but we all nod our heads yes. We sit there in the heat with the bags of groceries piled in the backseat squashing Mark. The plastic seat covers are wet with sweat from our legs, and we smile politely.

"I've known your grandmother for over thirty years, she's one of my best friends. Dorothy, these can't be your grandchildren, they are much too grown up."

"Well they are. Sandra here is my oldest, she's going to be twelve this October."

"Oh my, where does the time go? Last time I saw them, I think Sandra was eight. They had just moved here from Phoenix or California, something like that."

"Yes my babies came here and went to Fort Springs and lived in the old cabin."

"That's right before you married Duke. Dorothy, I think we're getting old."

Grandma laughs and Marge waves us on with a smile. She pulls her cart down the sidewalk, and the flowers on her summer dress blow a bit as we drive off. Her flabby arm continues to wave to her dear friend Dorothy. I look to see if Grandma's arms are the same. Thank God they're not. Grandma is never going to get old, I won't let her. We pass at least another ten friends as we make our way through town and down the neighborhood past her church. Grandma knows everyone, and it's important that they all know us.

Mark has found the popsicles, "Grandma can I have one before they melt."

"Oh my, I forgot we bought those silly popsicles. Why sure. Sandra, help him get 'em open and pass one to your sister."

I do. The box is damp and soggy, and Mark looks with bug eyes as he waits to see if the popsicles are still alive. I pull the paper off and lick at the same time.

"Don't ya'll get that mess in my car."

I don't know how not to, the missiles are melting faster than we can lick, slurp, and suck. Mark's popsicle breaks off the stick and falls between the seat and the grocery sacks. I reach around and try to help him, but it's gone. He can't say anything. He has to keep still, he doesn't want Grandma to know. I manage to eat mine successfully, and Shelly has only a bite a left. Mark is done before he starts, poor guy.

By the time we get home, Dad has left and Mom is sleeping. "Grandma, Mom is still sleeping." I quietly close the door. She lays there curled up and completely out. She's not napping, she's sleeping as if it's bedtime.

"Now leave her alone, she probably needs it."

I walk away and down the small hallway to the living room. Mom never sleeps like this, especially at Grandma's. I look at the clock—it's two o'clock. If she's not awake in another hour, I'm going to wake her up.

"Brooks and Regina are coming over for supper tonight. We're going to have ham, mashed potatoes"—Grandma looks to Shelly for a smile as she knows Shelly's favorite food is mashed potatoes—"and green beans with salad."

"Can we have pie too?"

"Now Sandra," Grandma points the spatula my way, "you're going to have to watch your weight. Grandma's noticed you've put on a few pounds."

I can't believe she said that. Mark and Shelly laugh at me. "Yeah fat cow."

"Now don't you worry, you probably got it from Grandma. But if you don't watch out, it will be worse when you get older."

Am I hearing her right? Does she *think* I'm fat? I wish she'd stop talking about my body.

"Grandma," Mark tugs at Grandma's apron, "if Sandra can't have any pie, can you still make us some?"

I walk out of the kitchen. It's as if the topic of Sandra and her potbelly is open for everyone to discuss. My body is none of their business. I don't eat too much. Why is my body always a concern around here? I know I'm bigger than Shelly, but it's not my fault.

Suppertime rolls around, and sure enough Brooks and Regina show up. Regina had the baby and Brian is his name. I get to hold him. I try to understand him as a cousin, but he feels much more like a nephew. After all, Regina and I were more like sisters than aunt and niece. Grandma fusses in the kitchen and Regina fusses with the baby. I give him back and wonder where my little baby brother is; is God taking care of him? I wonder if he is lonely up there in heaven. I only let the thoughts come in for a minute, and then I quickly change the subject in my head. I can't believe how much it still hurts to know he died.

"Come on you all, let's eat." Duke is the first in the kitchen taking his chair. He's a shadow most of the time, but when Grandma calls dinner, he shines.

Brooks holds out a hot pan of juicy green beans, "Hey Shel, want me to load up your plate with green beans?"

"Brooks, you stop it," Grandma hits Brooks softly with a pot holder, "If Shelly doesn't want any, she doesn't have to eat them. Besides she likes Grandma's mashed potatoes."

"Awe come on Shel, they're great."

"Brooks I don't want any."

Grandma takes the pan from Brooks. "Give some to Sandra, she needs to eat the green beans and stay away from the mashed potatoes." Grandma winks at me like it's our little secret. Secret my ass, she's done it again, announced that I'm fat and I eat too much. She doesn't even know I hate mashed potatoes.

Brooks gives me a "poor thing" look. He pats me on the back as some sort of encouragement. What is encouraging? The cat's out of the bag, and Sandra is fat. I haven't even got a plate. Mom says nothing, but she knows I hurt. Dad wants to join in but for some reason stops himself. All of a sudden I have a plate, and the whole table is glaring my way.

What will Sandra eat? I want to throw my plate at them all. I pick up my fork and cut a tiny piece of ham and chew thirty times before I swallow. Grandma tilts her head and is proud of me. Proud of what? I am pissed off and uncomfortable. How did this dinner turn into Sandra's last supper? I look to Mom for support, but she keeps her head down and avoids eye contact. Someone should stop this.

Dessert comes to all the thin people, and Mark, who is sitting next to me, exaggerates his lips and mouth as he smacks down his warm piece of pie.

Shelly sits across from me singing, "Umm Umm, this is so good."

Grandma cuts me a piece of cantaloupe, but what she doesn't realize is I hate cantaloupe more than I hate mashed potatoes. And worst of all, I hate all this attention around my plate. I wish I wasn't fat.

The next three days are spent at Grandma's while Dad hustles to find a job. Mom muddles around trying to contribute, but she's still tired. She's not in a bad mood but a quiet one. She encourages Dad when Grandma's in the room and cusses him when she's not.

"I want the hell out of here, Goddamn it. I can't stand your mother paying all the bills and buying us food. She's helped us enough already. It's not right. Find a job and get us out of here. An apartment will do."

"I will," Dad rustles the newspaper, "but it's not that simple."

"I'll get a job then, damn it."

"Ardell just hold on."

"I'm not kidding around with you, I've had just about enough of this shit. It's the beginning of August and my kids *will* be in a house when school starts." Mom is done talking.

"Look, I've talked to Dorothy. She's going to give us a loan to get us back on our feet. Go ahead and find us a place."

28

That evening Shelly, Mark, and I sit on the back porch swing. I can't help but look at the chains holding it. I know it can hold two adults easily, but I'm wondering if it will hold me. Grandma comes out and grabs a chair. She goes on and on about how humid it is and how her garden could use a nice rain. I sit there carefully, swinging gently, and listening for a crack from above. I've become paranoid in less than three days. Everything from this point forward revolves around my potbelly. I sit there sucking it in and trying not to breathe too loud, as Shelly kicks her feet back and forth without a care in the world. Grandma puts Mark on her lap and pulls his hair out of his eyes. "Boy, you need a haircut." Mark goes white, and I'm glad she has moved on to another target. Mom comes out just then with a cold Coke.

"Ardell," Grandma lifts Mark's hair, "this boy is going to go blind, he needs a haircut." I know where this is going to go, nowhere.

"Dorothy, Mark likes his hair long." I wish Mom would do that for me when Grandma attacks my body.

"I'm just saying we could take him to Duke's barber."

Mom protects him with all her might. "That won't be necessary." That little conversation ends right there.

"Grandma," Shelly points, "look at those clouds. Don't they look funny?"

I look across the backyard to the horizon along with Grandma. Shelly is right, the sky looks different. Grandma studies the sight, sitting there consumed by the swirling black clouds. The humidity suddenly evaporates into a chill. I'm intrigued. Grandma is still. "Shush, be quiet…hear that?"

I realize without a doubt she is right. Nothing. Not a bird, squirrel, or dog can be heard. It's a silence so loud I can hear myself breathe.

"Maybe we all better get inside." Not more than two seconds pass when a rain shower begins without a raindrop's warning. It goes from hot and humid, to cold and rainy.

"Grandma, what is it?"

"Get inside, it's a tornado."

We follow her and her suspicions into the house. Grandma goes in and turns on the news: "There is a tornado outside Stanville County. It is traveling due south approximately seventy-five miles per hour. It is advised you stay in your home and stay tuned for further updates. This is a tornado warning for all of Stanville County."

"Duke, why don't you close all the windows. I'll get a few things together to take down to the basement." Grandma pats Duke's arm and goes in the kitchen.

My head whirls with the approaching disaster. We just had a hurricane, now we get a tornado in the same week. What's going on?

Mom doesn't like the news, and Dad doesn't like tornadoes. Dad tries not to overreact.

"Oh hell, that thing could land anywhere, they have no idea where in the hell it'll go." How does he do that? Even if a dragon was in the backyard breathing fire up his ass Dad would remain calm, but it was more cocky than anything else.

"Duke," Dad stands up, "you want some beer? I'll go to the store, we need milk."

I turned around to see if my ears were still attached to my head. He knows he's not supposed to drink. Besides, we're at Grandma's. What is he going to do, go crazy in front of her? This is not right. I run to the back door to check on the clouds; they are still there swirling. Dad has picked up the keys, the jingle echoes above the thunder and rain. He stands at the door pulling up his jeans and tugging on his T-shirt. I can't believe it he's driving away.

"Duke...Where's Jack?" Grandma has a worried look on her face.

Duke, who is half gassed on Hamm' s beer, mumbles the words only a devoted wife could understand. "I don't know."

"Grandma, he went to the store for more beer."

Grandma looks at Duke and wants to kick him. Mom steps in and reassures her. "Dorothy he'll be back, he just went to the little corner store."

Grandma isn't buying it. I sit observing the storm outside and the one inside. Grandma's name is Dorothy, we must be in the *Wizard of Oz*. The tornado is here. Duke is Uncle Ed, Grandma is Aunty Em, Mom is the Good Witch from the East. And Dad is the Wizard of Oz. He's nothing but smoke and lights behind a giant curtain of bullshit.

The TV blasts: "Warning—the tornado is moving southeast at this time. Local residents of Pinesville must not leave their homes." Grandma clutches her mustard seed and prays to God. She prays silently to herself. She keeps that mustard seed in her purse for emergencies just like this one. I pray to God were not in trouble again.

Suddenly Dad yells from the front door. "I'm back. All they had was Coors, hope it'll do."

Duke sits smirking in the green recliner. Grandma stands there with the mustard seed in the palm of her hand, and Mom sits at the kitchen table.

"Jack, I think we better get the kids to the basement."

"You heard your grandmother." Dad hands Duke a beer. "Get in the basement."

We go to the basement and wait like good children. Mom decides the best place for her is in the basement too. Mom holds Shelly and Mark and we all sit on the bed. The wind hollers at the back door upstairs. The light flickers on and off as the storm comes closer and closer. Everyone is scared, and it is nice to be with Mom for a change instead of by ourselves when we're this scared. "Everything is going to be fine, we're going to stay here just in case the tornado comes this way."

"What about Dad?" Mark asks.

"Your father will be fine. If the tornado comes this way, Grandma will make him and Duke come down here. She's watching for it, believe me."

Waiting for a tornado takes a lot of patience. We sit there for forty-five minutes. "Come on y'all, it looks like the tornado has passed on by." We run upstairs and out the back door. I think I am going to see something, but when I open the back door, everything's fine. Every single thing is in its place. The bird feeder has fallen, but that is about it. All the neighbors are checking for damage. All I can think is, I'll be damned, that mustard seed did it again!

I sit on the swing outside and get lost in the rain. The smell of damp grass and wet trees fills the air. The humidity has still not returned, but it's trying. I feel the chill once in awhile, but mostly I feel the calm. It's dark, but I can see the beauty of everything. It's magical and mysterious.

Mom startles me when she opens the screen door, "Honey it's time to go to bed."

"But Mom it's so pretty out here."

She comes out and stands next to the swing trying to figure out what I'm talking about. I don't know if she does, but she stands there a long time looking for what I see. It's the first time in forever that I'm alone with Mom. It seems that all we do lately is fly around barely touching the ground or each other. The raindrops drip a little slower off the leaves, and the grass seems to smell sweeter. I hear a bird come back home to sing. And Mom standing there, alone, with me, seems to make everything a little bit more beautiful. She looks so tired, tired of it all, the traveling, fighting, and fussing we do. I wish she was Dorothy and that all she had to do was click three times and get us back to Kansas.

29

Everyone is up and watching TV with coffee in hand. The news is bad, real bad. The tornado had touched down later that night while I was sleeping. I see sadness, death, and devastation. The town of Zanesville has been destroyed.

"Zanesville has taken a mighty blow from last night's tornado. Without warning, the tornado suddenly turned due east and destroyed everything in its path. Fourteen people are dead and five missing. The survivors are without homes, power, and water. The emergency crews are not yet able to search, they must wait and secure the area first."

The newscaster keeps talking and talking, but all I see is a flattened town. Dead faces on people who are in shock. The mother of a little girl who is missing, and missing means dead.

I have to leave the noise of the TV. I walk down the creaking stairs to the basement. I hold on tightly to the wooden handrail and count each stair to the bottom. The sunlight has no way into the dark basement. My hand fumbles for the string with the single lightbulb attached. I pull harder than normal and the dim lightbulb turns on. I can see Grandma's housecoats and sundresses hanging from a wire strung across half the basement. The smells of dirty laundry, mold from the shower, and cold concrete fills my nose, and the familiar odors feel good to me. As I collect my thoughts, I realize this is home to me. One whole shelf against the back wall is full of her canning: tomatoes, beans, jellies, and pickles. I blow the dust off the shelf and see her handwriting on each jar: the date, year, and type of pickle— sweet, dill, bread and butter, whole, diced, and relish.

Next to the shelves is Duke's shop. Inside is every single fishing pole he ever owned. Some are broke, some are not, mostly they're old. They stand there ready to be picked up for the next outing, all of them holding on to the fishing stories they've collected over the years. I can practically hear them fighting with each other as to who has caught the most, the biggest, and who was the strongest. Out of the corner of my eye I see a weak thin pole with a rusted reel and no line. I can't help but feel a little sorry for that one. He's buried behind some shovels and rakes, and there's no chance that he'll ever see the river, a boat, or a hook again.

Boxes fill my path as I round the corner of the shop and peer into the storage side of the basement. Old pictures of people who are my relatives from long ago. I look into the faces deeply and then into the eyes, looking for the resemblance. Grandma's father is the largest of all the framed pictures. He is alone in the dark wooden frame. His face is familiar. They say he held me when I was a baby, but I don't remember. I wish I did…I hear that he was a great man. He lived in a modest home along the railroad tracks in a small town in the hills of West Virginia. He was honest, fair, and God-fearing. He worked hard and thought a lot of educating his children. A simple man with a simple life. He's the only one who my dad loved. I've tried to ask about my great-grandfather, but all Dad can do is look away and say that he was a great man and he taught him a lot. I carefully rifle through the rest of the other pictures, but they're not important to me. They're mere faces from stories I had heard. But my great-grandfather is a legend. I stare at his face for a long time, looking for something, but all I can find are his kind eyes staring back at me. I prop his picture up on the bookshelf and make sure he sees me. I want him to know who I am.

"Sandra, what in the hell is taking you so long?" The voice from above startles me and I feel like I just got caught.

"Nothing Mom, I'm just looking around."

"Well hurry up, we're ready to go."

I jump into the shower. I keep my hair out of the water. I'll wash it tomorrow. I dry faster than I washed and up the stairs I rush.

"Did you turn off the light?"

I turn around with a huff and back down the stairs I go. As I reach for the light, Grandfather's picture strikes me. There he sits on the bookshelf, watching me. I click off the light and darkness takes over. I run up the stairs before the darkness can catch me.

"Where are your shoes?" I think for a minute as Mom taps her foot. I search the living room while I pray they're up here. I find them shoved in a corner. "Just put them on in the car, your father is waiting." Mom and I are the last in the van. A lit cigarette hangs from Dad's mouth.

"Why can't I stay here with Grandma?"

Mom pushes my butt into the van.

"She needs a break from us." Dad puffs on his smoke.

What's he talking about? Grandma loves me, she doesn't need a break from me.

"What kind of house are we going to get?"

Mark opens his big mouth. Mom puts on her sunglasses and sighs, "I doubt we'll get a house. We're going to Circleville to look at apartments."

Mark closes his mouth. I watch the light turn green and think about this apartment thing. We've never lived in an apartment before.

Dad steps on the gas and the van pushes forward to the interstate where the sign reads, CIRCLEVILLE 12 MILES. "I'll be working at the Bent Bolt factory in Circleville," he shows us the direction of his new work. The next sign reads ZANESVILLE 17 MILES, with an arrow to the left.

"Dad can we go see…"

"No."

We pass by McDonald's and Shelly tries not to ask for a Coke, but fails, "Dad after we look at apartments can we have a Coke from McDonald's?"

"I'll think about it."

That's good enough for Shelly. Besides if he forgets, she's got the green light to ask him again.

Mom adjusts her sunglasses as she anxiously awaits her new future away from Dorothy. "What about those over there, they look nice."

Dad slows down and notices the vacancy sign. "Well what the hell, let's go look." I see kids playing inside the boring, tan complex. The apartments are set up four to a building, and there's about ten buildings in the complex, five on each side. Dad searches for the manager's sign and pulls up to the office. It feels like we should hide. "Wait in the car while your Mom and I go speak to the manager."

Shelly and I try not to stare, but we can't help it. Will these be our new friends? Will this be our new home? Will we go to school here? The questions flood our minds as our eyes wander around the apartments, looking for something great about this place. The longer we search, the less we find to get excited about. I want to stay at Grandma's house, at least I know the kids around there.

"The longer they're gone, the more I bet we'll move here."

Shelly's words ring true, and with that announcement, she twirls her gum on her finger. We wait for the verdict. Will we or won't we?

The office door opens, and Mom follows the manager, with Dad in tow, to an empty apartment. I watch for familiar body language for hints.

Mark kicks the seat. "Why can't we look too?"

"I don't know, that's weird," I say while my eyes examine Mom and Dad waiting to enter the apartment.

"I want to see." Mark rolls down his window.

"Mark knock it off, we're gonna get in trouble."

The manager is trying to open the door with the key—she drops it and laughs. She is a skinny middle-aged woman. Her pants are green and they don't match her blouse, which is purple with flowers on it. I can tell she likes living here; it probably gives her plenty of time to watch soap operas. And I'm sure it's a lot quieter than that old trailer park I imagine she lived in.

"This place is dumb, I don't want to live here," Shelly blurts out.

I couldn't agree more. It feels empty around here, the grass is fake and the neighbors look like they are hiding from something. It reminds me of prison but with bigger cells. Mom and Dad come out of the apartment door with smiles, nodding their heads yes. That's it, they've taken this place without our approval.

"So we can move in today?" I hear Dad ask from the sidewalk. Dad hands her a folded check from his back pocket.

The manager, whose name is Phylis, agrees. "Today will be fine as long as this check clears."

Dad sneers back at her and opens the van door. He flips back a sarcastic tone, "Well then I guess we'll be right back then."

Mom gets in and slams the van door closed.

"Mom why can't we see?" Mark hangs over her seat.

"We're moving in today, you'll see it then. Besides, it's nothing special, it's just an apartment with carpet and walls."

We park in front of Grandma's. I try to hold my head up as we march in, but I can't. The truth is, it's a dumb apartment with no trees to climb, cold cement, fake grass, and only a circle in the center to ride our bikes.

"How did you all do, find anything?" Grandma wipes her hands on a dishtowel.

"Yeah, we got a little apartment in Circleville."

"Circleville, are you crazy? Hell, it smells worse there than it does here."

I can't believe my eyes, Aunt Mozzell is here. She steps out of the hall. Her one-eyed crooked smile always makes me wonder if she's going to slap someone.

"Aunt Mozell, when did you get here?" Dad pulls Mark closer as a shield from the bullets being fired.

"Well since I never hear from you no more, Jack, Dorothy called to let me know you all were here. I know you don't care if you see me, but I'd like to see these kids once in a blue moon."

She reaches for a hug from Dad, while Mark's fright makes him forget to move out of the way—he gets squished in the middle. Mozell then slaps Dad upside the head, just a reminder that she loves him dearly. We all take our turns hugging her around the waist and hope that she doesn't hit us.

Grandma speaks up for poor Dad, "Now Mozell, I would have never invited you over if I knew you were going to act this way. You behave yourself. Jack's been traveling and he just got here." Grandma continues fidgeting with her dishtowel.

"Now I might be as old as the hills," Aunt Mozell snaps, "but I'm not stupid. Dorothy let's just get some supper started. Kids, why don't you all wash up and let me and your Dad visit."

Mom pulls on Dad's shirt. "I thought we were moving today."

"Just how in the hell do you expect me to tell Aunt Mozell we're leaving? One more night won't kill us."

The sun lowers, the conversation lifts. Aunt Mozell goes on and on about that crazy old George. "That man wasn't worth a plug nickel. Now Dorothy I know you loved him, but he wasn't nothing but a worthless old drunk." Any other time if Brooks and John were around, this would be a forbidden subject, but they're not, and it's full throttle. George is the main topic, and for some reason it's time for Aunt Mozell's true confessions. She must still have a broken heart over Dad being taken away when he was a little boy. After all, she's the one who helped raise him, and she never did have any children of her own. I can see the love for her "Jack" melt his heart.

Dad listens as she crucifies George. And because he wasn't Dad's real father, he wasn't my grandfather. He was George, the man who hated Dad. Grandma just listens quietly, picking her teeth, as Mozell continues to talk about their parents and the good old days when Dad was a little boy.

"You know Jack was the cutest little thing I'd ever seen, and he grew like a darn weed. Mother would worry something awful, and Father would carry him in his arms or on his back, and the two of them were thick as thieves. He never went anywhere without his little Jack."

Grandma sits staring as if she's ten years old and getting scolded for not doing her chores. She tries to ignore Mozell's words, but I can tell that something inside her hurts. "Now come on y'all, let's get us some dessert before it's too late."

Grandma excuses herself and fusses in the kitchen. The struggle between Grandma and her son and Mozell's little boy "Jack" is as apparent as the lightning bugs that appear and disappear in the darkness. Mozell knows the truth about what really happened to Dad when he was snatched from the life he knew with her parents and introduced to his new family, Dorothy and George. And Aunt Mozell isn't about to let anyone forget the past. As a matter of fact she stays there, she doesn't know her little Cracker Jack is all grown and meaner than hell.

Mom stays close to the kitchen with Grandma and finishes the dessert dishes. She listens in once in a while, but most of it she's already heard. Mom looks at the clock, "Come on you guys it's late, get ready for bed." We whine a little, but it is late and it is time. The worst part of going to bed tonight is the dreadful kisses good night. We all know that Aunt Mozell will be on the list. Mark runs down the hall for his bed and pretends he's already asleep. Shelly and I have to walk the other way right through the living room. We kiss Dad, Grandma, and then quickly kiss Aunt Mozell on the cheek; Shelly waits until we get through the kitchen and wipes off her kiss. I can't help but laugh out loud. "No screwing around girls, go right to bed." We do just that.

Mark runs into the kitchen the next morning looking for Aunt Mozell. She's gone. Grandma is outside and Duke's gone fishing. Shelly and I hear the footsteps from below and know it's time to get up and get moving. Mom is drinking her coffee with Mark half on her lap, and Dad is tying down the truck out front. "Good morning, did you guys sleep good?" I hear Mom's voice before I make it all the way up the stairs.

"I did."

"I did too." Shelly and I both sit down at the kitchen table.

"Well, your father is about ready to go. Why don't you girls get dressed and we'll get going." Going is all that we do lately, but for one reason or another this time feels especially bleak. Maybe it's the idea of living in an apartment. Or maybe it's not. I don't know anymore. I'm tired of guessing. Shelly and I follow instructions and quickly get our stuff together. Grandma is washing her tomatoes in the kitchen as we whiz past her.

"Hey, doesn't Grandma get some sugar this morning?" We stop in our tracks and give Grandma her well-deserved hug. She hugs me extra tight and pats me on the back. I take a moment to realize how much I love her and how much she loves us.

"Are you guys about ready to go?" Dad puffs away as he stands holding the screen door open. "Dorothy, we'll call you later. Thanks for everything."

Grandma shyly turns her head, "Now you stop it. I didn't do anything at all. You all get settled and I'll stop by later."

Dad leads the way and out the door we go. We follow the tired truck down the interstate and into the complex. The doors of the van open, and we wait to see what's next. I take a breath wondering what will it be like. I pretend it will be cute and cozy and full of furniture.

The apartment door drags itself across the carpet and leaves a repeated mark. It is nothing more than a motel with a kitchen and extra bedroom. I look to Shelly who sees the same thing, a motel. It takes less than an hour to unload the truck into the tiny two-bedroom apartment. I know why there wasn't any need for us to see the apartment first—there's nothing to see. The walls have a few nail holes that look like they were just put there; we don't have any pictures to cover them up. I continue to search out my new home; the fingerprints on the wall tell me not to. I can smell the previous tenants' aftershave in the bathroom, and I see a leftover bar of soap. It's not ours. Mom is in the kitchen throwing away a leftover box of minute rice. Dad can't help himself.

"Hey what are you doing? That might still be good."

Mom whips around and reminds him he's lost his mind. The apartment is used, it has a worn feeling and it reeks of temporary. Even if I tried to fool myself, I can't, the apartment tells me, *I'm only a place to sleep.*

It's one thing to share a room with Shelly, but now I have to share with both of them. This is unspeakable. The apartment has two bedrooms, two, that's all, and no matter how many times I count them, and all of us, it adds up the same. The apartment is also tan. As a matter of fact everything in and outside the apartment is tan. I think the grass is tan. I walk in the living room with one of the last boxes. "Mom where do you want this one?" She points to the small staircase that leads upstairs to the two little bedrooms. I think to myself, "You call this a staircase? I call it a joke." Besides the baby kitchen next to the toy staircase, there's no more except for an empty closet that would barely fit Mark in it. We unpack our stuff. All we have to do is stack our clothes in the corner of the bedroom. I decide to flip my box over and stack on top of it, at least it separates me a little from Shelly and Mark. "Mom, we're done," Shelly yells down.

"All right then, come help with the kitchen." The kitchen is just about as hard; three boxes and six cabinets—there's not a lot of room for error.

We have nothing: no furniture, no kitchen table, no beds, and no drawers. The apartment is so small that it doesn't even know how to echo. Mark thinks it's funny, I don't. A new TV that Grandma loaned us sits alone in a corner, and we use our pillows for chairs.

It's Sunday afternoon by the time we are done unpacking, Dad can now watch television. Mom goes upstairs and lays on the mound of blankets she calls a bed. It's time for us to go meet the neighbors and introduce ourselves. I'm not excited by this at all, as a matter of fact, it's old to me by now. I don't even care about having friends, it's all a big waste of time. Besides, we'll probably move again anyway. I go upstairs to put on some clean shorts. As I get ready to leave, I peek in on Mom. She's not feeling well. She's still really tired.

"Mom, we're going outside."

"Sandra, come here." Mom lifts her hand to me. I walk in and she holds my hand, "Hey, I know this looks pretty bad, but we'll get out of here. Do me a favor, don't bring anyone over, I don't want anyone to see this place. I mean it, honey. Don't"

"Are you okay?"

"Yes. I'm just a little tired," she exhales, "I'll be fine."

I accept her answer.

"I love you honey, have fun."

"Love you too." I shut the door behind me and pass by Dad propped up against the wall watching TV and eating some old Lay's potato chips.

"Bye Dad, we're going outside."

"Hey, don't go outside the apartment complex, and don't go inside anyone's house." Potato chip crumbs fly out of his mouth.

I shut the door as soon as he finishes his instructions.

Shelly, Mark, and I scope out the complex, wondering who everyone is and where all the kids might be. There's nowhere to go but in circles here, and it's far from the mountains of West Virginia. All the trees are babies with green plastic straps holding them up, the grass consists of narrow patches between apartments, no clovers, no weeds, no birds. We finally sit down and wait for our new friends to show themselves.

The longer we wait, the more discouraged we get. All that comes around are babies, kids Mark's age. That's no fun. I don't want to play with babies. Shelly and I sigh as another car comes home with another little kid.

We wave of course, but we don't care. Mark on the other hand is in kid heaven. Everyone here so far is made for him. This is not acceptable. Where are the bigger kids? By the end of the day we know it's true—no one is interesting.

"Sandra, there's no one our age." Shelly plops down on the hard grass.

"I guess people in apartments all have little kids."

By now, Mark is in the street playing kickball with a little guy named Tony. His father, Tony Sr., is a cop and his mother is pregnant. Her name is Marie, and she walks slow and bends down for her groceries just like Mom did when she was pregnant. I've met her twice now, she's real nice and she always takes a little time to talk to Shelly and me while Mark and Tony play cops and robbers. Mark is the robber.

Dad has been working now for over two weeks, and his paycheck is this Friday. According to Mom, everything will happen on payday. I don't remember ever having to wait this long and this intensely for a payday. Sure we've been broke, but not like this. At least before we had furniture and hamburgers to eat. Now all we eat is soup; chicken noodle for Shelly and tomato with crackers for me and Mark. Dad works all the time, nights too. But at least Mom is not sleeping as much. We still don't have any furniture, but what scares me the most is school. We're supposed to start school in a couple of weeks, and we don't have any school clothes. This is bad, real bad. Mom knows about school clothes and there's no way she'll send us without clothes. I don't have anything but shorts and one pair of play pants. I hope this paycheck is going for some clothes. I won't ask yet, but I'll have to soon.

Dad comes home finally. It's around ten, and he's tired, dirty, and frustrated. He plops on the floor and moans.

"Ardell, this is bullshit. Do you have any idea what I do all night? I stand at a machine making bolts. Can you imagine standing in one place for ten hours, for a measly four bucks an hour? I lift, sweat, and bend. My feet hurt so bad that on my break I take off my shoes and pray to God I can finish my shift." Dad rubs his swollen feet.

I wish I could do something for him, but I can't. We all sit around and listen to his stories of how stupid and ignorant his fellow workers are. And what a low-end job this is. The polio that had attacked him when he was a kid not only left him in braces for a couple of years, but his poor feet are permanently deformed. We were supposed to buy him some special shoes this summer, but I guess we forgot.

Mom walks in with no expression, "Do you want a sandwich?"

"No, I'm not hungry." Dad stays on the floor, "Come here Mark feel this." Mark puts his hands on Dad's stomach and Dad sucks in his belly and then says, "Bent Bolt." As he finishes the words, he hardens his stomach and forces Mark's hands off with the new muscles he has developed being a grunt. Mark laughs and Dad plays his little game again. Dad inhales, "Bent," and exhales, "Bolt." Mark tries to out-muscle the new muscles.

Pay-day comes and goes, and the only thing I notice is that we now have food in the house; fish sticks, macaroni, and hamburgers. School clothes didn't make the list. I really don't understand this, and I can't go to school without clothes. Maybe we're not going to school. We're supposed to start next week, I think. Shelly and I have now joined in with Mark and Tony on a few games of kickball. Mostly I just kick their butts with all my strength, they don't have a chance. But we all have to make compromises since Shelly and I don't have anyone else to play with.

Mom left us with Tony's mom today so she could go to the doctor. The color in her face is back to normal. She said she'll be home soon and told me not to worry. She must have seen it in my face.

She found this guy a couple of days ago who makes silk screens for "Thank You" signs and she bought them. She's going to start making them herself and selling them to small businesses. She thinks they'll sell. Her plan is to make them at home and cut the cost down to pennies and then sell them for ten dollars a piece. The sign is brown and the words are yellow, with a pleasant saying about how much the owner appreciates the customer's business. Right now we have nothing but brown and yellow paint with a bunch of two-by-three-foot boards all around the house. So far a couple of them have turned out okay, but some of them are pretty ugly. I think she's going to buy us some school clothes with the money she makes. Dad hopes it works so he can sell them and get out of Bent Bolt. I just want her to come home and tell me she's fine.

Dad's home early today, I see the truck bouncing over the speed bumps to the apartment. Mom isn't home yet. I run up to Dad and check on him. His feet still hurt and he doesn't feel like talking.

"Sandra, when your mother gets home, stay outside for awhile. She and I need to talk about a few things. It's nothing bad, we just need to talk."

The look on my face must have given me away again. "How long?"

"Awhile. I'll let you know."

I stand on the sidewalk as he lets himself in and shuts the door. Of course he needs to talk to her, there's nothing wrong with that. I shouldn't worry; heck I'll just go play kickball and pretend I'm fine. Except we have no furniture, no clothes for school, and no one seems very happy, but I won't worry. Mom spent all of our money buying the silk screens, boards, and paint. Hopefully everything will work out. Especially after she learns how to mix the paint properly. Exactly what temperature the house needs to be in order for the yellow paint not to gum up, and precisely how much paint to use on the silk screen itself, and how to stain the background of the boards so they look like real wood, they'll make us some money. Of course I'm not worried, I'm scared to death.

30

Mom is waiting for us on the floor with her back propped against a pillow. Dad sits on the lone chair smoking and tapping his foot. The "thank you" signs fill the living room, they're still drying.

"Hey, why don't you guys sit down? Your mother and I want to talk to you." Mark doesn't listen very well, and he almost starts to cry. I nudge him in the arm. I don't know what it is, but it has nothing to do with Tony or being in trouble. This is something new.

Dad reaches into his pocket and pulls out a ten dollar bill. "You see this, well it's all we got. And your Mother and I have been talking, and we think we could do better in California."

Mom is still and quiet while Dad tries to tell us something. Her hands squeeze one another tightly. Her face is round and her eyes are sad. I watch the expression on their faces and wait for the bomb to drop. I can't see, it but I can feel it.

Mom finally speaks in a low voice, "I'm going to have a baby." She looks directly into our eyes.

I think she said she's going to have a baby. What is she talking about? We're not supposed to talk about the baby. My eyes shift back and forth as my brain pounds. She's not going to have a baby, this is bullshit. I refocus on the room and look to her for some other explanation. She sticks to her words. She is pregnant. Mom offers no more, she's finished talking.

Dad jumps back in, "We feel it would be better for all of us if we went back to California and your Mother had the baby there. I can't make a living here. And this is no life for us."

I curl my toes tight inside my tennis shoes. I want to burst. I feel like a bomb went off inside me. I don't want another baby. I don't want it to die again. There's no way God's going to let us have another one. What in the hell are they thinking? Shelly sits Indian style pretending to tie her shoes over and over again. Mark stares at the front door.

"Don't you guys have anything to say?" Dad sucks on his cigarette with the long ash waiting to fall. No one says a word.

"Nope," we mumble and shake our heads.

A voice screams inside me. I have a lot to say, but nobody wants to hear it. I go back to the river, back to the tree, and back in time. Time held frozen by the pain of the baby. The baby that knew me and died for no reason. The one I never got to hold. And now this is supposed to make me feel good or something? Well it doesn't. I don't care. I hate it all, California *and* this baby stuff.

I'm not going. How about that? Nobody is going to make me forget what happened. I know what happened. How can they just sit there and tell me they're having another baby? What about the one that died? Does this make up for it? I wish to God I could understand how a baby dies; no one talks about it, no one even mentions what color hair. Or how long it lived, and what it's name was. Did he/she look like me? Aunt Carole had a baby that died, she talked about him once in a while, for God's sake. He had a name and she still misses him if you mention Sammy, her baby who died.

My jaw is tight when I realize where I am. The sun is going down. A light beams through the tiny crack in the living room curtains, the same curtains we keep closed so no one can see what we don't have. I breathe heavy to myself and watch the light beam creep across the floor almost touching Mom's knees. Everyone sits there waiting for someone to talk. Mom wants out, Shelly has stopped tying her shoes, Mark pets the dogs hard, and I look for the nearest spaceship.

Finally Dad finishes with a bang, "We're leaving with ten dollars in our pocket and a hundred signs. We have fifty now, and by tomorrow night we should have the rest done. What I'm telling you is, we have to sell signs in order to get across the country. If we hit a town and don't sell any signs, we stay in that town until we do. The same thing goes for food, gas, and hotels. Everyone needs to help. Do you understand? This is not a joke. We pack tomorrow and we leave tomorrow night."

At this point, I know the rest of the speech by heart. Pack only what we need and leave the rest behind. I don't ask about school, it's something we'll handle later I'm sure. After all, we still have two weeks. The family talk ends the same way it started, just the facts. Mom has Dad help her up off the floor and goes to the kitchen. "Go wash your hands for dinner," she says to the room. Excusing herself from the three open mouths that hang there.

I'm the first one up and out. I go to the bathroom and turn the water on full blast. I don't wash. Instead, I sit on the tub and let the water drown out the buzzing in my head. I wonder if this will ever end. Will we ever stop chasing Dad's imaginary rainbow and running from giants? God is pissed, I can feel it. I can't deal with him now. I will later, oh I know I will later, but not right now. I try to find some strength inside me. I desperately search inside and out. The strength to drive across the country, land in a new bed, and attend another new school. All of that I can handle somehow, but how can I watch Mom be pregnant, and wait for the baby to die? I can't. I'll crack this time, I know it. I want to talk to God about it. What am I thinking? He'll take it for sure. I know, maybe if I don't love it this time, maybe if I stay away, and pretend I don't care, the baby won't die. The tears well up in my eyes faster than I can wipe them away. I hurry to fight off the tears before God can catch me. What if I do love the baby by accident? Shut up! God can't hurt me if I don't love it. The steam rises over the mirror and hits my face evaporating my tears. That's it, I won't have anything to do with the baby. God won't even know Mom's pregnant. I'll make sure of it. I'll keep it a secret from him and maybe this time...Well we'll just see if God does or doesn't. The knocking at the door slams me back to the cold tub I'm sitting on with my new revelation. I've made up my mind I can be strong, and tricky enough too.

"Come on Sandra, Mom said dinner is ready. Hurry up."

I open the door to Shelly and Mark standing there. They have questions for me in their eyes, but now is not the time. Besides, I need to talk to Mom a little before I can tell them what's going on. Usually Dad presents the bomb, Mom explains it to me, and I interpret it for them. We finish splashing our hands and drying them on our pants while we pound downstairs. Mom's made Mark's favorite, macaroni and cheese with cut-up hot dogs. I can eat it, but it's not my favorite.

After dinner, Dad stacks the dry "thank you" signs to one side of the living room. "Hon, I think these are dry enough. What do you want me to do?"

"Just leave them there and start sanding the edges if they need it."

Mom takes out the big giant silk screen and lays it on the kitchen table. She mixes her paint by the sink and we take our places. We have to be quick about it, because once she starts running the boards, she can't stop or the paint will gum up. Dad sands every couple of signs where the edges are rough.

"All right Sandra, hand me one."

I do just that. I hand her a stained board, and she places it precisely under the screen and shuts it. Now the board just lays there under the silk screen waiting for it's paint. She takes the squeegee and pushes the paint down from the top and evenly across. She slides down the silk screen carefully. The yellow paint leaves a border on the brown board. It's done. Mom opens the screen and inspects her work. I grab it from the tray with my fingers and hand it to Shelly who props it up against the wall. Mom hand it off to Dad this time, and Mark sets it up. After twenty or so boards, Mom's arms are getting tired. She hands the squeegee over to Dad and reminds him how much pressure and paint needs to move through the screen.

"I know for Christ's sake." Dad snaps the baton from her and goes. The first one is thicker on one side than the other. We all see it, but no one says a word. Mom's boards are better. Mom hands off to Mark. Mark carries the precious cargo to the chair. We're out of space against the wall. I hear a scrap and turn. The board with wet yellow paint has lost it's balance and fallen. The assembly line grinds to a halt. Mark is scared and embarrassed. Shelly goes over to assess the damage. Dad can't stop to yell, but he's mad. Mom is exhausted; she wipes the sweat and her hair out of her face with her elbow. She gets a little paint on her cheek.

"Dad, here you go, redo." Shelly smiles and hands him the damaged goods. Dad takes it and puts it back in it's place.

"Goddamn it!" Dad lifts the screen. "It's starting to bubble."

"Let me see," Mom moves me out of the way. "Keep going." She adds a little thinner to the paint. "You guys stack them faster. Sandra, stay right here and help your father." Mom stands over him and pours the paint. We're almost done, ten more signs. Dad runs the last one as a bead of sweat falls onto the board. We watch it in slow motion to see where it will land. It lands safe, not on the yellow paint.

It's ten o'clock by the time we're finished cleaning up. The cleanup is horrible: the paint thinner, the big screen caked with gummy yellow paint, and the sink to small too work in. It all stinks. Fifty more signs stand half naked waiting to dry so we can finish them with white letters tomorrow. We all exit upstairs, yellow polka dots all over us. Mom is the last one up. She turns around to look at the living room below filled with her future, and flicks off the light.

Cautiously we make cereal in the kitchen, trying to avoid the cluttered living room from last night. Mom tests the signs and decides they are dry. We go back upstairs and quietly pack. Dad wants us to stay in today. I want out of the house and away from the smell. Packing takes less than an hour.

"We're done," I yell downstairs. Dad and Mom run the white batch by themselves. They barely notice us sneak out the front door.

Once outside, the quiet of the birds and distant traffic brings my thoughts back. Pregnant. Shelly sits down on the step.

"I'm glad Mom's going to have a baby."

I hear her, but I don't have anything to say back. The more I think about the baby, the more likely God will find out.

Just then, Mom opens the front door. "Come here," she yells across the street. We whip around and run back.

Mom has a cold glass of Pepsi. "Get inside, we're leaving tonite."

That evening as the sun goes down, Dad's plan takes form. He starts with one box and then another. Out to the truck we follow.

Mom stacks the signs, checking them for flaws. We'll load them last. The yellow border with white letters completes the sign and it looks perfect to me. The darker it gets, the closer we are to leaving the little town of Circleville, Ohio. Dad looks over his shoulder with each box and bag he takes out to the truck. There will be no good-byes at all. We are not to say a word. I'm not sure exactly what a gypsy is, but all of a sudden I feel like one.

We sit in the van with the dogs, waiting for Mom and Dad to load the signs. I remember three weeks ago when she brought home the magic beans. I never thought they'd grow into anything, but I was wrong. The highway seems to be the giant beanstalk. And California is where the golden eggs are. We're about to go find them. But what if we don't sell these stupid signs? What if Mom has the baby on the road? What if we can't eat? I don't hear any answers, all I hear are questions. They pile up in the back of my mind like the signs Mom and Dad pile in the back of the van. I feel the weight of each load as they stack the signs. "Last load guys, you ready?" Dad covers the secret treasure with a torn faded pink blanket. Then he crawls into the truck as quiet as he can and starts the loud engine. Mom does the same. Dad leads us out of the tiny village and up and over the speed bumps to the beanstalk ahead. The bumps hit hard. They remind me that we're not going to heaven, but rather, to go see another giant.

Dad drives long and hard, farther and farther away from Grandma, Circleville, and eventually, Ohio. I finally join Shelly and Mark in sleep. The van is a treat when it comes to sleeping, at least we can lay down and dream. I dream of the baby, the old baby, not the new one, but the one who floats above me and haunts me if I let it. I'm in the woods wandering around. Up in the distance, through the mist, I can see a basket. The closer I get, the more I realize it's the baby. The baby is alive, wrapped softly in a white blanket. All I can see is a round face and tiny hands. Hands that jerk and swing at the air. I walk faster and harder to the basket. I must get to the baby, it's all by itself. I have to tell Mom I found the baby. When I reach the basket, I'm stunned, I stop about four feet from the bundle, I can't believe my eyes. The baby looks like a she. And she has dark hair like mine. Mom said it was a boy, a brother, not a sister. I try to get closer to the basket where the baby lays squirming. She's a happy little thing, kicking and smiling. I want to touch her hands with my fingers. But as I reach for the basket, it floats away from me. I try again and again, but for some reason I can't reach her. Every time I take a step toward her, the basket swiftly jets away. The more I try, the farther it gets away from me. Exhausted and mad, I finally storm the tricky basket with all my might. I lunge into the air and fall to the ground. The basket with the baby disappears with a blink up into the trees. I beg for another chance, maybe even a glance, but she's gone, whisked away into the wind and hidden by the trees. Now, alone in the woods, I lean on the warm trunk of a wise old tree, which seems to know of my sadness. The tree hugs me and tells me over and over, *It's okay, don't worry, it's okay.* I sit down, look up into a million leaves twinkling above and wait for her to return…Am I wishing, dreaming, or seeing? It's all the same, I can't tell the difference.

The flashing caution lights wake me from the dream. Dad has to get a coffee and Mom has to stretch. It's really early morning, about five, and the dark time is waking to a glow in the horizon. I don't want to go back to sleep, I could, but I'd rather not. I lay there still, my eyes open. I know I'm being silly, but something says that was real, it was more than just a dream. I wish I could ask. I have so many questions for Mom. I want to know what she looked like, I mean him. What color hair? How did he die? I want to know what happened, I have to. Now is not the time, maybe later when she's not so tired. Right now she doesn't even know I'm awake. I think I'll keep it that way.

Later that morning, we stop for lunch. Nobody seemed to mind missing breakfast but me. Eleven o'clock and bologna sandwiches for everyone. Mom reaches in the cooler and grabs the sodas. The brown paper bag is full of peanut butter and jelly if you want something different. I hate it when the white bread sticks to the roof of my mouth.

Dad talks with his mouth full about how, after lunch we need to hit this town and sell. He nudges me, I ignore him. There is no way I'll sell signs to strangers, it feels too much like begging. I haven't told him that, but I will if I have to. Dad swallows hard and pounds down a grape Shasta. "Ardell, I think we need to go at least ten dollars on the signs." He finishes wiping the grape mustache with his arm.

Mom rolls her eyes, "Why don't we see if we can get seven and go from there. It's not worth losing a sale right now." Mom's point is heard. All I can think is, we'd better sell something in Peoria, Illinois, or else we'll be living here. Dad shuts up and finishes his sandwich. He's going to be the first to try to make a sale. God help him because he's just not a salesman. Dad throws on a little cologne, swigs off the Maalox, while Mom gathers the trash from the front of the van. Shelly takes it to the garbage, Mark runs around with the dogs, he knows it will be his last chance to get out for a while. I strain over the backseat and scrounge through a suitcase looking for a clean T-shirt. I have a big purple dribble stain down the front of this one. Mom gets back in and says with a sharp tone, "What are you doing?"

"Mom I spilled. I need a clean shirt."

"Just watch it. If you scratch those signs, I can't fix them."

These signs are starting to piss me off. Everything for the past few weeks are signs this and signs that. You'd think they were alive or something.

The car doors slam as we make sure our hands and feet don't get caught. Dad rolls on down the highway a mile or two until he sees the first exit sign that says, Downtown Peoria. He moves in carefully, picking the precise location to park the truck and the van. He grabs the first two parking spots on the right side of the street. The town is not complicated. It has a gas station at both ends. Woolworth's, hardware, Thrifty, auto parts, and restaurants. Population, fifteen thousand. According to Dad, it's a score. Dad walks around back and tells Mom to stay here. He crosses the street, slowing traffic just because he can. He has the sign tucked tightly under his arm and he looks stupid. He walks into the first business—it's a barbershop. A few people pass by on foot. It's warm, I want my shoes off. We try not to breathe as he performs his unseen magic. He pops out as quickly as he went in, the sign still hanging under his arm. He doesn't skip a beat, into the next and the next. Finally, the auto parts store buys one for seven dollars and fifty cents. He runs back to the van like a robber after a heist. Mom is chomping at the bit. She knows she could have sold them all. "Piece of cake," Dad huffs, "like taking candy from a baby."

Mom gets out and walks around to the back of the van. "Here, take this one." She selects just the right one. Dad blows on it for good luck and grabs three more. Back across the street, diving in and out of shops like a fly. He's out of sight. We wait. And wait some more. "There he is," Mark shouts, "He has one left, that means he sold THREE!!!"

Mom looks like someone has just let the air out of her and she can now relax. The signs do sell, *I'll be damned*, runs across her face. Dad tries not to run, instead he kind of skips and hops fast to the van. "I'll be damned." He reaches over me in the front seat and hands Mom a fist full of dollars.

"San, it's your turn. Want to give it a try?" He slaps my back. Mom must have seen the terror streak across my face.

"I'll go this time," she opens her door. Dad grabs her waist and gives her a tickle as he kisses her on the cheek.

"Be careful, there's a lot of money out there."

Mom has done it—saved our ass and made something out of nothing work. I've never seen him this happy. Finally cash, good old American cash. Dad whistles while Mom works the streets. He gets cocky, he can't stand waiting any longer. "Kids, I'll be right back. I'm going to hit the bar back there." He grabs a sign and I grab my heart.

Please don't let him do it, everything is going so good. If he goes in there and drinks, we're dead. Shelly and Mark don't know what to do, keep watching for Mom or wait for Dad? I watch for Dad. Every single step he takes toward Fred and Shirl's Bar with the neon sign flashing O-P-E-N, I cuss him out as the bar door slowly swings shut. He's in a bar with a fistful of cash and everything was going fine. My stomach tightens. I try to make it stop, but it won't.

"Mom's coming, look, she doesn't have any signs." Shelly slides open the van door and yells, "Mom how much money—-"

Mom shoots her a look to shut up. I can't relax, Dad's still gone, it's taking too long, I know it is. I keep my eyes straight ahead, and I'm yelling at him inside my head, *get out here right now.*

At that moment, the door flies open and he's got a smile from ear to ear—and no sign.

He's walking toward the van when, creeping up behind him is a black-and-white car. The cops. They're going to slow and stay behind Dad. Dad knows they are there. He slows down to match their speed. Mom gets in the van and shuts her door.

"Don't stare." She pinches Mark's knee behind her.

"What are they doing?" Shelly whispers.

Mom doesn't know and says nothing. Dad turns around and gives a nod to the officers. They pull over and Dad walks over to them. I can't hear them but Dad is bullshitting, I'm sure of it. I can tell by the fake smile and the way his hands move in and out of his pockets. Dad never plays with his pockets. After a few minutes, I hear Dad, "Okay officer, thanks." Dad swings his arm and jumps back onto the sidewalk. He comes to Mom's window, "Let's get out of here."

"What did they want?"

"Oh, some bullshit about a business license."

Mom wants to cuss, she's pissed. "What in the hell?"

Dad gets quiet and moves gently away from the window. "Not now, let's just get out of here before they come back and run the plates."

We leave with dollar bills spilling out of the glove box. Mom is concerned, Dad is driving carefully and obeying all the traffic signals out of town. Once we get on the freeway, the laughter returns. Mom is amazed at how much money we made. I count it over and over. Dad sold four signs, Mom sold three signs, that makes seven, and seven times seven is forty-nine dollars.

"Mom, we just made forty-nine dollars."

Mom smiles and reaches over and tickles my side. I reach for her, but she uses driving as some kind of excuse. "Don't."

We drive about twenty miles. Dad signals ahead, he's pulling off to a lone 76 station. Mom looks down and checks her gas. We don't need gas. We all wonder what he's doing. It's not like Dad to pull over so soon. We have to be in serious pain before he pulls over. He gets out and so do we. He has the map in his hand. He lays it down.

"Ardell, we have to be more careful, the next town is about sixty miles and we can hit it before they close." He unfolds the map and points it out. "But we're going to have to park separately and have the kids bring us more signs. We can't be running back and forth to the van. You'll hit one side and I'll hit the other. We need to get in and out quickly.

Shelly jumps in, "I'll do it."

Mark copies her. "Me too."

I keep my mouth shut, praying they don't ask me. Dad says something quietly to Mom about the van payment and the truck. Mom thinks to herself for a minute. She nods in agreement. They know what they are talking about.

We go to the bathroom, and Dad buys us a candy bar of our choice. Of course, I take too long and Mom yells to hurry up or she'll pick it for me. I choose a Big Hunk and tell the M&Ms good-bye. We all run to the van and rip open the treat. The next sixty miles fly by.

We pull into Calfax, Illinois, about four o'clock. The sun is setting over a range of mountains outside the town. Population twenty-two-thousand. Dad cruises slowly down the main drag. He eyeballs every potential customer. Mom chews on the end of her sunglasses with one hand and drives with the other. My feet are up on the dash as I coordinate the strategy in my mind. Dad turns left onto a small side street with a café on the corner. The sign reads BETTY'S HOMEMADE CHILI AND FRIED CHICKEN. I can't help but remember the smell of our chicken. Dad parks his truck in an alley and has Mom park the van closer to the corner so we can see them. Shelly and Mark finish putting on their shoes so they can run the signs out to Mom and Dad. I stay barefooted. My job will be watching for the cops and helping Shelly and Mark get the signs. Mom is at the back of the van. "San, why don't you act like you're taking the dogs for a walk?" I hook them on their leashes and mosey around in circles on a thin patch of grass next to the sidewalk. She's right, this doesn't look weird at all. Dad goes over the plan one more time with Mom.

"So, I'll hit this side of the street and go down, and you can cross the street and go up. Shelly can work with me and Mark with you. All they have to do is meet us when we're down to one sign."

Mom agrees and Mark is relieved he's with Mom.

Dad steps on his cigarette, "San you stay here and look like you know what you're doing. And have those signs ready for Shelly and Mark to run." I heard him loud and clear, I'm in charge.

Mom and Dad go their separate ways up and down the street. I keep an eye on them both. Mom starts with a beauty parlor first while Dad hits the hardware store. Mom sold one and Dad did not. They continue on to the next. Shelly and Mark stand there with their arms out, ready to fly.

"Stop it you guys, we're supposed to act normal."

They both drop their arms like I shot them or something. When I look up to find Mom and Dad, they are both looking my way. They both are down to one sign each. "It's time you guys." I reach in the back and hand them three signs each. They can't carry that many. It's too much. I take one back and hope it's the right thing to do. Dad didn't say how many. Mark starts running, he's so excited. He keeps his eye on Mom. I yell at him to stop running. As his foot steps off the sidewalk, a big blue car screeches to a stop. I almost faint it's so close. Mom heard the whole thing. She wants to kill me. Mark forgot to look and I forgot to remind him, that was my job. Mark backs up and waits for the light. But it's too late. The whole town is outside watching him, people are peering through the windows. He stands there, white as a ghost, with two signs.

I walk over, bend down, and whisper, "Don't run. Just act like everything's okay. Mom will wait for you." Time is running out, and Shelly has already met Dad and is back by now. She's huffing and puffing, she ran all the way back.

"Dad said for me to get ready, he's on a roll."

I look down the street, he's been in at least five places and nothing so far. I wonder what his concept of roll means. He's still got three signs. Mom sends Mark back, and I wait for him on the corner. He knows how to cross the street, but I better watch him just in case. I can't tell, but it looks like Mom has two left. She's moving farther and farther up the street. Shelly's adrenaline pumps as she waits for Dad to sell. "Come on Dad, sell 'em." She sounds like it's a game and he's up to bat. Mom sells another from what I can see; there's a car in my way so I can't tell for sure. I wonder if I should send Mark now.

"I'll go over to Mom, I'm faster than Mark." Shelly is like a bloodhound and she's got the scent.

Mark protests, reaching for his signs to hand off. "No you're not I'm going."

I give in to Mark. "Here just go, but go slow." Shelly waits and watches Dad not sell.

"I bet I can do it."

"Do what?"

Shelly bends down and pulls up her socks. "I can sell signs."

Dad has three signs, and his cheeks are red as he walks back. He reached the end of his territory. I get back in the van. Shelly waits on the sidewalk. Mom and Mark are done too; Mom has one sign left. I can see them both walking back with smiles on. Dad opens the sliding door and drops the signs on the seat.

"How's your mother doing?"

"I think she sold five. How many did you sell?"

"Three. It was really hot at first and then nothing."

Shelly listens to Dad and bites her tongue as long as she can. "Dad, I bet I can sell 'em." Dad keeps looking straight ahead, almost ignoring her. Then as if a lightbulb went on, he whirls around and smiles.

"You can, can you? Maybe you can give it a shot."

By now, Mom and Mark have reached the van. I can't believe it, Shelly's going to sell signs of her own freewill. She's crazy. I'd rather eat a bug.

"Mom, Dad said I can sell signs."

Mom is whipped. She looks at the clock. She barely hears Shelly as she focuses on the time. "It's four thirty, lets go park uptown a ways and keep going."

Dad agrees, knowing we have a half hour before this town dries up. They both get in the van and leave the truck parked. We drive uptown and pass all the stuff Mom just hit. Mom scouts out a section of new territory.

"Same thing, but this time we take four signs. I'll cross the street and you stay here on this side. We'll meet up around the corner."

"Mom," Shelly whines, "what about me?"

"Honey, some other time, I promise, but right now is not a good time." Mom shuffles the signs into her grip.

"Ardell, hell, let's just give her a shot."

Dad hands Shelly a sign. "Here go across the street to the auto parts store."

Mom gives in to Dad's little game, and the fact is she's tired. It'll only take a minute is Dad's logic. And inside his head I can see the wheels turning. He says nothing, but he's thinking something. Shelly loads up and with every bit of confidence and courage she has, she crosses the street. Mark's eyes are envious. Shelly pushes open the Auto Parts Center's door. It slowly shuts and she's gone.

No one talks while she's in there. We all feel for her. Wonder what she's saying and what they are doing? Do they buy one or tell her to get lost? The pressure of the unknown and speculation builds. The door opens fast and Shelly flies out with nothing in her arms. Her fist is tight and her smile reaches all the way over to the van. Dad grins from ear to ear as his little girl wins another trophy. Mom is shaking her head, she can't believe it. Mark blurts out, "I want to do that." Shelly gets to the van, her bloodhound instinct for selling puts her on the trail.

"I did it, I did it. Give me some more."

Mom can't argue. "Okay sweetheart, take these and go back."

"But I can't go by the auto parts store, they'll see me."

"What's that got to do with anything?" Mom takes off her sunglasses.

"I want them to think they're the only ones that have one."

"She's got a point. Ardell, drive her up a ways and let her work her way back down the street."

Mom does just that. Shelly jumps out of the van, arms full, and turns around.

"Mark, you want to go? I'll teach you." Mark is out the door with his own sign before Shelly finishes her question. They dart off into the sunset with twenty minutes and four signs between them. Mom, Dad, and me sit motionless as these signs make their way in and out of all kinds of businesses. Shelly takes Mark in, we wait, the door opens and Shelly exits. She gives us the signal, one. They sold it. The next and the next read the same. Every business—diners, hair salons, hotel, and vacuum repair—buys from Shelly and Mark. They run out of signs. Dad is bouncing in his seat, slapping the dash. "Hot damn. I knew it. Who can resist buying from these guys. They're perfect. You hear me, perfect."

Mom now realizes why Dad was so interested in them selling, it's brilliant. Shelly runs back to the stash. Mark is screaming, "I sold one all by myself." Shelly interrupts, "Yep, he sold the last one to that repair shop. He did it all by himself, I didn't say anything."

Mom and Dad are laughing. It's now five to five. Shelly wants one more fistful of money. She spots a restaurant down the block off main street. "Pick me up down there." Shelly walks off fast, Mark races to keep up. Dad's lap is full of money. Mom counts it with Dad. "Not a bad town, how many is that now? We sold eight and so far the kids sold five."

"Make that six." Dad flicks his cigarette toward Shelly and Mark who are empty-handed. "I'll be damned, thirteen signs in an hour."

Mom puts the van in gear and slowly goes to pick up her golden eggs. I, however, sit in the back with my arms folded and my foot on Big's belly, scratching him, noticing that unless I sell these stupid signs, I'll probably be left behind. I can just see it now. We'll stop at a rest area, and I'll have to fetch them water and walk the dogs while Shelly and Mark sit on lounge chairs. I'll be opening their sodas and washing out their socks. I feel like Cinderella but without the magic slippers. About then, the door opens and I feel my bare foot on Big. I look down, my toes are filthy. Shelly and Mark don't even wait for Mom to stop the van. Any other time that would be a serious offense. I lean over the front seat where Shelly and Mark spit out the stories.

"All I have to say is, 'Would you like to buy a sign?' Then they lean over and read it. Before I say anything else, I hear the ding of the cash register and it opens."

Mark reaches in his pocket just about then and pulls out two dollars. He hands it to Mom. "Look what the lady gave me, she said it was for us."

Mom looks down at his small hand covered in two dollars. "Oh honey, that's yours then, she gave it to you." Mark hesitates a second and then splits it with Shelly. Shelly takes it. She and Mark both did great, there's no denying that.

"I have an idea." Dad shoves the money in his pocket. "Why don't we ask eight dollars and Shelly and Mark get a dollar for every sign they sell."

Mom thinks for a minute, "Okay, but if we find that they don't sell at eight, we go back to seven and Shelly and Mark can have fifty cents."

I saw Shelly add the dollars so fast it made my head spin. Shelly turns around to me and with sincerity says nicely, "Hey Sandra, why don't you sell some? I'll show you how, it's easy."

I sink down in my seat and hope she'll quit talking about it. I feel like a retard she feels sorry for. I shake my head no and leave it at that. But inside I know I'm too ugly and fat to sell signs. The reason Shelly and Mark can sell is because they're little, cute, and blond. I'm tall, fat, and ugly. I try to talk myself into selling, I really do. The blood rushes to my head, I just can't embarrass myself. What if I do try? Is it really worth it to me to prove I can't sell? At least this way only I know the truth. If I go out there and fail, they'll all know the truth. Besides, Shelly and Mark have already established in twenty minutes that they are the chosen ones. I'm not.

We pull into a Jack in the Box and order. Everyone talks with their mouths full about what they're going to do with all their money. I kick the backseat knowing I don't have anything to say. Mom has already figured out with excitement, Shelly and Mark can buy their own school clothes when we get to California. I shiver at the thought. What am I going to buy? Nothing. I'm going into the seventh grade and I have nothing to wear. I'm so scared. I wish I could skip the first day. The first day at junior high, and I'll have cutoffs and a T-shirt. I wish with all my might that Mom will buy me some clothes with her money. I don't even know how much money I'll need or how much she'll have. Dad sits up front snacking on his hamburger. Shelly and Mark suck on their soda, and Mom looks back to see if I'm still there. I am, but not really. Mom must have felt how left out I am. She winks and smiles. I find comfort in her sensing my discomfort.

31

The road-weary dogs lie in the back with their tongues falling out. I feel the same way too. We sleep in this morning. After all, two days on the road and leaving in the middle of the night didn't help. We are all tired except for Shelly and Mark who can't wait to hit the next town and clean up. Dad reminds me of an organ grinder, and Shelly and Mark are the little monkeys dancing in the street. But one thing remains—Shelly and Mark are rich.

We should be in Colorado by this afternoon. I think it's taking longer to get across the country this time, mainly because of those damn signs. We stop here and there and everywhere, hitting any town that has a population. I've noticed that elevation has a lot to do with population; the higher the elevation the fewer people. I'm not sure why. Mom and Dad do the driving and Shelly and Mark do the selling. By now everyone is on the search for territory. Mom says that California is wide open. No one has ever been this far with these signs. The man who sold her the signs was just getting started. I think she bought the first silk screen. Dad is a lot more relaxed and he hasn't lost his temper at all. I don't think I can remember the last time he said yes so much. I bet he can't either. Mom has said nothing about the baby the whole trip, and I like it that way. My questions still hang around, but they're not bugging me as much.

There it is, WELCOME TO COLORADO. It's two o'clock and lunch is up around the next mountain. I'm starving. Shelly's not. Mark just wants to get out and wander around the next town and sell, sell, sell. That's just fine, but it's day three and I'm a little bored. The signs have been going like hotcakes. Dad says if we keep it up, we might have enough money to rent a house as soon as we get there. I hope so, I really don't want to stay with Aunt Carole. And I know I'll be the one they drop off. I overheard Mom tell Dad, she was going to call her sisters tonight. Probably to tell them we're coming and staying.

I can't quit thinking about school. "Junior High School." The name alone sounds scary; I've heard about what they do to the seventh graders—how mean they are and something about initiation. What is that? Well if anybody tries to hurt me, I'll kick their ass and that's that. Uncle John said, "If you don't take shit, you won't have to eat it." All I know is I'm scared to death. Shelly and Mark won't even be at the same school. I have to go there all by myself. I know Mom thinks I'm strong, but I'm really not. She has no idea how scared I am, and most of the time all I am is scared. Sure, I can handle it, but afterward I usually feel like throwing up.

Grandma said that those people back in California are crazy. I hope she's wrong. But no matter what, there's nothing I can do. I will go to a new school, and I am in the seventh grade. I thought about this long enough, I think I'll look at the mountains for awhile. The next town must be here soon.

Dad and Shelly ride together after the last gas station. He wants to stop in Denver, sell some signs, and get up tomorrow and sell some more before we leave. He said that this town was big enough for us to work a week. Mom shot that down immediately. She wants off the road.

Mark and I play tic-tac-toe. Believe it or not, he wins a lot more than he should. I pretend I let him, but I didn't.

"What the hell are they doing?" Mom screeches to a halt. The van goes wild as she pulls into the dirt shoulder. The tires smoke from Dad's truck as he and Shelly run into the desert. Dad has his coat and Shelly is running with him. I'm trying to get the door open and get out. Mom yells, "Stop it, just wait here." She opens her door and stands on the side of the road watching the two of them go crazy chasing something. I can't stand it, what is it? I open the door and get out. Mark is right behind me. In the distance, I see Dad throw his jacket onto the ground. He's got something. Shelly is helping hold it. My god, what did they catch? a wild dog, a rabbit, or maybe a baby wolf? Mom releases her hold on me and Mark and I run toward them. Mom marches behind us.

Dad and Shelly are petting it and struggling with a mysterious animal. I can't wait to see it. Mom doesn't know whether to be mad or what. She thinks it's stupid no matter what this creature is. "Get back Sandra, it doesn't know you." I stand back. Dad is slightly turned away while Shelly's face is hidden behind Dad's back. "What is it?" I demand. Mom finds this less and less funny as the thorns scratch her feet.

"Bill—," before Mom can finish, Dad twirls around and drops the beast. Everyone goes running and screaming from the deadly jacket. Our feet are as high as our voices. Running and screaming. Finally, I notice that Dad and Shelly aren't screaming, they're laughing their asses off. Dad is doubled up and holding his side. Shelly is bravely standing next to the lifeless jacket. I on the other hand, am twenty-five feet away with Mark in my back pocket. Mom is thirty feet away on top of a boulder, cussing. "You dumb son of a bitch." She climbs down while Mark and I go meet the jacket. Shelly is stuttering, "It was Dad's idea."

"Bullshit, I said we should pull over, I didn't say anything about running off into the dessert. You're the one who came up with throwing the jacket."

After the shock of it all, I can't help but laugh with them. It was the funniest thing I ever saw. All three of us so curious and then scared shitless, and then running like hell. We looked like chickens with our heads cut off. I should have known something was up, Shelly is usually a scaredy cat when it comes to stuff like that. It should have been me, that would have made it even more believable. What am I saying? I believed it.

The signs continue to sell. Shelly and Mark are starting to get more and more aggressive. Shelly practically maps our way to California. Mom drives and Dad follows, one town after another. The backseat and I hang out, I do word search. By this afternoon we should be in Nevada. That means only one day left until California. I hear Dad saying we are not going to stop by Grandma Lois's, we just don't have time. Mom didn't fight real hard to change his mind. Reno is on the way. It's not about time, it's that Dad doesn't like Lois and Red. I exhale a sigh of relief. Mom still hasn't called her sisters and I wonder why. Maybe she wants to surprise them. They'll be surprised all right. That's all we do lately; surprise people. I'm finding that there is nothing better than a hotel. At least I can get out of this merry-go-round. I have a headache from all the word searches. I'm grouchy and fed up—I want to get off the road. Shelly and Mark count. That's all they do is count their money, over and over again. Shelly has sixty-one dollars and Mark has forty-four last he counted. I pretend I can't hear them, but I do.

The day passes and by six in the evening we've entered Nevada. I hate Nevada, it's the most boring state I've ever seen. It reminds me of Utah but without the Mormons. Nevada and Utah were probably brother and sister until one day Nevada said, "Forget this; it's too boring here. I'm going to break away and make my own rules, watch this, God." And that's how Nevada was born. Except Nevada didn't get Salt Lake, it got Tahoe. Dad's favorite place is Tahoe. He said when we get rich, we're going to buy a place there. He says it's for us, but it's really for him.

Dad is a little lighter and brighter in the morning. He loves the road, being on it for some reason is where he feels at home. He loves the desert for some reason too. I can't wait until we're out of the desert. He stretches outside the motel door and drinks his coffee; a cigarette dangles from his mouth and his shirt's off. He seems to know the desert, almost like it's some sort of long lost friend of his. Something about the quiet and emptiness calls to him. I can see it in his blue, bloodshot eyes. His eyes don't seem to squint as much when he's in the desert. I bet it was hard for him to leave Phoenix.

Mom, on the other hand, has no particular love for the road or desert. She packs up the room and drops the key on the TV as she walks out of another motel with no name. Her belly is pouching out a little, but only I can tell. I look once in a while when I'm sure no one else is.

"Ardell," Dad stamps out his cigarette, "I was thinking. If we drive through lunch and eat some donuts for breakfast, we can make it to Tahoe by evening."

Mom holds open the van door until he finishes. "Are you serious? We need to sell signs."

Dad answers right away. "Hell, we have plenty of time, and besides we can sell there too. For Christ's sake we deserve a little fun after all this driving."

Mom knows it's either give in or fight, so she gives in. We all take our seats and drive all day as fast as we can to a place called Tahoe. I've heard of it, but I've never been there. I'd like to see it, Uncle Mal said it's the prettiest place on earth. Mountains, lakes, and trees taller than buildings. According to Dad we'll be there in about six or seven hours.

We stop three times to sell, go to the bathroom, and get a drink. Reno eventually shows up on a sign that says nine miles. Mom raises her hand slightly and says a silent hello to her Mom as we pass right on by. Her arm continues to hang in the hot wind as the white sand waves good-bye. Reno is now in the rearview mirror. Tahoe, however, is up ahead two more hours, Dad boasts. His voice is excited. He keeps his foot on the gas, and his eyes water while the wind races across his face and back through his red hair.

Shelly and Mark get a break from selling today, not much to do but wait to meet Tahoe. The most beautiful place on earth. I feel like I've been handed a secret key and I'm about to meet something grand, something I've never seen before, a place I've never been. Two hours go quickly, and the sun lowers just as fast. I wish the sun would hang in there a little longer, but it's sinking lower and lower. The closer we get to the mountains, the more the shadows grow. I watch out the window, my face so close I can see my breath breathing on the window. I don't want to miss a thing. The trees are tall, the mountains are grand, and I can't wait to see the lake. I love the water. I hope it's a big lake.

Dad seems to know exactly where he's going; Dad never knows exactly where he's going. Mom follows. We drive a lot slower, the four lanes have now turned into two. I see a few more motels on the side of the road. We must be getting close. The air has cooled and Mom's window is up. Dad crawls through the lights that are growing and growing. Traffic lights appear out of nowhere and cars multiply. I still don't see a lake. Before us is a strip full of huge hotels on both sides of the street.

Mom reads the marquees and knows everyone up there flashing, Tom Jones, Helen Reddy, and Al Green. She might have got down off the stage years ago and quit singing, but she certainly didn't forget how to sing. There are little men in front of the hotel doors who run around taking people's cars for them. People cross in the middle of streets, they don't care, they can't wait for the light to change. Dad's head swings back and forth, searching and searching. He's probably lost. I can't imagine a lake around here. It's dark. He flips a left in front of a car and Mom slams on her breaks; she can't make it. Dad has pulled into one of the fancy hotels. What is he thinking? We can't stay here, is he crazy? I'll wait for Mom to handle this. There is no way she'll let us stay here. Finally, the traffic eases and she makes a left. Dad sits there in front of the big hotel in his beat-up truck with boxes tied down in the back with tired, frayed rope. The little men aren't sure what he's doing and neither am I.

Mom pulls up, "What in the hell are you doing?"

"Just follow me to the parking lot. Hell, we're here, let's go inside for a minute."

Again, Mom stops herself from killing him. Dad's truck spits and sputters as we pass the little men. I sink low into my seat so they won't see me. They saw me. Dad parks way in the back, up against the fence.

Mom rolls next to him. Dad jumps out and pushes his hair back and tucks in his yellow T-shirt. Mom directs us from the front seat. "Get your shoes on, we're going in."

"But I have to go to the bathroom," Mark whines.

"You can use the one inside." Mom is restless and irritated. She seems to think we know where we're going. In there means nothing to me. Where is in there? Are we actually going inside this big hotel? I don't get it. Why?

I follow Mom and she follows Dad. We look like a mess, and the people passing me look so nice and clean. I can't help but stare and neither can they. I pretend like I know what we're doing. I notice right away, it smells like the mountains. The pines remind me and cold air tells me it's the mountains. But the parking lot and the big giant glass doors in front of me don't feel like the mountains. I want to hold Mom's hand but Shelly and Mark do. The closer we get, the bigger the doors are. I have to tilt my head back to see them. The little men in red and black greet us, half a smile creeps off their faces. One of them opens the door for us. I must be dreaming, this is not Denny's. Dad enters first, his chest fills with air and he's born again. His eyebrows lower and his head cocks with each and every bell and buzzer from down below. It looks like a party and everyone's invited. They're all playing cards and machines. No one even turns their heads to notice.

I stand there with my hands in my pockets. Why am I wearing these cutoffs? I look stupid. Shelly is wondering the same thing—now what?

Dad squeezes Mom's arm. He says something, but the noise is too loud. All I can hear is men's voices, buzzing, and constant ringing. Why doesn't someone shut up those damn machines? Mom points to where the restrooms are and tells me to take Mark and Shelly. She rushes down the stairs and finishes, "Get right back here and wait. Don't screw around. I'll meet you right here."

The restroom sign is two football fields away, through a million people. Mom goes to find Dad. He disappeared into thin air, and last I saw him he was standing right here. I don't know how I'm ever going to get past all those people, the smoke, the cocktails, and those irritating bells. Shelly and Mark follow me as we walk carefully trying not to bump into people, but they don't care. They walk in a daze with buckets of change tucked under their arms and drinks in hand. All I can see are cherries spinning and the word *jackpot* flashing in red, yellow, and blue. The floor has electricity to it, and if I don't keep moving, it feels like it will swallow me up. By the time we squeeze out of the way and through the maze, the restroom area feels like home base, and we're safe. I wait outside forever for Mark and Shelly.

One of the hotel cowboys dressed in white and black is coming my way. It looks like he's heading straight for me. I didn't do anything, so why is he coming toward me? I stand still and cross my arms and turn my head. He bends down, "Hey little lady are you okay?" What a stupid question, of course I'm okay. Do I look like I'm not okay. I stare back into his face for a minute. He really means it, am I okay?

I shake off the smart-ass inside me and answer politely. "Yeah, I'm just waiting for my sister and brother."

"Okay then, but you aren't allowed in here without your parents. You need to get out of the pit area."

Pit, now that's a nice word. I think of it more as *the pits*. I thank him and off he rides into the pit. I tap my foot and wish they would hurry up before I get in more trouble.

Does Mom know I'm not allowed in here? I see Mom's head in the crowd. Her black hair is unmistakable. She doesn't see me. She goes to the phone around the corner from me. I can't leave my post, I have to wait for Shelly and Mark. But at the same time I want to get over to Mom before she leaves. I move a little closer to the corner so I can see her and wait for them. She turns my way a little, and I hear her talking to Aunt Carole.

"Carole, it's me. Yes, I'm fine. We'll be there tomorrow. I know, but it's been real hard to get a hold of you. I wanted to write but I ran out of time. Carole I'm pregnant. Yes, Bill knows and the kids. Of course I'm going to keep it. But I'll need some help with finding a home.

I think I heard something unusual. I'm not sure. Mom's tone is shaky, and she's turned away from me. I can't make out all her words. The noise prevents me from hearing the rest. I see her walk away. What did she say? She's going to keep it, what does that mean? Can you give your kids away?

Before I finish, Shelly and Mark are ready to go. Me too. I walk back to the doors through the people and past the yelling steel machines.

The room is now tiny, and yet all the same people are here. I feel trapped, claustrophobia is moving in and my body wants out. I need to sit down, get away from all the strangers. My stomach hurts. The phone call is ringing in my head. Mom isn't here, where did she go? We stand in the way, getting bumped and excused at the platform entrance. The doors stand taller, and I'd give anything to get out.

The floodgates open as I replay Mom's words. I must be completely out of my mind. Mom always tells the truth. What happened, I don't know, but there's a secret growing slowly, just like the baby inside her. What is going on? Mom *decided* to keep me and Shelly and Mark? Did she just *decide* to give the baby away—she couldn't; it died damn it. This is terror. I want to know the truth, but I wonder if I really do. Maybe I don't. Maybe this should all shut up and leave me alone. I'm not understanding anything right now. All that's happening is my head hurts, my stomach aches, and I want to get out of this loud stupid place. Why are we here? Oh yeah, so Dad can play. I'm not having any fun, and I haven't even seen the stupid lake.

Shelly taps my arm and interrupts my terror. "I'm thirsty."

"What do you want me to do?" I snap and rip her head off. "I don't want to be here either. Tell Mom and Dad, not me."

She rolls her eyes in a way that says I'm an asshole. She's right but she's wrong. My arms fold tighter and tighter across my chest, it feels like I'm going to blow up. The phone call won't go away. It rings over and over. Something is missing; I know it. Mom shows up out of the crowd below; she's miffed and she can't find Dad. Who cares? Let's just get out of here. She walks up ten stairs.

"Sandra wait here, I've got to find your father."

"No," fell out of my mouth so fast I couldn't catch it.

She whirled around. "Excuse me?"

I stare straight into her dark eyes; I looked deep inside. I want the truth. Her black pupils lock tight and block my invasion. She doesn't blink. The black gets blacker, and we both know inside what this isn't about. She breaks the deadlock and takes control as she calls my bluff.

"What is your problem?"

I look down and fold, "I want to go wait in the car with the dogs." The answer comes naturally, and she ignores my mouth this time. We chalk it up to tired, hungry, and cranky. She agrees to let us go.

I turn around in fury, and my anger and terror blow open the giant doors. I walk out, and the doormen's eyes follow me across the red carpet. The carpet looks like blood, and the doors bounce to a close.

The wind stays out of my way, Shelly and Mark do the same. Mark thinks I'm going to hit him, and Shelly waits for a fight. But inside I know if I started, I probably couldn't stop. Anger and heat fill my legs, and they pound the cement parking lot as if it can feel. I approach the van. I can see the dogs' noses sweating on the side window. They knew I was coming. Shelly and Mark race freely to the door, calling the front seat. I could care less about the front seat, hell the farther away from Mom the better. And Dad too, him in there playing around like everything is just fine. He always acts like everything is just fine. IT'S NOT! Do you hear me? I scream wildly at the top of my lungs to myself.

At that moment, time stops, it falls away, disappears. I find myself dizzy looking up to the stars. That's it, the stars know what's going on. Please tell me, tell me what's going on. Am I crazy?

"Is this my imagination too, God?" I feel a tear inside the back of my throat, "Is it?" the tear would not drop out of my eye. Have the tears inside me forgotten how to get out? I hold my head back and fill my lungs with cold air and the scent of pine. The black sky and the pinholes of light keep my attention. I feel like throwing my arms out to the side and twirling. But there's no need, I'm already twirling inside my body. Around and around I go. The van soon disappears, the casino, the fence, and eventually the parking lot itself. Time comes in and out and eventually the Voice speaks, and loudly. It says with a full deep growl; *If the baby is born a boy, then She is alive.*

I listen closer to the voice. It repeats the words slowly, *"If the baby is born a boy, then She is alive."* I want to argue, but my words have no way out. The Voice closes, *"You will understand in a very short time. No more."* The stars come back and the twirling stops. The anger leaves, and now I'm very cold, standing in the empty parking lot. I walk the last fifteen feet back to the van. I shake off the cold and start to question what it is. It seems to be just like the snake who chased me, they said it must have been my imagination—I say it was real. It seems that imagination sits somewhere in the middle of the truth and lies. But then who is She? Mom said she, is she the one in my dream? Or is She the truth?

Mark opens the van door. He has Big on his lap and he's screwing around. He has a pair of Dad's shorts on his head. I grab the underwear off Mark's head and throw them outside.

"Hey! What in the hell do you think you're doing?" Dad flies out from nowhere and screeches like an owl.

I turn sharply and stand up and look at his big voice; waiting for him to hit me. I want to scream back, What in the hell are you doing?

Mom stands behind him quiet, hoping I'll keep my mouth shut.

32

The morning surprises us all; it comes way too fast. The smell of late morning is in the air. Mom and Dad aren't talking much. Actually, no one is talking much. We're all out of things to say. Besides, today we end this trip and start over. I'm not going to ask, but I know we'll go to Aunt Carole's first. We'll put our things down for the night and figure out the rest. Mom will be the leader for a while. It's her turn, and she knows it. Dad takes the rear as we drive down the winding highway. This will lead us straight to Aunt Carole's front door. I wonder where we'll live, what school, and if Dad will find work. After an hour, I remember it'll be a surprise. I'm getting good at surprises, actually I might be enjoying them.

The valley opens before us, and all that remains between us and the surprises are about forty miles. Mark catnaps and Shelly doesn't, her eyes are wide open. Mine are still red. Mom grips the steering wheel like she's trying to get away from something. Her thoughts are deep and wide. She looks like she's going down a swift murky river and she's looking for something to hold on to. I wish I could talk to her, but she's gone right now.

Aunt Carole is in the front yard with Jason who's now about four years old. He's beating up his dump truck and she's trying to stop him. Tanya is Aunt Carole's newest addition, she's about two and tugging at Aunt Carole's leg. Her round face and black hair remind me of Mom. She senses something and looks up: we're here. She and Mom meet before the van has stopped. I can't wait to see her. We pile out, stepping on each other, the dogs and the junk all over the floor. Dad pretends he could care less about seeing Aunt Carole, but he's happy to be in California. Shelly runs for the bathroom, she doesn't care about hugging and hellos. I wait my turn for my hug. Aunt Carole squeezes me tight, but only I can tell. She welcomes Mark who barely remembers her.

It's been three years. Mom reacquaints herself and goes to Jason. He likes her immediately. All the kids in our family like Mom. Mom is not like her sisters, she cusses and says it like it is. They all tell me how lucky I am to have her for a mom. Aunt Carole shows us the house and offers lunch. She and Mom sneak off into the kitchen, their old stomping grounds. Mom takes her old seat and Aunt Carole does the same.

Dad stays outside with us. We look across the street to the old house we used to live in. It looks exactly the same. I hear Aunt Carole from inside her house, "Darla should be back in a minute. She just went to the store." I hear it more as a warning. Darla, I almost forgot about Darla. Three years have passed and I wonder if she still hates me. I'll find out in a minute.

I go inside for a drink of water, and Mom is surrounded by papers that Aunt Carole has collected from the Welfare Office. Aunt Carole reminds me, "You know where everything is, help yourself. There's cold water in the fridge."

Mom jumps up to help me, "Here, why don't you take some to your brother and sister." Jason now wants some too. He reaches for a dirty glass off the sink. Mom trades him for a clean one.

"Carole, how old is he now?"

"He turned four in August."

Mom stops what she's doing. Aunt Carole catches something in the air and tries to dart the conversation away from Jason. "So I was talking to Revell last night, and she thinks she found you a house."

"I can't believe it's been four years since..." Mom stares out the kitchen window.

I see Aunt Carole get sad all over and she tries to brush it away. I catch more than a glimpse of something; it's a fast slap across the face that stings. Aunt Carole and I know, Jason and Mom's baby are the same age both born in August. I feel a stab in my back; it comes and goes quickly. This is the first time Mom has ever mentioned the baby in any way. I'm shocked. Before I know it, the water is spilling over the glass and onto the floor. It catches all of our attention and mention of the baby disappears as swiftly as it came. I watch what I'm doing, Aunt Carole goes back to shuffling the papers, and Mom dries her hands—they're not even wet.

Darla's coming, she's sweating from a long walk back from baby-sitting. I see her, and question whether or not I should go meet her. Shelly and Mark go with me. Darla sneers at first, not recognizing the three stooges before her, and then it clicks. Her cousins, they're back. She smiles and then really smiles. Darla is glad to see us and especially me. Her hands are full of bags and her forehead is beaded with sweat.

"Oh wow, Mom said you guys we're coming. How long are you staying?"

I shrug my shoulders, I don't know. Mark continues searching the slimy ditch for bottles or treasures. Shelly and I help Darla carry the groceries and trot home. Darla is in a good mood. She's still a very serious girl and laughing isn't her favorite thing to do. However Shelly gives it her best shot, and Darla cracks up by the time we reach the front door. Mom and Aunt Carole are still in the kitchen shuffling through papers.

Aunt Carole peels an orange and finishes talking to Mom, "You know this MediCal will cover you, the kids, and the baby. I'm sure you'll qualify."

Mom tugs and picks at her fingernails. She listens while Carole continues figuring out the future. Something about Welfare and a training program for Dad, it all sounds easy to me. Revell found a house and Carole found us some money.

Dad stays outside with Uncle Mal. They bullshit each other and I bet they would love a beer right now. But instead, they drink tumblers full of sweet tea outside by the old Studebaker that sits fat on its blocks. Mal's been working on that thing for as long I can remember.

That night, Uncle Mal barbecues hamburgers for dinner, he loves standing by the grill burning our dinner while Aunt Carole and Mom fuss in the kitchen with the ketchup, pickles, and toasting buns. We kids avoid the kitchen and stay far, far away. After dinner they make us do the dishes and clean up. Some things never change. The adults go to the living room. I listen carefully.

"We'll go with Revell to see the house tomorrow. She says it's for rent and they'll accept welfare. I guess she's already talked with the guy. It's not too far from her house. Shelly and Mark can go to the elementary by her house. It's better than the one in that neighborhood. Sandra can go to Will C. Wood. Junior High, she can walk from what I understand."

I've heard enough. I walk from the kitchen table to the dirty dishes and dry—as a guest I get to dry. Darla washes and Ross still isn't home, he has a basketball game or something. Shelly and I don't mind. Aunt Carole warns us that bedtime is approaching. Mom goes along with the plan to put us to bed. Bedtime is difficult. Darla sleeps with Jason and Tanya in their room. Mom and Dad get Ross's bed. We sleep all over the living room. And Ross gets the camper outside.

Morning shows up like it always does, and Shelly and I stay put on the couch. Mark gets in the way of brushing teeth and eating breakfast. Mom and Dad sleep through it all. Aunt Carole offers us Froot Loops. Darla's pissed, she has to eat Shredded Wheat. Froot Loops are for weekends. It's Friday. Ross says two words, hi and good-bye, and he's out the door. Darla doesn't say a word, but I can tell she's thinking a few. Tanya is cute and round. She's lost in the mess of it all and eventually Aunt Carole scoops her up, pulls her thick brown curls in a high ponytail, and gives her a hug.

"Darla, you stay here with your sister and brother while I go with Ardell to see the house. Turn on cartoons if you want to."

Shelly, Mark, and me just stare at each other. There's nothing to say, we want our own house. We hate sitting around here. We feel out of place and lost. I for one am a lot more comfortable in the van. I don't know about Shelly and Mark but they look like they just had a bad dream. I know I'm having one.

After showers and coffee, we pile in the van. I change my mind and jump in with Aunt Carole. She's usually serious, that's probably where Darla gets it. But not with me. She talks to me when we're alone, and I forgot how much I missed that. Aunt Carole gets on the freeway and checks her rearview mirror a hundred times, making sure no one gets lost.

"Sandra, I'm so glad you're back. Are you glad to be back?"

I think about her question long and hard. I know she wants me to say yes, but my home is back in West Virginia. "Yeah, it's okay." All I can do is try not to lie and try not to hurt her feelings. She doesn't know about Grandma, Uncle Brooks and Regina, or Uncle John. She doesn't know how much I love them. This is Mom's side of the family, and Dad's side isn't part of them. I know all about sides and I also know I'm in the middle. I hate picking sides.

"Are you excited about junior high?"

The answer flies out, "No."

She turns her head around and looks my way. "What's the matter?"

"Aunt Carole, I don't know anybody and well—I'm not..."

Her heart pops open and she lets me off the hook, "Honey don't worry, you're going to do fine. You're funny and pretty and smart. The first day might be hard, but after that you'll make friends and the nervousness will pass."

She's right, that's what I am, nervous. I'm not scared, I'm nervous. I hope I'm going to be okay.

Aunt Carole changes the subject. "And what do you think about your new baby brother or sister? It'll be here soon."

"I know, it's great." I play with the door handle. "Yeah me, Shelly, and Mark were all born in Phoenix."

Aunt Carole changes lanes, "And this little one will be the first one in your family to be born in California."

My eyes open wide and then pop out of my head. I look at her as if she's lost her mind. "What?"

She thinks about the last five words out of her mouth and adjusts her back deep into the seat. Her eyes never meet mine. The hesitation and nervous fidgeting take over the road, Aunt Carole looks away, "Oh, I mean the second one born in California."

"Aunt Carole, did you see the baby?"

I feel her slam on the breaks—the car keeps moving but this conversation has gone too far. Aunt Carole can't lie. She knows how, but she can't. Her face swells and her voice cracks. Her eyes move like moths trying to get to the light, and her lips tighten. The detective in me knows I've done something.

"Honey, what makes you ask such a question? No."

"I heard Mom say once that it had dark hair like me."

The car stops on a dime, bumping the curb in front of Aunt Revell's. She gets out of the car and out of the way. Heading straight for the door, she yells for Aunt Revell. Aunt Revell has kids galore, more than last time. She now has a little one named Lori about three, Kristie is five, and Julie is eleven, Shelly's age. Then Jeff who's my age, twelve. And last but not least the two giants, Steve and Allen. They're even bigger now. They remind me of soldiers that guard castles.

Aunt Revell is in the aftermath of the kitchen. It looks like a tornado touched down. Bowls everywhere with Cheerios half stuck on and French toast dripping down the hot grill. Underwear on the floor like dead bodies and two little ones opening the cupboard doors below her feet. She cleans frantically, trying to get it done before we get there—too late. We are here, the troop. Aunt Revell smiles long and hard as she looks us up and down. Shelly's beauty takes her back. Shelly remembers Aunt Revell and returns a sweet smile to her.

"Oh my goodness, look at you guys. Come here and give me a hug." She reaches for all of us and hugs us to death. Aunt Revell is the only family member on this side who sincerely hugs us. She rubs our backs and finally lets go.

"I'm so glad you're back, I missed you so much." Aunt Revell includes all of us, then looks up at Dad, "How are you Jack?" She stays on her side of the kitchen counter using it as a barrier between them. She's on one side and Dad better stay on his side. "Okay." She wipes her hands. "Lets not waste any time. Let me finish getting dressed and we'll go." She abandons the mound of dishes piled all over the sink.

Lori and Kristie look like they've seen a ghost. They stand up and stare. Mom tries to get them to come over. No way. They know Aunt Carole, but they sure as hell don't know us. We all take a seat and wait. Aunt Revell returns and so does the conversation. "Carole, why don't we all ride over in my van, it's not far." She gathers her little ones, Jason holds onto Aunt Carole's hand. The big blue Dodge van holds all of us, no problem.

We drive out of her neighborhood and go south. I notice the farther we drive the browner the lawns get, the more cars fit in the yards, and the windows have big black bars on them like cages. I look over to Shelly; she sees it. We cross a big intersection next to a pink cemetery. The gates are iron and the headstones go on and on. It's the biggest one I've ever seen.

I wonder if that's where they buried the baby. The thought floats in and out, then I remember Aunt Carole. Why did she say that? *It'll be the first baby born in California.* What? She forgot? How did she forget something like that? Maybe it doesn't count because it died.

Aunt Revell makes a right at the Goodwill. Duke's Bar sits next door. And then she stops right away. "There it is." She points out of her window.

The yellow cinder block house sits vacant on a dirt front yard with a quarter-high wall decorating the cement porch. The front door is aluminum and painted brown, the scratches and scuff marks resemble footprints. The mailbox hangs crooked, reading 4848 ALCOTT DRIVE.

Alcott, I don't know what that means, but it ain't West Virginia. Mom doesn't want to get out and Dad clearly doesn't care. Shelly and me look at each other and close our mouths.

Aunt Revell bounces down and rips the girls out of the van by one arm each. They swing to the ground. The brown grass, yellow house, and cement blocks stare at me, and I stare back. Revell and Carole go inside, Mom and I don't. She holds onto my shoulder, I can feel her leaning on me. Mark and Shelly stay on the sidewalk next to us. We make sure we stay off the dirt. Dad wanders through the broken gate and goes to the backyard. The gate stays open and he vanishes.

Mom tries to fill up with pride before her knees give out, and stands tall, all five feet and three inches. Her words form carefully and her lips don't move. "You guys listen to me," she scoots closer, "this is only temporary, nothing is forever. We may have to live here now, but we're not going to stay. I promise you that. I'll get us out of here, somehow." She folds her hands gently across her mouth, I know she's not, but it looks like she's praying. "Remember, whatever happens you guys, I raised you better than this. And this place is not who you really are. It's just for now."

She's the boss and we know it, and so does the house. We move together in a huddle, Mom enters first. I want to close my eyes until I turn eighteen. The yellow cement on the outside immediately turns bright white on the inside. The living room, the kitchen, and the three bedrooms are tiny. One of the bedrooms is part of the hallway—I don't understand it. The bathroom is dark pink. Forest green bleeds through the white walls here and there, and I think they forgot to clean the place. The kitchen floor is muted gray brown. Not a pretty sight. The closets have left over hangers strangling themselves. And the carpet is green with patches of brown worn spots. The house is a box, with corners called bedrooms and an unhappy kitchen. The living room is tired of being a living room. And the house isn't breathing at all. There are no ghosts, there isn't any room for them. The house feels young, about twenty, but a depressed twenty. It functions alone and can't remember how to have fun. I don't think it ever has, and the other houses don't like it very much.

Mom closes one eye and listens halfway to Revell and Carole offering this and that: a couch and bed, a dresser, and so on. No one cares about the furniture; it's not going to change a thing. Mark goes outside to study the neighborhood. He throws dirt clods at the single tree with no leaves. Everything needs water. The bushes are thin and wiry. The backyard is weeds, tall mean weeds. The garage is dark. I stand alone in it, looking for something good. The house settles it, and simply says, *"You're here now and you better get used to it."* I want to argue, but I can't.

That weekend we move in. Revell and Carole stop by with this and that. We add it to the ratty, mix-and-match decor. The couch is soft and the two chairs sag, but the kitchen table is sturdy.

Mark stands on the table when no one is looking just to make me laugh. I run after him and push him, he trips and lands on his ass. He looks up and his eyes almost fall out. "What's the matter with you?" I laugh.

He gets up slowly and bends over resting his hands on his knees. He's in pain, but I didn't push him that hard. His mouth is open and he can't speak.

"What's wrong with you?"

He stays bent over and reaches quietly around to his back pocket. His hand comes out with three crushed walnuts he had in his back pocket.

"Hey what's going on?"

"Sandra pushed me down and I fell." He holds out the walnut dust and Shelly laughs first with the rest of us. I look around at all three of us laughing and then stop when I see how ugly the house really is. I hope Mom's right, I hope this doesn't mean we're poor and dumb. I shuffle back into the tiny cell block trying to ignore it.

On Sunday afternoon, Mom and I walk over to Goodwill and shop. She has a little money and no more. I'm trying not to look disappointed, pissed, or humiliated, but I am. She is too; we both keep a stiff upper lip. She tells me we're just getting a few things, we're not school clothes shopping. But we are.

"Honey with the check we get next month, I promise the first thing I'll do is get you some real school clothes."

I nod to myself and kick the loose gravel on the pavement. Mom holds the door open and we enter the Goodwill—it's official, we are now poor. I try not to make eye contact with any of the other poor people inside. I barely have the strength to shove the clothes over on the racks before me. Mom sifts and sorts trying her hardest to find stuff not too worn or ugly. I pray she can, because I can't. I give up before I try. I don't want to be difficult, but I can't help it. She's asking too much of me. My first day of junior high and I'm wearing rags. I have nothing in me to fake my feelings. Mom's heart is broke, and she is just as devastated. But she's not the one going to a brand new school and introducing herself as poor. Mom shows me this and that. She finds a brown and baby blue pair of cords, they'll do. I find a few summer shirts that look halfway decent. The pink paper tags with handwritten black pen read twenty-five cents. The pants are fifty cents. Mom and I keep the talking down to one word sentences, yes, no, and sure. But the truth is, I have a lot to say.

Mom says it all, "I'm sorry honey." She grabs the paper bags full of faded clothes that sort of fit. "I know how hard this is for you, and I hate myself for making you do this." Her words soften my edge but the chip on my shoulder stays put. I understand her side and I know my side of it, but nothing makes it better. It's the worst day of my life and tomorrow will outdo today.

We get home and there's no need to show Dad what I got. It's not cute and I feel like a fool. I don't say it out loud, I don't want to hurt Mom's feelings, and as for Dad, I can't say he has any. According to him, *I should just be glad I have a roof over my head and food to eat.*

Yeah, the creamed tuna on toast is a real treat. The chip is growing and if I didn't know better, I'd think it was a second head sitting on my shoulder. I try to make it go away, but I can't. It sits there reminding me that tomorrow is Monday, 4848 Alcott Drive is my new address, and I better keep my mouth shut. I can't talk to Mom or I'll make her cry, and if that happens, Dad will make me cry. The circle flies over my head like distant vultures in the mountains. I grab the wire hangers out of my closet and rip open the bags. On the bed lies the truth. I hang the clothes up crooked; I don't care. The shirts act difficult, and fall off the bent hangers. I step on them hard to show them who's boss. Like I said, I don't care.

That night the weeds blow in the backyard. They sound like rice paper scraping together. The tree sways back and forth and its shadow dances on my bedroom wall. It tries to rock me to sleep, but I toss and turn like my stomach. The kiss on my cheek from Mom still smells like her. Eventually I give up and my mind closes. I drift off next to Shelly, who's curled up and gone.

Monday morning surprises me, it came so fast. Shelly and Mark are not yet awake. Mom is and Dad's gone to interview for some job—they're going to pay him to go to school. I see Mom in the kitchen in her faded pink nightgown. It's thinner in some spots than others and the neck hangs loose on her chest. She's good at hiding her belly and it barely shows. Mom hears me coming and puts down her glass of water. "Hi Honey, are you ready for the big day?"

No hits the floor as I try to say sure, and the words get all mixed up and nothing comes out. I shrug my shoulders.

"Why don't you go shower before I wake your brother and sister." She moves my way to give me a hug. My body stiffens. If she hugs me right now I'll start crying, I know it. I back up and leave the kitchen without a word. I walk back to my room with my dirty socks half on and half off. I look down and decide not to pull them up. The toe parts drag, flip, and flop, they act the way I feel. I walk past Mark who sleeps in the hall in a scratched-up twin bed. At least I'm not him; I have a bedroom. Next, I see Shelly almost awake. I say nothing, she knows I'm there picking out my clothes. She stays turned away, good thing or I'd probably hit her. I grab my new old brown cords and a white sleeveless shirt. It's trimmed in red and I love red. And it's not that bad, I'm the only one who knows it's used. I'll just pretend that I decided to dress this way because junior high's not that big of a deal. I can be brave and fake my way through this day. I shower while the rest of them beat on the door begging for me to hurry. I shouldn't have locked it, but I did. Mom finally bangs and instantly the water turns off. I wrap the towel around my dripping body and go down the hall to get dressed. "Hey, get out of my room," Mark yells from the couch.

"Shut up." I slam his door. Mark doesn't get it, his room is only his at night when he goes to bed. During the day, it's the dirty clothes room, hallway, and dressing room. His room has a patch of gold carpet; Shelly and I have a cement floor. I can't stand getting dressed in there, the dirt sticks to my damp feet.

Mom scoots Mark over on the couch, and Shelly sits in the chair waiting for me. Mom's going to drive us to school. They look like they're getting ready to throw me to the lions. I brush my hair for the last time and grab a pencil and the notebook Mom bought me. I'm the first one out the door. The door slams shut behind them. I try not to look at the dirt front yard as we load into the car. I sit in the front seat; everyone knows not to fight me for it today. I have that look. Mom drives at her careful pace, and each light we approach means I'm that much closer to school. All I can think is, maybe we'll get in a wreck and I can miss school. No such luck. There's no one on the road but us. Mom makes the last left and sucks up in line with the rest of the tired mothers. They all wait their turn to drop off their precious package. Finally, it's my turn. Mom reaches over, kisses me, and whispers, "You're going to do fine."

I don't believe a word she says, but I nod anyway and jump out of the car and into the crowd of kids. I wave but I don't think she saw me.

I work my way up to the front of the first building. It's very modern looking, nothing like the mini prisons back in West Virginia. I know the name of my homeroom teacher, Mr. Lewellen. I search the glass windows with all the teachers' names and room numbers. I find it, thank God, right there, Room 103. I enter the main hallway. I'm shocked; Will C. Wood is beautiful. The hall is like an atrium. The second floor is exposed and I can see everything. The school is big and open, and the center of the hall looks right up to the sky. The planter boxes are full of flowers and plants. It's easy to get around. I chug down the long hall, excusing myself from one face to the next. Watching the numbers on the classrooms get smaller and smaller. I see small groups of kids here and there hanging around, laughing. There are others like me, alone, we keep to ourselves and work our way to our homerooms as fast as we can. Homeroom, what is that? My mind is quiet and my heart beats fast. I'm not scared anymore, I wish I knew somebody, but I'm not scared. The bell rings twice, maybe a warning bell or something. I'm close and definitely not lost. Just then, a small girl with a plaid dress and white face taps me on the back. I turn around and look down. "Can you help me? I can't find my class." She holds out a card, "Mrs. Worthing, Home EC, room C101." I study the card and look around trying to understand what the *C* might mean.

"I really don't know, maybe it's outside in those buildings." The look on her face tugs at my heart as I point outside the hall toward the football field. "Look, come with me and we'll ask my teacher, my homeroom is right here." She follows behind me like a little sister as I open the door into my homeroom. I spot the teacher sitting half on his desk, with one leg thrown over the side. His relaxed manner makes me feel safe. I walk right up to him, a smile appears from under his beard and mustache. I know that smile and it's real, I like this teacher. "Hi, my name is Sandra Vaughan. I'm supposed to be in your homeroom."

He quickly looks for my name. "Yes you are, now go ahead and take any seat you like."

"Mr. Lewellen, this girl is lost. Can you help her?"

He looks behind me at the frightened puppy and soothes her with a pat on the back, "Here honey, let me see." He walks her outside and shuffles her off.

Next thing I know I'm being stared at by all the kids, and they look mean. I'm frozen, I can't move. Maybe it's my clothes. The room suddenly gets twice as big and the eyes in the room triple. I scope out the front rows, but they're all full. I look to the right. All I see is a blond girl with lots of makeup, blue eye shadow, she's too colorful and she scares me. Then I notice a seat to the left by the window. My armpits are sweating, what is going on? My armpits never sweat. I slide my body over the chair and squeeze into the desk. The classroom follows me, and as if a storm cloud entered the room, silence takes over.

I fold my arms tightly in front of me, and my face looks forward. I find a scratch on the blackboard, I stare a hole in it. The longer I stare ahead the more I can feel the class pick me apart. Maybe it's the way I talk—West Virginian—maybe I have another one of those damn accents.

About then, Mr. Lewellen, in his hip corduroy tan suit, begins his hello to the classroom. He goes on and on. I hear most of it as I try to stay focused on his words. But all the strangers around me distract my attention. I hear him end the speech, "I'll pass out your classes, and if you have any questions about where you're going, I'll help you." He closes and winks at me. I feel a waterfall of cool water splash over me. He likes me. I sit up a little taller and finally stop sweating.

As he passes out the cards, I hear whispering and someone says, "Ouhh girl…" I don't think she's talking to me. After he's done, he sits back on top of the desk. "Okay, now lets find out who you are. I want you to tell me your name and what school you came from."

Then I see the blond with too much makeup stand up. The boys hoot and holler. She acts like she's just been crowned Miss America. She twirls back and forth with a fake sheepish grin, knowing full well who she is, "My name is Leeesa. I'm from Peter Lassen." She sits down carefully so as not to knock her boobs into the desk. Where in the heck did she get boobs?

Then I hear the girl up ahead one desk talking very slow. "I'm Kanisha, and I'm from Washington Elementary." She has an afro with a big comb sticking out of the back of her head. She's taller than Mr. Lewellen and her lips are blood red.

Now it's my turn, I don't know what to say, so I say it all, "My name is Sandra Vaughan, I just moved here from West Virginia." I sit down faster than I spoke. I hear snickering. Next I hear a sassy attitude behind me, "My name is Alisha and I'm from Washington too." She sits down hard. Her hair is curled on top and slicked back on the sides. She has a little plastic bow that says she's a girl, it holds back her slick black bangs. She has on a glittering shirt, tight shiny pants, and platform shoes. Her shoes are so big that she can't get them under her desk.

The bell rings and I file out with the rest of them, on to the next classroom. Mr. Lewellen stands up as I'm about to pass by and taps me, "Hey, come here." The rest of the class has gone. "So you're from West Virginia? Let me give you a piece of advice. You're not like the rest of the kids, and things work a little differently here, so be careful. By the way, I like your accent." I wonder what in the heck he's talking about. I say good-bye and get out of there. I run through his words one more time and try not to trip on my own feet. I walk less afraid to my next classes because I know where they are. So far, I'm doing great. I have all my body parts and only gym class left to go.

During lunch, I sit alone by the beautiful flowers on the ledge of the giant planter box, my feet dangling freely, and I eat my ice-cream sandwich. I notice a few kids who are starting to look familiar. A couple nod or smile, but mostly I observe. I heard that the ninth graders sometimes pick on the seventh graders and take their money and even beat 'em up. I have a quarter left over from lunch, and I'll be damned if some ninth grader's going to take it from me. I reach in my pocket and shove it down just a little bit farther. I wish I had a pair of platform shoes, all the girls are wearing them. I look down at my scuffed-up Keds and stop swinging my feet. I tuck them back underneath each other.

The bell rings, and now all I have to do is get through gym and the day is over. I hop off my perch and try not to skip, skipping is for kids. I manage to make my way through the locker room, straight to the gym. I sit cross-legged in the second row of girls on the floor. I wait for the teacher and listen to the girls giggle around me. I hear about this boy and that boy and who likes who and who doesn't. Then I can't help it, but I hear a familiar voice. I can't turn around, but it's driving me crazy, who is it? With a bragging tattling voice I hear, "Oh yeah sure, I've done it. Lot's of times. It's not that big of a deal. No, it doesn't hurt."

I knew it, it's that Lisa, the one with all the makeup. I'm not going to turn around; I'm not. She's bragging about sex. I don't belong here, maybe that's what Mr. Lewellen was talking about. Well, it is wrong, just plain wrong. I'm in seventh grade, I'm not going to have sex. No way. Now some others are chiming in, they aren't virgins either. Hell, I am. If they find out I still play with dolls, well, they're not going to. But, if they do, they'll laugh me right out of here. I've got to quit playing with dolls and I'm going to have to grow up fast.

Mrs. Koomers walks in with her whistle bouncing from one boob to the other and her clipboard held tight

"Class, this is only an orientation. This will be considered a free day. You'll need to bring in a check for six dollars and ninety-five cents for your gym clothes. It is your responsibility to care for your clothes. You'll have ten minutes to dress for class and ten minutes after class. Do you understand me? Menstrual cycles are no excuse not to dress."

Just about then, I feel my ears start burning. Periods? I don't have a period. Oh my God, this is gross. First, I find out that no one's a virgin but me, and then they all have periods too. I stay quiet and to myself. I'm afraid if I do open my mouth, I might just say, *So have you seen the latest Disco Barbie?* I hope Mom's out there waiting for me when this bell rings.

The bell finally rings and my foot's asleep. Really asleep. I can't feel it. The class leaves me behind as I try to wake up my foot. I stand slowly, the tickling pain overcomes my embarrassment, and I walk with a gimp. By the time I hit the locker room, I'm unable to control the foot that drags behind me. I look at the lockers lined up and say a quick hello to number 245, I'll see you tomorrow, and enter the madness of the hallways. Kids everywhere, screaming, hitting, teasing, and running. I'm free, all I have to do is get outside and this day is over. I trot for the door when I feel a push from behind—I fall forward just enough. I don't look back, it had to be an accident. I feel it again. I look back.

There's Lisa with a gaggle of girls chewing gum standing in a half circle. All I can see is a wall of pastel colors, ditto hip-huggers, and platform shoes.

Lisa smacks her gum, "So you're pretty tough huh?"

I stand upright, wondering what in the hell she's talking about? My foot's asleep, I have on old brown cords and dirty Keds, and she thinks I'm tough? I'm so close to the door I can touch it. All I have to do is make a dash and run like hell. The standoff continues. Lisa throws her hand on her hip, "Well, you sat with the blacks, not the whites."

By now I'm fed up and furious. What in the hell is she talking about?

"In homeroom this morning, you walked over to the black side of class and sat with them."

Oh my God, she thinks I what? I race back to homeroom in my mind and replay the morning. She waits for my response. I didn't see some black or white line, and I didn't intentionally cross it. I just wanted to sit by the window, and besides, she and her makeup scared me. I pop back ready to defend myself. "I don't know what you're talking about, I just took the closest seat."

"Well if I were you, I'd be moving my seat tomorrow." She snaps her fingers and disappears. I'm outside, the sun beaming hard in my eyes, I squint and search for Mom's car. There she is, her fingers tapping on the steering wheel as if I'm lollygagging and she's tired of waiting. Little does she know I was fighting for my life just now. I slide in and Mom starts in with all the questions you'd normally ask, except I don't have normal answers. "Mom, things aren't right here."

She turns the wheel carefully away from the curb. "What do you mean?"

"I don't know, I guess I messed up." I start chewing the ends of my hair. "Well, the white kids are mad at me for sitting next to the black kids in homeroom."

"Oh Jesus, that's ridiculous."

"Mom it's not. Some girls just came up to me and warned me."

"Who are they? What did they say?"

"They said I better move my seat tomorrow." I roll down my window.

"No dumb little twit is going to threaten you, you hear me. I'll go with you tomorrow and straighten them out." Mom speeds up and beats the yellow caution light.

The truth is, my life would be ruined if she walked down the hall with me. Her solution is a problem. "No Mom, you can't do that."

"All right then, here's what you do. First, only move if you want to, not because someone threatens you. Tell the teacher and see what he says. And if something happens, go crazy, people are much more afraid of crazy than they are of strong."

"What are you talking about?" I mumble.

"I mean if someone is going to hurt you, act crazy, all the way crazy. They won't know what to do."

That night, things around Alcott Drive soften. Dad's got the job and he'll be going to school. The state is going to train him to be a psychiatric tech. He'll be working with the mentally ill. Dad raises his fork and fills his mouth with macaroni. "And after six months, I'll start working for the California State Mental Hospital." He seems happy about that. "And then, I'm guaranteed benefits and cost-of-living raises. We're on our way."

I sit on the couch wondering about life and death, mine. I have to go to school tomorrow.

"Ardell, did I tell you? MediCal will take care of you, the kids, and the baby. It's all paid for with this program."

Mom acknowledges him with a quick glance. Shelly and Mark spin the knob on the TV. It's eight o'clock. The peacock is black and white and the music for tonight's TV movie is blaring. The miniseries *Roots* is starting. I can't wait to see this, I've seen the previews all week. Mom gets up and says, "Nah, it's going to be too violent." Mom flips to *All in the Family*. Mark goes to bed early, trying to claim his room as his own. Shelly and I take to our side of the freezing cold waterbed—thank God Mom found the foam rubber piece to lay on the waterbed mattress or Shelly and I'd be frozen solid. Dad says it's just a matter of time before we get a heater for it.

Tuesday morning is here and school is all I can think about. What will happen to me? Should I move or what? I have been warned and now it's up to me. Mom sees my shiny forehead and I wipe away the sweat and get out of the car.

"Don't worry it'll be fine." Mom pats my leg.

The curb empties slowly as the cars depart. I look around wondering who's going to ambush me. I clutch my empty notebook close to my flat chest and head for homeroom. No one is here, not even Mr. Lewellen. I don't know what to do. I'm going to the bathroom. When I return, the whole class is before me, staring at me, the line-crossin' country bumpkin. *I have to choose*, echoes in my head. And now I can see the line. The left is all black and the right is all white. I never saw that. I can't move, that'll be rude.

"Good morning," rings out of Mr. Lewellen's mouth. "Go ahead and take your seat." He pushes my way. I look to Lisa and the empty seat next to her. Just then, a little wandering soul appears. He's lost and thinks he's supposed to be here. The rest of the class is settling in and just as I turn to the right I hear, "There you go, sit right there." The seat is gone, the wandering soul has been given the seat next to Lisa. I turn without hesitation and go back to my seat. I walk with a cocky step, knowing I tried to but I just couldn't. Now Lisa can get off my back, and I can sit comfortably where I want. Kanisha, the tallest girl in the world, accidentally trips me, her foot got tangled with mine. I laugh it off and turn to her and apologize. "Oops."

"You better watch it," she says, so only I can hear.

What did she say? You better watch it? She's the one tripping me. I take my seat behind her and the giant cake-cutter comb with growling teeth. And right in front of Kanisha is her best friend Alisha. Alisha looks like a sparkler today. I feel the room quieting down, way down, and even more. Mr. Lewellen senses something and so do I. It's like a time bomb ticking real slow. The bell rings; I jump and so does half the class. I hear rumbling in the halls, something about *Roots* and a riot. I really don't understand. I think they're saying the blacks are going to kick the whites' asses. I try not to be affected, in fact I don't care, this is crazy. I didn't even watch it last night. Besides, we all know I had nothing to do with slavery.

Then I remembered West Virginia with the thick humid air and the friends I had, including Martha and her family. This stuff just doesn't go on where I'm from. Martha never hated me because I was white. I never felt bad because of it. She didn't care who I sat with or where. She'd never stand for this. I can hear her now, "Honey, the sun rises and sets in everyone's front yard. It's all just the same, ain't no difference."

That's it, I've had it, I'll sit where I want and no line is going to choose for me. The truth is, I wanted to sit by Kanisha and Alisha and I felt more comfortable over there. I made my choice. I don't care if they don't like me, they don't even know me. And as for Lisa and her hip-hugger gang, well all that makeup must have affected their brains.

The following Monday morning and it's time to go to school and time to take my place. *Roots* ended last night. Mr. Lewellen and his beard will be there smiling, I'll be fine. He's the only one who likes me anyway. The bell rings and half the class runs in and scrambles for their seats. I'm the last one in before the door closes. Kanisha is ahead of me, and it looks like she's in a bad mood. She walks down the aisle slowly, she drags her feet, and passes by her desk, then plops down in my seat. She's made a mistake. Alisha is close behind me, she pushes me right into Kanisha. I stumble and try not to fall. I whirl around trying to regain my balance but Alisha pushes me again—I fall—right on top of

Kanisha, who's in my seat. I push myself up and off her with my hands pressing on her shoulders. This isn't good. Kanisha then grabs onto the neck of my shirt and yanks me down to her face. All I can think is where is Mr. Lewellen? He should be here by now? "You listen, this is my seat now, go find another one."

I look into her eyes; her face is solid. Alisha is behind me, breathing down the back of my neck, still shoving me into Kanisha. The adrenaline is now the master, it takes control, running up and down my spine. Then like a puppet, my mouth opens, "This is not your seat, it's mine, move." The words terrify me as they finally stop; they roll out of my mouth and onto Kanisha's lap. She holds on tighter, squeezing and pinching the skin around my neck. Probably an accident but whatever, she's gone too far. She's hurting me. I shake loose like a mad dog and free myself from her grip. Standing up alone in the middle of a war, I flip around to Alisha. My face to her face, I watch her eyes, ready. Her nose flares. She's going to kill me. Then without a word, I sit down with all my might on Kanisha's lap. I watch Alisha in front of me; her mouth shuts. By now I announce to both of them, "This is my seat, and if you want to share, that's fine." I cross my arms and push my whole body on top of hers. I sit there stubbornly and wait for her next move. I can't see Kanisha, but I can feel her underneath me. She's boiling, she has no idea what to do. The longer she sits there the stupider she looks. Alisha moves back out of the way. Kanisha struggles and tries to kick her legs free, she wants to get up. I bounce off her lap.

About that time the door opens. Mr. Lewellen is late, but it's not his legs that walk in, it's a substitute, a nondescript substitute with no voice, no face, and no backbone. I'm dead. Kanisha takes her seat in front of me and I take mine. Alisha blows hot air my way and bumps my shoulder hard as she passes on by. The tag team takes their seats.

Half the class has their mouths open. Silence, dead silence. Not a word floats through the air. And right then a fist comes from behind and lands right across my face. Alisha has taken a full swing from behind and hit me so hard that I get dizzy. The right side of my face and head are sizzling, and then they go numb. I reach for my bottom lip and wipe my hand across it. Blood. I sit there staring at the blood for two long seconds and then I hear Mom's words, "Go Crazy."

I start screaming. *"No one hits me in the face, I'll kill you!"*

I stand up with the strength of King Kong and reach back on my desk. I know I have to kick the shit out of both of them, and I'll probably lose. But I pick up a stack of books anyway. I lift them high over my head. Alisha dares me with her eyes. I throw them with all my muscle right at her face. I knocked the shit out of her, but my face throbs and I want more. She leans back in her desk, trying to get up. I stand next to her, blocking her. I pick up the front of her desk and heave her backward in it, throwing her to the floor.

Now I'm done, and she's all done, laying on the floor in a knot. I feel the shadow of Kanisha coming up behind me. I scream violently at the top of my lungs, not breathing just screaming. And then I reach for my desk, the desk that started the whole thing. I hear people scooting out of the way and yelling, "She's crazy." I don't think anymore, I pick up my desk and hold it up over my head. Kanisha trips and falls over someone, and she's on her ass. She looks up at me, her eyes pleading with the desk that's over her head. I bend down and yell, "You see this, it's my Goddamn desk." I want to throw it in her hate-filled face. I hold it up as long as I can and then I smash it as close to her as I can. The back seat breaks off and lands on her chest. Kanisha is in shock; she makes sure she's not broken. Alisha is back there behind me, up against the wall, not moving. Tangled in her desk like a fly in a web, she's waiting to see what's next. My face isn't numb anymore, it's throbbing so hard I have to get to the nurse. I whirl around to Alisha, pick up my books, and scream at her, "No one hits me in the face."

I walk, run, scream, and stomp myself to the nurse's office, still screaming at the world. I'm so mad I could smash something, anything—glass would work. I hear doors open and I feel teachers following me. I want out of this stupid place called Will C. Wood. Who is he? I'll kick his ass too! The nurse jumps, the secretary squeaks, and the principal bursts out his door. The whole office is afraid of me. I sob out of control, "I want to call my mom."

"Now listen to me, calm down, what happened?" Mr. Price puts his hands on my shoulders.

I sob harder and harder, "I'm not talking to anyone but my mom." I shake loose of his resting hands. "383–8267, get my mom, right now," I speak through my clenched teeth.

My face hurts, my lip is bleeding, and I don't know what happened back there. My body is shaking and the nurse puts a blanket on me. I refuse to sit. She hands me a cold blue thing. I hold it and wait for Mom to pick up the phone. "Yes, Mrs. Vaughan, there's been a situation here at school. Your daughter…Mrs. Vaughan, Hello. Hello." The secretary, with her star necklace and matching earrings, hangs up the phone. "I think she's on her way."

The door opens and in flies Alisha, Mr. Kann, the next-door teacher, has her by the collar of her tight glistening red long-sleeve shirt. He throws her down in a chair. "Now sit there."

She folds her arms and tries not to look at me. I stand in the corner by the tall, long wooden desk, waiting for Mom.

In minutes Mom bolts through the door and stands there like Superman, her cape flying out of control. She almost drove the car into the office. She walks over to me in one step and rips off the blanket. She pulls my hand down off my face. The pain hits me so hard my knees buckle.

"Kanisha knocked the shit out of me."

Mom looks into my eyes and searches me over. She hovers over Alisha. The secretary frantically calls Mr. Price on the intercom. In a crackling voice, "Mr. Price, Mrs. Vaughan is here. I think you should come out. No, I think you'd better get out here."

Mom rolls around and stabs her finger in Alisha's face. Shaking it back and forth, "Are you the one who did this, are you?"

Alisha is barely able to move.

"Why? Why did you do this?"

Mr. Price interrupts, "Mrs. Vaughan."

"You wait one minute—" She turns away from him and back to Alisha. "I said, Why did you do this? What did Sandra do to you?"

Alisha's not a sparkler anymore, her face grows lonely and scared, "Nothin'. She didn't do nothin'." Alisha fizzles as the lump in her throat gets bigger, I can feel it all the way over here. My heart is starting to ache when a tear finally leaks out. Alisha looks at me and my swollen face and swallows, "I'm sorry." She puts her head down.

"All right Mrs. Vaughan, would you like to press charges?"

Mom looks at me and I shake my head no.

"But I would like this girl's mother to know what she did to my daughter, and I want to talk to her."

Alisha and I accidentally look at each other. Alisha turns white. Mom grabs my arm, opens the door, and without another word, she snaps me out of the office.

We drive home, the sound is gone, nothing makes a sound. Mom is ashamed, I'm embarrassed, and the car quiet.

"Are you okay Honey?" Mom pats my leg.

"Yeah." I move my knee away.

"You know Sandra, it's not what people think, it's what you think. Sometimes you do have to fight for yourself, wrong or right." Mom softens her voice, "I'm so sorry this happened to you, and I know how bad you feel." She takes a deep breath, "But you can't let this stop you from being who you are and who I love."

I choke on her words and cry and cry, I want to stop it but I can't. I'm so sad, I want her to be my mom for the rest of my life, I don't want to grow up. I don't want to fight.

She brushes my hair off my face and continues, "Sandra you are the beautiful little girl I know, and when you grow up you're going to be a very special person. I have watched you, and you will be fine, I promise." She turns the corner and parks in front of the house, "And let me tell you a little secret, you have strength in you that I have never had. I am so proud of you." She puts her head down, and her fingertips grip onto the steering wheel, and she cries with me for the first time.

33

Fall turns to winter, not as drastically as West Virginia, but it does. The sky stays gray and the wind blows cold. It doesn't snow, but sometimes it feels like it should. Dad goes to school and, surprisingly, does well. He studies at night, and in a few more months, he'll be at the crazy house working with the nuts. I'm still not used to using food stamps; every time I go to the store for Mom, I make sure no one's in line. I don't want anyone to see me dig out the colored pieces of paper buried deep in my pocket. I'm not sure, but it seems the other people who use them are fine with it. I'm not. Mom rarely goes to the store herself, probably because she's tired from being pregnant, and she doesn't like using the monopoly money any more than I do.

Her body is round, and the baby is coming whether I want it to or not. I can't say I'm happy about this yet. In fact, I don't think about it at all. The more time passes, the closer it is, but I won't believe it until I see it. I've stayed as far away from God as I can. Actually, it's been nice these past few months; he stays away and I don't have to think about him. It's easier that way.

Alisha is the same way. She stays over there, out of sight, but I can feel her checking over her shoulder, making sure I'm not in trouble. She says nothing with words, but I can hear her say hi once in a while. Lisa, however, treats me like a novelty, she's still trying to be my friend.

I'm nice back to her, but she's just too full of herself. I keep my distance and walk by myself. I have a couple of friends; they aren't very smart or pretty.

Shelly and Mark go to the same school, they always have each other. I don't get to play with them as much now that we're here in California. Shelly has her friends and Mark hangs around Shelly more. Ever since junior high, things seem to be changing. Mom worries about money, Dad concentrates on school, and Shelly and Mark blissfully go down the street to ride bikes without me. I don't know why, but I don't quite fit in like I used to. I fight a lot more with Shelly and Mark, and I'm always pissed off. My body hurts and for no reason I get pains in my legs. Mom says it's growing pains and brushes me off. That's weird, my body grows a lot more at night.

Later one morning the door bell rings. It's Aunt Revell with bags of groceries and some Pepsi. She barges in with a smile from ear to ear. "How's my favorite sister and my nieces and nephew?"

Mom follows her to the kitchen where Aunt Revell cheerfully makes herself at home. "We're fine. We're just getting the day started."

"Well, how are you feeling?" Aunt Revell pats her.

Mom says with a tight lip, "Just fine."

By now we're all in the kitchen waiting for Mom to pour us a Pepsi for breakfast. Aunt Revell teases Mark and brushes his long blond hair out of his face. "For goodness sake, how am I supposed to see how cute you are?" Mark's heard it a thousand times and ignores her as he moves toward the front door.

Mom hollers, "Get your ass back in here, and clean up your room first."

Mark shuts the door and smiles back to Mom.

"Ardell," Aunt Revell turns toward her, "Are you sure you're okay?"

Mom squirms a little and shrugs her shoulders. I stay in the living room and listen. Shelly sits listening on the couch.

"Is there anything I can get you? Do you think Jack will be around to take you to the hospital?"

I look at Shelly, even the word *hospital* can make Shelly faint. She turns light green and swallows hard. I don't recognize the worry in Aunt Revell's voice. Is she talking about the baby? Why is she so concerned? It's not that big of a deal, is it? I never thought about that part.

Mom assures Aunt Revell, "I'll be fine, don't worry, and if I need you I'll call."

This baby is real—it finally hits me—Mom is going to have a baby. The baby, a baby, another baby. My head twirls and now I feel sick. What's going to happen? This doesn't seem real. Is there really going to be a little, tiny baby in the house soon? As I continue drowning in all the questions, I hear Aunt Revell.

"I've been thinking, it would be a good idea if I start taking Sandra to church with me on Sundays."

I choke on her words, and Shelly sits up with my discomfort. What in the hell is she talking about? I'm not going to church, how dare she even mention it? Is this some trick? Is this what you had in mind God? Send Aunt Revell over? You get out of here! Shelly shoots me a look that says, *Don't worry, Mom will help you.* I hear Mom scoot her chair out a little bit.

"That's not necessary, but if Sandra wants to go to church with you she can."

"Sandra, come here," Aunt Revell whispers. My body goes cold—the Mormon of all Mormons has summoned me into the kitchen. Her eyes are weepy and her cheeks blushed. "Honey, I'd really like it if you came to church with me. You don't have to, but you might like it, and maybe meet some friends."

I look to Mom, then to her round belly, and back to Aunt Revell. I'm trapped, if I say yes, then God will find me for sure, but if I say no, then God might take this baby. I wish this would go away. Shelly stays put on the couch praying for me. She knows me, she feels me, and she's afraid for me. The fear leaks out of my body and runs onto the floor. I feel like Jesus on the cross, my palms are sweating. Aunt Revell's eyes stay pounded on me, I can't get away.

Mom breaks the trance, "Revell, let her think about it, you don't have to know right now."

"Oh no, not at all, you just let me know, sweetheart. Church starts at ten o'clock. Just give a call and I'll come and get you."

Mom and Aunt Revell go on and on about this kid and that one. I excuse myself and slip out of the kitchen. Shelly whispers, "What are you going to do?"

I shake my head, "I don't know."

"You better go or you'll hurt her feelings." Shelly pulls her knee up and her T-shirt over her knees. I yell back at her, "Shut up," but she doesn't hear me. It was just thunder that roared.

The day is all wound up the wrong way. The rain has started and Christmas is only a week away. Tomorrow is Sunday and Aunt Revell wants an answer. I want out. I stay outside on the porch while Shelly and Mark pop in and out. They want to play or do something, but it's a boring day. Nothing to do. Mom stays busy trying to beat the laundry down. She never does. She's getting ready for something, and cleans all day. Her back hurts and she's short-tempered. She doesn't want to talk. She makes spaghetti during the day, a big pot of it, so big it looks like we'll be eating spaghetti for a month.

God's been tapping on my shoulder all day. He won't leave me alone. He keeps asking me about the baby. Which baby? I don't know. I run away and he finds me. I finally end up in my bedroom closet. I pull the dripping string and the lightbulb flashes on. No one's here. I sit down. I can hear the TV in the living room drowning out the noise in my head. God taps away at me. He won't leave me alone.

Shut up. Do you hear me? I'm not ready for this, I'm not! Mom is going to have a baby. And when this baby comes home, I'll know. I'll know the truth. And I don't want to. I want you to stay away from me. I will not go to church, no matter how much they beg. I will not. I don't worship, I wonder. I wonder about you and the baby boy that lays dead in a grave with no name. No Name, do you hear me? The day the baby didn't come home. I don't know if the baby is dead. Do you know what that means? It means I didn't fall for the tricks and lies. The one question you can't answer, the same one Mom won't, is still alive in my heart. Why? I remember that day. You laughed. I heard you. I was there.

Now you knock on the door asking to come in, so when I answer, you can hurt me. Now you knock again, asking me to do the same. Sitting quietly pounding, all the time pounding at my head, what do you want? I listen to you, I know the answer; you gave me the answer, remember? You took the baby and now you give one back. I'm supposed to love you and the baby with no name and the one that's on the way.

You know I will not bleed for you again. The day is approaching, and the dream said, the *dead baby is not a boy* but rather a *living girl*. If this is true, the baby is alive and she is a girl. Then you will be forced to give us a boy, and I'll know once and for all if it's a lie. I hate you. I hate you.

I hear Shelly, she's coming in the room. I wipe away any hot tears that might have fallen onto my cheeks. Both hands are wet. "Hey, what are ya' doin?"

"Nothing," I swallow. I stand up before she sees me on the floor.

"You going to church?" she teases.

"No," flies out of my mouth and hits her on the forehead.

"All right, I was just asking." She falls onto the bed. "When do you think Mom's going to have the baby?"

"Soon," I plop down next to her.

"What if…?"

"Don't worry. It's not…" I sharply answer her thought.

"It's going to be a little Christmas baby, I can't wait." She kicks off her tennis shoes.

I chew on my hair, "Yeah, me too."

34

It's Sunday morning and the phone is ringing. Mom answers, "Nope, she's still asleep. Yeah, maybe next Sunday."

Mom hangs up the receiver with a thud. I turn over and sigh and thank Mom for saving me from going to church today. The last person I want to deal with today is God. I can't stand the thought of someone standing up there behind a little wooden box telling me what God is thinking. I know him personally and I still haven't figured him out. I push the loose strands of hair off my face and untangle the others around my neck that are strangling me. I concentrate on keeping my balance as I creep to the bathroom; I don't feel like fully announcing I'm awake to the rest of the house. Mom is in the kitchen; she's very quiet, and I don't know what she's doing. The TV is off, that means Dad is still asleep. I love that. Waking up to a sleeping house even for a few minute feels much better than waking up to the chaos of everyone all at once. I take the cool water from the sink and splash my face, Mom taught me that. She doesn't fuss with makeup, but she always wakes her face with cool water and puts on a thin oil to moisturize. I can't wait to grow up and look like her. She's so beautiful. Her face is smooth, not wrinkled. No fake black lines on her face anywhere; no eyebrows or eyeliner. Her cheeks are pink where they're supposed to be, and her lashes are thin but noticeable. I go to the kitchen where I can see her sitting alone at the light blue Formica table. She sips soda and slowly chews on a piece of toast dripping with butter. Butter is her favorite food. She says she knows it's bad for her but it's the truth. Her knee-length pink thinning nightgown open at the top with her cleavage spilling out reminds me of who she is: my mother—my world.

"Sandra, what are you doing?" She catches me staring.

"Nothing, just waking up."

"Make some toast." She nods her head over toward the sink where the tired greasy toaster sits surrounded by crumbs. I hate to tell her I don't want toast and I'd rather have Cocoa Puffs. I pop in two pieces of bread and sit down with her, shoving the paper, dirty glasses, and junk out of my way. Silence sits next to us. I want to talk to her; she wants to talk to me, but the words float around our heads and nothing is said. We breathe, she moves the kitchen window curtain over and looks outside—not for anything particular, she just does. The toaster pops and now I have something to do. First I slather it with butter for her and then spread peanut butter on it for me. I open the fridge for a cold glass of milk, but all that's left is a drink, and I know better than to drink the last drink, it's some strange ritual around here. If you drink the last of the milk then it's your fault we're out. I shut the door, grab water instead, and join Mom back at the table. The silence still sits there with us not saying a word. I eat my toast while Mom sips her soda. I notice her hands and then her index finger nail that slightly curls down, and then look I at my fingernail that does the same exact thing.

Eventually the rest of them wake up. Mark stumbles in first for a hug and pretends it's Mom who wants a hug. Next, Shelly, who hates mornings, goes straight to the couch, flicks on the TV, and stays there for at least a half hour before she deals with anything. And finally Dad comes in and pushes Shelly off the couch and onto a chair.

The day rolls on by; everyone keeps to themselves. Dad stays on the couch, he's tired. The newspaper buries him alive. He tosses and turns while he catnaps all day. He groans and stretches out loud. "Ardell, why don't you sit down? You've been running around here all day."

"Yeah, maybe in a minute. I just want to finish up the dishes," she yells back from the kitchen. Shelly and I know what's coming next.

Dad lifts himself up. "Goddamn it, you girls get in there and help your mother." We scramble for the kitchen. The lion has roared. Mom is bent down hanging over the sink. "Mom," Shelly talks faster, "are you okay?"

"I'm fine." No she's not, her stomach hurts. Dad knows something's wrong and he's up off the couch. He looks at her and waits for the pain. She takes a deep breath. "Is it time?" Dad moves closer.

"Yeah, I think we better get ready." Mom pushes herself off the sink. "Sandra, you guys stay here while your father takes me to the hospital. He'll call you later. Now don't worry." She wobbles to her room and packs a few things. Dad is already at the front door waiting for her. She walks by herself to the car, and he follows behind her and drives them both away.

Shelly, Mark, and I are alone in the living room. I look past them to Mom's room. The white baby crib sits still. The triangular pale green diaper bag hangs low off the door handle, full and waiting to be used. The giant baby powder bottle stands up tall on the crowded dresser, making room for itself. I notice them all staring back at me and feel a sharp stab. These baby things weren't around the last time. I don't remember a crib, a diaper, or baby powder. Nothing was waiting for the baby last time…

That night we put ourselves to bed. Dad calls two hours later, but he doesn't say much. He sounds like a stranger. "Your mother's fine and so is your new little brother." The words hit hard and fast. I want to ask again. *Brother?*

Shelly grabs the phone out of my hand. "His name is what?—Beau, oh it means beautiful." Shelly can hardly stand it, her voice cracking as she repeats it, "Beau Jacob Vaughan." Mark fights for the phone, but Shelly will not share. She and Dad talk back and forth, I think Dad wants to get off the phone. Shelly repeats everything while she twists and turns the phone cord in between her fingers. I'm afraid of the phone, I don't want to talk on it. I feel sick and unbelieving. I think they're really going to bring the baby home this time. He was born over two hours ago, and he's been alive for two hours, I think the other baby died after a couple of hours when it was born. God I hope this is the baby from before coming back to us.

The night woke me up a hundred times. What's going on? Is Mom okay? Is the baby…here? Mark went to bed sad; he and Mom have something unseen for each other. Mom is his best friend and I can see he is already struggling with his new baby brother and where that might leave him in the order of things. Shelly goes to bed giggly, she does that when she's nervous. She fidgets all night.

I go to bed, but I don't stay there, I go a million miles away. Back to the tree, along the river, past the mountains where the nightmare began. And back into Mom's arms where it all started. She's holding me when I was a baby. I feel her rock me gently back and forth. I lay perfectly still, knowing exactly who she is. She's not sure, and she searches for who I am. I feel her soft hand across my cheek and her lips kiss my forehead softly so as not to wake me. I'm not asleep, I'm alive in her arms, breathing her soul. I love her. She loves me. I miss her. I'm growing up, I can't stop it, but I want to. I look back to her black eyes with knowing, but now she has to send me out into the world. She fights with herself as she finally looks away. I wobble and fall, but the nudging is persistent. She holds me lightly until I'm on my feet, and then with a clap, she applauds my great strength. I hear her whisper a faint, *I love you*. I turn back to hug her, I want just one more, just one more chance to be her baby again and give her my love. She stands alone holding no magic and having no answers, she simply reminds me who I am and not to forget to tie my shoes, and then puts the world at my feet. And once more I hear *I love you* as she blows me a kiss that flings open the door. I snatch the kiss, hold it close to my heart, and then twirl around to the blackness of her eyes and suddenly realize the truth of who I am.

The room is now empty. Mom's hand falls. The baby is born, a girl. She's tiny, real tiny. She screams and hollers, wanting to be heard. Mom can't get to her. I want her to, but she can't. Why can't she? Then I see Mom on the porch, holding her empty stomach, aching as she spits out the Lie. "*The baby has died and I don't ever want to talk about it again.*" But this time I see far and deep into the strain, the tone, and pain of those words. I continue tossing and turning, curled up yet stretched out of my mind. My heart pumps thick oil. The baby is alive! How could the truth hurt so bad, cut so deep, and never end? I can't understand. Sleep finally penetrates my body, and I give up. The night and its mirrors end with the sound of a drum that concludes its song.

That afternoon around three o'clock the house is spic and span. Shelly and Mark wait by the door. I sit on the couch with my feet planted firmly, waiting hopelessly. Finally, I see the hair on Mark's head rise—his little brother is home. Dad pulls the car up gently in the driveway and parks. I'm scared. Is he the one in my dream? Or is he his own person to be? Dad shuffles around the car and opens the door for Mom. I peek through the curtains; I think I'm going to be fine. Mom smiles from inside out, her face looks long at the bundle in her arms as she scoots carefully out of the car. Shelly can't breathe. I think she'll be sick. Who is this Beau? My brother, my baby brother! I'll know in a few minutes. My heart pounds deep.

Dad walks in first, the proud papa of his brand new redheaded son. He drops the bags on the floor next to Shelly, squeezes her shoulder, and cracks a big grin. They both stand there biting their nails as Mom quietly walks through the door.

Beau enters the room on Mom. She hands him over to me, the keeper I am. I study his face. It looks like mine. He finds my finger and gives it a squeeze. I hold him up close to my chest but at a safe distance. I want to be his big sister, but I'm just not sure I can. If I love him too fast then I might not be so sure of who this baby is and if he has returned. I feel a strange distance. Then his warm body squirms. He needs me, I need him, I can't help it, I'm falling in love with him. I watch his little eyes with a glaze over them, as he struggles and fights to open them and then sees me for the first time. I take another deep breath, and right then my heart skips a beat, and he captures it quick, quick like the wind. Now his heart beats for two, harder and faster, but his breath is still soft, I can feel him alive. He's *not* the one I dreamed about. He is *not* alone. We have just met, and he has yet to become. And from now on I love this new brother we call Beau.

Still lurking over my head, above the trees and between truth is the question in the distance, *Where has my baby sister been all these long years?* Last time I saw her, she sparkled away in a dream, back to the trees, among their soft leaves, resting safe in a basket with each leaf that twisted and turned. God can rustle the wind and he always knows. Is she out there? In my heart she is. I saw the *look* on Aunt Carole's face, her story unraveling like a ball of twine. I felt Mom not tell the truth. I know the difference: the truth glides, lies are sticky. Why didn't those baby things sit there before? It only took two hours for Mom to have Beau, not three weeks. And what about the baby's name and the grave? They don't exist. I heard her say she has dark hair like me. The time is not now, but it will be someday.

* * *

"Happy birthday to you, Happy birthday to you…Happy birthday dear Beau, Happy birthday to you." Shelly sings and I muffle as we all finish singing to Beau. The cake has a yellow lion on it with its mouth open, a giant green number three, and written in red icing it says: Happy Birthday Beau. Beau has grown, and according to him he's not a baby; Beau hates being littler than us. His hair stayed red, his round face freckled, and he's become the most important thing in my life. I love watching him fall asleep on the couch, his little hand curled around my finger. Or when he fights with the front door when he's trying to get out, and especially when he runs fast across the front yard and jumps up into my arms and squeezes my neck with a hug.

I'm sixteen now. Mom raises Beau, grocery shops, and sells signs for extra money. Mom is alive but different. Dad is gone, working in Stockton. I see him on his days off, but not much. Shelly and Mark play softball. I watch as they eventually forgive and forget about West Virginia, but not me. I remember everything. I let the past die slowly and the baby live silently in my heart, in the tree, and in heaven. I don't think about it as often, and some days not at all, that is until Aunt Carole comes to pick me up from school one Friday. The heat is relentless; the sun burns my arm as it hangs out of the car window. We're going to Oregon to pick up a friend. I'm the likely one to go because I love long drives; I can help her with Jason and Tanya, and she loves my company. The drive starts off normal: chitchat, Diet Cokes, and rest areas. News of the 1976 recession repeats itself over and over again in the background, gas prices and interest rates. Who cares? The highway is straight, and rises up and down once in awhile when we get out of the foothills and into the mountains. Aunt Carole slows down a bit as a truckers' convoy is right next to us. I see at least fifty trucks. I hear the song lyrics "Convoy" in my mind. I tap my foot to half of the song rambling around in my head. *Okay good buddy, ten-four,* and something about *a rubber duck.*

Tanya and Jason are asleep in the back with their mouths open, eyes closed, and a sweaty dead soda between them. I trip out at the thought that Jason is seven, seven years have passed since…

"Hey Aunt Carole, I've been thinking. What did Mom's baby die of?" It should be a simple question, especially after all these years. Besides, I still can't go to Mom, she never lets that door open, not even a tiny crack, for me to walk in and ask.

Aunt Carole avoids the question, pretending she doesn't hear me; hoping I'll go away or accidentally fall out of the car. At fifty-five miles per hour she's stuck.

I ask again a little louder, "Did the baby die?"

She darts into the slow lane behind the truckers single file in front of us. I keep my eyes focused on her as the peaceful ride takes a sudden turn and hits some sort of wall.

"Sandra why are you asking me this?" she grunts.

"You were there?"

"You need to ask your Mom." She spits back like a slingshot.

Something snaps, I snap. A loud mean voice roars out of me, "PULL OVER! AUNT CAROLE PULL OVER RIGHT NOW!" I grab the door handle and squeeze the life out of it. What does she mean, *Ask your mom*? There's nothing to ask. The baby is dead! She's supposed to look over at me and say, *"Honey, the baby died of a rare complication…"* But she didn't; there's something else, and this is not my imagination.

Aunt Carole slides the car carefully over onto the gravel shoulder. I'm determined to go to battle, but I have to get out of the car before I choke. I jump out before the car is stopped. Aunt Carole jumps out next. She and I are ready. We're both squaring off; she picks her side and I pick mine. At that moment I see the wall she puts up in front of her, and her face is stone. I should be scared of her, but I'm not.

"That baby's not dead." I feel like I'm going to explode in two. "That's why you can't answer my question." My breath is short. I want to hit something.

"Sandra now just calm down." She keeps her distance and tugs at her bottom lip not sure what punch to throw next.

"No I won't. Tell me right now." I throw my Diet Coke into a barbed wire fence.

Aunt Carole puts her head down, and her voice talks strong. "I cannot tell you. I promised your Mom!" She wants me to stop it right now. "You have to ask her."

"Promised her what?" I scream at the top of my lungs, at the road, at the heat, at the lie. I want to stomp on Aunt Carole and make her say it. Her heart snaps as she stands upright in between Mom, the promise, and me.

Aunt Carole answers me, "That if you came to me I would…"

A car drowns out the words she won't say and the ones I don't want to hear. Her pause, her honor, and her sweat scares the shit out of me. This is not happening, I'm not supposed to know this. Too late, I do. After all these years the doubt has just evaporated like that. I'm naked standing next to the raw truth, it has teeth, and it goes for my throat. I whip around toward her, open the car door, and grab my purse. I have to get out of here. I start to walk off. I'll fucking hitchhike home! I'm so mad I can't even look at Aunt Carole. With sweat beading down my face and stinging my eyes, I point back to her.

"You tell Mom I just got my answer." I end the conversation with absolution, "If the baby is really dead, you could have said it."

I storm up the highway toward the next exit. My head is throbbing as my feet smash against the tiny hard rocks and I wail, no tears just noise. I don't know what I've done, or what to do. I certainly didn't know she'd say it, but she did. Mom lied, Mom really lied? I brush my hair off my steaming red face and out of my burning eyes. All I can think is that I need Shelly.

Aunt Carole runs back to the car. Now she's creeping up behind me. She passes me slowly and stops. I will not divert my path. I pound straight ahead.

"Get back in the car," she demands.

I ignore her, because if I look at her I'll start bawling, and it takes everything I have to stay upright.

"Sandra," she gets out and blocks my path, "please, please sweetheart, I'm so sorry. It'll be fine, I promise." She's no longer a soldier, she's just as wounded as I am.

The pain finally catches up to me as I stop; the cars passing by are silent. I hurt so much I think I'll break. My back is tight, my neck is weak, and I can't walk anymore.

Fighting back the tears I lean on the dusty white Ford. I will not cry. I stand there with my arms folded. Aunt Carole's words can't find their way out. They're all lost and so am I. Finally I brush the dust off my ass, open the car door, sit down, and slam it shut. Aunt

Carole stays outside a little longer than she has to as cars whiz by. Eventually, the gravel growls as we drive off to finish the long drive to nowhere.

I have my answers. I know the truth. And it's much more than words. I sit with it tightly tucked on my lap, not sure how to hold it, as I stare deep into the blues of the distant mountains. Now what? How will I find the baby?

I know I'll tell Shelly, I'll tell her we do have a sister, I'm positive. But then she'll look at me as if I were crazy. They all think I'm crazy anyway. I can't tell Mark, he's too young. What about Mom, how will she react to the lie? It's not like I can walk up and say, "Oh by the way, Aunt Carole told me you lied about the baby."

I can't live the lie, I saw what living a lie did to Mom and something dies. I just can't. I want to shout to the world, but what…? I haven't the words. I need the words. What happened? Where is the baby girl? God, I don't know. I remember the day, the smell of that hot humid August day and the morning dew still on the grass as I stood there looking up to Mom for the baby, but it was so long ago and I can hardly reach the truth anymore. If only I could ask Mom. But then it's her baby, her lie, and her heartbreak.

My head swirls and churns as I stay close to the shoulder of the road watching mile markers pass by for the next two days. Suddenly Aunt Carole stops the car and I find myself at my driveway. Aunt Carole drops me off as quick as lightning. She has to go home, she can't come in, so Mom stands there at the door, greeting me and waving goodbye at the same time. Her round face, black hair, and Beau around her ankles remind me of what it might have been like that day; the day the baby didn't come home. I find a smile and throw it her way. She looks at me from the porch and sees it in me, and she knows! I try to hide it, but it's too late. It is now seven years since I saw her on the porch that day in West Virginia, without the baby in her arms. Time freezes as we both go back to that horrible moment of the truth. She is fighting me, oh yes; cursing me the whole way I'm sure. Both of our memories drift far, far away, to a place, the place, where we divided and broke in two. On the way back I see her look at me, and say, "Sorry, sorry I can't help you."

Now I'm back in time on the porch in the mountains. Mom is there, and she's standing with all her might, her hands closed tightly to her side as she's reduced to a mere shell, and trying to talk, I can see it. I can see *the look* on her face. Her pain is oozing out, her arms aching, her life emptied as she spits out the words, *"The baby died and I don't ever want to talk about it again."* But this time I'm taller than her, my back is straight, and my eyes focused. Her hair is a little grayer, her body still cold, her voice hoarse, and her face the same. I go beyond the words she speaks, and this time instead of running to the river, I stay with her and watch. I watch the whole thing and then realize she still lives on the porch everyday in pain; she never left. While the years have fluttered by like a butterfly, and time has erased the dark edges of my memory, I have grown up strong and tall. But she is the one who stayed there, paralyzed, unwilling to leave her baby. I can see her, rocking and cooing the child from before, safely tucking her little secret to her breast while she raises her children with a watchful eye. And now that I revisit the grave image for the first time with Mom, the image softens as I remember her, not me. Then without a word, Mom looks up to me and her eyes plead for me not to hurt her anymore. For the first time I feel her, her heart and her child. Mom fights the truth alone, batting at it like a persistent gnat getting in her way. I hurt so bad for her I want to run. I can't stand it. Then she shows me how the pain and sadness is the baby she loves, her baby, and how no one will ever take that away from her, not me, not anyone. Her strength has been the mask all along, and for that split second I see the invisible truth of my mom.

Beau tugs and wants to be tickled. I try to hug Mom, but her shoulders stiffen and her body language tells me to stay away—but not too far away. I pick up Beau and give him the long hug instead of Mom. She keeps her distance, she's afraid of me, of it, and if she gets too close I just might kill what's left of her. Beau squirms to get down and I plop him down and reach for the doorknob. Mom reaches for it at the same time, her hand soft on top of mine. She looks away; I feel the warmth of her palm on my hand and that's all it takes to break the truth. My eyes well up, a tear starts to fall, she bends forward and says softly without looking at me,

"I just can't talk about it yet, please give me some time, I know what you want."

I take a chance and look at her. Her chin starts to quiver, she's not going to fall apart, she's not. She swallows hard.

"I have always known what you want, but this is mine. I'm begging you, let it be in my time."

I nod, grab the handle, and pause as the sadness rolls over to me and I get it. It was hers, not mine and the truth can be very ugly, hard, and unforgettable. I wipe the single tear from my cheek and for now I leave the truth on the porch where I found it.

35

Shelly swings back and forth up the street toward the house, her hips curve out perfectly from her tiny waist accenting her walk. She's the envy of every wannabe woman in the neighborhood. I, however, have been jealous of Shelly ever since I can remember; it's nothing new for me. But now she's getting boobs and of course I'm not. After junior high Shelly's body flowered, and mine is still somewhere between part man and part elephant. The boys at school told me once that if they could put my face on Pam Boyd's body I'd be a fox. I had to scrounge a compliment out of it somehow so I told myself well at least I have a pretty face. Shelly has packs of boys that hang around in front of the house like junkyard dogs. They all want to be her boyfriend, even if it's only for one day, hell that's good enough for them. Shelly breaks up with them if they try to kiss her, talk dirty, or if their hair's not combed right. She's still picky, always been picky. Me, on the other hand, if I could get one guy to look my way, the last thing I'd be is picky, I'd be lucky. At night when I lie in bed I pray for boobs, just a little something. "Dear God if you have mercy you'd do this one thing for me please give me boobs." Hell, it's my only chance to get a boyfriend.

It took awhile but after three years Dad's training through the state has finally turned into a real job and we're not on welfare. He's a psychiatric technician and drives an hour everyday to Stockton to work with the mentally insane, criminally insane, or just plain insane. Mostly he gets a kick out of it, he says it's not hard as long as you don't take it too seriously.

Dad puts his worn-out feet up on the coffee table. "Hell, if Joey eats with a spoon and not with his hands it's a good day. And if Joey decides not to eat and rubs his food all over himself and the cafeteria, that's a bad day." But there is a much darker side to the mental hospital, and that part he doesn't want to talk about.

Dad continues on about work, "It is all a bunch of bullshit; no one gives a shit if the clients improve. The thing that kills me the most is the kids who get dumped off because they're physically handicapped or a little slow, and the parents who say they are too much of a burden. That's horseshit, they're embarrassed that's why." Dad snuffs out his smoke. "It breaks my heart that this one kid Joey, a sweet kid but a Mongoloid, everyday he stuffs his little suitcase and waits for his mother. He's been there since he was five; he's thirty now. He tells me how pretty and sweet she is and that she's coming to get him today. I nod and agree with him, hell, some days I sit and wait with him."

Mom listens in the kitchen with half an ear, Beau sits coloring at the table. Mark brushes his long hair out of his eyes, and Shelly continues working on her math problems when Dad finishes.

But the tension in the house remains, Mom stays away from Dad and Dad mostly forgets to talk to her anymore. Dad quit hitting Mom when Beau was born, now he just knocks the shit out of me, I still think it's because I look like her.

The last time he hit me was for being late from church. It was nine o'clock on the dot, I walked in with my stupid dress on and plastic high heels that were killing my feet. The house was dark except for the TV. The introduction music to *The Waltons* was playing. Mom sat huddled with her feet underneath her in the chair and Dad was lying back with his feet up on the couch and his hand resting on a beer. My first thought was to run, I could tell I was in trouble before I got the door shut. Mom was silent, Dad was brewing inside when he opened his mouth, "What time is it?"

"Nine."

"It's after nine, I told you to be home at nine." He sits up. "What in the hell do you think I am, a fool?"

"No, I…"

Dad jumps up and screams at me. "When I say nine it means nine. Do you hear me?"

"Yeah." I don't agree, my face scowls, I hate this. I'm not late. Aunt Revell picked me up and dropped me off, what am I going to do, tell her to drive faster? *The Waltons* start at nine and the theme music is on.

"What do think nine o'clock means? *The Waltons* have already started." He points out the ridiculous.

Dad must have seen the look on my face. He reaches up with his body and punches me in the face. But this time, I don't take it, I come back at him and before I can shove him, he steps back.

"You're not going to pull that shit on me." He's serious. I run for my life. "Get back here."

Mom is back there somewhere, not stopping him, just screaming, "Bill leave her alone!" By now he's got me, the world turns bright white, and I can only feel him behind me grabbing my long tangled hair and trying to throw me to the ground.

"Bill stop it! Again Mom screams from the doorway, afraid to get too close to the animal attacking her kid.

I fight him off as he takes the last of his might and heaves me through the closet door that breaks as I fall to the ground. He sits on top of me and hits me over and over again. I cover my face and take the punches on the head, chest, and shoulders. I hear nothing, not his words or the pounding, just Mom.

"You're going to kill her for Christ's sake." Mom cries and begs, but she can't get him out of the trance. I can't feel anything; I lift out of my body and see me on the floor with a strange man on top of me beating the shit out of me. He's beating the shit out of everything, it's not me he's hitting anymore, he's lost his mind and is fighting some other creature that stirs inside him.

Now I'm terrified, he is killing me, and it, at the same time. I can't move. I have to get up. I roll over and kick him in the back with my heel, he loses his balance and finds it and then snaps out of his trance. He loosens up, I push him off me, and I hear a thump. I get up and run to my bedroom. Mom doesn't touch me, she moves out of my way. Shelly is wrapped tightly in the blankets, waiting for me; she's hysterical on the inside, on the outside she knows to be quiet or it might be her next. I'm hurt. She can't look at me, no one can look at me. No one helped…

I shiver at the old thought still hanging around, besides if he ever hits me again I'm leaving, for good next time. No one can stop me. The TV is loud when Mom walks in from the store and announces, "I'm taking Shelly and Mark to sells signs tomorrow, we're going up to Sonora and if we do well we might spend the night and hit it some more the next day."

Shelly shuts her math book and huffs just loud enough for me to hear.

Dad grunts, "Yeah sure."

Our lives are becoming more and more separate.

She picks the last load of dirty laundry from the bathroom, shoves it in a pillowcase, and returns to the front door where the other four hundred loads of dirty laundry lay waiting. Thursday night is when we all share in the torture of the Laundromat. The Laundromat represents two things: one, just because we're not on welfare doesn't mean we don't act like it, and two, the neighborhood is dark and people are hopeless, which means we might end up here forever if we're not careful. We heave, drag, and huff and puff the dead weight to the old white Oldsmobile in the driveway. What is an Oldsmobile anyway? We're the only ones who have one.

"Come on kids lets go." Mom gathers Beau, any loose quarters, and the keys last as she shuts the front door just a little harder so Dad knows we're going now. We pile, push, and shove ourselves around the limp and loose laundry that manages to get in everyone's way inside the car, and Mom tosses Beau across the front seat like a little rag doll and he lands on top of the mounds, giggling. We drive slowly and cautiously across Fruitridge Road, the meanest, widest four-lane street that ever lived. We drive four blocks. First, we pass the bar where old creepy drunks live, and then the Foster Freeze where we get real Pepsi with ice once in a while, not that cheap Shasta stuff like at home. Then finally we drive past Fruitridge Market, a grocery store that has absolutely nothing to offer.

Mom makes a right into the narrow parking space as she pulls up close to the front door of Fruitridge Laundry. Can't anyone think of a more original name for their business? How boring, Fruitridge this or Fruitridge that, I'd call it something fun like Sally's Soap and Suds or Lazy Laundry. Mom turns off the car but the engine continues to sputter and spat, clink and clank. I'm never quite sure when to get out, when she turns off the engine or the engine decides to finally turn off. The damn thing is possessed if you ask me, it reminds me of *The Exorcist*.

"Shit." Mom stomps on the gas pedal trying to kill the engine.

We wait until the last of the engine noises are gone; it's the polite thing to do. And with a cough, a hack, and a low rattle it finally dies. Door handles fly open and legs spill out of the car as the dreaded laundry baskets, swollen and overstuffed, fall over.

"I swear if anyone sees me, I'll never do laundry again." Shelly swears and picks the underwear and socks up off the ground, "And they can't make me either." She hurries the thought. Mark could give a shit. "Mom can I hold the quarters?" he loves money.

I lump two baskets on top of each other with one arm and strangle another by its neck. "I don't know why I have to carry all the heavy stuff." I talk to the baskets.

Shelly flips back with a dirty sock between her fingers and opens the door. "Cause you look like a horse."

The dirty Laundromat door with the sticky kid fingerprints all over it has a nice welcome sign scratched deep into the plastic glass with a pocketknife: "*Fuck You.*"

We all agree on one thing: it's so much easier to do this if we are alone. Too bad, the usual mothers with unhappy faces stuck on them are here. And what a treat—their screaming tots with snotty noses are here playing chase. This will surely add to the night's misery. The smell of sweaty dryers and musty washers mingles with the sight of gum wrappers and smashed cigarette butts on the floor. Mom is in charge of soap and keeping Beau tucked by her side as he fights to go play with the other kids. She nods politely to the other mothers sitting in the blue plastic chairs flipping through the pages of the *National Enquirer* with cheap smiles, while they flick their cigarette ashes on the floor like it's some sort of country club around here. They glance in her direction as if sympathizing: "Yeah we know."

What they don't see is when Mom turns her back around and her eyes roll so far backward she looks like Linda Blair and she snarls underneath her breath, "Like hell you do." She exhales through her nose controlling herself and measuring one cup of Tide for each washer.

Beau squirms his final squirm as Mom lets him have it, "Sit down right now and don't move!"

Shelly and I continue separating darks from whites from the endless mounds before us.

"Mom what about these?" Shelly holds up her light blue Dittos, not sure which pile to put them in. I want to scream, "Darks you moron!" She just loves showing off all her brand new Dittos. The pink ones, the baby blue ones, the tan ones, that's all I ever hear, 'Dittos this,' and, 'Dittos that.' I hate Dittos. They're stupid girl pants, with that horse-shoe stitching around the ass in those pastel colors; how could they fit anyone except Shelly? From behind I look like a pink elephant with a ring around my ass. Not Shelly though, she looks like a hooker.

36

Mom pulls the clean clothes from the baskets and packs for the trip today; I'll put the rest of them away this afternoon while they're gone. Shelly and Mark grumble as they get up and get ready for work. I eat breakfast with Beau, he wants Cocoa Krispies. He says so with a pretend smile; he knows that I'm going to give him his way. I pour the last of the milk over Beau's cereal. He's so darn cute with his crooked smile and freckled nose and red hair. He loves his big sister and I remind him constantly. I consider him as my very own baby brother, and I love him so much that I wish he was all mine. Beau is much more than a little brother; he is the only thing in the house I enjoy. He makes every single bad thought disappear and every morning beautiful when he climbs on top of me to wake me up or when he chokes me with a bear hug around my neck. I love holding his hand and answering all of his "Why" questions. I watch him eat, spill, and slurp like a little trooper, he's not a baby, he's a big boy. Beau is four and independent as hell; he wishes he could be big like Mark. He's the only little guy I know who carries a yellow plastic bat everywhere he goes instead of a blankie. Without Beau around I don't know if I could stand this place much longer.

"Come on honey, finish up we have to go." Mom taps Beau. She enjoys leaving, I can see it in her eyes, and she hates coming home, I can see that too. She reminds me of Dr. Jekyll and Mr. Hyde. When she leaves, her personality, laughter, and beauty returns, and when she walks backs in her face scrunches up and she scowls. I don't even think she knows she does it. Dad, on the other hand, lays in bed and snores on his day off. I can hear him from the kitchen while Shelly brushes her teeth and Mark shuffles around the house in circles scratching his head not sure what he's supposed to be doing.

"Sandra you need to clean out the garage today, and be careful I've got wet signs in there, make sure they're dry before you stack them," Mom bosses.

"No duh," my eyes roll to the back of my head.

Mom catches the wisecrack. "What the hell did you say?"

"Well, I'm not stupid, I know."

Mom doesn't have time for this, she goes outside to check the oil; she opens the heavy hood and props it up with a stick, bends over, and yanks the dipstick out. Usually men do that, but not around here, Mom does. I hear the hood slam shut and follow Shelly outside, she's pissed, not talking and in a very bad mood. She doesn't want to go.

I love it, as I hold the front door open for her I smirk, "Too bad Shel, guess I'll see you tomorrow."

The house is sloppy; I look around at last night's ice cream bowls in the living room. I walk past them to pick up the nightgowns on the hall floor from this morning and I see the tired yellow, pink, and purple toothbrushes hanging off the edge of the bathroom sink as if they're ready to jump. The limp and soggy towels thrown halfway over the moldy shower curtain reminds me that no one gives a shit. In a way we've all just accepted it, *it* being the dreamless life we've been living. No one's trying anymore, we used to try all the time, but those days are over. I turn to Dad who's lying in bed with one leg hanging over the edge too. I watch him for a minute, wondering how we ever made it this far, and I wonder: Is he happy? Is he dreaming right now? About what, I wonder? Is it the daily double at horse races, or the exacta, or maybe the slots up in Tahoe waiting to finally pay him off.

He rolls over and grunts a little, I catch myself being stupid and caring. I'm not supposed to do that. I snap up Mom's nightgown and I hold on to it a little longer than I should and practice not caring. With a fling, I toss it in the hamper just past the toothbrushes daring to jump.

Dad moves from his bed to the couch; it must be afternoon. I have a plan, as soon as I'm finished with the damn garage, I'm walking over to Denise's house. The signs are dry and sitting over in the dark by themselves. I finish shoving all the old boxes of crap, broken lamps, ratty furniture, and worn-out clothes over to the other side of the garage, which gives it some sort of a clean feeling. I brush off my dirty pants and push up my sleeves. I bend down with my arms straight ahead of me, and I grab hold and shove the last dusty thing, a heavy, old green trunk.

As I sweep up dirt where it sat, I can't help it, I keep noticing that trunk, it's not in my way but something about it bothers me. I tell myself no, not to do it. It's Mom's old trunk from when we used to live in Phoenix. She says to leave it alone. She never opens it, but for some reason she always made sure it traveled with us no matter where we went. Hell, I've seen her leave behind a perfectly good coffee table just so we'd have the room for her trunk. She says it's all she has left of Phoenix and it's hers. I fuss, sweep, and kick a dead sock from around it, but finally I can't resist it. What's in this damn thing? What is calling my name?

I crouch down carefully next to it and listen hard for any signs of life. It's quiet, but the trunk calls my name louder and louder. I HAVE to open it. The latch is strong, not locked, just strong. The lock is Mom telling me to leave it alone, it's hers. I shoo away her wishes and pop the latch up, and with a deep breath I shake my head and open it. The first thing I see is her old self staring back at me. There are beaded necklaces, a shiny pink one with big black squares, four or five deep purplish ones, and some long pretty ones; the ones she used to wear that dangled on her fancy dresses when she performed up on stage and sang to the audience below. I remember those and her, the mother with lipstick kisses and butterscotch donuts for breakfast. And all the crazy dances she did at home. I put on each one of the necklaces, and a dozen memories fly by.

I dig farther just a little at a time, I don't want to miss a thing. Then I see a picture, a large eight by ten glossy of her and the old gang, the others she called friends and the ones she performed with. I remember them, the silly guys and pretty girls, and I catch myself smiling back at each one of them like I used to when they shot me a wink down in the audience at the Flamingo Club. I used to get so embarrassed when they did that.

How did Mom's trunk ever end up on the garage floor on Alcott Street? I blow back the annoying thought and with it, a few straggling hairs. I search the trunk with my mom locked in it. I don't want to go any farther but I have to, something is urging me on like baseball fans yelling to the next batter up. Next I find me, lots of pictures of me when I was the baby, her only baby, the first baby. I look quickly through them, but that's not what I want.

I move a small box over and keep digging until I reach her clothes; small dresses in bright colors and low V-necks and a pair of sparkling high heeled shoes that tap perfectly when I put them down on the garage floor. Here are her rings and bracelets; my God I forgot about the rings and bracelets she wore back then. What happened? When did she put her stuff in the trunk and why? Did it happen fast or slow, or was it just one thing at a time...? A deep pool of regret seems to be at the bottom of this trunk and I'm not sure I can look any farther. I pause for a moment and look more closely at Mom and her lingering, hanging on, dusty and cold stuff. The subtle smell of mildew and sadness penetrates my heart. Then I remember. She never wanted to be ordinary, she wanted to be a star, a shining star with glitter and gold.

But now she's not the girl in the trunk or the woman she's become. From the ugly brick house with yellow weeds called a lawn to checking her oil in the light of day and four kids who call her Mom, this girl from before has accidentally turned into a woman and locked up all her dreams in a trunk. All she can do now is struggle not to open the trunk while at the same time refusing to let it go.

I stop the regret with a tug and pass by the fear of going on. I lift up the white feather boa that her friend Donna gave her a long time ago at one of Mom's birthday parties. Donna threw her the party at our house and the people . . . oh my God there must have been a hundred. Dad was gone then but I remember how Mom looked that night; she looked like a princess with jewels dripping around her feet. Donna was a blond Marilyn Monroe with her own ideas and a make-believe style. She was Mom's best friend. I know Mom wonders about her old friends. I've heard her say it before, but it's a quick thought and then a short good-bye. "Those days are gone and hell, they probably don't even remember me." I grab an old snapshot of Mom and some guy, God she looks so happy as he squeezes her tiny waist. On the back, handwritten, it reads, "Love always, Jim." I blink and a flash appears, I remember Jim, he was Mom's friend when Dad—was—gone. No way, love always . . .

I want to close up this terrible box with nothing but torment and broken dreams in it. This box of junk is cruel and heartless, it sits here laughing at what could have been. The lifeless trunk is tricking her, it says, "I'm holding your other life safe Ardell," but what it really means is, "I'm holding you prisoner for failing."

Goddamn this box. Don't you think I wish with all my heart that Mom *could* have had it all, and that she *could* be a star, and that she *could* dance again for no reason. Mom hurts all the time, I can see that, and on some days she hurts so bad that she's not sure if she'll make it. I know that too, you stupid little box. I fucking know that! I see the sorrow and dried tears that have left their ugly marks on her. And you don't think it kills me to hear her beautiful voice locked away inside this green tattered trunk? And for what? So you can sit in the dark holding all her secrets hostage while playing her songs and toying with her heart. Fuck you box! She will sing again . . . I slam the lid hard, and one of the long beaded necklaces around my neck snaps as the lid clamps down. The tiny beads fly everywhere, bouncing and rolling away trying to hide from me. I want to smash the hell out of the green monster with his big mouth finally shut. But instead I open it again to untangle the long mess around my neck. And there in the back tucked in the corner I see it. A hospital bracelet with Mom's name on it, and before I can run away I read, "August 16, 1969." I have to get out of here. I should have never opened this. Oh my God...

Dad is exactly where I left him, on the couch.

"Dad, I'm going over to Denise's."

"I guess." He fixes the pillow behind his head.

He hardly listens and asks no questions.

"I'm spending the night." I run off to my bedroom and grab a few things that fit in a grocery bag. I have to get out of here. I drag the brush across my hair and pick up my toothbrush.

"Bye, hon," I hear him say as I reach for the door.

Hon, that's what he used to call Mom sometimes. Uhh, I look at Beau's toys upside down in the dirt and the garbage cans with the crooked lids on the side of the house and then to the uneven number four at the top of our address next to the door, and the dingy pink house with no hope.

The walk is familiar and I break it up into three parts: Part one is leaving my street, Alcott is some forty miles long. Part two is just as long but it's nice, with lots of big trees lining the street standing tall on the green grass with perfectly edged lawns. It takes me up to Sixty-Fifth Avenue where my new high school sits, Hiram Johnson. I squint, practically closing my eyes when I pass it, I just can't think of high school right now. Part three, things shift a bit, the liquor stores are every two blocks, and the waist-high chain-link fences keep barking mighty mutts from biting me. The windows of the houses have thick black bars on them just in case; just in case the poor decide to rob the poor. I feel my skin crawl, I wish Denise would hurry up, she's usually here by now.

I walk a little faster and keep my eyes down, I don't want to make any unnecessary eye contact with those walking past me. In this neighborhood there's no real racial problems; everyone has a problem, no one is to be trusted. They call this place Oak Park. I don't know why, I certainly don't see any oak trees; I see sticker bushes, heaps of junk, and garbage like old mattresses and stuff begging to be picked up one day. I look up ahead to Stockton Boulevard less than ten blocks away. Where in the hell is Denise, I'm not crossing over Stockton Boulevard without her.

I finish my thought as I push the button to cross the street, the same street I swore I wouldn't cross without Denise. But hell, I don't have a choice now; I can't turn back. As I wait to cross I hear, "Sandra."

I look around but I don't see her. I hear her again. I look behind me to the red shack called Willy's, the local bar that sits on the corner. There's Denise standing next to the front door smoking a Marlboro 100. She's my age, sixteen, but Denise is much older. From the way she holds her smoke, to the way she talks, this girl has seen it all. One of the reasons she likes me so much is because I haven't.

The baggy jean shirt tied at her tiny belly hides the red halter top underneath and her loose jeans. She knows older people, way older, drunks and hounds are what I call them, but to her they are family. Mostly from what I've seen so far, they're harmless old guys and mean used-up women.

"What are you doing?" I wave to her and yell over the sound of traffic flowing.

I walk up to the black padded door of the bar where she fidgets and stamps out her cig.

"Oh Goddamn it, Mom didn't come home last night. I sent Shirl in to see if she's here. I know she is, she came here to cash her check last night and then called drunk out of her mind. She got that extra Social Security check she's been waiting for. I'm so pissed, she knows I need a couple of pairs of jeans and she owes me thirty dollars."

I listen wide-eyed to the problem.

"If I don't get her out of there she's going to spend all the money on those assholes inside. Especially that pig Hank."

Shirl pops her head out.

"Is she there?"

"Yes Denise but Dolly said for you to go home and leave her alone, she's fine."

"I don't give a shit about her, tell her to let me hold some money for later."

Shirl, with her hair ratted high on top of her head, follows Denise's orders like a waitress. Shirl is Dolly's best friend and a second mom to the girls. Denise has four sisters and she acts like the oldest. She hates drugs and alcohol and she won't smoke pot but she cusses like a man most of the time. I don't think there would be food in the house half the time if it weren't for Denise. She is serious and the sober one of the bunch and for some reason I love her. I met Denise in junior high and we've been tight ever since.

Shirl returns with her fist closed. "Your mother said fine." She hands Denise forty dollars.

Denise snatches it and snorts, "You tell her she better not spend it all and to come home tonight."

"I'll make sure she does." Shirl reaches back to open the bar room door.

Denise is still pissed and whimpers to me, "Like hell she will, she just wants to drink for free like the rest of them."

We start off toward home. It takes Denise a little while before she has anything to say, and I don't blame her. We walk and walk. All I can think is how in hell am I going to get out of here when I turn eighteen?

In the morning I call Mom and ask her for a ride home. She huffs and puffs a little and then agrees to pick me up. I really don't want to walk home anymore. I can't tell her all the reasons why. I just don't want to, is all I tell her.

Mom picks me up and waves to a happy and hungover Dolly who is standing on the cracked porch full of broken chairs and the trash that Sherry needs to dump. Denise walks me to the car and says good-bye. I jump in and wave to them all as if I just left a slumber party at the Brady's. Behind it all is a whole other world far from slumber or a party. Thank God Mom doesn't drink.

"Did you have fun honey?"

The question has only one answer, "Yeah, it was great."

"What'd you do?"

"Nothing, just played cards and watched TV." I'd love to see her face if I told the truth. *Yeah Mom, Dolly came home smashed with a couple of drunks and then she ate a bunch of pills to get high. How about you, what'd you guys do?*

When Mom and I get home, the TV is loud and Shelly and Mark are quiet. Sundays are so boring: Dad sits, Mom putters around, and we do everything we can to get the hell out of here.

"Dad can we go down the street?" Shelly asks.

"No. Help your Mother around the house," he barks out for no reason. This is bunk, we already did. Now what? You can't say we already did, because that would be talking back.

Shelly comes to me. "You try."

"Hell no, not right now, he's not in a good mood." I sit on the windowsill and light up a cig.

"Are you crazy, Mom will smell that."

"No she won't, she'll think it's Dad's." I open the window and tuck up real tight to the windowsill making sure to exhale all the smoke out the window.

"You make me sick. Why do you smoke anyway, that's so dumb." Shelly sits on the bed. I don't listen to her; instead I take a long drag to show her who's the boss. I'm the only one who smokes in the family except for Dad. Maybe that's it, I want to be like Dad. I choke and sputter on the thought as I cough on my cigarette.

I finish fighting with Shelly and go to the kitchen for a sandwich. Mom is on the phone with Aunt Carole. The air is stale now that we've all learned to stay in our corners and away from each other.

Beau wakes up from his nap. I see he's still sleepy when he walks into the living room and stands there, he looks groggy. Dad puts his arms out and Beau starts to walk toward him on the couch. Beau loses his balance and falls. Dad waits for him to get up with his arms stretched out. I go back to my sandwich, thinking after I'm done eating and Beau wakes up all the way I'll take him for a walk.

"Ardell get in here, there's something's wrong with Beau."

It hurts immediately, I don't know this pain, but it shoots like a dart. Mom drops the phone and runs to the living room.

"What's the matter with him?"

"He won't get up," Dad is bending down beside him on the floor. Mom's hands are all over Beau. I freak out, I knew this was going to happen. God's going to take him away. I can't watch, I can't help, and I don't know what to do.

Mom screams, "Beau, Beau!"

He won't answer. He won't answer, and his body falls forward in a slump. I can't believe this.

Dad puts his head down on Beau's chest. He looks so small, what's the matter with him?

"He's not breathing!" Dad scoops him up. His limp body falls around Dad's arms like a dead rag doll.

"Fuck." I cry and the panic sets in like a fire.

Mom screams to Shelly, "Call the hospital and tell them we're on our way."

"Sandra get in the car!" Dad yells running with Beau smashed up to his chest and holding him for dear life.

"Is he breathing?" Mom screams over and over.

I'm in the backseat listening to him not breathe. I don't know what to do.

Mom is driving fifty miles an hour down our street, honking and screaming for people to move. She is crazed.

Dad is crying, "No God, No."

"He's turning blue! Bill, do something!" Mom begs and pounds the steering wheel with her fist, "He's turning blue! Don't let him die!"

Dad bends down and puts his mouth to Beau's and starts to breathe for him. I cant' believe what I'm seeing.

Mom drives faster, her body lifts as her foot smashes the gas pedal with all her might. She screams for Beau's life and honks the horn wildly, warning people she'll kill them if they get in her way. She will.

"Oh my God, he's not breathing yet." I say to myself out loud.

Mom turns to me frantic, her eyes fill with rage, and she grinds her teeth my way, "Don't say that." She wants to slap the shit out of me.

She turns to Dad, "Just keep breathing for him, don't stop."

I watch Beau's chest fill with each one of Dad's breaths and then fall, when is it going to catch? As Dad lifts up for some more air, Beau remains asleep and blue. His eyes are shut, and his mouth hangs open waiting for some more air, he's gone. He's really leaving.

Mom swerves, a car horn cusses her out long and hard as she just misses hitting it.

"Don't fucking wreck, we have to get there." Dad is stern as he softly bends down to give Beau another breath.

He talks to Beau's unconscious body, "You're okay Beau, you're going to be fine buddy." Beau's head doesn't move in Dad's hands.

I leave the backseat and chase Beau's spirit with everything I have. I can see his tiny spirit fluttering in the distance. I can't stand it, I will not let him go.

"Beau come back!" I turn back to see his body in Dad's lap one final time. I have to go get him. What if he gets away? Mom and Dad don't know how bad this is. I do. I go straight to God and I blow open the door.

"You FUCKING give him back!!!" I cry out loud and hard. "He's not going with you this time. Give him back right now! Please." I stand my ground and wait.

God stands his ground and doesn't budge. I'm helpless. God is mad and I'm mad. This whole fucking thing is mad.

"Why?" I scream. "What do you want?"

Over the roar of the engine everything goes silent. The car moves, Dad breathes, and Mom's hands shake as she tries to steer the desperate car. But I can't hear the panic, the crying, or the torture in the car. Dad starts shaking Beau and Mom is rubbing her hand on his tiny leg.

This is it, God's in the car. I can feel him.

I fold my hands tightly, squeezing the life out of them; I begin to plead, "Dear God please help him! I know I need to be more loving. I will, I promise you. Give me another chance. I'll do anything you want, please don't do this..." I feel myself begging for mercy and the hot tears streaming down my face, but I don't know if *He*'s listening.

I talk faster and faster as time continues to take Beau further and further away from me. I hurt all over, I can feel Mom, she's terrified, she loves Beau so much she'll die if she loses another. And Dad, I can feel him too, he feels guilty for everything, and his pain is deeper than the breaths he sucks in. And me, I feel ashamed, ashamed that I never told God, "Thank you," for such a beautiful gift like Beau.

I bow my head and rock back and forth sobbing to God, "I'm sorry, I'm so sorry. Please give him back, Please."

I feel the car jerk as Mom turns hard into the emergency driveway. Dad is out of the car, the nurses grab Beau from Dad, and they all run through the doors that know they'd better fucking open. Mom leaves everything behind, her wallet, her keys, and her terror. She's the last one to bolt through the doors and disappear into the white halls with red letters. I look around, I see people staring, they nod a sad smile, and under their breath they say, "*Thank God* I'm not the one with a dying child." I don't want their pity; I want Beau back. I gather Mom's stuff off the front seat, Beau's blue blanket from the ground next to the car, and myself as I prepare to go inside the whiteness. I walk in with my arms stuffed and the blanket over my shoulder. I smell Beau, he's here, I can feel him. I try not to cry in front of the nurse as I ask where they are?

She hates doing it, she tilts her head and says, "I'm sorry. You'll have to wait out here."

A wide sea of people who have nothing to offer sit before me as she points to the waiting room. I mind her orders and sit. I listen and look for anything, breathing, crying, nurses talking, and hope while Beau's back there somewhere. I fold my hands tight around Mom's wallet and remember Beau on his first pony having his picture taken on his last birthday. He sat up so proud, not moving an inch and smiling at me when that guy snapped the shot. Shelly is holding Beau as I tease him, "I'm going to get your tickle spot." And the walks with just him and me, and every dirt clod on the way that I let him throw hard. I love him so much.

"Sandra." Mom touches my shoulder.

I jump back from my soothing thoughts and into the hospital. And then God is standing next to me and I hear him breathe, "Your brother can stay."

"He's going to be okay," Mom says. "He's breathing on his own."

"What's the matter with him?"

Mom wipes her eyes and sighs to me, "They don't know yet, maybe spinal meningitis. Your father's in there with him now, I can't watch." Mom looks like a scared little girl, "They have to stick a needle in his spine and do some tests and see what..."

I hear Beau scream before she finishes. Mom cringes, her heart breaks all the way, and the last of her love spills out.

We both feel him kick, struggle, and fight the doctors with the sound of his tears. Mom's hand closes over her eyes and she rubs the tears around and around her blotchy face. She turns to hide her face as her little boy yells for her one last time. I want to run in there and grab him and wrap him in my arms and give him back to Mom. Just leave him alone, he's fine now I know it. I want to tell Mom to stop them, but I can't, she didn't talk to God and she doesn't know Beau will be fine.

"Mrs. Vaughan, you can come back now, we're done." A nurse with a pen in one hand and a file in the other instructs. I look up to Mom and she reads my mind.

"Excuse me," she says to the nurse walking away, "is it okay if my daughter comes in?"

She thinks for about a minute, "I guess, but make it quick."

Mom takes some of her junk I've been holding and Beau's blanket. "Oh shit, I completely forgot about my wallet."

The curtain in Beau's room is half closed; I can't see him yet. The room is a mess, I see the machines they used with fallen hoses and I hear them beeping for no reason. I see Beau's tiny red tennis shoes and dirty socks lying on the ground empty. Dad hears us and moves the curtain quietly. Beau is naked; Dad whispers in his ear what a big strong boy he is. Beau doesn't move, his eyes stare past Dad, he's tired. His red hair is sweaty from the pain and he doesn't look like Beau. I want to cry so hard, but I can't, instead I fake a smile and rub his back. Dad scoots back just a little so we can get closer to him. Mom kisses Beau over and over.

"His fever is down and they said they'll be right back." Dad sucks in air and shakes his head. He's been crying.

Mom suddenly turns back into a mom, and she wants answers now as she bites her lip, taps her foot, and waits.

I see Dad look up to Mom and for the first time in years they are in this one together. All Dad wants is his baby boy to sleep a little bit until this mess is over. Beau is drifting off with nothing but a little Band-Aid on his back from the stab wound called a spinal tap.

Mom covers him and rubs his hair back off his forehead while we wait.

"Mr. and Mrs. Vaughan, I'm Dr. Loren." The doctor walks in with a concerned look and a little smile tucked inside you can just barely see.

"It seems the tests are normal. Your son does not have spinal meningitis. His fever is down and he's not in any danger."

"What happened to him, why did he quit breathing?" Dad stands up to the man.

"Sir, I'm not sure. We ran all the necessary tests and your son has no signs of any problems."

"I think it's one hell of a problem when a kid of mine quits breathing." Dad starts a fight.

"He's a strong boy and I've seen fevers spike so high and so fast they can cause the younger ones to go into shock, his body just couldn't fight."

Mom picks up her armor; she's not buying it for a minute; she didn't put Beau down for a nap with a raging fever.

The doctor continues, "You can take him home, or we'd be happy to keep him overnight for observation, whatever you'd like."

Mom doesn't move a muscle while she thinks about the fever, Beau, and *her* decision. "I think we'll take him home and keep an eye on him."

The doctor smiles and pats Beau's arm, "That would probably be best, he's been through a lot today."

The drive back home is filled with so many thoughts of blame there's practically no room for Beau.

"You know those doctors don't know shit." Dad drives the car and his point home. "That was the hardest thing I ever did holding my baby boy down while they taped him down like that and tried to talk to him while they stuck that fucking five-inch needle in his back."

Mom agrees. "A fever my ass, well you can be damn sure that it'll be a cold day in hell before he ever gets a fever again."

Beau wants his shoes tied, the rest of his popsicle, and off Mom's lap. His cheeks are rosy and his spirited ways are back, and Mom won't tell him no, not for at least fifteen years.

It was three hours ago when I sat back here with God asking why for no apparent reason Beau was going die. For some reason Dad knew he had to take me with them; he didn't know what was going on around him once he had Beau in his arms. The whole thing makes no sense, but I was there when we all held Beau by one foot as he almost slipped away. I realize it was everybody's fault and yet you can't really blame anyone. The doctors didn't bring him back, hell they don't even know why he left in the first place. I couldn't catch him, he was to far away. Mom tried to drive fast enough, but did she? And even Dad breathing air and love into Beau over and over again didn't do it.

The car stops with a thud, we're home. Shelly and Mark are outside on the porch; they look like wrecks. Shelly fidgets with her hands and she's frozen solid as she waits for us to get out of the car.

Mom reaches out for them both and hugs them, "It's okay you guys, he's fine, look he's fine. It's all over."

Shelly finally cries when she sees Beau up close. She cries so hard, I don't know if she can stop crying right now.

37

High school is in its third week, and that afternoon I go to English class, Mrs. Seymour. She can't see shit, she's blind as bat and I swear she's ninety-five years old if she's a day. And she weighs about the same. I don't mind this class, it's a snore, and all you have to do is take roll and pretend you're reading for the next fifty-five minutes as they slowly pound away.

I sit when the bell rings and Mrs. Seymour stands up. It's the last class of the day for everybody. Most of the class gets a pass for the restroom and they never return. I sure wish I could do that. As I read one paragraph over and over about prepositional sentences, not knowing what the hell it is saying and trying not to fall asleep, a girl walks in. The whole class looks at her as she tells Mrs. Seymour something about a transfer. I've never seen her before. It doesn't matter though; she's gorgeous. She's petite, with short brown hair, a real bitch I can tell. I go back to the English book, which is written in Greek, and ignore her.

Kim sits down, she smiles at me. She didn't have to do that. She probably feels sorry for me or something. I smile back.

Silence grows as the interruption disappears and then she taps me on the back.

"Hey, what are we doing?"

"Reading chapter four and trying not to fall asleep?" I say as a matter of fact.

Kim laughs a little, "Okay, but then what?"

"Pray the bell rings," I say to myself.

The second hand moves like taffy for the next twenty-two minutes. The bell rings and the day is finally over. We scoot out of the desk/chairs that don't fit anymore, and escape into the noisy hall. Lockers crash, people yell, and the crowds shuffle outside. I walk by myself close to the hall wall thinking about the long walk home and all these damn books I have to carry. I don't mind the walk. I mind all the books. A tap on the shoulder hits me out of the blue, I quickly turn to see who is it? I don't know anyone here. It's Kim. I ask her sharply with a look, "What?"

She hesitates, "Thanks a lot for your help in there."

What in the world is she talking about, I didn't help her.

"Yeah," she finishes, "I was really nervous, thanks."

"Sure. Hell I'm nervous all the time around here."

Kim laughs, she isn't used to laughing I can tell. She's kind of serious.

"I was just wondering if you want to have lunch with me and my friends tomorrow?" She shifts her books and holds them up a little higher.

"Yeah, I'd love to."

"Okay we usually meet in the parking lot and go to Jimboy's Taco or Tahoe Park."

"All right, I'll see you tomorrow." The crowd pushes me on and I float with them in the opposite direction to this new girl called Kim.

I walk, run, and skip home. I can't wait to tell Mom I think I just made a new friend. She's going to be so happy for me. I replay every sentence that fell out of Kim's mouth and mine. Did I sound stupid? Too eager? How come she didn't see that I'm an ugly dork? I bet it sounded like I was desperate. What about her friends? I wonder if they'll like me? What did she say, they go Jimboy's or the park at lunch? You can't walk to either one of those places, I bet we're going to drive. The thought of a car is so exciting that I must remember to act cool, like it's no big deal. I can't believe I might actually have friends who have a car. I walk faster so that nothing wrecks my joyride.

"Mom, Mom, guess what?" I drop my books on the couch.

"What?" She answers with no curiosity at all.

"I think I might have made some friends today. This girl came into class and..."

"That's nice honey, I knew you would." She interrupts the noise of me babbling.

"But Mom you don't understand."

She raises an eyebrow and I can tell she doesn't want to hear the rest of my incredible story. She's busy figuring out bills, stirring the spaghetti, and listening to *Sesame Street*. I give up when I realize how childish this is of me to be excited over friends.

"Honey would you wash the dishes and put them away?" She goes back to her world.

"I thought that was Shelly's job."

"Look, don't argue with me right now." Mom puts her foot down. "Shelly has practice right now and I don't want to hear it."

And before I know it, in just the count of ten, Mom and I are fighting for no reason.

Shelly grabs her glove and kicks my ass on her way out to softball practice with all of her friends.

Mom and I don't talk as the hot water bubbles in the sink before me. I hate this. I feel sorry for myself and try to understand why Mom doesn't like me anymore. She's always in the mood for a fight, even if I'm not. Maybe she's been fighting for so long that's all she hears. I shake my head and wash the milk stain ring from the glass and try not to think about it.

The next morning I throw all my clothes on the ground and then the bed desperately searching for something cute to wear. I don't have anything cute. I stomp around, the more stuff I try on the more I sweat and swear. It's no use; everything is ugly, I'm ugly, I look fat, this is stupid, forget it I'm not going. Shelly's gone, thank God or else she'd be laughing at me right now. Mom doesn't have any idea how important this lunch period is for me. I sit on the bed, beaten by my ugly clothes, and decide I'll just hide today and forget about it.

"Mom, I'm not going to school today." I walk in her bedroom.

"What the hell are you talking about, yes you are." She looks straight at me.

"Mom please, I'll clean the house."

"What's the matter with you?" She pulls the blankets up on the bed.

"Mom, I don't have any clothes and I look stupid, I hate school."

"Listen, is this about that new friend? Honey, she's either going to like you for who you are or not. There's not a damn thing you can do about it. Just go and give it a shot. What's the worst thing that can happen, she doesn't like you?" Mom taps me on the knee hard and reaches for the door. "Whatever you do in life don't ever look back and ask yourself, 'What if?' Don't do it." Mom wipes her hand down my stiff arm and nudges me out of her room.

Lunch went great, so great in fact, that I now belong to my very own clique. We ate, smoked, and giggled together, I found out what a best friend is: Kim. And she found out what it was to laugh. I made her laugh and she made me feel welcome. I forgot about my past and barely cared about anything but them, my new friends. For the rest of that year and the next summer all that mattered was getting a job, staying a virgin, and drinking beer without throwing up.

Mom and Shelly come home after they went to Revell's and stopped at Belair Market. I pop down off the car trunk to go help them carry in the groceries. Shelly made it to All-Stars and she'll be pitching the games. If she wins, which she will, the Fruitridge softball league will be number one in the state division. The whole neighborhood is talking about it. Shelly is so popular now that I'm known as "Shelly's sister Sandra." Plus the more Shelly grows the more beautiful she becomes, and now that she's the All-Star pitcher everyone knows her and all the girls around here hate her. I may not like Shelly either, but I'll be damned if anyone touches my little sister for any reason.

"Sandra, guess what? Mom and I just saw a house for rent down the street on Whittier." Shelly hands me the heavy bag. "And she's going to ask Dad if we can move."

"Which one?"

"You know the brown one on the corner with the lawn that slopes down and the planter box in front of the porch."

"I like that house." I turn back to Shelly.

Dad's home from work that evening, and he's tired and grouchy, he doesn't want to talk. He goes straight for the shower. We know as soon as he brightens up, Mom's going to ask him if we can move. Dad finishes his shower and joins us for dinner. He eats his spaghetti slowly in the living room and from the kitchen we hear: "Bill I've been thinking, now that the money is good and we have all the bills paid, why don't we move? I found a nice house down the street for rent. It's not that much more and it's nice, nice backyard, three bedrooms, and it's safer for the kids. Especially Beau, we won't be next to Fruitridge Road, it's a lot quieter." Mom waits for Dad to swallow.

"Wait a Goddamn minute here." Dad starts to blow.

Mark almost drops his fork; the tone of Dad's voice is familiar. Shockwaves move invisibly through the walls. We weren't expecting this.

"I asked you last month to move to Stockton and you said no. Now all of a sudden you want to move down the street. What the hell's wrong with you?"

Mom slowly picks up Beau and moves him into the kitchen with us. Beau sits on my lap, oblivious to the waves that are curling up ready to crash. I notice where each one of us is sitting and how fast I'll be able to get them out if this thing blows. It's going to blow. The garage door winks at me and through the garage and out the side gate is my plan.

Mom returns to the living room, "That is bullshit. I told you I would not move the kids down to Stockton. Sandra is in high school now and for the first time all the kids have friends and are doing well in school. I don't care how much gas money we'll save."

Dad is pissed and not listening. He erupts, "I'm the one busting my ass, driving two hours a day to work, and living in this shit hole." He throws down his fork.

Mark sits up on alert, Beau squirms to get down, and Shelly rises just a little. Not me, I wait for the big bang.

"The kids my ass, you don't give a shit about school, you just don't want to leave your sisters."

"Now you listen to me…" Mom stands her ground, she's not backing down. "…we have followed your ass all over the country. No more! We stay here, I'm not dragging the kids to another new school, a new city, they're going to finish school here."

Dad stands, "Get outside!" He yells at us.

We don't move, what's he going do, beat up Mom?

He yells again, "I said go outside."

"Go ahead kids, Sandra take Beau," Mom directs and prepares for battle. I see it in her eyes she's not afraid this time, she's going to fight for us, and this time she's going to win.

As we leave through the front door, shame follows us. Another fight, I thought those days were gone. I hear Mom growl: "I'm warning you, don't you dare. I will take the kids and leave your ass so fast your head will spin."

The door shuts, the bell rings, the fight begins.

"I'm so sick of your shit, always feeling sorry for yourself. Guess what, it hasn't been a picnic for any of us. Do you hear me?" Mom lets him have it; her words fly out of her mouth so furiously he can't move.

I hear Dad throwing things, smashing the house up, but he's not hitting her. He yells, "You fucking bitch, I'm the one who has to live with a whore. You don't love me, you never have."

"I've put up with your bullshit and your jealousy for seventeen years. You can't stand the idea that I won't be common, so you can feel better about yourself. Living off your mother, lying, and cheating everyone around you. You're the one who's common."

The neighbors peer out of their windows, step outside to make sure we're okay, and pretend they can't hear Mom and Dad fighting.

"Well if things are that bad then why don't you just leave then.?" Dad is clear as a bell. I've never heard him say that. He wants us to leave. A roller coaster of emotions whips, turns, and dives and then chugs up through me.

Mom slams the bedroom door. "I *will* get my kids out of this shit hole if it's the last thing I do. I don't give a shit if it's with or without you, we're moving out of this house!"

The night is almost warm as we stand together on the sidewalk; Beau plays with his trucks in the dirt and we don't. There's nothing to say, we don't know what just happened, but the wind has been knocked out of all of us. I see Dad's shadow sit back down and turn on the TV.

38

Shelly won the All-Star game again this summer and we moved up the street. I learned how to smoke pot, roll a fat joint, and which liquor store I can buy beer at. Budweiser. I also learned the importance of tanning; the only thing that should be left white is your teeth and eyeballs. Our skin is so dark that Kim has to take a break today, her mother said so. I lie on the living room floor in a dark blue tube top and white shorts, admiring my tan lines and watching cartoons with Beau. Mom is at work.

She found her independence on the road selling signs, she takes care of us and herself now. She opened her mouth and shut Dad up when she packed up the house and said, *We're moving, you can either come with us or don't*. He came and she got a job at Wells Fargo doing something like processing, whatever that is. I work at the Sub Shop, I'm the night manager. I spend every dime I make on gas, drugs, and concerts. Dad leaves for work at 4:30 a.m. and I usually wait around the corner for him to leave the house so I can sneak back in. I see him early in the morning, he doesn't know I watch him jump on his Honda Gold Wing and ride. I heard him say once it's his only freedom.

As for Mark he's got friends and runs the streets, he's tall and lanky and eats like a horse. I usually see him in the mornings till about noon and then I'm gone or he's gone, basically we're all gone except for

Beau. He goes to the babysitter's or stays home with one of us. He's learning to swim this summer.

"Sandra," he tells me with his little hands on his tiny hips, "I'm not wearing my floaties today."

"Oh yes you are."

I take his hand and together we cross the hot street. We're going to his girlfriend Nicky's where he can swim. He's going to marry her. Beau has on his tight little red swimming trunks and two big yellow floaties suffocating his upper arms. Heck I don't blame him, I wouldn't want to wear those things either. His tiny little butt and big arms look so cute I feel the love for him tug at me, and a tear wells up for no reason as he runs to climb the ladder and jump in. I wipe it away and think how silly, and then I remember how it felt to plunge into the water when I was a kid.

Over the fence I see Mark leaving. He's by himself and I watch him and wonder what's he going to do today; I should try to talk to him, we hardly ever talk. I hear Shelly start up her white Cutlass Supreme with its chrome wheels and tinted windows, she's going to work today. I see her slink into her seat as she pulls around my rust-colored Dodge Dart with tape holding in the stuffing of the front seat and my front tire that needs air. I think I've done something great even having a job and getting a nickel raise to night manager, and then she pops home last week and announces she just got another one during the day at a warehouse working in shipping and receiving. Oh sure I'm the night manager, I manage making tuna sandwiches and mopping floors all night. After Shelly ships and receives all day, she makes BBQ and regular chicken at Picnic-n-Chicken at night.

Beau splashes me when he kicks.

"Beau let me show you." I reach for his slick body in the pool.

"What?" He dog-paddles away.

"Let me show you how to swim." I tug and finally get him over to the side. "Now first you have to kick with your legs out."

He holds onto the edge and kicks.

"That's it, kick hard." I instruct and cheer. "Now put your face in and blow bubbles."

"Why?"

"I don't know, just do it."

He kicks, blows bubbles, and splashes with his arms. Nicky swims all around like a turtle waiting for her friend to hurry up and learn. From the side of the pool I show him how to cup his hand, reach up over his head with his arms, and pull down through the water.

"Now kick Beau—use your arms—keep your head down," I yell to the giant tadpole in front of me swimming his strokes. God he's getting so big.

Then a chilling thought runs through my body: I don't have much time left with him. I'll be graduating soon and moving out. Mom has told us all that at eighteen it's time to be on our own, and she means it. I always planned on leaving but not this soon, it happened so fast and back then I didn't have Beau to consider. Panic takes hold as I look to Beau who's bouncing, kicking, and gulping unintentional mouthfuls of water. How in the world will I live without him? I know I'll miss so much of him when I go, and I know I won't be back. I try to hide from the lighting bolts of truth hitting the ground around me. My little brother won't be waking me up in the morning; he won't ask me for more bubbles when I'm in the middle of watching a good part on TV. He won't be able to show me what he drew today at preschool, and I won't be there for him.

I have to go, I can't let him see me crying for no reason in the backyard in the middle of the day. "Beau, I'll be right back."

Beau splashes me back with an okay.

I run across the street and slam the bathroom door, sit down on the bathtub, and turn on the shower so no one can hear me cry. The fear and pain of leaving them all is unbearable, I want to stop crying but I can't. I wish to God I didn't have to do it but I do. It's so unfair that I have to leave and I think Mom wants me gone, Shelly could care less and Mark doesn't even know what's happening. How in hell can

I stand there and say good-bye to my family? Goddamn it I didn't know about this part, no one prepared me for good-bye. I have said good-bye so many times before and with them it was a fake I'll see you later. But to say that to my family, I won't make it to the door, even the thought of it starts ripping out my heart. I catch my breath, wipe my wet checks off with my shirt, and sober up before I loose it. For God's sake, it's not for another couple of months. But Beau, he's the one I wish I could stay and protect from Dad just a little while longer. I don't want him to know or feel the things I have. I just want him to be a little boy who wants to find a frog.

I get home from work; it wasn't busy but steady. I'd rather have it be busy all night and then dead. I open the door and Shelly is pacing back and forth. Mark is in his room with the door open, and I see him nervously cleaning his room. It's eleven o'clock and Mom and Dad are in bed, with Beau crashed out next to Mom. Shelly fidgets and fights with her long blond hair, Mark stays away as Shelly finally settles down long enough to talk to me.

"What's going on around here?" I turn the TV down and look at Shelly who looks like she killed someone.

"Oh man San, it got bad around here tonight." She twists into a ball with her legs up on the couch. "It wasn't my fault."

"What happened?"

"Dad got mad. Really mad." Shelly thinks about it and tries not to cry. "Mom told me to do the dishes, so I did. Now I just got home from work and I really didn't feel like it. Maybe I was a little huffy but I didn't say anything."

My heart pounds as I try to help her tell me the story quietly. My eyes lower and I listen.

"I was in the kitchen, I finished the plates and glasses and I was doing the silverware when Dad came in. I didn't even look at him. He picked up a spoon from the dish rack and was starting to make a sandwich and then yells at the top of his lungs, 'Goddamn you. Look at this shit!' He shoves the spoon in my face. I must have missed a spot. I didn't know what to do, and then I got mad."

Shelly's face is tortured as she holds back her fear of what happened next. I sit next to her without expression knowing that if I show any emotion right now she'll crack and start bawling and won't be able to finish the story. She takes a deep breath through her nose and exhales softly.

"I yelled back, I couldn't help it, 'What's your problem?' And I pushed his hand with that stupid dirty spoon away from my face. By now Mark is under the dining room table and Mom drops her glass and is running in the kitchen. Dad looks like…" Shelly stops and I wait for her words to return. "…he looks crazy, he looks like he does when he's hitting you." Shelly loses it, she's scared to death.

"It's okay." I reach for her but I'm afraid to touch her.

Shelly speaks through her cracked voice in a whisper. "He raises his hand to hit me, I don't know if he was going to slap me or punch me. I felt him come at me when Mom ran in, grabbed his arm, and practically threw him across the kitchen. Then she just started screaming at him, 'Don't you dare touch her! You son of a bitch, I've had it. Get out! I mean it this time! Pack your shit tomorrow and get out.'"

I can't believe what Shelly is saying, this has never been said before. Mom is kicking Dad out? No, no way.

Shelly finishes; I hear Mark in his bedroom listening and sniffing at the same time. "And then Mom looked him straight in the eye, he wanted to kill her but he couldn't move for some reason, he just listened. 'And I want you to know one more thing, I've stood by and watched you beat the shit out of one of my kids and I have to live with that, but I'll be damned if you ever touch another one of these kids. First it was Sandra and now it's Shelly, what next, Mark?'"

I sat there with nothing to say and a lot of feelings leeching out of my body. I hated Mom for not helping and hated being Dad's punching bag. I sat numbed by the words Shelly spoke. It was as if Shelly was telling me some strange story about how she's sorry. And for the first time in my life I understood that Mom couldn't stand up for herself, the baby, or me. It seems so long ago. I wonder, does it even matter anymore? And then with a sharp stab to my back, I feel *yes* penetrate straight to my heart. All that ever matters is the truth. How and why are simply parts of the journey, the strength is measured by the truth.

Tonight as I lie in bed, I feel different, sort of like a turtle who feels safe while sunning himself by a pond. No hissing sounds inside my head, no rattling, just the quiet sound of empty that puts me to sleep.

"Girls get up, your father and I need to talk to you." I scratch my head and Shelly moans as we roll out of bed. Mark is already in the bathroom. He comes out in his underwear and a long T-shirt. Dad is dressed, and looks like he's going to church, Mom is stern, her face void. Beau sleeps as we all sit together waiting for the talk. It's probably that Dad is sorry and it will never happen again, that sort of stuff. I wish they'd hurry up and spit it out. I want to go back to bed.

"Girls, Mark, your mother and I have been talking and we think it's time..." Dad chokes up. "We've had a good life together with a lot of up and downs."

My mouth drops, I hear the words before he says them: he's leaving.

"We think it would be best if your mother and I divorce."

I feel the roof of my mouth dry and the back of my throat close. This isn't happening.

Shelly cries first and Mark is right behind her, "Dad you mean you're not coming back?"

I don't listen; I know he's not. He's going to fucking leave, forever this time I can feel it. I pound out the need to grab him and hold him and beg him to stay.

He continues, "I want you all to know I fucked up in a lot of ways, but I will never stop loving you guys. You're the best thing I ever did in life."

Mom sits controlled, motionless, and hurt. She feels the room spin, we all do. No one can talk except Shelly. "Dad we love you too."

"I want you guys to know this is not anyone's fault, not your mother's although she put up with a lot of my shit," he tries to lighten up the darkness in the room, "and certainly not any of yours. I just have to go."

I want to hit something; I want him to stop saying that…I don't know what to do, my body tightens afraid to feel. He stands up before the tear falls and he changes his mind. He bends down and reaches for each one of us and hugs us to the bitter end. Mark isn't breathing and Shelly isn't moving, I am, I'm moving as far away from this awful place called truth.

"Mark, now you stop it big guy, I'll see you guys," Dad cries as he tries to blow us a kiss good-bye. "I love you guys." His hand drops to his side and he finds one last smile and gives it to us as he shuts the door.

I get up and put on my clothes, I have to get out of here. I walk and walk to nowhere for hours and find myself back at home. I feel like the worst kid who ever lived. How could I have not seen this coming. How could I have let this happen? I should have seen it. Shelly and Mark look like broken toys where I left them on the floor. Mom is in her room with the curtains closed. She is in her room laying on the bed with her feet hanging over the edge. "I had to Sandra. I just couldn't live…"

I want to say something like it's okay or you did the right thing, but no words can form and no reasons to form them come to mind. I touch her arm and turn to leave; the closet door is open. It's so empty, all of Dad's shirts and pants I hung up a thousand times are gone; every single one of them. I stand there, broken, I didn't get to say good-bye. It hits me so hard I fall forward, my stomach aches and my hand trembles; my dad is gone.

Somehow I manage to get ready for work, it's Saturday and it'll probably be busy. I don't know if I can work, I really don't know if I can.

I have a sign on my face that reads *leave me alone and don't talk to me*. Everyone reads it immediately when I walk in. The sauces need to be stirred and someone took my apron home last night. I find a hat and open the register and count the twenties, my day to work the counter. I stand at the counter asking large or small, and with or without onions, waiting for the feelings to seep back into the hole so I can be normal, they are dripping deeper and deeper into my heart.

"May I help you?" I look up.

"Yes, I'd like..." Dad stops when he sees my face. "Honey, how could I leave without telling you good-bye." He smiles. "Hell, you were my first."

"Dad..." It feels like someone is holding my arms behind my back and another is punching me in the gut. I can't look him.

"Come on honey, you can do this. Hell, I've put you through harder shit than this."

Dad leans forward, "Honey, I just want you to know you are the best daughter a dumb Dad like me could ever have. I love you Sandra."

"But..." I choke on the welling tears and press my clenched fists hard against my eyes. *Don't go!* is what I want to say, but I can't, he is leaving. The sadness reaches over the counter, I want to touch him so badly and say I'm sorry this hurts so much.

"I have to go." He turns to leave before I break in two. I run out after him.

He hugs me and whispers, "We're going to make it, sweetheart," and squeezes me hard. "We always do. You're going to do just fine. I'm not leaving you, I'm just moving."

If he lets go I'll fall to the ground; my knees are so weak.

He lowers his head and holds back his tears with a strong smile. All I can do is cry inside. Cry for the past, the love, the good-byes—all of it.

I leave work and Dad leaves Sacramento, and it's one of the worst days of my life. I grip the hot steering wheel with both hands, holding my body tightly upright as I drive home. I think about what it took for Dad to come and face me. I saw it in his eyes; it killed him saying good-bye to me. It's the same look Mom had in her eyes when she told me her baby had died.

I stop at the red light near a busy intersection and loosen my grip, my knuckles are white and my fingers are stiff. I just have a mile to go before I'm home. I glance into the rearview mirror and see my tear-stained face. I look away and something catches my eye, a glimpse of something, and I look back. I see Mom in my reflection staring back at me. It reminds me of how she looked to me from the backseat with her dried tears and sunglasses as she drove. I look down at my hands holding onto the steering wheel, they too look like Mom's. I look up again and blink; looking for my face, it's not there, and I'm not that little girl anymore, wondering where I'm going. I'm the one who's driving now.

A car honks. I step on the gas and drive through the intersection. I look back to the mirror and this time I see me. I am not Mom, but she gave me her love, her sense of strength, and understanding, and I am not Dad either, although searching is in my soul.

Dad admitting his failure as a father and telling me the truth of his love for me was actually him releasing me from the chains of his life, and from his own father's hate. Mom's reflection was her telling me softly that I have what I need to find my own image. It's my turn to understand, to gather strength, and find myself. I'll find my way because Mom and Dad have both shown me that starting over is a part of life. And when I find these things, I'll be free to find the baby from long ago. And I will find her, I will…

39

Four years later Mom remarried a sincere man with a tan face and a salty beard named Daryl, and together they started a brand new life in a real a home outside of Lodi, with a washer and dryer, and laughter. Mom left Sacramento and never looked back. Ten years later she's still in love with Daryl. Later I found out that the woman Dad lives with was also the one he was having an affair with for years before Mom and he divorced. No one really talks about that, Mom said she knew it the whole time, but didn't care. Dad is still content living with Laura, working for the state, and watching TV. I guess it's okay, but still, I look at him and wonder, how could he? Shelly works hard at two jobs and lives with her boyfriend. And Mark works for Mom so he can eventually own his own business. Beau graduated from high school and is going to be a famous musician one day.

Sunday afternoon I sit at home in LA with a pen in my hand jotting down the address and hang up the phone. It's time. It's been a year since Shelly, Mark, and I all had the dream, the same dream I felt and that chased me all these years. But this time they saw her too, a teenage girl sitting on the back of a green pickup truck looking, just looking off into the distance. When Shelly and Mark both told me of their dream last year on Christmas Eve I'll never forget the look on Mark's face when he said, "She's looking for us, you have to find her."

How could I argue? Not only did we all dream of her, but on the same night as well. I promised them I would find her, hell I promised myself that long ago.

That's finally when I had to talk to Mom, and we met at a coffee shop outside Stockton. I didn't tell her what it was I needed but I suspect she knew. She was already sitting in a booth next to the window looking into the drab gravel parking lot of Rocky's Coffee Shop, a favorite of the truckers who travel on I-5. The big semis sit in a perfect line next to one another facing the exit. I park and look in the mirror at my face for some sense of right and wrong. I can do this. It's Mom for Christ's sake she'll be okay. I walk up to the door, I see her back facing away from me, I know she saw me pull up, but she's not looking at me. The waitress eagerly greets me with a menu in her hand, I shake my head and dismiss her warm welcome when I point to Mom over there. I smile to the young gal and leave her standing at the register.

"Hey, Mom." I drop to the rust-colored vinyl and use the paper napkin to wipe the sweat off my forehead. Mom is tense, and she slowly and deliberately takes a long sip of her Diet Coke.

"So, what's this about?"

I don't know what to say; everything I practiced for the past week, the words, the courage, and intent is all gone, evaporated. I sit there twirling the ice in my glass around and around with my finger. She won't talk. She waits for me. "I don't know I just wanted to ask you..."

"Then go ahead, ask." Her eyes are dry and black; she never blinks.

"Well then," I look in her eyes." "What happened to the baby?" I can't believe I said it. I turn away from her as soon as the forbidden words are spoken.

Mom's eyes go first, she looks away and then back, but this time filled. Her hand clenched over her lips. *Never mind!* I scream out in silence. Next she goes; her whole body sucks in all the air she can and still she looks like she's suffocating. "What do you want to know?" She opens just a crack and bleeds.

"Why did you say the baby was a boy, it's a girl. Right?" I talk low trying not to kill her, but her face turns red and angry, she hates me. And then she shuts up and tries to escape. She sees something, maybe the baby, and when she returns, the look on her face is pitiful and tears spill out one after the other. I want to reach over and touch her, do something but I can't, she's like ice. She tries to talk but she can't breathe and her cold voice cracks.

"Mom..."

"Don't." She hears my voice. "You don't have any idea..." She stops herself, her jaw clamps. "I did what I thought I had to do. It was a girl..." Mom's pain is sour and contagious, I can't look at her, she's making me cry. "Do you know what it was like to see the look on your face that day...to see you looking up at me?" Mom rubs her eyes with one hand, "Christ, it was bad enough, and I never thought about the lie. Until I saw you standing there waiting for...I panicked. Mom's eyes stay away from mine. "I couldn't say that my baby girl died, that's why I said it was a boy."

I sit back without a word. The world I thought might be is so, and now I'm sitting in a booth with the colorless truth on one side and Mom on the other. She tries to hide from me as I hide from her. I've never seen Mom look like this, a woman, crushed, ashamed, and guilty. I'm sobbing to myself while I watch her finish crying old, dark tears.

She lifts her head and sees my sadness, and the mom in her rises, "I'm so sorry I did this to you." She swallows hard, "I never thought about you and what I've put you through when I made the choice..." I want her to stop. "If I had, I wouldn't have been able to go through with it. It was too late, by the time I saw your face that day..." She cries, "I couldn't get her back." Mom reaches for my hand and squeezed it. "I never thought about her being your sister, I just thought about her..."

I can't talk or think, all that I wanted to ask or say is in the past and Mom is right here. "Okay."

"Listen," Mom sits forward and dabs her swollen eyes. "I'll tell you whatever I can to help you find her, but in my heart I don't feel like I have any right, but you do." She stands up. "I have to go."

* * *

The day is clear and crisp, not too unusual for December. The eucalyptus trees swing and moan outside my door. They're about forty feet tall and creek like old bones. I swear one day they'll snap like a twig. I keep one ear open for a cracking sound as I pour myself a cup of coffee and fantasize about the day all the scattered pieces will fall back in place. I'll write the officer like he asked when I have the birth certificate in my hand. I need it to continue the last of my search. When I called the courthouse last week, I convinced the lady, Loretta, to help me find the birth certificate. After hearing my story she finally said she would. I am too close to fail, every phone call, every letter and conversation brings me closer and closer. Soon I'll know my sister's name.

How does one start this fantasy, the dream, and the nightmare? You don't. You let each dream talk to you and let every angel direct you. You feel the pang of nothingness until one day the truth is available. It's as if the world has stopped for a brief second and you take your first real breath, for the first time you can taste the crisp sweet air. That is the truth and no more.

I find my search resembling a rainbow; every color imaginable bleeding into the next became a new feeling. My intent is clouded daily with new thoughts of how I'm going to disrupt other people's lives. The more I looked at *them* the longer it took to see me. I finally found the truth staring back at me through my mother's eyes; I'd grown up and I need to find my sister.

The biggest issue is how this will affect Mom's world, which is bound and gagged. I had no right, or so I'm told. I felt disgusting pawing at the truth. But then quietly the familiar voice of God says, "Find her." And with that, I have to search. I no longer concerned myself with the, *what-ifs*, I focused on *what is*…

There's no need to run anymore, I just need to turn around and look, look at the land covered with stories before me. The race, the characters, and the madness are all a part of the magic. After awhile you get tired of battling right versus wrong. Besides, there is no such thing. It's just life.

I wait impatiently as a child on Christmas Eve, closing my eyes and begging for sleep. That morning, sure enough, Lorretta sends the birth certificate, it's an old, green tattered paper and the typewritten black words are all here. At first I opened it like it was nothing more than a statement. Until I realize what I'm looking at. The hospital name is Charleston General, date of birth, August 16, 1969, the time of birth, three thirty-two p.m., weight, six pounds, ten ounces, and mother, Ardell Vaughan. I feel clammy and my brow tightens, this is it. Then the most disturbing thing of all—next to *father* the word *unknown* is typed hard and crooked. I read it ten times, this can't be right. I sense an angry old nurse beating on the typewriter keys as she fills in the blanks describing the cold fact about the nameless baby. And then Mom, in there all alone, I know she saw the baby, I overheard her say dark hair like me. I feel something, a new color seeping in this rainbow I call a search. A dark yellow hatred and confusion takes over, and all I can find inside me is a faint memory that is stronger than this ugly pea-green piece of paper. It's too hard; I can't go on. But I can't quit.

I put on my sweater and my slippers; my hands are freezing as I type the letter. The kitchen is quiet and the yellow fear slowly turns to courage as the sunlight reaches in the kitchen window and takes over. Nothing is going to stop me, not the black words, the reddish lie, or the yellow fear. I will not give up now, not for anyone. I read the letter back to myself before I shove it in the envelope and mail it to a stranger who will help me.

December 5, 1994

Kanawha County Sheriff Dept.

Law Enforcement Division
Attn: Detective Sergeant JW Johnson
PO Box 70587
Charleston, WV 25375

Dear Sergeant JW Johnson:

Thank you for taking my call last week. As I mentioned I am Sandra Vaughan, and I live in Southern California and I need some help locating my sister. We were separated as children in West Virginia.

I have followed up on all the contacts and agencies you suggested and did find the birth certificate. She was born in Charleston and grew up in the town of Clendenin, West Virginia. She was born August 16, 1969.

I hate to bother you again, but I have no other sources to find her. If you could please take the new information and help me I would really appreciate it. Enclosed is her birth certificate that I recently found at the Kanawha County Court house. Also there is a copy of my driver's license for verification.

I could use any help you can provide me with. I thank you for all your assistance with my problem.

I look forward to hearing from you.

Sincerely,

Sandra Vaughan

By now it's raining in LA and that's unusual, I don't know what woke me first, the rain or me sweating. The phone rings, I jump. A deep calm man's voice greets me. "Miss Vaughan."

"Yes..." I lean back against the living room wall, the wall is cool on my bare skin.

"This is Sergeant Johnston. Do you have a fax?"

"Yes." The wall holds me. "Why?"

"I think we have..."

"What's her name."

"Melinda, Ma'am. Melinda Kay Lane."

A tunnel opens and I'm swept away. Melinda...

They have located my sister. The call from Sergeant Johnston said she's not that far from here. Charleston. He said she got married and that he had gotten a copy of the marriage certificate. That's how he found her. He said some more stuff about the parents and that Melinda's married name is now Henline. I could get the phone numbers through information. The fax from the sheriff's department came in that afternoon. It all happened so fast that a floating fuzzy feeling took over from that point and it's been with me all day.

I call information and ask for Melinda or Richard Henline and of course before I can grab a pen off the shelf the computer voice rings out her number. I listen to the repeated numbers. I wish this would stop. Why is this so fucking easy? In less than two weeks not only do I have her name, but I'm sitting here about ready to dial her, for God's sake. Why in the world was she so easy to find? I dial the numbers slowly and pray she won't answer—if she does I'm hanging up. After three long rings the machine picks up and I hear it, a girl's voice saying, "You've reached Melinda and Richard..." I slam down the phone, dropping it as if it's burning a hole in my hand. I sit there unable to breathe. I just opened the box I was forbidden even to see, let alone open, for the past twenty-five years. I don't know how to say what it's like hearing my sister's voice for the first time. It's can't be possible.

A rabid thought strikes me: what if I have the wrong number? The only way to know for sure is to verify Melinda's married name with her mother and that way I can put it off a little longer. I call her mother and pretend to be an old friend.

"Hello, is this Arline?"

"Yes it is."

"Hi, I'm so sorry to bother you, but I'm an old friend of your daughter Melinda."

"Yes..."

"Well, I kind of lost track of her since college." I try to keep my voice steady and try not choke on my lie. I do know she went to college, the sheriff's report mentioned it.

"Oh you went to Perdigo?" She continues like a water fountain. "Well, you know she married Richard?"

"Yes, I just forgot her last name and I wasn't sure where they moved to."

"It's Henline."

I try to hold on and pretend it's fine, and the nice woman spills out everything I need.

"She's right over in Charleston, on Preston Street. I have her number right here. Would you like it?"

I want her to stop talking, now I think Melinda's going to walk in for a visit at any second and her mom's going to hand her the phone. Worse, Melinda might be there. I don't know. "Oh yeah that would be great."

"304–555-1223."

"Thank you so much." I practically hang up on her but not before I hear what I knew was coming next.

"May I tell her who called?"

I click the button that ends the little conversation between us. There's not a doubt left in my mind, not one single bit of hope that I found the wrong person, the number her mother gave me was exactly the one I got from information. And she said Henline, clear as a bell. There are not two Melinda Henlines in the city of Charleston, West Virginia. The voice I heard on the answering machine was my sister's. I call back, but this time I just listen to the recording with my heart.

Her voice is soft, and she sounds like Shelly. The rest of the afternoon is a blank.

No one knows yet, I'm not sure how to tell anyone; right now, I'm not sure about anything. I turn on the nightlight next to my bed and lie there unable to move, I want to go back to sleep and deal with this tomorrow, but the name, her age, and the fact that she's married are far too real. This whole thing went from a silly childhood wish to a serious game of hide-and-seek and before I could count to ten, that was it. This is not a game or a wish, it's my sister.

What should I do, call her or write her? The question won't leave me alone, not for one minute. I toss the heavy covers off me, flick on a light, and go to the living room. My legs feel like they're filled with lead and the light hurts my eyes, I have to shut it off. I sit in the dark wanting to be happy or at least pleased about what I've done. Nothing, I feel nothing. It's like a sad movie and I'm in a crowded theater and not allowing myself to really cry as much as I feel like it. I think what's shocking me most of all is that I had this goal or purpose my whole life, and now that it's here, I'm numb.

Now what? How far do I want to go with this? I can't sit here knowing she's out there and not try to contact her. What is the matter with me? I lift up and drag myself to the kitchen table. Just the thought of facing my fear and writing her this letter begins to tap an old, faraway emotion. *I'm so sorry* repeats itself over and over. This is stupid. How did I ever think I would be able to do this? I can't write a letter. I go back to the living room and wait. Wait for what, I don't know, but I need something else, more than a childish wish to write a letter that will change everything forever. A warm tear spills down my cheek, and then I ask myself one question. What scares me more, finding her or losing her? The answer is simple; it shoves me back into the kitchen.

I sit hunched over the table for hours trying to assure a stranger with mere words and a whole lot of magic that I'm her sister and that I love her.

December 16, 1994

Dearest Melinda,

It's 3 a.m. and I cannot sleep, you see I just learned your name yesterday. Now I sit here with a thousand questions that won't let me sleep. I don't know where to begin, and the truth is I am scared. I've loved you for twenty-five years and missed you my whole life. I began actively searching for you about three years ago.

My name is Sandra Lee Vaughan, and I am your oldest sister. I don't think you could have known how many people have carried you with them. The important thing is your feelings. Along with my own need to find you, is the fact that you live in many people's heart. You have another sister Shelly, and a brother Mark. You also have a younger brother Beau.

This tragedy leaves so many unanswered questions that I find it impossible to begin. I don't pretend to understand anyone's feeling but my own. I have lived without you in my life as long as I could. Now I need to take the chance that you might have some desire to know us. I guess what I am saying, is simply, I am here. It's strange to dance around in this letter not knowing how you'll react, because for me you are my little sister and that is what you have always been. I find it a shame to pretend a minute longer.

Two years ago on Christmas Eve the ongoing dreams about you intensified. Shelly, Mark, and I all dreamed about you that same night. We all saw you as a young girl with dark hair sitting on the hood of an old green pickup on a farm. Mark said that he thinks you're looking for us too and he insisted I find you now.

I was finally able to put all the scattered pieces together. I went to Mom and explained our dreams and from a distant place inside her soul she agreed to do what she could to help. I cannot begin to tell you Mom's story, although I know it well, but I know that you were never rejected.

I was eight years old when this all came about in my life. I have lived in two separate worlds since the day you did not come home. It took twenty-five years to finally learn your name. And again I wait, but this time, for the day I can tell you my story.

Love,

Your sister Sandra

40

A week after I sent the letter to Charleston endless amounts of nervous energy filled me. I do errands, hell, I make up errands just to keep busy; meaningless chores like taking out all the spices in the cupboard and wiping down the shelf, I even start making those annoying piles for my taxes, anything to avoid waiting. Every morning before my first cup of coffee the same thought assaults me: wouldn't it be something if I got a letter from Melinda today? It's sort of like the lotto—you know better then to dream about winning it, but you do it anyway. At first I was tickled, I did it! But now I'm so tired of me and my thoughts; it's torture.

I see the mailman coming up the street, but I'm not going to check right away, nope, not this time. It's New Year's Eve day and I'm not going to do this to myself today, she'll write me back when the time is right. The mailman steps into my driveway toting his blue-gray bag and I dash for the shower. I'm not going near that silly mailbox, I promise myself out loud three times and shove back the shower curtain, turn on the hot water, and strip. See, I'm fine, I'll check the mail later when I get around to it. As I shower my thoughts drip and spray all over me, I wonder if Melinda has even received my letter yet, probably not with the holidays and all. But if she did, what is she thinking? She'll think I'm some crazy chick from California who's trying to deal with her inner child bullshit. But what if she freaks out, maybe I scared her, no that's not it. She's going to tell me to go to hell. Fuck, what would I do? I don't know, I guess I'd have to forget about it. Go on with my life...Oh my God, she might never want to...I don't want to do this pretend shit anymore. I want her back.

I must have been out of mind, how could I have sent her that letter? What if she got it and threw it away or maybe she won't read it at all and returns it to sender. Oh my God, that's what she did, she looked at it and threw it away. Butterflies flutter and the anxiety binds my guts in a knot and I double up. If she doesn't write back then what do I do? I wait...I'm so sick and tired of waiting! Just give it to me, good or bad, I can handle it, it's the waiting I can't stand. I start to hear the statistics repeated to me by the experts when I was searching, and they rumble loudly over the shower. *In over seventy percent of all searches the adoptee is either unresponsive or angry. You shouldn't get your hopes up. We see many cases in which the birth family is rejected and the adoptee feels threatened and does not appreciate any further contact.*

But...this is different. She has to know it's different. Last week when I called Mom and told her I found the baby and her name is Melinda she dropped the phone and didn't speak to me for five days. She didn't speak to anyone, not even Aunt Carole. She simply went to her room, closed the door, and remained there. Daryl said she doesn't want to talk. Mom has never ignored me in her life. I don't know what I did to Mom when she heard her baby's name for the first time, but it was much worse than I ever expected.

She finally called and asked for some details in a voice made of stone. I didn't even recognize the voice; this was a voice I'd never heard before. She cleared her throat three times before she asked, "You're sure it's her?"

"Yeah."

"Then you need to do what's best for you. But I can't be strong like you right now." Her voice crumbled, "I really hope you get what you're searching for." Her pain clamped down on her words, "I never thought…" The phone went dead.

I reach for the towel and dry off; I need to get out of here and go vacuum out the trunk of my car. Or maybe Rob and I can go to Malibu Canyon and hike for a while. I know he's studying but I'll call him anyway. I'm driving myself insane, this has got to stop. I've been sitting here cooped up all week, waiting for the phantom letter that will confirm that it's okay I blew the gates to hell wide open. I sent her the letter last week and that's that, I can't undo any of it. So I better just shut up. I could have listened to the more logical voice inside my head: "Leave it alone, just be happy with what you have, or you could lose everything." But I can't play it safe. *Safe* to me is the most dangerous word in the world. It makes you believe that taking the risk is the danger, but in the end is that right? I don't know. I'd rather be wrong than safe.

I finish dressing and call Rob, my boyfriend. I fell in love with him a couple of years ago. Hell, I couldn't help it, he's tall as a lumberjack and gentle as a deer. Big smile, deep voice, and warm hands.

"Hi. Do you want to go for a hike?" I walk to the front door with the phone hanging from my ear.

"Yeah, but after lunch, I have to finish this."

"Come over when you're done." I lean out of my door and open the mailbox and reach in for a handful of junk.

"What, no I love you?" Rob jokes.

I smile. "Yes, I love you…"

"Me too." Rob hangs up.

I pour a cup of coffee and walk over to the kitchen table next to the trash to throw all the junk mail away. The Company Store— trash, Visa-Platinum application— trash, Southern Pacific Gas

Company—save, something Resident—trash, Sandra Vaughan from Melinda Henline…

Oh Fuck!

I drop the letter almost throwing it across the table, and now the room tilts. I run from the kitchen to the living room where I'm safe. I don't know what to do, I'm falling apart and each second that ticks the louder the buzzing sound gets all around me. What's happening? I'm not ready!

I run to my bedroom trying to shake the letter off me. I sit on my bed, shaking off the touch of the letter. I get up and then sit back down gripping the blanket with both hands, then I'm up again, pacing from the living room to the bedroom, I don't know where to go, I don't know what I'm feeling. Then a knife slices the air: yes I do. I fall to the couch and cry like a death has occurred. I can't stop it. I rock back and forth, my body hot and knotted. A secret valve has been opened and floods the whole room. I miss her so much. God I missed her. I lift from my body and look down on me, rolled in a ball and hysterical. I feel so sorry for me, but I can't do anything. It hurts more now than when I lost her. I'm so confused, in pain and helpless. I observe from above. *Just stop it!* I want to yell down to her. But there's no use; she's a mess.

I pull myself up and go to the bathroom to throw cold water on my face, try to sooth the burning tears. It feels like acid. I have to pull it together, stop this right now, I'm stronger than this, and then I think about opening the letter. I burst out of the bathroom before it starts all over. I've never been so afraid in my life. I have to have help…

Please pick up, please.

"Hello?" Thank God.

"Aunt Carole…"

"Is this you Sandra?"

"Aunt Carole," I whisper.

"Honey, what's the matter?"

"It's all wrong, I screwed up really bad this time." I rock quickly back and forth.

"Sandra, it's okay, just tell me please."

"She wrote me back."

"Who?"

"Melinda. My sister."

"Oh my God! Already? Honey, are you okay?" She feels it too.

"No...I don't know what to do."

Aunt Carole cries out, "Sandra you're going to be fine, just hold on a second."

"Aunt Carole, I can't..."

Aunt Carole takes a moment to think. "Honey, listen to me, you didn't do anything wrong." Her voice is raw.

"But I did." And the pain rears its head again, I'm reduced and ashamed. "I did this!"

"Stop for a minute and take a deep breath."

I follow her instructions and breathe one time in and then out. I find another breath and take it quickly. The noise quiets outside my head and the buzzing slows down.

"Now tell me honey, where are you?"

"I'm in my living room at home in LA." My hands vibrate uncontrollably.

"All right, you don't have to do anything right this second, just calm down. Nothing bad is going to happen, I promise." She's crying to herself. "What do you want me to do?"

"I don't know." I wipe my face and rub my forehead.

"Just go get the letter, I'm right here, I'm not going anywhere."

I drop the phone on the couch and walk stiffly to the kitchen. There it is, the letter sitting right there on my kitchen table, a past that holds a new future. What do I do now? My hands still shake uncontrollably and I can't stop them. I can't do this and I brace my hands on the countertop with my back to the letter. I thought I had a month or so to prepare, process whatever, but it's already here. Why did she write back so fast? I knew it; the only reason could be that she wants me to go away and leave her alone.

At least pick up the damn thing! shouts at me from behind. I see the single envelop on the table and stare at the return address, MELINDA HENLINE, CHARLESTON, WEST VIRGINA. I see my name in the middle of the letter, SANDRA VAUGHAN, LOS ANGELES, CALIFORNIA. My mind twists and turns the addresses around, and I breathe a brief sigh of relief, this is my letter returned, thank God. But then *no* catches me off guard; this is her writing me back. My knees buckle instantly while my eyes refocus hard on the reality that this is not a return to sender, it's a response.

"I have it, it's right here. It's her." I babble fast as the fear begins to build back up. "What is Mom going to say? She's going to be mad, I know she is."

"Honey, she'll be fine. She gave you permission, right?" Aunt Carole's voice is quieter, "Sandra it's going to be fine. Just open it."

"Call Mom for me please…I can't tell her." I beg like a child.

"All right, but promise me, you're not going to blame yourself for any of this."

"I'll call you back…" I hang up. My head is throbbing, my heart racing, and my lips dry. You wouldn't know that I'm thirty-three years old because right now I feel about eight and it's all happening all over again. I had no idea what I'd do if she wrote me back or how much it would hurt until this moment. And all I have to do now is open the letter. God help me, I didn't know, I swear, I didn't know or I wouldn't have ever done this.

There's *her* handwriting. She's real. I move closer to the letter and look at her handwriting, she writes just like Mark, slanted to the left and straight, and no curlicues. I smoke a cigarette and pour another cup of coffee and wait. The letter sits there, terrifying me. Finally I grab it and snap it open like ripping a Band-Aid off a deep wound. I must do this; I have to. The traffic outside my duplex is hushed; I sit there stunned. Not a single sound reaches me. I open the envelope, I pull out the letter, and read:

Dear Sandra;
I never would have dreamed that all these years I had a sister who thought of me so often and cared about me so much.

Seven pictures drop to the floor, and a giant swell of stinging tears stream down my face; the teenage face stares up at me off the floor. I try to shake loose the tension from my hands and snatch up all seven pictures at once. There she is, a five-year-old in a long nightgown, the one that makes you feel like a little princess, it's just like the one I used to wear. Round face, small nose, and long brown hair down to her butt, she looks exactly like me. I shake my head and continue. Then the next one is a ten-year-old, who hates taking pictures, her smile is forced, she looks embarrassed just like me. Her smile is like Mom's, but everything else is me. Now she's twentysomething next to an old truck, I recognize the picture, it's close to the dream we had, but worse, now she looks exactly like Mom.

My mouth is so dry and I sip my cold coffee and I flip over to the next picture behind. I hesitate and then swallow hard and written on the back in pen is, *The day I came home from the hospital.* Nothing prepared me for this: the image of the baby wrapped tightly in the arms of a stranger. A bitter cold grabs me. What have I done? No, I can't…The cold moves up through my chest and into my heart, and the harsh reality of what I've done knocks the shit out of me. I thought this was about finding the baby but it's not; it's about Mom. I continue reading the letter:

I've always known I was adopted. My parents told me so when I was about five years old. Over the years the questions have mounted in a pile in the back of my mind. Why did she do it? Where is she now? Do I have brothers or sisters? What are they like? Where are they now? Does my father know about me? I want to get to know all of you very much. What I'd like to do is take this slowly. I need time to digest it thoroughly and maybe you do too. I'd love to get letters from you and all the others and learn about your lives piece by piece. There's so many emotions behind all of this, that I'm hesitant to jump in too quickly. Tell me about yourselves and I'll do the same. I have twenty-five years of stories just waiting for you!

Melinda (Mel for short)
PS: Please let our mother know that I have no anger toward her.

I hold the innocent baby picture full of shadows on my lap and tightly close my eyes. What in the hell did I ask Mom to do? Give me back my sister? Or admit she made a mistake? I have to put these pictures away so she doesn't have to see the baby. What have I done? I have to stop before I hurt Mom anymore. Fuck, this is ugly!

I really thought I could do this alone and be a hero. I created a world where I was right and Mom was weak, and through *my* strength I could make *her* live happily ever after. How stupid! Now it's all backward and I have no idea what it takes to be a mom or a hero. I pace back and forth, I want to call her and apologize for being so stupid and self-centered and beg her to forgive me. But what I really want to say is. "Help me Mom, please. I'm so sorry. I can't do this."

I have no choice, it's too late to take it back, the letter is the truth and I've already opened Mom's heart for everyone to see in. A woman who spent her whole life hiding herself will now be on display for everyone to judge. And it's my fault; no excuses, I'm the one who did it. I can't change what I did, I feel horrible. I sit here alone reliving each and every single moment Mom gave to me. Her views on independence, her beauty, her last ten bucks so I could go out with my friends, and her love. The way she looked at me with total wonderment each time I tackled another difficult task growing up and becoming a woman. Maybe one day Mom will understand why I did it—because I love her. Probably the same reason she had to do it.

And no one can be judged when love pulls you in directions beyond the rainbows through all the colors with no names. There's a faint line between the colors of crazy and magic. It's when you come through the colorless side of the rainbow and still see the beautiful colors; that's called magic.

I unfold the paper and begin to read my sister's letter again.

Epilogue

Heart pounding, the airplane lands and I find the courage to unbuckle the seat belt and stand up. It's hard knowing that in a few hours, I will be right back to where this whole story started: West Virginia. I am not eight years old; I am thirty-three, and I try telling my heart that, as I exit the plane. Melinda wanted to get to know us, but she had rules to protect her family and herself, and I had to respect her request to go slow. Of course that was hard, I am a film producer now and *slow* is not a word we usually use in the film business. But we did go slow, eking out small bites of information and bits and pieces of our personalities as we tried to get to know each other. And all to get us to this point, the point where I fly to West Virginia and meet my lost sister for the very first time.

It's unquestionably August, hot and muggy. I roll down the window and stare at the city whizzing by. My boyfriend, Rob, has joined me on the adventure. He tries to keep it light, "I can't wait to meet a real, live hillbilly," he says as he turns on the blinker and turns off the highway heading up the mountain to Fort Springs.

"Yeah, they usually keep them in cages on the side of the road for tourists." I puff on a cigarette as the jet lag heightens my inner turmoil. He doesn't know my whole story; he just knows I have to go to Fort Springs first, before I meet Melinda on her birthday. At the time

I made the reservations it all sounded so perfect, go back to the old cabin along the river and then go back down the mountain to meet her in Charleston... Now of course, I want to kick myself. What the hell was I thinking? I shake my head, "Damn it."

"What?" Rob turns.

"Nothing. I just don't know…"

"San, you can do this. She's probably just as nervous." He pats my leg. "I'm right here for you. If you want, I'll go with you."

"Na, she wants to meet me alone, no one else the first time."

"I get it." He keeps driving.

Three hours later we're there. The sun is setting as he turns left onto the old river road. I know exactly how far down the road it will be from this corner because of all those long walks with Mom when she was pregnant and I was a kid.

As soon as he turns and I see the riverbank, I feel weird, nauseous and cold. There they are, all the little cabin-like houses lined in a row across from the river. Memories flood. I see Mark saving furry caterpillars, Shelly holding Mom's hand strolling down the road. I see it all.

"Stop!"

Rob hits the breaks. "Is this it?"

"Hold on." I look at the cabin, the river, and back to the cabin, and even though the color has changed, I know. "Yep."

"Wow. Tiny." Rob pulls over and parks. "Are you going to go up there and ask to see inside?"

"No." Again, I unbuckle my seat belt, this time tougher than the last. "I just want to go to the river."

"Want me to come with you?"

"Sure."

We get out of the rental car. I look extra carefully before crossing the scary road, something ingrained in me early on due to all the giant coal-mining trucks that could have easily splatted us.

I look down the road, nothing is coming and nothing to be afraid of, it's clear as I take Rob's warm hand and dash across it.

Immediately, my feet sink into the deep sand again, just like before. It's all so dreamlike. As I walk down the riverbank to the river, I look up, I can't believe what I see. It's still there, the old rope swing, tattered of course, but it's still there. It immediately brings to mind Paul with his curly long hair, smiling crookedly as he eggs us on to jump, him treading water below as our safety net when we finally take the plunge. A smile must have crossed my face as I drifted off into those memories because the next thing I know Rob is yelling from the river's edge.

"Hey babe, look at this!"

I look and see him flipping over an old wooden rowboat. "You think we can take it out? It has the oars and everything."

I walk over to him, "Rob, really? That's somebody's boat. You can't just jump in it like that."

Stumped, he puts it back down. "I thought someone left it or forgot it."

"No dude, it's someone's boat. Around here, no one's worried about someone stealing their boat, ding dong."

I take off my shoes and walk over to cool my feet in the river... When my toes hit the water, I can finally breathe and relax. The water feels good on my feet, the air is clean, and the river looks so pretty. I am here. I made it. And right then as if God was winking, I see them, two thousand minnows swimming all around my feet, as if teasing me to try; just try once more to catch them. I smile and wiggle my toes just to see them dart around.

It's true; I did live here, I did catch minnows, and I did live this life. As with everything in life, things fade, distance becomes the new normal, and memories float between here and there. But standing here with my toes in the river and the cabin at my back, I knew I needed to be here for some reason.

I kick the water off my feet, put on my sandals, and head up the riverbank back to the road. Rob is down river poking around, still looking for a hillbilly when I stop and rest. Watching him, I put my hand up and lean on an old oak tree. Suddenly, I feel it—a sensation that rocks my soul and takes over, I knew it before I saw it, why I am here! A fever builds, flushed, I move my hand down the side of the oak and there it is. The burned-out hole in that old tree from that sadder time; I had forgot. The same tree I put my happy self in those long years ago. The same tree where I promised I would come back for her after this whole mess was all over and I found the baby. I put all my love for the baby and myself in this tree when there was nowhere else to go. The self who could not cope, comprehend, or accept that moment in time when our worlds splintered into pieces.

With hot tears filling from my eyes, I forced myself to look back, across the street, to the innocent cabin where I see Mom pull into the driveway without the baby, and know that she died her own kind of death when she has to tell us that horrible lie.

And now here I am standing right here, remembering a silly childhood promise I forgot I had made to myself that horrible day. "You go live there with the baby in the tree and I will stay out here live and when I find the baby, I will come back for you, I promise."

Shocking as it sounds, there I am standing before the tree, the old promise and the truth untangled. I had no idea why I had to come to Fort Springs; I just had a gnawing sense that I could not ignore. I thought it was to ground or something, or maybe to prove to myself that I wasn't crazy and that this story really did happen before I went to meet my sister.

But truth was, I had worried that time had faded my memories like it does with most things and that I was crazy for caring so much and for so long. In that moment, with my hand on the hole of the oak tree, it became clear. My spirit had guided me here to keep that promise to free myself so I could finally meet my sister.

So, with the burning truth in front of me, and Rob hanging out by the car twirling a stick he had found, it was time to go to the hotel and wait until tomorrow at three o'clock on the dot. At a mall in Charleston, West Virginia, at that exact time, I would meet the truth untangled—my sister.

One thirty my stomach aches.

Rob bounces into the room from swimming, not a care in the world, "Hey, babe, want to get some lunch before you go meet—"

I chop him in half. "No! I am so freaking out right now."

"You want me to come with you?"

My stomach tied in knots and in a clammy sweat, I rock back and forth, staring out the sliding glass door. "You can't help me!" I shake my head, fighting back the tears. I open my suitcase and dig like a mad woman to pick out what I'm going to wear. Still ranting, "I'm sorry, but I'm fucking scared. I need to be alone!"

Rob comes over to comfort me and gives me a bear hug. "Babe, you got this. If you need me I'll be down by the pool. Just breathe." He tries to be sweet.

But he's damned if he does, and damned if he doesn't. I shoot him a look, hating him for leaving me but I'd hate him if he doesn't.

He kisses me as he leaves, ignoring my display of insanity and my emotional roller coaster. We both know he's going to be the target of all my stress.

I slam the bathroom door shut.

Alone, I trip out. In less than one hour I will be standing face-to-face with a sister I searched for and carried in my heart for twenty-three years from this exact day.

I begin to plead. "Dear God. I can't. I can't do this."

The closer it gets the more I think about what is about to happen, and soon panic sets in. I know this feeling all too well, the room closing in, breathing is labored, and sweat beads on my forehead. I open the bathroom door for some air. The panic attack throws me across the room. I fall on the bed and cry but the pain of the secret and truth are convoluted, the wounded sound in Mom's voice haunting, and all the years lost are finally catching up to me. I feel trapped, like a wild animal with the claws tightly clamped shut on its leg, in pain, and scared, it can't escape.

Stop it. I say to myself, *it's okay, you're going to be fine*...Lie, lie, lie. It doesn't help, the madness of it all is unbearable. Again, the questions shoot at me like a machine gun—*tat, tat, tat*—what have I done? Why did I go this far? Who the fuck do I think I am?

Truth is, it was too much for me to handle, but how would I have known until this moment alone in the room, forty-five minutes from seeing her? I can't do it alone.

I looked at the stupid birthday present and card I bought her, and it feels ridiculous, she isn't going to like it anyway.

"Damn it! You have to take a shower." I say aloud. "You're running out of time." As I begin to undress, a tidal wave hits from behind and knocks me down again, but this time I can't get up, I am undone, frozen, and hysterical. I cry so hard I can't breathe, and the more I think about walking into the mall the more I lose it. I really can't do it. Game over.

I manage to dig my cell phone out of my purse and dial. Shaking, I fumble the words, "Mom—"

Sandra is that you?"

I swallow, unable to speak.

"Sandra. What's the matter? Are you okay?" She waits.

"No-no I'm not—"

Mom starts to lose it, "San, God, I am so sorry—I never meant to—"

I nod, tears roll down my face, "I know—I gotta go. I'll call you back." I drop the phone and finally take a deep breath. I guess just hearing her voice pulls me back from hell and gives me the strength to get up and splash cold water on my face and take a shower.

In front of a water fountain, I stand exactly where I am supposed to in the mall with a small gift bag that screams Happy Birthday. Again, I feel like an idiot. "Why, dear God, did I do this on her frickin' birthday. Really?" I can see in every direction of the mall from this location; that sucks too because I have to look in all four directions for a stranger/sister. I watch for any signs of her coming, but I know I will know, but will I really? The thoughts bounce around and around as a slight dizzy feeling consumes me. I don't feel well, mostly because of the torrential outpouring of my tears and emotion thirty minutes earlier, but also of the enormity of standing in the middle of the final chapter of my quest.

And there she is…a smaller version of me walking toward me with a half smile. She cheated; she came armed with a baby and a husband.

Shit, not fair.

The closer she gets the more I see it—a sister. Not a half-sister, but a 100-percent sister. Same hair, thick brown and healthy, but wait a minute…

She reaches out and lets me hug her; she's exactly like my mom!

"Wow, you're so tall," Melinda speaks first and smiles.

I am suddenly fine, I have no more tears, and all my fears vanished as soon as she spoke and made a joke.

"I know some of us are tall."

We both laugh.

I reach out and hand her the gift. "So, Happy Birthday. I know it's dumb, but . . ."

"No, no, that's fine. I like presents." She takes it from me and again removes all the awkwardness. Then she looks at her husband Richard and nods, "Okay then, we're going over to Chili's Bar and Grill over there and I'll call you when we're done."

Abrupt as it was, it doesn't bother me, because I knew that personality; she is just like Mom and Shelly, exact and to the point. And, I knew that now she saw that I was normal and not a crackhead, she is comfortable having lunch with me alone.

Sitting at the table I find myself staring at her like a brand new doll. Everything from the part in her hair, down to the way two of her fingernails bent forward exactly like my mom's. I can't believe what I was seeing.

"What?" She suddenly asks.

"Oh God, I'm sorry but it's so trippy how much you look like Mom, I mean my mom, I mean Ardell. Shit this is weird."

"I know. Man, I mean I've always known that I had a birth mom—"

Hearing those words, *birth mom*, my heart skipped a beat. They feel like such a slap—ouch. Was I that, too? A *birth sister*?

She continued, "Yeah, but I never thought about having sisters or brothers."

The waitress comes to the table, "Are you ladies ready to order?"

We nod and she looks at me, "Do you guys eat a lot of salads back in California? Because, I don't, I'm a potato skin kind of girl."

Of course you are, I think to myself and smile. "We are too."

The waitress takes our order. I have soup and salad, my stomach is a little queasy from all the emotional commotion, and she orders the chicken with a potato.

The waitress asks, "What kind of dressing would you like?"

Melinda replies, "French dressing please."

And there it was—the big bang, nurture verses nature. I had traveled the world and met with a thousand-plus people in my line of work and there are only two other people on the planet who have ever openly ordered French dressing—Shelly and Mom.

When the words *French dressing* come out of her mouth, I choked on my water and start laughing.

"What now for God's sake?" she smiled. "Tell me."

"All right, there are only two other people on the planet who actually eat French dressing, Mom and Shelly."

She understands instantly and we both laughed.

"Hey, would you mind, can I feel your hair?"

Melinda gives me a queer look. "I guess, but why?"

"Well, we all have really good hair, and I want to see if yours feels like ours." I reached across the table and sure enough, good hair, thick and healthy.

That day we sat at the table for four quick hours babbling about all our likes and dislikes, and joked our asses off. I told her all about Mom and how she and Mom were going to trip out when they finally met each other one day.

But underneath it, I could tell she couldn't believe I loved her. It bothered me, but again, what did I expect, she didn't know about me or us, and I can't be that silly as to think she'd love me just because she met me. But deep down I did, I thought the connection would be there instantly, no matter what.

When it was finally just too late to keep going, we both knew she had to go and it was over. Everything moved in slow motion for me, from standing up, her grabbing her gift off the table, to paying the check.

One question moved rapidly through my mind: *Now what?* What do I do now? Say good-bye or—

Now, outside the restaurant, we hug each other good-bye. It was a standard hug, not big, not little. Just a hug, which really said nothing.

Sadly, I smiled at her once more and then I turned to leave and start to walk away. Then she calls out—

"Hey, Sandra! I really would like to hang out some more...Can you stay another couple days? Maybe come over and have dinner?"

My heart leaps from my chest and I look at her, "Hell, yes. I'd love that."

She laughs and we both smile, relieved we weren't saying good-bye just yet.

But more importantly, I saw it—a glimmer, not the big instantaneous sister moment, but a glimmer inside that her spirit really did know mine.

On the plane ride home, it all seemed so surreal: she and I had met, she and I connected, and she and I are sisters.

Once back in LA, I start writing her the longest love letter ever. I know she didn't know me, but I was going to show her that I did know her, and tell her who we all were and what we were doing while she was gone.

That love letter turned out to be my first book, *Two Thousand Minnows*.